MAKING

MILWAUKEE

MIGHTIER

MAKING
MILWAUKEE

Mightier
Planning and the

Politics of Growth

1910–1960

John M. McCarthy

Northern

Illinois

University

Press

DeKalb

All Rights Reserved

Design by Shaun Allshouse

Maps by Mapcraft

Library of Congress Cataloging-in-Publication Data

McCarthy, John M.

Making Milwaukee mightier: planning and the politics of growth, 1910–1960
/ John M. McCarthy.

  p.   cm.

includes bibliographical information and index.

ISBN 978-0-87580-394-4 (clothbound: alk. paper)

1. Urban renewal—Wisconsin—Milwaukee. 2. City Planning—Wisconsin—
Milwaukee. 3. Milwaukee (Wis.)—History. I. Title

HT177.M48M33 2009

307.1'2160977595—dc22

2008052754

Contents

To Ann,

For everything

Preface

Contemporary observers of urban America often struggle to make sense of twentieth-century policies in light of what industrial restructuring and suburbanization have wrought. If, for example, freeways accelerated suburbanization and middle class urban abandonment, why did cities so willingly build them? If urban renewal ruptured viable city neighborhoods, why did city leaders so eagerly bulldoze large swaths of the inner city to accommodate redevelopment agendas? If public housing both failed to provide decent shelter for the urban poor and in fact warehoused the less fortunate in isolation from the rich and middle class, why did cities pursue such planning strategies? All of these questions are valid and volumes of scholarly literature exist to engage them; nevertheless the common perspective that infuses these questions with urgency and even tragedy comes from the embattled postindustrial city.

Similarly, a fundamental shift in how many planners view cities has raised a difficult set of questions as to how reformers approached the problems of urban industrialism. In 1960, a New York City resident and neighborhood activist named Jane Jacobs published *The Death and Life of Great American Cities*, a devastating critique of urban renewal that challenged decades-long planning assumptions about cities. Far from being deleterious to quality of life, density was, Jacobs argued, the lifeblood of urban ecology. The vitality of informal street life, observed by Jacobs in her New York City neighborhood of Greenwich Village, could not be "planned" in the top-down manner that seemed to characterize urban renewal. Jacobs also defended the urban grid for the very reasons many planners abhorred it. Jacobs's not-so-implicit message was simple: modern planning techniques were undermining the very fabric of urban life. Past reformers thought to be radical in their own times also appeared in Jacobs's writing as unwitting agents of the modern destruction of urban life. Jacobs castigated the Garden City theories of famed British reformer Ebenezer Howard for ignoring the complexities of city life and even setting in motion "powerful and city-destroying ideas."[1] The position Jacobs wrote from, that of an embattled neighborhood activist, makes her urgent denunciations of planners understandable. Jacobs became one of the most important urban activists in the United States, fighting to preserve neighborhoods threatened by urban renewal and helping inspire a future generation of urbanists to embrace historic preservation and the assets of city life increasingly lost in the deluge of modern American suburban sprawl. Her original work remains canonical reading to professional planners and thousands of other defenders of city life. It also preceded (and heavily influenced) a broader planning movement, now known as "New Urbanism," that embraced many of Jacobs's assumptions about how cities work. New Urbanists promote the creation and preservation of compact urban neighborhoods, mixed-use communities, and mass transit as alternatives to sprawling suburbs that are rigidly zoned and exclusively reliant on the automobile. In the wake of *Death and Life*, critics of planning from the New Urbanist perspective sometimes became even more shrill in their criticisms. Cultural critic James Howard Kunstler, a fellow traveler of Jacobs, less tactfully has observed that modern American city-building, aided and abetted by planners, had "nearly wrecked the human habitat in America."[2] Within the planning profession, more muted criticisms of past planning practices echo these principles, but regardless of tone, in obvious ways New Urbanism is a reversal of how many early twentieth-century reformers framed urban problems and proposed solutions.[3]

Perhaps it is not a coincidence that in the city of Milwaukee, Wisconsin, one of the most eloquent and vocal New Urbanists, John Norquist, was elected mayor four times between 1988 and 2003. With Norquist's encouragement, Milwaukee became something of a laboratory for New Urbanist ideas. Planners under Norquist have encouraged catalytic design principles. Norquist introduced plans for an ambitious light rail system that he hoped would reduce the region's reliance on the automobile. Though the push for light rail eventually failed, Norquist was able to claim at least partial victory by persuading local and state governments to tear down the Park East Freeway, a spur north of downtown built in the 1960s that was never finished, but had been a symbol of short-sighted planning for years. Norquist stepped down in the middle of his fourth term as Milwaukee mayor at the end of 2003, assuming the presidency of the Congress for the New Urbanism, the movement's largest institutional arm, that same year. Norquist chronicled his mayoral efforts and broader observations about cities in a book titled *The Wealth of Cities*, published in 1998, and in many ways meant to be an embodiment of New Urbanism at the municipal level. In the middle of his book, Norquist pointedly refers to Mayor Daniel Hoan's inaugural address to the Milwaukee Common Council in 1916. In it, Hoan pointed out that congestion was a "serious problem" for Milwaukee, and the only way it could be overcome was by the "spreading out of the population." The planning policies that followed this philosophy, observed Norquist, essentially "backfired" and the consequences were dire for urban America.[4]

Norquist's observations are not inaccurate. They evoke a fundamental question that anyone living in or near a struggling city might raise. From the perspective of Norquist—a mayor trying to revive a city that still hemorrhaged population—Hoan's attitude was clearly endemic of wrong and short-sighted planning ideas. Why would any mayor, but especially the mayor of a city that had only twenty-six square miles and was almost completely built up in 1916, call for "the spreading out of the population"? During the course of my research as a graduate student living in Milwaukee, I came across a similar set of statements favorable to decentralization from a later mayor, Frank Zeidler, and they raised the same question. This book is an attempt to answer it.

The planning ideas that help explain why Hoan (and later Zeidler) advocated "spreading out" the urban population are rooted in the reform environment of the Progressive Era. In the early twentieth century, American reformers, deeply concerned about the adverse effects of urbanization, immigration, and industrialization, began to embrace professional, comprehensive city planning as a catalyst in developing better communities, redeveloping older neighborhoods, and bringing prestige to cities. Most histories of this era observe that planning became more important to cities as a tool to enable orderly development, economic growth, and civic beauty. In the process, as historians John Bauman and Edward Muller have recently observed, "Most progressive planners steered a more conservative social and political course."[5] As planning matured in Milwaukee, its advocates embraced the tenets of the new profession, but often for strikingly different ends. Early visionaries such as Charles Whitnall viewed planning as a weapon to attack social ills, especially urban overcrowding, and to achieve social ideals even at the expense of capitalism. To that end, Milwaukee planners did not follow the more familiar national trend during the Progressive Era of abandoning housing reform, nor did they create any of the grand, comprehensive city plans in the mold of Daniel Burnham's vision for Chicago. Instead, city planners and other public officials emphasized land use controls, cooperative housing, and decentralization. An aggressive annexation program would allow the city space to grow while "spreading out" its population, as Hoan put it in 1916.

What is striking about these ideas is not that they were unique. Milwaukee's planners and reformers who openly admired the British Garden City movement and the German innovations in land use controls were also directly linked to American housing reformers whom one historian has framed as "the City Social" and later oriented themselves to the tenets of regionalism advocated by lead members of the Regional Planning Association of America.[6] The way these reformist streams manifested in Milwaukee never completely reflected the aforementioned movements either. But the broader goal of planned decentralization in Milwaukee survived the divorce of planning and housing that seemed more common in most of urban America.[7] These "metropolitan visions" dictated that Milwaukee extend its borders at all costs, with annexation as a primary tactic and some form of metropolitan government as the broader goal. This eventually failed when outlying communities in Milwaukee blocked city growth, incorporating as independent communities immune to consolidation with the larger central city. Suburbanization—that is, the emergence of separate communities outside the central city and increasingly less dependent on it—eventually overwhelmed the capacity of Milwaukee to take the physical form that its leaders and planners had hoped for. Each new suburban incorporation furthered a process unintended by Milwaukee's planning visionaries but familiar in the United States: metropolitan fragmentation.

The second way that the twentieth-century planning ideas and their ultimate manifestation in Milwaukee are worthy of consideration is that they took root in the city during the insurgency of the Socialist Party, were informed by socialist principles, and ran their course throughout the three Socialist mayoral administrations, Emil Seidl's, Daniel Hoan's, and Frank Zeidler's, between 1910 and 1960. Because the local Socialist Party declined in Milwaukee in the 1930s and Socialists rarely enjoyed pure majorities in the Milwaukee Common Council that could reinforce mayoral policies, it seems there is little to link these administrations together beyond fiscal stewardship and pro-labor political rhetoric. No study of Socialist governance in Milwaukee in its totality between 1910 and 1960 exists. This book is not meant to fill that gap; it is not a political history of socialism. However, the planning efforts that make up a significant part of this book drew much, though not all, of their inspiration from ideals decidedly to the left of more conventional reform Progressivism in America. Milwaukee's planners and their supporters frequently adopted conventional policies with unconventional goals. They embraced zoning, annexation, parkways, and arterial highways, for example, all because such endeavors promised to help attack the debilitating social effects of urban congestion. Other, less conventional ideas, such as cooperative housing, planned communities, and scattered public housing, also thrived in Milwaukee as components that could transcend the overcrowded conditions wrought by the industrial city.

This book follows the germination, maturation, and ultimate unraveling of these policy efforts, which together cohered as a distinct set of metropolitan visions for twentieth-century Milwaukee. The first chapter situates Milwaukee's nascent early twentieth-century planning movement in its national and local contexts. American planners abjured housing as a planning concern during the Progressive Era, a divorce that never completely took place in Milwaukee. Locally, the Socialist Party's seizure of the mayor's office provided a forum for planning ideas that emphasized land use controls, cooperative housing, and an impulse to look outside the crowded central city for urban salvation. The second chapter traces the implementation of zoning, platting, parkways, and other initiatives that were all designed to foster decentralization. It also introduces annexation as the vital component of decentralization, promising to reduce Milwaukee's shockingly high population density while ensuring that planning ideas targeted at the urban periphery would remain firmly under city jurisdiction. This book's main title, *Making Milwaukee Mightier*, in fact borrows from a city report from 1929, in which annexation was vigorously defended as a metropolitan solution. The third chapter chronicles the detour of Milwaukee growth policies during the Depression, as the city wrestled with seemingly intractable housing issues, joined the advance guard action in the national urban movement to move the Franklin Roosevelt administration to address housing, leveraged its growing reputation as a planning leader by attracting a New Deal greenbelt project, and tried and failed to achieve city-county consolidation. Chapter four discusses the 1940s, when an eight-year Socialist absence from the mayor's office mirrored growing concerns that Milwaukee's inner core had aged and new growth policies were needed to attract reinvestment downtown. It also traces the emergence of the third and final Socialist mayor, Frank Zeidler, whose planning ideas reflected his Socialist predecessors and provided a distinct counterpoint to urban renewal. Chapter five chronicles Zeidler's early years in office, when Cold War civil defense concerns revitalized the idea of planned communities and the city tried to gain control of one such community—Greendale—and tried to plan a second one entirely outside of Milwaukee County, enabled once again by annexation. Both plans failed, but in the wake of the second failure annexation was thrown open into an even more hotly contested growth exercise that circumscribed the ability of planning to foster regional equality. The final two chapters examine the devolution of metropolitan planning into municipal mercantilism in the 1950s as new suburbs rapidly incorporated, rendering annexation a partially fulfilled achievement. Fragmentation also gave an inequitably spatial shape to the polarizing issue of race that divided city and suburban residents further along class lines.

Municipal government is a somewhat rare place to find metropolitan visionaries. A city known for "sewer socialism" and austere civic projects is perhaps a surprising place to reflect upon the ability (and inability) of planning to act as a social force, and the implications of trying to remake an urban agenda into a metropolitan one via the blunt force of annexation. Civic observers in twentieth-century Milwaukee have, at varying points in time, decried its political leaders' apparent disinterest to become a truly great city. These criticisms often appear in evaluations of Socialist leaders of Milwaukee, whose stewardship admittedly paid far less attention to showcase projects that may have gained national attention for the city. Fiscal thrift did not inhibit planners' imaginations, however, and the absence of prototype downtown projects copied by other cities should not be mistaken for a lack of metropolitan ambition. Few other mayors of American cities would have predicted that their cities would annex, build, own, and control satellite cities in five neighboring counties, as Frank Zeidler did in 1951. Understanding what motivated Zeidler to make that prediction, and earlier made Daniel Hoan call for one of the smallest cities in America to "spread out" its population, can help us make sense of past decisions in their own historic context, and concurrently better understand our postindustrial cities today.

MAKING

MILWAUKEE

MIGHTIER

Charles Whitnall—Charles Whitnall served on Milwaukee city and Milwaukee county parks and planning commissions for several decades Image Courtesy of Milwaukee County Historical Society

City Planning and Social Progressivism

In May of 1911, the Third National Conference on City Planning gathered in Philadelphia amid a growing split in America's nascent city planning movement. The conference's two strongest factions were about to part ways. On one side were advocates of professional planning and on the other were reformers and activists who wanted to use planning to address the nation's urban housing crisis. The planners, led most notably by Frederick Law Olmsted, Jr., and John Nolen, sought to refine the movement's technical aspects, create professional standards for the young discipline, and fight for city planning's legitimacy within municipal government.

The Olmsted/Nolen faction had emerged from the turn-of-the-century "City Beautiful" movement, where planning had gained notoriety as the enabler of higher forms of civic art and urban beautification. While City Beautiful advocates were perhaps the most vigorous in their defense of the young profession's legitimacy, they had not originally called the national planning conference. That clarion call had come from the housing reformers, driven primarily by women who had come from the settlement house movement like Mary Simkhovitch, and journalists like Benjamin Marsh. These reformers cared less for civic beauty, and instead drew their inspiration from the increasingly congested urban environment itself. The overcrowding of large American cities had grown so acute—Marsh often said—that comprehensive, professional city planning was necessary to attack the environmental problems that seemed to underlie every social ill urban America faced during the Progressive Era. Marsh had challenged planners from across the country to meet to address urban overcrowding, and in 1909 the First National Conference on Congestion was held in Washington, D.C.

During the subsequent two years, Olmsted worked quietly and diligently to wrest control of the national movement away from the housing reformers, filling the executive committee with allies of planning, shifting the conference program from presentations of slums and their influence to more technical matters of planning, and finally changing the name of the conference itself, eliminating the word "congestion" from the title by the time of the third conference in Philadelphia. Thus the housing reformers that gathered in Philadelphia in May of 1911 felt the planning movement drifting away from social reform. They responded, in part, by declaring themselves "insurgents," and they held events outside of the regular conference committee. One such impromptu event was a tour of Philadelphia's slums. Among the "insurgents" on the tour were famed British Garden City planner Raymond Unwin and Emil Seidel, the Socialist mayor of the city of Milwaukee.[1]

Seidel's presence at the conference and especially his participation in the housing insurgents' tour is not a coincidence of history. Instead, it provides the first small hint that Milwaukee's fledgling city planning movement would deviate in important ways from the national movement. As historians Jon Peterson and Peter Marcuse have already noted, after the 1911 conference, the American planning and housing movements separated.[2] As this opening chapter will demonstrate, in Milwaukee comprehensive planning and housing reform grew together throughout the decade of the 1910s, driven by two interconnected motivations. First, the city's socialist movement gave Milwaukee its most important planning reformer, Charles Whitnall, and eventually a mayor in Daniel Hoan who shared most of Whitnall's planning assumptions. Second, as the decade progressed, Milwaukeeans generally grew alarmed at the city's overcrowded conditions, and remedies to alleviate "congestion," which included cooperative community building, land use restrictions, and eventually annexation, originated in the distinct social progressivism of Milwaukee's planning community. By the early 1920s, Milwaukee had a comprehensive zoning ordinance, a government ready to build a cooperative housing project, and a planning mentality committed to metropolitan development instead of inner city reshaping.

City planning emerged as a direct response to the rapid urbanization of late nineteenth- and early twentieth-century America in general and Milwaukee in particular. Incorporated in 1846, Milwaukee originally enjoined two formerly competing frontier settlements, Kilbourntown, on the west bank of the Milwaukee River, and Juneautown, which was located east of the river and west of Lake Michigan. The rivalry between the "east" and "west" sides was fierce in the 1840s, and it would remain long after the city outgrew its original boundaries. Milwaukee steadily grew out of its frontier town status, first as a commercial center for agricultural exports, and then as a producer of manufactured products. The city's population stood at 71,234 in 1870 and at 124,000 in 1880, and had mushroomed to over 373,000 by 1910. Immigrants from Germany, Poland, and Eastern Europe, attracted to the city's diverse metal-working, tool and dye, and precision manufacturing establishments, filled the growing neighborhoods that radiated along streetcar lines north, west, and south of Milwaukee's original urban core. Freight also moved down the Milwaukee River, which fed into Lake Michigan, connecting the growing city to America's emerging national economy. Two major railroad lines, the Chicago, Milwaukee and St. Paul—commonly known as "The Milwaukee Road"—and the Chicago and Northwestern also served as carriers of the city's commercial and industrial products.[3]

Progressive Era Milwaukee's morphology deviated from that of cities on the East Coast. While cities like New York built multi-story tenements and Philadelphia and Baltimore built tightly packed brick row houses, the most common residential structure in Milwaukee was the balloon-frame wooden house or bungalow, more common for the urban Midwest. The built landscape of Milwaukee was thus easy to characterize as orderly, well spaced and free of the "slums" that were alarming reformers in much of urban America. Booster groups such as the Merchants and Manufacturers' Association of Milwaukee proudly nicknamed their locale a "City of Homes" that had "no congested slums or tenement districts"; and indeed, homeownership rates were somewhat higher in Milwaukee than in many of its urban counterparts.[4] Furthermore, the city's two most numerous immigrant groups at this time—Germans and Poles—both placed a cultural premium on home ownership, and thus even impoverished districts of the city like the Polish South Side Fourteenth Ward contained higher numbers of home owners than their economic status seemed to afford.[5]

Milwaukee's Health Commission, first organized in 1867, steadily gained a reputation as one of America's strongest such institutions, giving Milwaukeeans another reason to enjoy perhaps false security that the city's urban problems did not approach the magnitude of those in its more celebrated counterparts like Chicago and New York. During the Progressive Era, a variety of reformers—from journalists to settlement house workers—made New York City the paradigm for urban congestion, with its multi-story dumbbell tenements. In 1905, an inspection of Milwaukee neighborhoods observed that "no definite tenement districts" existed in the city. Four years later, in 1909, the Wisconsin state legislature passed a restrictive tenement house law as well, but since builders in Milwaukee favored duplexes and single-family bungalows, it had little effect on development.[6]

During the Progressive Era, intellectuals placed strong emphasis on environmental factors—especially poor housing—as causes of urban poverty. It was convenient for visitors who spent little time in Milwaukee's immigrant neighborhoods to infer that without tenements (or true row houses) the city was without slums. This stereotype lasted well into the twentieth century. On a visit to Milwaukee to research her book *Modern Housing*, Catherine Bauer, impressed with the city's "Germanness" and "orderliness," told Clarence Stein, "There are almost no slums in the city."[7] Edith Elmer Wood, another nationally renowned housing reformer used to crusading against the ill effects of multi-tenant apartments, mentioned the Wisconsin tenement law as an example of Milwaukee's progressivism and urban prosperity.[8]

Despite the cosmetic appearance of an orderly city without "slums," several factors made Milwaukee increasingly compact. First, the city did not require building permits until 1888 (when the city already had over 200,000 residents), which allowed developers to carve out small lots. While this made home-owning more affordable, it also created tightly packed neighborhoods that were to become targets of Progressive Era reformers, who believed overcrowding and poor planning were cities' greatest weaknesses. Secondly, due to a lack of coordinated annexation, Milwaukee's ability to take in new land and thus continue to grow horizontally had slowed. In 1910, Milwaukee comprised only twenty-six square miles, far smaller than St. Louis, Cincinnati, Cleveland, and Chicago. Third, immigrant Milwaukeeans' cultural premium on homeownership in spite of steep economic odds led many urban dwellers to improvise. In the Polish South Side wards, residents often took in boarders to help pay mortgages, increased their living space by raising their basements, or built homes that included these extra floors. These distinctive "Polish flats" helped make homeownership rates in the South Side disproportionately high and also negated the need for dumbbell tenements.[9] Yet, they also made South Side wards far more crowded than their building types appeared to accommodate. As the 1910s progressed and Milwaukee's borders remained relatively static, overcrowding here and in other neighborhoods became a problem that drew the attention of reformers outside of the conventional circles of public health.

It was in this urban-industrial milieu that professional city planning first took hold. As Jon Peterson has noted, "planning" as a deliberate effort to shape landscapes is as old as cities themselves are. However, institutionalized, comprehensive city planning grew out of several diverse "special purpose" planning endeavors in the nineteenth century, primarily the movements for sanitary reform, urban parks, water and sewage, and civic beautification.[10] Milwaukeeans undertook all of these "special purpose" planning endeavors during the nineteenth century. In 1867, the city established the Board of Health, and during the subsequent decades, citizens began to embrace public health both in broader terms and as a function best served by municipal government, not the free market. In 1878, the Board of Health became the Health Commission, with its own separate department in city hall. As Judith Walzer Leavitt has demonstrated, both health officials and a growing number of civic betterment clubs largely succeeded in both reducing Milwaukee's mortality rates and raising public awareness of the need for better sanitation.[11]

As the Health Commission's conceptions of public health broadened, it also began linking sanitary reform with the need for better housing. Smallpox outbreaks, common in nineteenth-century cities, were more likely in overcrowded neighborhoods. Health officials first made the correlation between mortality and the built environment, which was an argument that the larger American housing reform movement frequently made as well. One of the key functions of Milwaukee's early city planning efforts, zoning, was motivated at least in part by these sanitary concerns first raised by health officials.

Similar linkages between public health and the need for better city planning are found in Milwaukee's early efforts at securing clean water and disposing of its waste more efficiently. The city's Board of Water Commissioners, first organized in 1871, gradually extended water lines to the growing city in the late nineteenth century. As Roger Simon has noted, water service across Milwaukee was uneven. Wealthier neighborhoods on the city's east and northwest sides usually received water and sewage extensions quickly, and poorer immigrant neighborhoods like the Polish South Side often opted out of the higher assessments that accompanied water lines, instead preferring to use the money saved to pay off mortgages more quickly. Furthermore, by the 1900s, Milwaukee politicians realized they could use the city's waterworks as a source of municipal revenue if they instead sold water at a profit to newer suburban communities such as Shorewood. The uneven distribution of water services to city neighborhoods was an issue of growing political importance, and it was poised to be a key issue that the city's growing Social Democratic Party would exploit in the 1910 city election.[12]

The newest realm of special purpose planning—civic beautification, or the "City Beautiful"—spawned the professional city planning movement in most of urban America. Two events had the strongest impact on City Beautiful. The first was the Columbian Exposition in Chicago in 1894. The

Exposition's legendary "White City" inspired architects across the country to seek out more ambitious projects, and thus was clearly a precursor to the Progressive Era's emphasis on urban beautification. Interestingly, Milwaukee's proximity to Chicago did not guarantee the Exposition would have a heavy influence on planning and architecture to Chicago's northern neighbor. Milwaukee leaders saw the Exposition less as a turning point in beautification and more as an opportunity to promote tourism to Milwaukee and showcase the city's leading businesses. The city's two leading brewers—Schlitz and Pabst—both created large exhibits to display at the Exposition. Efforts to build a Milwaukee city display fizzled, however, and the mayor of Milwaukee, Peter Somers, as well as the governor of Wisconsin, George Peck (who was also from Milwaukee), instead arranged a visit to the city for the foreign press who covered the Exposition. Tourism to Milwaukee noticeably picked up in 1893.[13]

The Exposition did, however, precede a growing interest in Wisconsin in classical architecture in particular and urban beautification in general. In 1904, the state of Wisconsin commissioned George Browne Post, an architect who had worked on the design of the Columbian Exposition, to design the state's new capitol building. The building's dome and Corinthian columns were typical of classicism in the early twentieth century. A far more important link between the Exposition and Milwaukee's design community is found in the design work of architects George Bowman Ferry and Alfred C. Clas, who emerged in the 1890s as the city's most renowned classical architects. Ferry designed the Milwaukee Public Library during this decade, and he also formed an architectural firm with Clas that designed many of Milwaukee's most ornate homes.[14] Clas's interest in classical architecture also accompanied a growing personal interest in civic beautification and urban parks throughout the city as a whole. During the 1900s, he became the most notable City Beautiful advocate in Milwaukee. Clas joined the movement's largest national body, the American Civic Association, in 1904. He also began writing a series of articles in local newspapers and making speeches before a variety of local organizations on the subject.[15]

Like many of Clas's contemporaries across the United States, his clarion calls for urban beautification grew far more vocal after the monumental publication of Washington, D.C.'s McMillan Plan in 1902. The plan—originally spawned to coincide with Washington, D.C.'s hundredth anniversary—is widely regarded as the first comprehensive city plan in the United States. Not only did it call for a rearrangement of public buildings around that city's famed mall, but it also included a broader system of parks that covered terrain across the city as a whole. The plan's release coincided with

Charles Mulford Robinson's emergence as national proponent of civic beauty through his contributions to the *Atlantic Monthly*, and especially his two books, *The Improvement of Towns and Cities*, which was published in 1901, and *Modern Civic Art*, released in 1902. In these works, Robinson called for the varied local civic improvement groups in America to recognize that their efforts were, as Jon Peterson wrote, "not many, but one."[16] Robinson argued that voluntary cooperation outside municipal government was not sufficient for the task of rebuilding American cities in accordance with the movement's higher civic standards. Furthermore, trained experts were desperately needed to bridge the gap between the high ideals of the movement's architects and the political realities these plans faced in city hall. Robinson's books had tremendous impact on the nascent movement, and his emphasis on expertise and public support were cornerstones for the broader shift toward professional planning.

As the 1900s progressed and the movement's advocates faced increased difficulty in retrofitting their beautification plans with the fiscal realities of municipal politics, men like Frederick Olmsted, Jr., Robinson, and John Nolen began placing more emphasis on the "City Practical," which accepted the aesthetics of City Beautiful but sought to utilize trained experts to study more closely traffic patterns, street-widening, and public costs of building projects. As Olmsted, Jr., admitted to the city of New Haven during his study of that city's needs, while his professional background may have qualified him to tell the city "what to do," nothing qualified him to tell the city "how to do it."[17] These tensions within the original planning movement were never fully resolved, but the effort to mediate them played perhaps the central role in the creation of municipal city planning commissions.

The transformation from City Beautiful to City Practical is apparent in Milwaukee as well and is linked to the fourth important "special purpose" planning initiative, the push for urban parks. The city first formed a Park Board in 1890, whose tasks were to buy land and develop it into city parks as well as to promote more aesthetically pleasing roadways, usually wider "boulevards." The board's early leading member, Christian Wahl, a wealthy retired businessman, hoped to create a system of boulevards and parks that would have encircled the entire city. But during the 1890s, the Park Board's efforts focused almost entirely on the affluent lakefront neighborhoods on the East Side of Milwaukee. The city hired Frederick Law Olmsted's firm to provide designs, but the Park Board chose the sites.

The three largest parks developed during the 1890s all reflected the class interests of the elites who dominated the Park Board. Lake Park and River Parks were about four miles north of downtown. Lake was situated directly in the path of the affluent East Side's steady growth along the bluffs above Lake Michigan, and River was just a half mile east along the Milwaukee River. "West Park," renamed Washington Park in 1900, was located four miles northwest of Milwaukee's center. Olmsted criticized the Park Board for choosing sites far away from Milwaukee's major population centers. But any hopes that early park planners such as Wahl clung to for expansion to correct these flaws ended with the Depression of the 1890s. Building activity slowed, city finances constricted, and park development temporarily ground to a halt. Wahl's hopes for a grand system of boulevards linking his network of parks also failed to materialize. The only such road built during the 1890s was Newberry Boulevard on the city's wealthy East Side, which linked Lake Park to River Park and was lined down its middle with large shade trees.[18]

Efforts to make civic beauty a practical governmental undertaking stepped up noticeably after the publication of the McMillan Plan and as the national economy picked up again in the 1900s. Clas began urging the Milwaukee Common Council to sponsor a comprehensive study of the city's park system, with hopes of both extending parks over a wider urban terrain as well as linking them via roadways to a new civic center. In 1905, David Rose, the city's colorful but corrupt mayor, urged the Common Council to follow Clas's suggestions along "similar lines in other American cities."[19] Crucial support also came from Charles Whitnall, a Socialist, who in 1906 self-published a long report on the value of parks as a necessity for working-class residents to gain some measure of relief from the overcrowded conditions of their city neighborhoods.[20] Whitnall was soon to play a foundational role in the city's planning efforts, but in 1906, with the Milwaukee Social Democratic Party still aspiring to the mayor's office, Clas was the city's key advocate of civic beauty and—by his membership in the American Civic Association—link to the national City Beautiful movement. Urged on by Clas, Whitnall, and Rose, in 1907 the Milwaukee Common Council adopted a law that created a new planning agency in the city. The new body was named the Metropolitan Park Commission, a confusing title since the city also maintained the Park Board, which it had created in 1892. The ordinance called for the Metropolitan Park Commission to consist of eleven members, one a member of the Common Council, another from the Park Board, the city engineer, and eight nonelected citizens who were to hold no other official positions.[21]

Clas authored the Metropolitan Park Commission's first report, which was submitted to the Milwaukee Common Council in early 1909. The report reflected both conventional City Beautiful arguments that early planners made about American cities and Clas's more idiosyncratic concerns with Milwaukee's riverfront. The city's narrow streets no longer could carry the heavy streetcar, horse, and auto traffic of modern cities. A more logical, aesthetically pleasing, and efficient system of streets was needed. The report referred to these new streets as "parked ways" and called for their width to be a minimum of 130 feet. Clas linked the new roadways with real estate development, noting that the modern roadways "make the real estate man's 'mouth water' and will stimulate private enterprise in replatting, particularly in residential districts, to conform to the convenience, comfort, and consequential economy of the parked ways."[22] Most importantly, the parked ways were to radiate outward from a new civic center. The report called for the new public buildings to be built downtown, just west across the Milwaukee River, with new buildings lining a grand boulevard and culminating with a massive courthouse at Ninth and State streets, at the crest of a hill above the Milwaukee River from city hall.

Befitting the growing calls for practicality, the Metropolitan Park Commission hired the "City Practical" movement's two greatest proponents, John Nolen and Frederick Law Olmsted, Jr., to review Clas's civic center plans. In July of 1909, Nolen and Olmsted, Jr., sent the Commission their review, generally approving of the efficient grouping of Milwaukee's public buildings, but calling for the location of the civic center's capstone building, the courthouse, to be on Cedar Street (now Kilbourn Avenue) instead of State Street, so travelers on Milwaukee's main downtown shopping street, Wisconsin Avenue, could have a better view of the structures.[23] The commission modified its plans to cohere with Nolen and Olmsted's recommendations, and incorporated them into two more reports it made to the Common Council, in November of 1909 and in April of 1910. The third report, made in 1910, reflects Clas's concerns for beautifying the city's three rivers, the Kinnickinnic, which flows into the Milwaukee River just south of downtown, and the Menomonee, which flows east into the Milwaukee and separates the city's north and south sides. It included photographs of waterfronts in European cities like Vienna, Nuremburg, and Dusseldorf, which featured pedestrian walkways along riverbanks and ventilation via the planting of trees along the water banks.[24]

Clas's early plans for the civic center and beautification of urban waterfronts are the height of City Beautiful in Milwaukee. The painfully long execution and modification of his plans reflect the relatively minor role the movement played in Milwaukee's planning history. The civic center project was largely ignored until 1919, when a new report called for traffic to circle the proposed civic center instead of going through it. The plan also fell victim to squabbling between downtown business interests on the east and west sides of the Milwaukee River, which reflected the frontier conflicts between the two oldest sections of the city. Although the ultimate location of the civic center remained west of the Milwaukee River, the political infighting delayed the project. The county courthouse was not completed until the 1930s, and Frank Lloyd Wright eviscerated its grandiose design as a "million-dollar rockpile."[25] Land assembly for the project also proved difficult, and it took eminent domain proceedings to ultimately acquire many of the smaller buildings and homes located along Kilbourn Avenue in the 1930s. The delays stretched into and beyond World War II. A city report in 1947, reviewing the civic center's checkered history, concluded that Milwaukee had "failed miserably" to execute Clas's original plans. It also noted that the only time that an outside, unbiased party of "top-ranking professional planners" had scrutinized the plan was in 1909, when Nolen and Olmsted, Jr., submitted their brief report.[26] Clas's calls for the beautification of the city's rivers took even longer to come together. Owners of buildings that abutted the Milwaukee River downtown showed virtually no interest in retrofitting their structures to accommodate leisure and tourism. Clas had foreseen a time as early as 1916 when Milwaukee would—ideally—be noted for its urban beauty as much as its vaunted manufacturing, urging a civic group that year to "waken to the realization that we must manufacture one article for our own comfort and pleasure, and that is a Milwaukee Beautiful!"[27] Nevertheless, the city did not take Clas's riverfront plans to heart until the 1980s, when other efforts to revamp downtown made the project viable. After Clas moved to Florida, the civic center project stalled until Daniel Hoan's mayoralty, when city planning became ensconced as a central function of municipal government.

Milwaukee's City Beautiful projects and plans appear even more modest when the experience of other American cities is considered. Many industrial cities of similar size and ethnic makeup embarked on far more ambitious—and costly—civic projects. Pittsburgh's civic leaders hired Frederick Law Olmsted, Jr., to devise a plan for that city's downtown, and Olmsted produced a lengthy report that included eighty recommendations for traffic improvements, and a series of ambitious waterfront improvements. Pittsburgh's city council acted far more quickly on at least some of Olmsted's plans as well. In 1912, only a year after Olmsted's plan was released to the public, the city council passed a $3 million bond issue that removed a large hill located downtown, thus paving the way for the widening of some key streets near downtown's growing civic center at Fifth and Grant streets. With help from several elite families, the city also accelerated the building of its cultural and education center, Oakland, with the completion of the entrance to Schenley Park in 1923. Milwaukee's somewhat more abortive efforts at beautifying its center contributed to its reputation for conservatism and caution in the realm of grandiose civic projects, and an apparent abhorrence to major urban changes. This reputation lasted throughout much of the twentieth century and is now embedded in many historical interpretations of Milwaukee. Cities such as Cleveland, Pittsburgh, St, Louis, and Detroit all contain concentrated cultural centers, often called "second downtowns," that are remnants of the early twentieth-century impulse toward neoclassical architecture, grand civic designs, and gifts of the industrial elites who gained great wealth during America's age of great city urbanism. No such secondary center exists in Milwaukee, and many of the civic elites who may have hoped to fund and guide a similarly elaborate project in Milwaukee frequently found their efforts frustrated.[28]

Clas's 1909 plans for the civic center and riverfronts arrived just before a monumental political shift in Milwaukee. In 1910, Milwaukee became the first large city in America to elect a Socialist mayor, as citizens voted in Emil Seidel, along with eleven aldermen to the Common Council, Daniel Hoan to the City Attorney's office, and Charles Whitnall to the position of city treasurer. The election was the culmination of thirteen years of organization-building. Milwaukee's Social Democratic Party first formed in 1897, largely through the efforts of Victor Berger, who quickly emerged as the party's most crucial leader. Milwaukee's huge concentration of German immigrants, by far the city's largest community of Europeans, tended to have less cultural opposition to socialism. Berger and his cohorts, many of them German immigrants or offspring of immigrants, leveraged the city's ethnicity in their favor. However, it was the corrupt administration of Milwaukee Mayor David Rose that eventually helped the Socialists the most. Rose implicitly tolerated vice, once famously saying of prostitution, "men are, and always have been, men."

However, most damaging to Rose politically was his change of heart regarding The Milwaukee Electric Railway and Light Company (TMERL), the city's private transit operator. Rose originally campaigned for mayor as an opponent of the "streetcar ring" but abruptly seemed to change his mind once in office. In 1900, TMERL executives, already under public scrutiny for their attempted weakening of the local transit workers' union, cut a deal with Mayor Rose and the Common Council, agreeing to lower fares to four cents a ride, but in exchange for an extension of the company's franchises until 1934. Berger's Social Democratic Party (whose members were commonly referred to as "Socialists"), first organized in 1897, hammered away at the TMERL deal. Many party leaders had been members of the city's Federated Trade Council, the largest trade union group in Milwaukee. TMERL's reputation for short-changing labor, combined with its pattern (replicated by most private transit companies) of extending streetcar lines first to wealthy neighborhoods, and only to working class neighborhoods as an afterthought, made it an ideal target for Berger's class-conscious Socialists. Moreover, Rose's apparent personal corruption opened the door to reform, and in the 1900s, the Socialists gradually won more votes. In 1904, Berger ran for mayor, and gained 25 percent of the vote, with nine Socialist aldermen winning seats on the forty-six member Milwaukee Common Council. In 1910, thirteen years of gradually building up the party and honing its reform message paid off. Milwaukee voters elected Seidel, already an alderman and owner of a small pattern-making shop, mayor and sent twenty-one Socialist aldermen (out of a shrunken total of thirty-five) to the Common Council.[29]

More remarkably, Milwaukee was governed by Socialist mayors for thirty-eight of the next fifty years, and the focus of its planning community also ultimately shifted in the wake of Seidel's election. However, little if any attention has been given to the relationship between planning and socialism in the city. Instead, attention shines on ideology, party politics, and the meanings of "sewer socialism," a phrase that originally was used to denigrate the party in Milwaukee as overly pragmatic and procedure-driven at the expense of radicalism. This narrative pattern has taken the form of both endorsement and critique, but it is generally accepted that there was little revolutionary about the city's Socialists, and while the party brought efficient government to Milwaukee, its fiscal policies also *contributed* to the city's civic reputation for caution, thrift, and deliberate action. Bayard Still's still iconic history of Milwaukee, published in 1948, perhaps set the tone by concluding that the 1910 election of Seidel as mayor "was a political, not a social event."[30]

It was the party's dogged organizational activities, Still argued, as well as Milwaukee's large Germanic population and subsequent cultural tolerance for socialism, that accounted for the 1910 results. Party leader Berger, a hard-headed, nonideological master of organization-building, was the national face of socialism in Milwaukee. The second most prominent Socialist, Daniel Hoan, also was a pragmatist at heart—always conscious of political reality—and rarely advocated the type of radicalism idealists dreamed of. Hoan's refusal to endorse the American Socialist Party's resolution protesting American involvement in World War I is perhaps the most obvious example of this realism in action. Political reality, historians have concluded, constricted radicalism and moderated the socialist message. To appeal to the middle class, whose votes often swung in the favor of whatever candidate seemed the most "progressive," Seidel, Berger, and Hoan often used rhetoric indistinguishable from that of other reform mayors in this era.[31]

The attention lavished on party politics, voting statistics, ideological debates, and stances on national issues such as World War I teaches us much about what Socialists believed and how they won and lost elections, but little about what they did while in office. An obvious reason for this is that in most American cities, Socialists only held power for a few years, and thus had scant time to implement long-range policy. This is especially apt in the relationship between municipal socialism and city planning, since planning efforts require years of implementation and (usually) some type of public consensus. Milwaukee's Socialist mayors rarely enjoyed majorities on the Common Council, and the Socialist organizational apparatus eroded in the decades after World War I. The decline of socialism in party politics has thus distracted attention away from Socialist policies. Finally, with the exception of John Gurda's magisterial urban biography of Milwaukee, the efforts of the Socialists' most important planner, Charles Whitnall, have gone virtually unmentioned in scholarly literature. Thus the link between municipal socialism and city planning has yet to be made. But Milwaukee's Socialists did fervently believe city planning could better the city and act as a tool for social justice. In this regard, planning in Milwaukee closely, but not exclusively, mirrors the outlook of anticongestion reformers Marsh and Simpkovich, active on the national scene but written out of the larger planning movement by Olmsted, Jr., and his cohorts at precisely the same time Seidel, Whitnall, Hoan, and eleven aldermen won Milwaukee city government for the Socialist Party.

The 1910 Socialist sweep held America's attention for a brief but arresting moment. Newspapers such as *The New York Times* and *The Wall Street Journal* wondered whether this was an example of creeping radicalism in the country. Party leaders were quick to play down the Milwaukee election's national impact. Berger, ever the pragmatist, said, "There will be no utopia, no millennium, none of the wild antics our opponents have charged us with."[32] For his part, the victorious Seidel promised his first action as mayor would be to "reassure the people and relieve their minds of an apparent fear that our victory means an entire overturning of business on our city."[33] In a 1913 essay on socialism, Walter Lippman assumed that any Socialist administration would seek to redistribute wealth via increased taxes on property that would be used on a variety of social policy initiatives aimed at helping the poor.

The writings of Seidel, Hoan, Whitnall, and other Socialists do feature rhetoric that favored wealth redistribution, but this never manifested into the type of fiscal policies predicted by Lippman. The fiscal conservatism of so-called "sewer socialists" is often used as a primary example of the absence of radicalism in Milwaukee. Practical political and class concerns informed this fiscal conservatism. Milwaukee's socialist base of working-class homeowners bore the greatest burden if property taxes rose dramatically. Mayor Seidel and, later, Mayor Hoan instead preferred to preach governmental efficiency and honesty, not necessarily to shine their moderate "progressive" reform credentials, but as the most realistic way to avoid alienating their political base and yet still manage to use the savings gained from austerity and prudence to modestly increase spending.[34] The second major piece of fiscal "conservatism" associated with Milwaukee Socialists, eliminating municipal debt, also appears to be another example of moderate policy in action. Hoan, the second Socialist mayor of Milwaukee after Seidel, initiated debt amortization and carried it through even the Great Depression. By 1943, Milwaukee achieved zero debt status, much to the chagrin of growth advocates who sought to use city bonds to redevelop downtown Milwaukee. While these cautious fiscal practices are today associated with conservatism, Milwaukee Socialists saw complete solvency as freedom from capitalist banks and flexibility to experiment in times of economic crisis. No matter what the political motivation for these fiscal policies may have been, they clearly inhibited Milwaukee from executing ambitious City Beautiful projects that were becoming the norm for much of urban America in the 1910s and 1920s. Civic ambition and long-range city planning, however, were not absent from municipal socialism. Instead, they were redirected to address the excesses of urban industrialism in more subtle ways during the 1910s. Planning in Socialist Milwaukee reflected not only the "City Beautiful" impulse of mainstream American planning, but also what historian Susan Marie Wirka has called the "City Social" that acted as a counterpoint to the emerging professional planning movement.

The roots of the "City Social" lie in two key places: America's growing social welfare professions, in which women played a crucial role, and radical critiques of urbanization, which called for unprecedented levels of state intervention in the city building process. As urban overcrowding increased in the 1900s, women settlement house workers began framing the problems of poor neighborhoods as environmental instead of behavioral. As Florence Kelley, one of the City Social movement's key leaders, famously stated, "Instead of assenting to the belief that people who are poor must be crowded, why did we not see years ago that people who were crowded must be poor?"[35] Kelley and Mary Simkhovitch, both settlement house workers, played crucial roles in the formation of the New York City–based Committee on Congestion of Population (CCP). Journalist Benjamin Marsh, who was gaining a reputation as a vigorous advocate of wealth distribution, served as the Committee's general secretary.

In 1909, the CCP sponsored a "Congestion Exhibit" in New York City that drew attention to overcrowding and the lack of recreation facilities, playgrounds, and parks. City planning promised to ameliorate these conditions. Marsh, already an advocate of Fabian Socialism and Henry George–style tax reform, was deeply impressed by European planning ideas, with which he had become familiar after a 1907 visit to the continent. That summer in London, the International Housing Conference met, and its attendees concluded that congestion could only be prevented by cities if they obtained the "power to forbid the erection of any new buildings except in accordance with a general plan for developing all uncovered land within the city boundaries."[36] Marsh also strongly admired German planning efforts, which gave municipalities broad powers to exercise land use controls, which served as precursors to modern zoning ordinances.[37] Counterparts in the City Beautiful like Nolen and Olmsted, Jr. also took many cues from European planners and certainly came to favor German-style zoning for American cities, but they were not motivated as strongly by Marsh and other housing reformers' almost singular focus on congestion, nor did they emphasize population dispersal to the extent Marsh and his social progressive allies did.

Similar links between neighborhood-level housing reform and anticongestion impulses were present in Milwaukee, and they contributed to the formation of professional, comprehensive city planning. Milwaukee's first large, professionally operated settlement house, the Wisconsin University Settlement Association (WUSA), was established in 1902. The WUSA was an extension of what came to be known nationally as the "Wisconsin Idea," which linked technical experts—often from universities—to a variety of public and private enterprises. The University of Wisconsin alumni who founded WUSA, most prominently Herbert Jacobs, sought to develop this kind of synergy between higher education and the state's largest city. WUSA's original board of directors consisted of ten Milwaukee residents and five directors in "active connection with the University of Wisconsin."[38] For its original location, the settlement house's founders chose Milwaukee's crowded and primarily Polish Fourteenth Ward. Like most settlement houses of this era, more than a hint of paternalism informed its founders. Jacobs called WUSA "a school of citizenship" and most of the activities

WUSA sponsored—such as housekeeping, cooking, saving money, and English language—clearly sought to make Fourteenth Ward residents better American citizens.

But WUSA also became a crucial generator of policy advocacy. Jacobs became a vocal proponent of child labor restrictions and workman's compensation, two measures that Milwaukee's Socialist Party also vigorously pushed for. Furthermore, WUSA enabled many professional (and volunteer) females to become involved in city politics. One of WUSA's workers was Anne Gordon Whitnall, the wife of Charles Whitnall, one of the founding members of Milwaukee's Socialist Party. Anne Whitnall became a passionate advocate for publicly funded "social centers," places where children could play and adults could discuss politics and enjoy simple entertainment. Anne Whitnall used this issue to win election to the Milwaukee School Board in 1907, with support from the Socialist Party, which she officially joined in 1909. While on the School Board, Anne Whitnall worked with fellow board member Meta Berger, wife of Socialist Party leader Victor Berger, to help make the social centers a reality. The Socialist Party platform of 1910 included the provision of social centers under its call for the improvement of public schools. Two years later, in a referendum, Milwaukee citizens voted to spend $20,000 to fund social centers in local schools, which became popular neighborhood gathering places for decades to come.[39]

Emil Seidel's mayoralty lasted only two years, from 1910 to 1912, but that proved long enough to begin orienting planning in Milwaukee toward the City Social. While the Socialists campaigned most strenuously (and successfully) against corruption and for municipal efficiency, they also linked housing and planning. The 1910 Socialist platform's eighth plank called for "better homes and living" and hinted at a metropolitan approach to planning by promising to annex enough vacant land on the periphery to allow for "experts" to ensure healthier conditions "in the organization of homes, factories, schools, and playgrounds."[40] Once in office, Seidel and his cohorts attacked the housing problem in much the same way Marsh's CCP did, mainly by drawing attention to it as an environmental problem. Milwaukee's housing problem was featured in a December 1910 issue of *The Survey*, which was published by the Kellogg brothers, who had recently completed their groundbreaking "Pittsburgh Survey," perhaps the most comprehensive survey of social conditions yet made of an urban industrial American city. Milwaukee city clerk Carl D. Thompson authored the article, which refuted the widely held view that Milwaukee's absence of tenements was equated with an absence of a housing problem. Herbert Jacobs, WUSA's head, observed, "What we have in Milwaukee is tenement and slum conditions in the cottage dwellings of the city."[41] Thompson also challenged city boosters' claims that Milwaukee's home ownership rates were as high as was claimed, noting that 35 percent of Milwaukeeans were home owners, which was, he noted, actually a lower proportion than in such Midwest cities as Cleveland and Detroit. "But how can it be said even of such a city, 'It is a city of homes?'" mused Thompson, since "only a trifle over one-third of the people have a place which they can call their own."[42] Thompson's article also called attention to the problem of cheap transportation, noting that a main goal of the Seidel administration was to gain municipal control over the city's streetcar and interurban transportation system. Here, too, Thompson framed transportation as a means to reduce congestion. "Solve the problem of cheap and rapid transportation," he wrote, "and the working people may live by the rivers, amid sunshine and shade, the melody and song of nature's open fields." [43]

International reform-oriented journals also took notice of the Seidel administrations' early efforts to highlight housing as a planning problem. In 1911, *American Review of Reviews* author George Allan England hinted that Seidel's administration wanted to plan a metropolitan-wide park system, and even to build municipally owned homes on the urban fringe. Under the Socialists, England noted, "all plans are based on the idea that the first consideration should be to make the city a better home for those who do the work of the city."[44] In 1911, Mayor Seidel also attended the National Conference on City Planning's third annual meeting in Philadelphia. Seidel apparently eschewed the sessions organized by Olmsted, Jr., and his cohorts, who were in the process of seizing control of the city planning movement from social progressives like Marsh. Marsh's New York Committee on the Congestion of Population organized the only session Seidel officially attended.[45] Seidel's administration also succeeded in persuading the Common Council to change the name of the Metropolitan Parks Commission in 1911 to the "City Planning Commission," which more accurately reflected that body's activities.[46]

No one personifies the relationship between social progressivism and city planning in Milwaukee more than Charles Whitnall, who served as city treasurer during Seidel's administration and emerged during this time as the most influential planner in the city's history. Like many "pioneer planners" of the early twentieth century, Whitnall was not professionally trained. The son of a prominent local florist, Whitnall was born in 1859 and raised at a home four miles north of downtown, along the banks of the Milwaukee River, in what was a decidedly rural environment through the 1870s and 1880s.[47] The juxtaposition of the nineteenth-century Whitnall home between a verdant rural riverbank and a growing city bears some similarity to the boyhood home of famed Scottish regional theorist Patrick Geddes, who came to see his family home as a "middle ground" between city and country and who, like Whitnall, allowed this tension to inform much of his writing.[48] The flatlands west of the Whitnall home—better known as the neighborhood of Riverwest—filled up with working-class German and Polish residents in the 1880s, allowing Whitnall to witness, firsthand and not without reservation, the forces of urbanization, industrialization, and immigration. In the 1890s, Whitnall, who had taken over his father's floral business, grew attracted to socialism, eventually coming to the Milwaukee Social Democratic Party via a much different route than Berger, Seidel, and Hoan. The source of most party leaders and the rank and file was the Federated Trades Council of Milwaukee, the city's largest labor organization, and Milwaukee's large working-class German population. Whitnall, native born, of British lineage, and a business owner, was not a direct participant in the Federated Trades Council, and perhaps for this reason has received strikingly little historic attention. But like his eventual fellow travelers, Whitnall, too, became interested in socialism in the late nineteenth century, joining, along with his first wife, Anne, Milwaukee's small Fabian-inspired "Ethical Society" and eventually getting elected president in 1899.[49]

Fabian societies, by far most numerous in England, were perhaps best known for their gradualist, incremental approach to reforming capitalism, but in the 1890s, heavily influenced by the writings of American reformer Henry George, they also accommodated an increasingly shrill critique of urbanization.[50] Ebenezer Howard, the English Garden City visionary, attracted a great many Fabians to his cause after the publication of *To-morrow: A Peaceful Path to Reform* in 1899. Howard also gleaned many of his own insights about industrial urbanism from the writings of Americans such as George and Edward Bellamy. American reformer William Dwight Porter Bliss cemented the connection between English and American Garden City idealists and Fabianism when he became the president of the American Fabian Society in the 1890s and later also founded the Garden Cities Association of America.[51]

Whitnall's ideas on politics and urbanism developed on a similar trajectory, first as a Fabian Society member, then as a charter member of the Milwaukee Social Democratic Party in 1897, and by the early twentieth century as a clear believer in Garden City planning. His writings indicate an eclectic blend of influences—the land reform ideas of Henry George and Benjamin Marsh, the conservationist regionalism of Patrick Geddes, and the town planning principles and utopian socialism of Howard. Like George,

Marsh, and Howard, Whitnall came to believe that urban real estate development was inherently exploitative. Real estate values were the highest in the most crowded places in cities. Because of this, the owners of land in these congested urban spaces relied not on the land itself for their wealth but on the high volume of people who occupied or passed their property and made these places so congested—and accordingly so valuable—in the first place. Therefore, Whitnall frequently concluded, the recipients of this wealth had not come by it honestly. This "unearned increment," the term that George had used to describe inflated real estate values and one that Whitnall made liberal use of as well, encouraged population congestion as a way to maximize land values. Unregulated capitalism had created congestion; and Whitnall, more than any other Milwaukee Socialist, charged municipal government with the task of reversing the trend.[52] Whitnall was Milwaukee's most vocal proponent of decentralization and served on both city and county parks and planning commissions from 1907 to 1945. His dual political vantage point was a rarity in Milwaukee politics and made Whitnall one of the few local leaders whose positions dictated that he transcend boundary politics.

Whitnall first grew interested in city planning during his involvement in the formation of the Milwaukee County Parks Commission, which formed in 1907, the same year that city leaders created the Metropolitan Parks Commission (a misleading title, since the body only had jurisdiction over city park development). A year earlier, in 1906, Whitnall authored his first important treatise, an eight-page publication that drew attention to the relationship between city and country, and the use of parks to mediate these spaces. Cities had, Whitnall charged, "vitiated" the nurturing influences of vegetation. City builders had completely ignored the landscape in the platting of residential streets, which almost always followed the grid pattern that many planners had grown to object. Whitnall linked the grid pattern to the exploitation of real estate speculators, who thus maximized corner lots, "because they fetch a higher price."[53] Furthermore, Whitnall was suspicious of the utility of placing small parks in a congested environment, "for what is a park but an island of normal atmosphere surrounded by physical disintegration?"[54] Whitnall's untitled report helped inform the County Parks Commission's activities, and he was a charter member of the commission when it formed in 1907. Furthermore, Alfred Clas's civic center plan for Milwaukee, which was made two years later in 1909, hinted at a system of "parked ways" that would cover a much broader swath of territory than the small "islands" of green space Whitnall charged were insufficient to city dwellers' needs. While the civic center project struggled to come to fruition for years, Clas had provided Whitnall with a ready-made blueprint for a far more ambitious system of parks, which he utilized when he emerged as the Socialists' key planner during the 1910s.

Whitnall's park plans were popular enough to earn him inclusion on the 1910 Socialist Party ticket, and he joined Seidel in municipal government as city treasurer from 1910 to 1912. In 1911, Whitnall, who remained a member of the newly dubbed City Planning Commission, authored his second major statement on urban development. Like his 1906 treatise on parks, Whitnall's "Milwaukee City Planning" was not a concrete set of policy objectives, but instead a highly polemical statement on the "aims and principles" of planning that guided the Socialists and a broad outline of future plans he hoped Milwaukee would undertake. Echoing Marsh, Kelley, and Simkhovitch, Whitnall began by noting that individuals did not create their environments; their living conditions greatly determined human development. "It is important to understand," Whitnall noted, "that about all the ills of a large city, for which remedies are continually being advocated, are directly or indirectly caused by congestion."[55] The mixed-use streets of the unregulated built environment, where land uses varied from building to building, had caused chaos, discord, and ultimately, gross capitalist exploitation. For planning to be effective, Milwaukee needed to follow German planners' lead and establish "special city ordinances" on future vacant lots, where land uses could separate commercial, industrial, and residential buildings. Whitnall expressly linked planning to housing reform in the last section of his report, which he titled "Model Homes or Garden City Additions." Since landlords—collectors of rent—were inherently exploitative, it was necessary for the *city* to "set the good example and provide these model homes, so as to give each an equal opportunity at the outset."[56] Whitnall hoped Milwaukee would look "far into the future" and plan for development on the city's outskirts, thus avoiding "the extra effort to rebuild, which is now necessary within the old city limits."[57]

The "aims and objectives" of Whitnall's 1911 report shaped much of how the future Socialist administrations of Daniel Hoan and Frank Zeidler approached city building. Urban problems were chiefly environmental, not behavioral. More conventional progressive reformers believed much the same, but to Whitnall, the "criminal class" was not the "court victims" of the judicial system, but "the ruling class" of landlords and speculators that exploited slum dwellers.[58] Civic beauty of the type pioneer planners like Charles Mulford Robinson and John Nolen offered could not remedy urban problems. Whitnall's report never even used the phrase "City Beautiful" and made no mention of civic centers or grandiose architectural designs that supposedly inspired citizens and brought fame to cities. Instead, Milwaukee could lead the way in building cities "with foresight and wisdom in the interest of all the people." To that end, it was the periphery of the city, not its center, that held the greatest promise. Planners could shape vacant land with highly regulated use restrictions, and workers could move out of crowded slums and into "garden neighborhoods" where natural light, fresh air, and access to the healing natural environment were more easily attained. Whatever transportation mode was to be utilized, be it rail, streetcar, or even automobiles (which Whitnall briefly mentioned), needed to facilitate decentralization. Though Whitnall did not explicitly mention it, the orientation toward the periphery and the emphasis on the social aspects of planning hinted at a regionalist conception that Lewis Mumford, Clarence Stein, and other planners explicated in the 1920s, and that Milwaukee's broader planning community slowly began to embrace.

A familial connection gave Milwaukee an unlikely but strong planning link with Los Angeles. Whitnall's son Gordon, also a Socialist and an aspiring planner, admired his father's plans. In 1910, Gordon Whitnall moved to Los Angeles, doing so, he claimed, "expressly for the purpose of inaugurating planning" in that rapidly growing western city. Gordon Whitnall eventually succeeded, helping to create Los Angeles's first planning body in the 1910s, and serving as Secretary of the Los Angeles City Planning Commission in the 1910s and 1920s.[59] Gordon shared Charles's vitriol toward congestion and his regionalist planning mentality, and the Whitnalls remained very close throughout the next thirty years, frequently visiting one another and keeping each other abreast of developments in both Milwaukee and Los Angeles. Late in his own life, Gordon recalled of his professional relationship with Charles, "Although we represented different generations our interests, our work, and our careers both technically and officially paralleled each other in a striking manner. We see-sawed back and forth in pioneering certain phases of planning efforts."[60] To Charles, one of those "pioneering" moments had clearly been his 1911 report of planning for Milwaukee. Three decades after its release, an elderly Charles sent a copy of the report to Gordon in California, reminding him, "You will notice this article was written in 1911, thirty years ago. Some of the recommendations therein made, I would not make in 1941, as they have become unnecessary by the advent of the auto truck and a few other modern experiences, including auto parking. But, fundamentally, the objectives of 1911 remain."[61]

Whitnall's 1911 report eventually provided broad outlines for planning in Milwaukee across a metropolitan terrain, but at present Emil Seidel's mayoralty fell into jeopardy. Both the Republican and Democratic parties, "deeply embarrassed by the Socialist victory of 1910," sought to regain control of city government with a renewed vigor.[62] For the 1912 elections, Republicans and Democrats decided to join forces, putting forth a "fusion" ticket of candidates from both parties. Key fusion candidates reflected the city's three most numerous ethnic groups: Gerhard Bading, a German American and the former city health commissioner, was the mayoral candidate; Louis Kotecki, a Polish Catholic, ran for comptroller; and J. P. Carney, an Irish Catholic, ran for treasurer. Bading's presence on the ticket, especially, helped give the fusionists reform credentials. Accompanying the temporary Republican-Democratic merger was an initiative for "nonpartisan elections" put forth by a variety of civic organizations in Milwaukee, perhaps most notably the City Club, a reform-minded group of citizens that first organized in 1909. Election reform of this type was common in the Progressive Era, and as numerous scholars have demonstrated, often served as a tool by middle- and upper-class urban residents to minimize the influence of both political machines and poorer immigrant newcomers to cities. While many criticized Victor Berger as a "party boss" of a radical stripe, it was more difficult to label Seidel's efficient administration as corrupt. Absent this conventional rhetorical weapon, the fusion candidates promised reform, but also an escape from "Red rule."[63]

When the results were counted in April of 1912, Bading had defeated Seidel by nearly 13,000 votes. Moreover, Socialists lost their majority on the Common Council and Whitnall vacated his post as treasurer. A month after the election, the Wisconsin legislature voted to reform municipal elections in Milwaukee, eliminating party labels from all future ballots. Politicians obviously maintained party allegiance, but voters no longer saw these affiliations on election ballots. The 1912 election reforms clearly targeted Socialist Party influence, and no 1910 sweep of Socialists into so many city government positions occurred again. Individual candidates affiliated with the local Socialist Party, however, continued to play crucial roles in formulating policy, and Whitnall, who remained on the City Planning Commission after the 1912 election, had established himself as a key voice for planning.

Large-scale planning was now a more prominent part of the public conversation on city building. Seidel and Whitnall's explicit links between planning and housing had gained traction, and it became apparent their appeal was not solely within the confines of the Socialist Party. In 1915, the Wisconsin state legislature authorized the City Planning Commission as the permanent, official planning agency for Milwaukee, under yet another name: the Board of Public Land Commissioners (BPLC). The new name reflected the work Clas had already done in civic center planning. While the 1915 legislation fell short of providing land use controls of the type

Whitnall hoped for, it did provide legitimacy to the city's planning activities. In Milwaukee, civic groups otherwise opposed to socialist ideology but concerned about urban overcrowding, chaotic development, and the urban growth of Milwaukee, temporarily picked up the planning baton after Seidel left office. In 1915, six organizations, the Wisconsin chapter of the American Institute of Architects, the City Club of Milwaukee, the Milwaukee Real Estate Association, the Westminster League, and the South Side Civic Association invited Werner Hegemann, a German planning proponent of growing international stature, to author a report on the importance of city planning for Milwaukee. Their choice of Hegemann further demonstrates the roots of social progressivism in Milwaukee's early history of planning.

Hegemann has recently been referred to as "Germany's Lewis Mumford" and his background personified social progressivism as a transatlantic force.[64] Born and raised in Germany, he moved to the United States in 1904, enrolling briefly at the University of Pennsylvania. At Penn, Hegemann studied economics under Simon Patten, the renowned progressive scholar who had previously mentored Benjamin Marsh.[65] Hegemann eventually earned a doctorate in political science in Germany, but he grew deeply interested in city planning through his exposure to Patten's teachings and during his frequent visits to the United States between 1904 and 1913. It was also during this time that Hegemann, who had no formal training in architecture or engineering, became interested in city planning. Hegemann greatly admired the New York Committee on Congestion of Population's 1909 exhibit, and he played a crucial role in the Universal City Planning Exhibits in Berlin and Dusseldorf in 1910.[66] At the German exhibition, Hegemann played host to American planning intellectuals like George Ford, Jr., a frequent advocate of housing reform, and Frederic C. Howe, an ardent single-taxer. After the Berlin and Dusseldorf exhibitions ended, Howe invited Hegemann to the United States as a guest of the People's Institute of New York City. After a lengthy lecture tour, the cities of Oakland and Berkeley, California, invited Hegemann to author a planning report for those locales, which he published in 1915, with Howe authoring the report's preface. With World War I's outbreak and the subsequent backlash against German culture growing, Hegemann's popularity in the American West waned. An Oakland newspaper even accused him of studying the East Bay harbor as a spy for the German government.[67] Hegemann thus arrived in Milwaukee in the middle of 1915, and he found the heavily German city far more receptive to his talents. The six aforementioned civic groups, on behalf of the City Planning Commission of Milwaukee, agreed to fund Hegemann's planning study of Milwaukee, which he completed in 1916.

Hegemann's report, *City Planning for Milwaukee: What It Means and Why It Must be Secured*, was built off Whitnall's 1911 planning statements, and differed noticeably from the Clas-influenced *Preliminary Reports* of 1909 and 1910. Like Whitnall, Hegemann attacked the original street grid layout for Milwaukee, created in the 1830s, as "shortsighted" and "thoughtless."[68] The extension of these "checkerboard" streets had allowed for congestion and prevented "the healthy spreading out of land values."[69] The *Preliminary Reports* had completely ignored housing; Hegemann dedicated ten pages—about a quarter of his report—to the city's housing problems. He highlighted the tension between boosters who promoted Milwaukee as a "city of homes" and reformers who claimed Milwaukee was "one of the most congested [cities] of its size."[70] One of the "greatest responsibilities of city building," Hegemann wrote, was to regulate "the proper subdivision of land."[71] The small lots carved out of the original street grids of Milwaukee, which often measured only twenty-five feet wide, were no longer adequate to meet the needs of modern industrial workers. Hegemann's report frequently used German cities—where land subdivision was more heavily regulated—as examples of good planning. Furthermore, Hegemann wrote that working-class neighborhoods needed to be oriented away from factories and toward nature, and he hinted that municipalities could promote future urban growth along these lines by exercising land use controls that would separate work and residence more clearly.

Like Whitnall's 1911 planning report, Hegemann provided no concrete plans for Milwaukee. Nevertheless, his report proved useful to the city because it implicitly endorsed a planning mentality that was already ascending in Milwaukee, namely, the notion that city building needed to be thought of broadly, not solely in terms of civic beautification; that the creation of decent housing should be promoted for all sectors of society and was a crucial part of planning; and that planning should guide growth away from the urban core. Whitnall's report had already expressed these sentiments, but Hegemann's international status and familiarity with planning theory and vocabulary gave these ideas a professional legitimacy, which seemed especially important after Seidel's 1912 defeat. It also cemented a local reputation for Hegemann in Milwaukee, which he parlayed in 1916 when he was hired by industrialist Walter Kohler, Jr. to build a "model village" for Kohler's workers north of Milwaukee, near the city of Sheboygan. Hegemann worked with several local architects on the project, but his most fruitful collaboration on Kohler, Wisconsin (as the village came to be known), was with a young landscape architect from Boston named Elbert Peets. Hegemann and Peets formed a close and lifelong friendship,

and they also worked together on the development of Washington Highlands, a 133-acre subdivision carved out of land owned by the family of
Milwaukee industrialist Frederic Pabst in Wauwatosa, a village adjacent to
Milwaukee's West Side.[72] Washington Highlands, with uniform setbacks,
heavily wooded and curvilinear streets, and huge lots, became one of the
Milwaukee region's premier residential neighborhoods, and probably made
more palatable Hegemann's planning ideas as they related to Milwaukee.

While Hegemann was releasing his planning report in early 1916, Milwaukee Socialists were rallying around a new candidate for mayor—albeit
a technically "nonpartisan" one on the ballot—Daniel Hoan. Originally
elected as city attorney in the Socialist sweep of 1910, Hoan held on to his
post even after Seidel lost to Bading in 1912, and again in the 1914 election.
Already a Socialist in his early twenties, Hoan earned a law degree from
the University of Wisconsin and passed the bar in 1908. In 1910, at the
age of twenty-nine, he assumed the duties of city attorney with a pub-
lic-minded vigor, gaining prominence as a vocal critic of The Milwaukee
Electric Railway and Light Company, and was the Socialists' most viable
candidate for mayor by 1916. Hoan defeated Bading by a slim margin,
and assumed office in 1916 as the second Socialist mayor in Milwaukee.
Hoan remained in office for twenty-four years, the second-longest tenure
in Milwaukee's history, and gained national renown as a reform-oriented
mayor. A recent poll of urban historians ranked Hoan as the eighth-best
mayor in American history.[73]

Hoan's effectiveness in office, however, usually is emphasized in terms
of pragmatism and efficiency. It is Hoan whose governance is most closely
associated with "sewer socialism," and scholars usually evidence his effectiveness in terms of tight-fisted policies (Milwaukee's municipal debt practically disappeared under Hoan's regime), steady guidance during the Great
Depression, and a populist style that ingratiated Hoan to a non-socialist
base of voters.[74] It is also Hoan who seemed to guide Milwaukee Socialists
away from radicalism. In 1917, during World War I, the national Socialist
Party explicitly denounced America's entry into the war. In a now infamous
political decision, Hoan, under heavy political pressure at home to demonstrate loyalty to the state, denounced the platform and asserted his support
of the war. This decision, probably more than any single incident, orients
Hoan away from socialist radicalism and makes him appear to be a more
conventional and moderate politician. Less noted, however, is the Hoan administration's role in promoting city planning under the guise of planned
decentralization and a regionalist mentality. Hoan's political style, notably
less ideological than many of his socialist contemporaries, falls well short of

leftist radicalism, but his support of Whitnall and other social progressives' planning ideas gave Milwaukee a national reputation for city planning and ensconced a metropolitan growth policy in local government that remained largely intact well after World War II. Furthermore, Hoan took a deep personal pride in his and his allies' ability to promote this planning mentality.

When Hoan took office in 1916, Milwaukeeans seemed to remain generally disinterested in planning. No major initiatives had resulted from Clas, Whitnall, or Hegemann's planning reports. Hoan hoped to change that, and according to historian Frederick Olson, "espoused the cause of planning on every occasion" during his first four years in office.[75] To better promote planning to a citywide audience, Hoan enlisted several local civic organizations to create a City Beautiful Committee. Thirteen such groups participated, and they joined representatives from the Board of Public Land Commissioners and the Park Board on the committee. The list of organizations that sent representatives to the committee was diverse and influential, including the Milwaukee Press Club, the American Institute of Architects' local chapter, the South Side Civic Association (who had sponsored Hegemann's planning report), and the Federated Women's Club.[76] The new group "spread the gospel of planning" through the affiliated organizations until World War I curtailed their efforts. Though the committee's lifespan was short, it also helped Hoan form two crucial alliances—one institutional and the other personal—that proved valuable to his later planning efforts. The institutional link was with the City Club of Milwaukee, a committee participant whose reputation as a nonpartisan reform-oriented group was growing in Milwaukee. The City Club supported many future Hoan planning initiatives, helping to depoliticize policy. The personal link was with William Schuchardt, a local architect who served on Hoan's City Beautiful Committee on behalf of the Milwaukee Art Institute. Schuchardt had visited Europe several times in the 1910s and was enthralled with the English Garden City planning movement led by Ebenezer Howard and Raymond Unwin. Howard's Garden City, and his calls for decentralization, worker communities of human scale, and exposure to nature, as well as his latent socialist rhetoric, provided a clear template for Milwaukee's planners. By virtue of his professional status and his visits to Europe, Schuchardt had the most technical knowledge of English Garden Cities, and Hoan mined it to great use.

World War I halted the City Beautiful Committee's efforts, but it also ultimately drew broad attention to the main problem that housing advocates and planners like Whitnall and Hegemann identified for planning to solve: congestion. Milwaukee's population continued to grow in this decade, from 373,857 in 1910 to 464,689 by 1920. Annexation of new land remained slow, and much of this growth took place within already crowded neighborhoods. Making matters worse, the war temporarily halted building activity, as capital diverted to war industries and away from new housing. Local agencies took notice. In its annual report in 1915, the Milwaukee Sewage Commission counted 75,492 housing units in the city for the city as a whole, 5.023 persons per unit. The Fourteenth Ward, which encompassed much of the Polish South Side, housed on average over eight people per unit, and other wards near the central business district had densities of six to seven people per unit.[77] In 1916, the Health Commission issued a report on slum housing that explicitly linked disease to overcrowding. However, the report did not reflect Whitnall's fervent belief that environment dictated behavior (and health). George Ruhland, city Health Commissioner, admitted that sickness and "delinquency" concentrated in the areas of Milwaukee where housing was the worst, but "it is," he told a local newspaper in 1916, "quite another to state that because a person sick with tuberculosis lives in a poor house, the poor house is the cause of his tuberculosis" since these diseases also existed in better-off homes.[78] Local newspapers like the *Milwaukee Daily News* put it more bluntly:

> Not that we would condemn all those who live in poor homes as lazy, shiftless, or improvident, but a goodly portion of them can live better if they make the effort. The poor we shall always have with us; the deserving poor deserve to be helped; those who are poor through their own folly or vices must be taught to work out their own salvation.[79]

While the causes of poverty and overcrowding remained contested, it was impossible to avoid the problem. As the *Milwaukee Journal* wrote in 1917: "The housing problem is not confined to one district; thirteen out of the 25 wards in the city have poor housing.... It is pointed out that since one-half of this area lies in districts of high land value, the economic loss to the community through non-improvement of the property and the consequent inadequate taxation, is considerable."[80] Slums seemed to be becoming an economic problem that threatened the vitality and wealth of the entire city.

In 1918, Mayor Hoan responded to the wartime housing crisis by creating a Housing Commission. The purpose of the commission—the first quasi-official agency in the city's history that was to specifically target housing—was to study how other cities in America and Europe had attacked the housing problem and to make specific recommendations to Hoan for a plan of action in Milwaukee. The commission included eleven members, many of whom were familiar with both planning and housing issues. Schuchardt, the commission's chair, and Whitnall both served as representatives of the Board of Public Land Commissioners, and Herbert Jacobs represented the Milwaukee settlement house community. Other members included John Hume, a prominent local real estate speculator, William George Bruce, secretary of the Milwaukee Association of Commerce (the largest business organization in the city), a local attorney, a merchant, a banker, and Ruhland, the city health commissioner.

The commission submitted its report to Hoan in the fall of 1918, and it provided one of the clearest expressions of social progressive planning's link to housing. Schuchardt and Whitnall's influences over its content were obvious. The report proposed five solutions to Milwaukee's housing problem. First was the "elimination of speculative land values." Speculative building had, the report argued, not come close to providing decent housing for urban workers. The most effective method to supercede this lay in Europe, where "large tracts of land" were often owned outright by municipalities. Without explicitly saying it, the commission was evoking English Garden Cities like Letchworth. Raymond Unwin had designed Letchworth, and Milwaukee socialists and planners had at least some contact with these ideas through Seidel's presence at the Third National Housing Conference in Philadelphia, Schuchardt's visits to England, and Hegemann's familiarity with Garden City planning in his various international endeavors. No less important were the report's other solutions. Second to ending speculative building was a much-needed extension of the Board of Public Land Commissioners' powers to include land use controls in "outlying districts" that would be "consistent with a general city plan." Third, "waste" could be eliminated from construction by focusing on larger-scale projects, and if the savings gained from improved techniques accrued to the "occupant and not to building speculators." Fourth, housing cooperatives promised to circumvent the "unearned increment" and also, the report argued, lessened foreclosure risks by spreading out the costs (and benefits) of home ownership throughout all cooperative members. Finally, the report called for legislation to "stimulate the erection of wage-earners' homes." Here was an entirely new form of city building that called on government "to put the welfare of the whole above the welfare of groups or individuals."[81]

The Milwaukee Housing Commission's report quickly gained attention, and it launched Milwaukee's ideas into a distinct national conversation that sought to reify housing's place in planning. The Milwaukee report arrived just as many architects and planners, responding to the national wartime housing shortage, began calling for more direct state intervention in the housing industry. New forums for these ideas began to proliferate. The American Institute of Architects' journal was now under the editorial direction of reformer

Charles Harris Whitaker, who was like Whitnall an avid believer in the writings of Henry George, and like Schuchardt a deep admirer of English Garden Cities. Whitaker had already begun to call for governments to house war workers before the Milwaukee Housing Commission issued its report.

As the war continued, Whitaker gradually became disillusioned with capitalism's ability to address urban problems, orienting his writings toward cooperative developments.[82] When news of the Milwaukee Housing Commission report reached Whitaker, he ecstatically wrote to Schuchardt, "God be praised! A housing commission has at last written a human report. This is the first one I ever saw that squarely and fairly attacked the problem at its roots."[83] In the February 1919 edition of Whitaker's *Journal of the American Institute of Architects*, the Milwaukee report appeared in full text.[84] Clarence Stein, a landscape architect and Whitaker protégé who in 1919 served as secretary of the Reconstruction Commission of the state of New York, also wrote Schuchardt asking for suggestions to deal with New York's housing crisis.[85] A frustrating stint on a second New York housing commission inspired Stein to collaborate with Whitaker, and later Lewis Mumford and many other key planning voices, in creating the Regional Planning Association of America (RPAA), which became the preeminent source of regional planning ideas in the country in the 1920s. Stein's knowledge of the commission piqued his interest in planning in Milwaukee. He remained in contact with Schuchardt and Whitnall, speaking with the latter at a conference on cooperative housing in New York City in 1924.[86] A crucial link to an important voice in American planning had been made.

Locally, the Housing Commission report also garnered attention, but not an uncritical reception. Among commission members, the report's harsh criticism of capitalism had not gone unchallenged. John Hume, the commission member who represented real estate interests, disagreed with the report's conclusions. Hume filed a "minority report" to Mayor Hoan that questioned municipal ownership as a housing solution.[87] The city's largest business organization, the Milwaukee Association of Commerce (MAC), commissioned its own housing study in 1919 as a response to Hoan's housing commission. The MAC report surveyed employees who worked for member companies, and claimed to have received over 20,000 surveys, of which only 248 indicated an inability to "find suitable living places." The MAC concluded that no "emergency situation" existed in Milwaukee's housing market.[88] Schuchardt, chair of Hoan's Housing Commission, vigorously disagreed with the MAC's report. The question was not merely whether the supply of homes kept up with demand, but "whether there are enough clean wholesome houses where people can live decently and where children can be given the opportunities they are entitled to, to grow up into physically and morally fit citizens."[89] In that context, Milwaukee's housing problem was chronic; the lack of decent housing had preceded the war and was sure to remain after the war ended unless a fundamental change in city building took place. Milwaukee's building inspector, William Harper, also disagreed with the MAC's conclusions. Thousands of homes in Milwaukee did not meet the city's minimum requirements, Harper told a local paper, and he had intended to initiate demolition on many of the homes if "families living in them had any place to go."[90]

The Housing Commission report was the blueprint for the Garden Homes, one of the first municipally funded housing developments in American history. The wartime housing crisis had given a sense of urgency to the need for affordable dwellings. Mayor Hoan and other city officials understood this and initiated efforts at cooperative housing almost immediately after receiving the Housing Commission's recommendations.[91] The initial plan called for both the city of Milwaukee and Milwaukee County to invest in the cooperative housing scheme, which first required state enabling legislation to be legal. Eager to stimulate the economy in the midst of the postwar recession, the Wisconsin State legislature came through in the summer of 1919, authorizing the creation of a nonprofit, municipally funded housing corporation to purchase and then plat land strictly for residential purposes. To guarantee that public money would be invested in affordable housing, a clause inserted into the bill capped the cost of any homes to be built at $5,000. The entire project, dubbed the "Garden Homes," was to cost $500,000, with half of that amount raised by selling preferred stock. Both the city and the county appropriated $50,000 and hoped to raise an additional $100,000 through private subscriptions.[92]

Initially, these efforts met with difficulty. The city's local business community, reticent about the cooperative principles behind both the Housing Commission and the Garden Homes, proved slow to invest in the project. The recalcitrant MAC announced its own plans for a large-scale housing development. The urgency of the housing shortage, however, transcended politics in this case. In 1920, the MAC agreed to abandon its construction program and relinquish to Hoan's Housing Commission the responsibility for addressing the housing shortage. A year later, the Garden Homes Company was incorporated and capitalized at $500,000. Schuchardt, the chair of Hoan's Housing Commission, served as principal architect for the project. The company chose twenty-nine acres of land just outside of Milwaukee's northern boundary and broke ground on the Garden Homes in September of 1921. By 1922, the first family moved into the project and, a

Garden Homes under Construction—One of the first publicly financed municipal housing projects in the United States, the Garden Homes was intentionally located outside of the Milwaukee urban grid. Courtesy of the Historic Photo Collection / Milwaukee Public Library

year later, 105 single-family homes, ten duplexes, and one apartment house were completed for a total construction cost of only $50,000.[93]

The social progressive ideas of Milwaukee's reform community inspired the city to make land use controls an even more important long-term attempt to implement planning in the city. Both technically oriented planners like Nolen and Olmsted and social progressives like Hegemann and Whitnall agreed on the need to copy German cities and give municipalities the power to zone. The growing popularity of zoning in the 1910s coincided with urban real estate interests' discovery of zoning as a capitalist tool. While on one hand, allowing the state to police land uses threatened to delay the development process, on the other, zoning promised to reorder the city into a more pleasing, safe, and efficiently trafficked place. Zoning also acted as a conservative force when examined within the broader progressive impulse to impose order, both moral and geographical, on the chaotic urban industrial landscape.[94]

The tension between state intervention to further (or even save) capitalism and state intervention to redistribute power from the "land interests" to stewards of the public interest largely made up Milwaukee's early history of zoning. When the Wisconsin state legislature legally sanctioned city planning in Milwaukee in 1915, it also entrusted the newly reorganized Board of Public Land Commissioners to make a comprehensive land use survey of Milwaukee and to adopt a zoning ordinance. Roland E. Stoelting, the BPLC's City Planning Engineer, compiled the land use survey. Stoelting's background was not in planning or architecture, however, and for technical expertise in drafting the ordinance, the city looked for outside help, hiring Boston landscape architect Arthur Comey to consult on drafting the ordinance. Comey was a protégé of Frederick Law Olmsted, Jr., and had recently worked as a town planner for the U.S. Housing Corporation in 1918 and 1919. What impressed Milwaukee's planners about Comey, however, was his stint as town planner for the state of Massachusetts's Homestead Commission, which had made plans during World War I to construct a cooperative housing project in the industrial city of Lowell. Comey created the Lowell project's subdivision plan and was also involved in the design of its cottages until the Commission's funding dried up in 1919.[95] While not a radical, Comey had also written favorably about "co-partnership" housing in national trade publications.[96] The Milwaukee Housing Commission had already lauded the Massachusetts experiment in its reports, making Comey a favorite of social progressives such as Whitnall. Together, Comey and Stoelting worked with the BPLC in late 1919 and 1920 to create the ordinance.

To further promote zoning efforts publicly, the city twice invited Edward Bassett, the primary author of New York City's 1916 zoning ordinance, to speak on behalf of the initiative. Bassett's justification of zoning differed markedly from those of Marsh, Whitnall, and Schuchardt. The problem of real estate speculation was not that it encouraged inhumane conditions, as social progressives frequently pointed out. Instead, without land regulations, it created uncertainty in investments, since "there was nothing to prevent a garage from going up on the next lot" next to a home. Also, as Bassett pointed out during one of his visits to Milwaukee, unregulated land use meant that industrial districts could and did seep into upscale shopping areas. On New York City's Fifth Avenue "crowds and crowds of garment workers" had chased away shoppers, apparently spoiling a genteel part of Manhattan.[97] Bassett's implication was clear: if conservative-minded business leaders felt threatened by the way that the Socialists framed zoning, he had provided an entirely different motivation for the same goal: zoning could also keep "undesirables" out. In the short term, the contradictory message probably broadened zoning's appeal. Bassett spoke to the Milwaukee City Club and the Common Council during his visits, and the BPLC finished Milwaukee's comprehensive zoning ordinance in 1920. Mayor Hoan and the Common Council approved it with little revision; in fact, the Common Council suspended its rules on the hearing of bills to rush the measure through. Zoning was voted into law in November of 1920.[98]

Milwaukee's first zoning ordinance is especially notable because of its extremely stringent controls on land use in the name of reducing congestion. The authors of the zoning ordinance defined congestion as debilitating in two important ways. First, congestion in terms of overcrowded neighborhoods facilitated the spread of diseases, which were "most prevalent in congested localities and people living in congested districts most always show diminished power of resistance to disease."[99] With the Spanish influenza having recently racked American cities during the war, zoning as a way to limit overcrowding gained even greater urgency. As Comey observed in the BPLC's report to the Common Council: "Zoning makes for an orderly city and it can be shown that this will have a marked effect on the physical fitness of the city's inhabitants."[100] The second way congestion could be reduced lay in the type of future economic growth that could occur in Milwaukee. Before zoning, "the hap-hazard development of our city was ruinous" as land uses overlapped, factories stood on residential streets, and apartment buildings crowded next to single-family homes, all of which made the city—in the eyes of planners, at least—a most dysfunctional place. Zoning could arrange land uses into a functional harmony that would provide for a more efficient metropolis. If factories represented "blight within the residential section," zoning them into specific districts would "make it possible for industrial property to develop unhampered."

In the same way, strictly residential districts could make these neighborhoods more peaceful and quiet and, as a caveat to landowners, "increase property values on such streets." To that end, three types of districts—use, area, and height—regulated land uses in Milwaukee. Use districts regulated types of uses to which buildings were put; height districts dictated the height of buildings in identified parts of the city; and area districts were "designed to establish and perpetuate conditions of adequate light and air, avoid congestion wherever possible, and prevent an undue decrease in light and air, and an increase in congestion in those sections where intensive building has already become general."[101]

Four different types of "use districts" were identified and organized: residence, local business, commercial and light manufacturing, and industrial. As in other cities, residential districts were segregated from industry to end the days when, as Milwaukee historian John Gurda has written, "A tannery was located next to a house."[102] Beyond that functional logic, use districts

Poor Planning, Early Twentieth Century—As evidenced by this image that appeared in Milwaukee's first zoning ordinance, planners in the Progressive Era usually frowned on diversity within the built environment, regulating even the mildest differences in the height of buildings. Courtesy of the Legislative Reference Bureau

promised to contain the growth of slums as well. Future residence districts were to be subdivided into lots with minimum sizes 40 feet wide and 120 feet deep for single-family homes, to further ensure that congestion would not continue on the city's periphery.

"Height" and "area" districts were even more stringently regulated. Downtown was to have no building erected at a height greater than 125 feet. "High-rise" apartment areas were limited to two places: Milwaukee's main thoroughfare, Grand Avenue, and parts of the city's East Side near Lake Michigan. No residential building in these areas was to exceed eighty-five feet. The vast majority of residential districts were limited to buildings no taller than forty feet.[103] The draconian height restrictions of Milwaukee's zoning ordinance were not uniformly popular when public hearings on zoning were held in 1920, as the BPLC pushed for passage of zoning. To better explain its rationale, the BPLC released a seven-page report, "Restrictive Heights of Buildings," in advance of the zoning vote. The report insisted that aesthetics were not the sole reason for the height limits, since the iconic European cities of London, Paris, and Berlin, whose beauty the BPLC admittedly said was worth emulating the most, had capped building heights at well under one hundred feet. Rather, the report argued smaller buildings, even in downtowns, were more profitable, and thus within the interests of landowners. The height restriction remained at 125 feet in Milwaukee. While height restrictions were argued for under the aegis of economic expediency, area districts, which regulated the amount of a lot that a building could take up, were clearly designed to make congestion a thing of the past. Here, planners placed the most obvious restriction against overcrowding, as the ordinance required that in areas where it was legal to build apartments, "not more than 50 families may be housed per acre, thus preventing serious congestion." Nationally, planners openly expressed doubt at the utility of area restrictions, and it is clear that Comey's opinion was overridden in the final draft of the ordinance.

A year after the Milwaukee ordinance was complete, Comey told an audience at the National Conference on City Planning that "density restrictions are not necessary" and that most cities had no interest in family-per-acre restrictions.[104] But the Milwaukee ordinance made it clear that a main goal of residential districts was to prevent the creation of tenement apartments and to promote Garden City living as endemic to the highest quality of community life. The hope of creating zoning limits on families per acre was that residence districts "will be in effect garden suburbs, in which it will be a lasting satisfaction to own a home or own an interest in a co-operative group, an ideal generally acknowledged as fundamental to the highest type of citizenship." While the city's ultimate control over the nature of community development on the fringe was, of course, limited outside the constraints of its land use authority, local planners like Whitnall could still hope that projects like the Garden Homes might influence developers toward more judicious platting.[105]

The architects of Milwaukee's zoning ordinance had paid careful attention to growth on the periphery, but they failed to consider much of the inner city as a place of residence. Virtually every low-income neighborhood surrounding downtown was zoned "yellow" for commercial and light industrial use. Furthermore, it is obvious that Milwaukee planners used class, not distance from the central core, as the main criterion in the creation of use districts. The wealthy "Yankee Hill" neighborhood, just east of downtown on high ground between the Milwaukee River and Lake Michigan, remained a "residential" use district, as did the wealthier sections of the city's

East Side. Poorer neighborhoods located near the tanneries that lined the Milwaukee River north of downtown had their "residential" status stripped. The justification for this dramatic change in future use clearly departed from socialist principles, and demonstrates the contradictions inherent in early American zoning, which was justified as both a radical redistribution remedy for ailing cities and a means of capitalist development. Comey attributed Milwaukee's discriminatory land use restrictions to market logic, arguing that light manufacturing could move out of downtown where real estate values were inflated and "utilize that very considerable area which is becoming less and less desirable for residential purposes."[106] Milwaukee's zoners did not expect commercial developments to replace old residences overnight or involuntarily but, instead, hoped that when residents left neighborhoods adjacent to downtown, they would move gradually away from the core, freeing up those zones for nonresidential uses.

Nevertheless, this type of restriction was not benign. Planners in Progressive era Milwaukee largely ignored rehabilitation of inner city neighborhoods in favor of cultivating growth on the urban fringe. The only exception to this pattern was in the modest City Beautiful plans the city had made, and even here, inner city neighborhoods seemed more like obstacles to civic beauty than viable neighborhoods where diverse citizens lived and worked. The partial revival of Alfred Clas's civic center clouded the future of the crowded immigrant neighborhoods west of downtown. In 1919, the BPLC issued a report defending Clas's choice for the West Side of downtown for the civic center location. The Common Council decided to ask Milwaukee citizens for official approval for the site in a 1920 referendum. In April 1920, the measure passed by more than a two-to-one margin, settling the issue of location. The neighborhood adjacent to downtown, where the proposed civic center was now to be located, was part of "Kilbourntown," the name given to the half of the city that sat west of the Milwaukee River. This neighborhood, part of the city's Sixth Ward, had originally served as an entry point for Milwaukee's vast German population and since 1890 increasingly housed Southern and Eastern European immigrants, especially Greeks and Jews.[107] Milwaukee's small but expanding African American community lived in the Sixth Ward as well, which earned parts of the area derisive nicknames such as "Nigger Alley" and "Black Bottom."[108] After a tour of the neighborhood, Milwaukee's Health Commissioner reported that in the Sixth Ward "approximately 20 percent of the sleeping rooms are overcrowded. . . . Bad housekeeping is quite general among all foreign people throughout this area."[109] Although no report on the civic center explicitly stated this, clearly the poor conditions of the Near West Side made the location of the civic center there an easier decision. Both Whitnall and Schuchardt also favored the

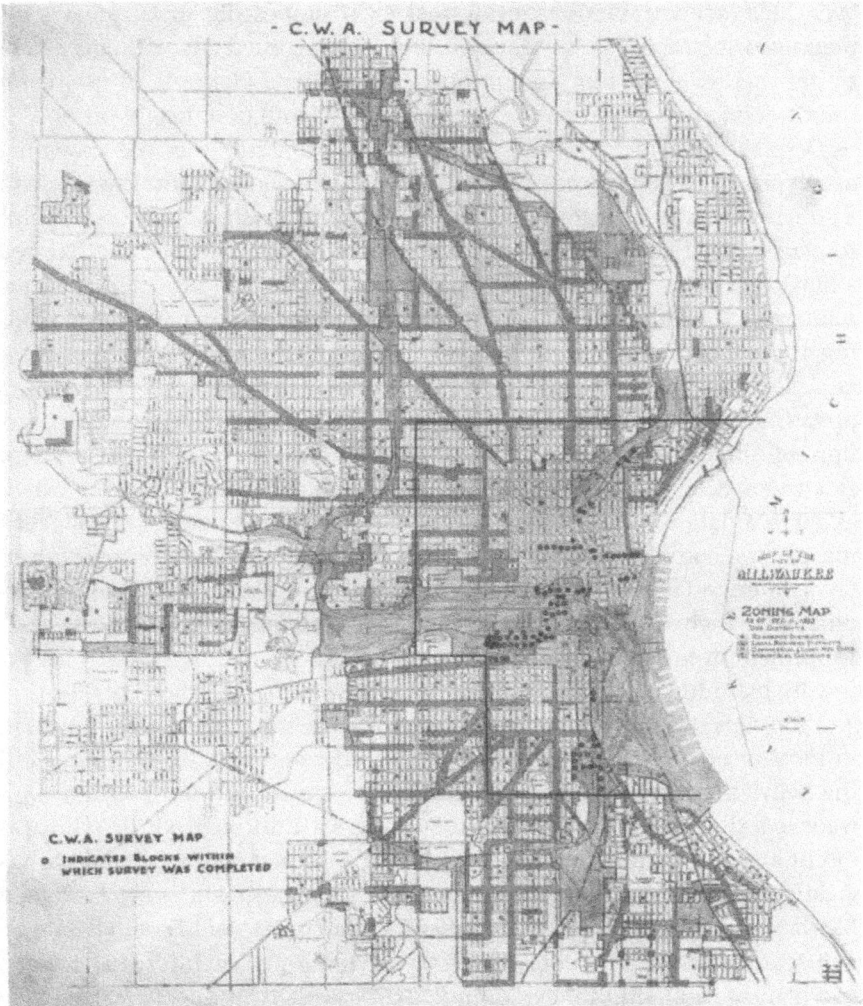

Zoning and "Use Districts"—The vast majority of shaded areas on this zoning map were not "commercial or light industrial" in 1933 or 1920, when the zoning ordinance was written but, instead, encompass most of Milwaukee's poorest residents and oldest housing stock. Planners hoped that zoning would push the urban core's poorest residents—mostly southern and eastern European immigrants and African Americans—out of the central business district. Courtesy of the Milwaukee City Archives / Milwaukee Public Library

West Side location, demonstrating that even supposedly social progressive planners were so obsessed with rupturing the congested city with any weapons at their disposal that they prioritized peripheral planning of new communities (via zoning) far ahead of preserving old and poor neighborhoods.

Despite these shortcomings, the zoning ordinance was the crowning achievement of Milwaukee's nascent planning movement, and it was last in a growing number of planning victories Hoan and his supporters could point to between 1919 and 1920. His Housing Commission had not only created a blueprint for an experimental housing project, but had provided a unique framework for community building that had gained national attention. Zoning, though moderated by the necessity of making it economically appealing, also seemed to give Milwaukee unprecedented control over the city building process. Even City Beautiful ideas survived, as the location (but not construction) of Alfred Clas's civic center finally was settled via the 1920 referendum. Hoan took deep personal pride in his promotion of planning. In 1919, when asked in a national survey, Hoan called his greatest moment as Milwaukee's mayor "the complete crystallization and functioning of popular opinion in favor of city planning."[110] Capping it all was the passage of the zoning ordinance, which Hoan later characterized as "perhaps the greatest single advancement ever made by Milwaukee."[111]

City planning had gained a foothold in Milwaukee, but the City Beautiful and City Practical movements had not played the same major roles they had in most of urban America. The National Conference on City Planning, still the bellwether for the national planning movement, did not mention Milwaukee a single time in its proceedings from 1912 through 1920. Yet it was essentially during this same time period that a distinct metropolitan vision—greatly informed by both progressive and socialist ideals—began to emerge in Milwaukee. Pioneer planners Hegemann, Schuchardt, and especially Whitnall feared congestion more than they championed architectural beauty, and blamed capitalism for exploiting urban inequality more often than they championed its civic virtues. Most importantly, Milwaukee planners looked to the urban periphery, not the center, for civic salvation. The indispensable component of social progressive planning, whether explicated by Benjamin Marsh, Werner Hegemann, Charles Harris Whitaker, or Charles Whitnall, was a city's ability to cut new decentralized urban patterns out of a rural cloth, where land was less expensive, and industrialism had yet to vitiate nature's healing influences. One historian has characterized this planning orientation as one of the alternative "roads not taken" in America, and indeed it largely faded on a national level after 1911, as the nation's housing and planning movements split.[112] But such planning *was* a road traveled in Milwaukee, and it ultimately took the city in directions never intended by its practitioners.

Decentralization by Design

For planning to take the shape social progressives demanded, cities had to look away from their crowded center to the periphery, where new communities could be planned free of the deleterious features that wracked the industrialized city. Milwaukee's planning community had strongly oriented itself to this mindset by the close of World War I. Mayor Daniel Hoan's Housing Commission had eloquently outlined a type of community building that would foster decentralization. Werner Hegemann's clarion call for planning in Milwaukee also characterized the modern American cityscape as exploitative and inefficient. Charles Whitnall, who was emerging as Milwaukee's most public proponent of decentralization, had made it clear that urban salvation lay in the city's ability to reduce congestion. Nationally, in the wake of World War I, reform-minded planners, architects, and theorists began to embrace the concept of regionalism. The 1920s are not generally noted as a fruitful decade for inventive city planning ideas, but regionalists such as Lewis Mumford, Clarence Stein, Henry Wright, and others did emerge as unique American planning voices, and they generally departed from their predecessors in their frequent calls to plan regions, not just cities. Congestion was still the symptom, but if decentralization was the answer then planning needed to have influence over a far more vast terrain than the immediate central city.

"Regionalism" became a planning buzzword in the 1920s, but it meant very different things to different people. To planning officials, who worked directly for municipal governments or who served on planning commissions, regionalism was a way to accommodate what appeared to be an inevitable process of urbanization; as cities ate up more undeveloped land, regional planning, accompanied by "modest decentralization," would rationalize this growth. Such regionalism is perhaps most famously embodied in the Russell Sage Foundation–sponsored Regional Plan of New York, a massive study of the future of America's largest city led by famed British town planner Thomas Adams. The plan, mostly created during the 1920s but not completed until 1931, drew criticism from Mumford, who thought it reinforced conventional settlement patterns and did not nearly encompass a broad enough territory. Mumford, Benton Mackaye, Patrick Geddes, Stein, and other reformers directly or indirectly associated with the RPAA, viewed regionalism as liberation from industrial urbanization, not a logical outgrowth of it. They admired the traditional village life of the preindustrial West, favored master-planned English-style Garden Cities, and supported cooperative ownership to make housing affordable and transcend the "unearned increment" of real estate speculation. Mumford, MacKaye, Stein, and Geddes all contributed articles to the famous "regional planning number" of *The Survey Graphic* in 1925, which became iconic to the RPAA mindset.[1] But planners who worked directly under municipal governments never managed to capture the spirit of RPAA–style regionalism. With cities embracing zoning and desperately trying to accommodate the now omnipresent automobile, planners found themselves trapped in the "mole work" of examining zoning variances and managing street-widening, ironically fulfilling the aims of the City Practical but largely forfeiting the high ideals of civic design outlined by City Beautiful advocates. The proliferation of the automobile also challenged planners to accommodate this new and clearly vital form of transportation. Milwaukee reflects both regionalist trends. Whitnall clearly favored radical decentralization, and had little use for the annoyances of enforcing zoning. Furthermore, the city built the Garden City–inspired Garden Homes during the 1920s, one of the nation's first municipally funded (and cooperatively owned) communities. Whitnall's twin roles as county and city planner sped the design of a metropolitan-wide park system, replete with roadways. The more conventional strain of regionalism, dictated more directly by politics, was also present in Milwaukee, as Hoan and other city officials began to envision an urban population dispersed throughout Milwaukee County, but under a single, metropolitan government.[2]

What ultimately gave all of these disparate activities a common purpose was the troublesome land question. Regionalists like Mumford and Geddes, detached from city government, could theorize about new settlement patterns and outdated municipal concepts. Whitnall, idealistic and frequently impatient with the machinations of city government, often thought little about the pragmatic political implications of his plans as well. From the perspective of city officials like Mayor Daniel Hoan, who cared equally deeply about the overcrowding of city centers, planning on a metropolitan level came with no incentive unless the city became large enough to benefit from these reforms. By 1920, precisely the opposite was true. Virtually every city whose population was comparable to Milwaukee's dwarfed it in physical size. Minneapolis had grown to just under fifty square miles, St. Louis exceeded sixty square miles, and Cincinnati and Detroit had passed the seventy-square-mile marker. Chicago was over 190 square miles by 1920. Milwaukee, at just over twenty-five square miles that same year, lagged far behind its Midwest counterparts, and was, with the exceptions of Newark and Jersey City, New Jersey, physically smaller than each of the remaining twenty-four largest cities in the United States.[3] Any kind of regional planning that encouraged decentralization would make little sense to city officials if Milwaukee failed to grow. If new roadways were going to funnel people away from or around the urban core, they would travel to communities not within city jurisdiction. The Garden Homes—which were fundamentally a scheme to house workers outside crowded inner city neighborhoods—could not be built within the existing city borders. Zoning, so crucial to Hoan and Whitnall in shaping decentralization, was worthless as a municipal exercise without open space on which to exercise the city's new powers of land use regulation.

For these reasons, Milwaukee's policy makers made an aggressive annexation program a central part of their urban policy, and along the way made the concept of metropolitanism a city-driven political exercise. Annexation functioned as the most crucial tool that would enable planning and zoning to work in the ways their advocates called for. As with other aspects of urban policy, private actors supported or opposed annexation to the degree that their own interests were either furthered or hindered. To make annexation workable, city officials had to collaborate with the very developers that planners like Whitnall took to task for fostering urban inequality. Nevertheless, in purely numerical terms, annexation proved successful in Milwaukee during the 1920s, as the city's size increased from twenty-five to forty-four square miles. In another important way, annexation in the 1920s carried growth politics to Milwaukee's neighboring communities, often formerly rural in character but at that time rapidly developing. Many of these suburban and rural communities strongly opposed Milwaukee's efforts to grow and gradually became permanent actors on an increasingly divided metropolitan political landscape. "Runaway industries" that had located outside the city's borders were also put off by the tactics the city used, hinting at a growing distance between public and private interests regarding the economic growth of the city.

This chapter outlines the maturation of planned decentralization. During the 1920s, Milwaukee gained a national reputation for innovative planning strategies, and city leaders grew more confident that physical growth could eventually lead to some form of metropolitan government. The Garden Homes became a blueprint for the ideal form of community. Zoning—in theory—promised to further decentralization, although it became hotly contested and politicized. Whitnall and other Milwaukee planners actively collaborated with developers to form platting guidelines that lent technical advice to builders. Transportation plans accommodated the automobile and sought to solve traffic congestion. Annexation, however, was the tool to ensure that guided growth remained under control of the central city, and it began to complicate the metropolitan visions of Milwaukee's leaders while galvanizing outlying communities who previously had had little in common with one another.

The 1920 U.S. census also revealed that among America's twenty largest cities, Milwaukee was the second most densely populated, trailing only New York City. Local debates over whether Milwaukee did, in fact, have "slums" or if it was a "city of homes" became somewhat superfluous in the wake of this revelation. One local scholar recalled a "widespread feeling of civic shock" after the census figures became known.[4] Planning officials, already long convinced that congestion was Milwaukee's most vexing problem, offered new statistics as further evidence of the land crisis. Over 450,000 residents crowded into twenty-six square miles. In 1893, 57 percent of the land within city borders remained undeveloped. By 1918, the amount of vacant land in Milwaukee had dropped to 5 percent, and four years later, only 3 percent of the city's area, *including* rivers, remained vacant.[5] The BPLC's City Planning Engineer, Roland Stoelting, estimated that Milwaukee's housing shortage had reached 7,000 dwellings. Moreover, Stoelting reported a "notorious shortage of sites for new industries."[6] The lack of industrial space in Milwaukee had already caught the attention of Mayor Hoan during the war, when an alderman told him that at least sixteen industries had bypassed Milwaukee due to the spatial crunch.[7] Hoan's socialist principles did not interfere with his conviction that "the progress of our nation depends upon the gradual development and expansion of our business and industrial areas," which by 1920 had virtually run out of space within Milwaukee's borders.[8] Charles Goff's study of intergovernmental relations in Milwaukee, conducted in 1952, recalled that many city administrators had concluded after World War I that Milwaukee could do one of two things; it could annex new land or die.[9] Key private interest groups, often at political odds with Hoan's Socialist administration, began to advocate a more aggressive annexation policy. The City Club of Milwaukee became an early advocate of annexation because "most of the land in the suburbs and townships is empty lots. If the city were allowed to expand, people would not have to crowd so closely together." Annexation would also dramatically increase Milwaukee's population, possibly making it "one of the great commercial cities in the world."[10] The Milwaukee Real Estate Board, the city's largest organization that represented the interests of developers, also saw annexation as a good investment. If vacant land adjacent to the city were annexed, it would receive valuable and cost-efficient water and sewage installations. A city report investigating annexation's feasibility noted with some astonishment that just beyond the "numerous rows of homes, typifying congestion of population," were miles of empty farmland that could be transformed into better-planned city communities.[11] Where city policymakers saw function, land developers saw dollars and became crucial proponents of annexation for this primary reason.

While the need to annex became obvious, the legal means Milwaukee could use to achieve it were less apparent. Prior to 1893, acts of the state legislature brought new territory into the city, but a Wisconsin Supreme Court ruling that year permitted cities to annex territory without state interference only at the request of property owners. In 1898, a new state law required a majority of property owners in a given area to sign a petition asking the city for permission to be annexed. This cumbersome procedure was difficult, according to a city report, because "private individuals cannot afford the time and expense involved in petitioning the city for annexation."[12] As a result, from 1893 to 1920, Milwaukee had virtually doubled its population, but had grown by only four square miles. Technically, the task of annexation was left to the BPLC, but it largely relied on the initiative of residents outside the city to circulate annexation petitions, and they often fell victim to legal scrutiny when left in the hands of "amateurs." To streamline the process in the future, in 1923 the BPLC recommended to Hoan and the Common Council the creation of a separate division of annexation staffed with a core of professional solicitors whose jobs would be to identify property owners outside of the city and circulate the proper petitions to legalize annexations.[13] The Common Council, eager for the city to grow, agreed, and created the Department of Abstracting and Annexation that same year. For once, Socialist and Nonpartisan aldermen alike agreed

CHART 2-1	Population Densities, Twenty Largest American Cities, 1920

City	Population	Size (sq. miles)	Pop. per sq. mile
1. New York City	5,620,048	299.0	18,796
2. Milwaukee	**457,147**	**25.3**	**18,069**
3. Newark	414,524	23.3	17,791
4. Boston	748,060	43.5	17,197
5. Pittsburgh	588,343	39.9	14,745
6. Philadelphia	1,823,779	128.0	14,248
7. Cleveland	796,841	56.4	14,128
8. Chicago	2,701,705	192.8	14,013
9. Buffalo	506,775	38.9	13,028
10. Detroit	993,078	77.9	12,748
11. St. Louis	772,897	61.0	12,670
12. San Francisco	506,676	42.0	12,064
13. Baltimore	733,826	79.0	9,289
14. Minneapolis	380,582	49.7	7,658
15. Washington, D.C.	437,571	60.0	7,293
16. Cincinnati	401,247	71.1	5,643
17. Kansas City	324,410	58.4	5,555
18. Seattle	315,312	58.6	5,381
19. New Orleans	387,219	178.0	2,175
20. Los Angeles	576,673	365.7	1,577

that the city desperately needed vacant land. The vast majority of annexation petitions sailed through the Common Council. In both postwar eras, annexation remained the one issue that council members (and Hoan and later Mayor Frank Zeidler) almost uniformly supported.[14] Milwaukee's elected officials had made annexation more efficient, but they had also taken it out of the hands of planners. While this freed up Whitnall and Stoelting to concentrate on more technical planning issues, it also placed the process of city growth—so crucial to the planning visions of social progressives—largely in the hands of exuberant bureaucrats who eventually found themselves on the front lines in the battle over urban growth.

Land near Milwaukee's borders contained far more than empty lots and farms. A report issued in 1921 titled "Annexation—The Concern for the Entire State" contained a map of Milwaukee's boundaries. To the north, west, and south, on all three sides of the city (Lake Michigan lies to the east), dozens of manufacturers had located just across the city limits. The list of industries included some of Milwaukee's largest employers. The A. O. Smith Corporation sat alongside the Chicago, Milwaukee, and St. Paul Railroad (Milwaukee Road) railway corridor to the northwest. At the west end of the Menomonee River Valley, just along the river's northward bend and alongside the Milwaukee Road, sat Miller Brewing, Pawling & Harnischfeger, and the Falk Corporation. To the south lay Nash Motors and Nordberg Manufacturing, among others. All told, forty-one large plants surrounded the city. Convincing this ring of industry to join Milwaukee was the first priority for city policymakers.[15]

In 1921, Hoan wrote to each manufacturer, asking them "in view of the present congestion of the city of Milwaukee and its present smallness compared with other cities of the same population" about their interest in being annexed to Milwaukee.[16] A few manufacturers welcomed annexation and the improved water installations it promised, but the vast majority objected. Of the twelve industries whose responses are included in Hoan's files, nine unequivocally opposed. The Evinrude Motor Company echoed the majority opinion that annexation "would undoubtedly bring about higher taxes."[17] Hoan's appeal to civic greatness also fell on deaf ears. The president of the South Side Malleable Casting Company initially wrote of his great excitement over the proposal to add manufacturers currently outside Milwaukee's borders to the city because annexation would truly make Milwaukee an industrial powerhouse. South Side Malleable's Board of Directors, however, wrote Hoan back, explaining that their president did not have the authority to make corporate decisions. They opposed annexation.[18]

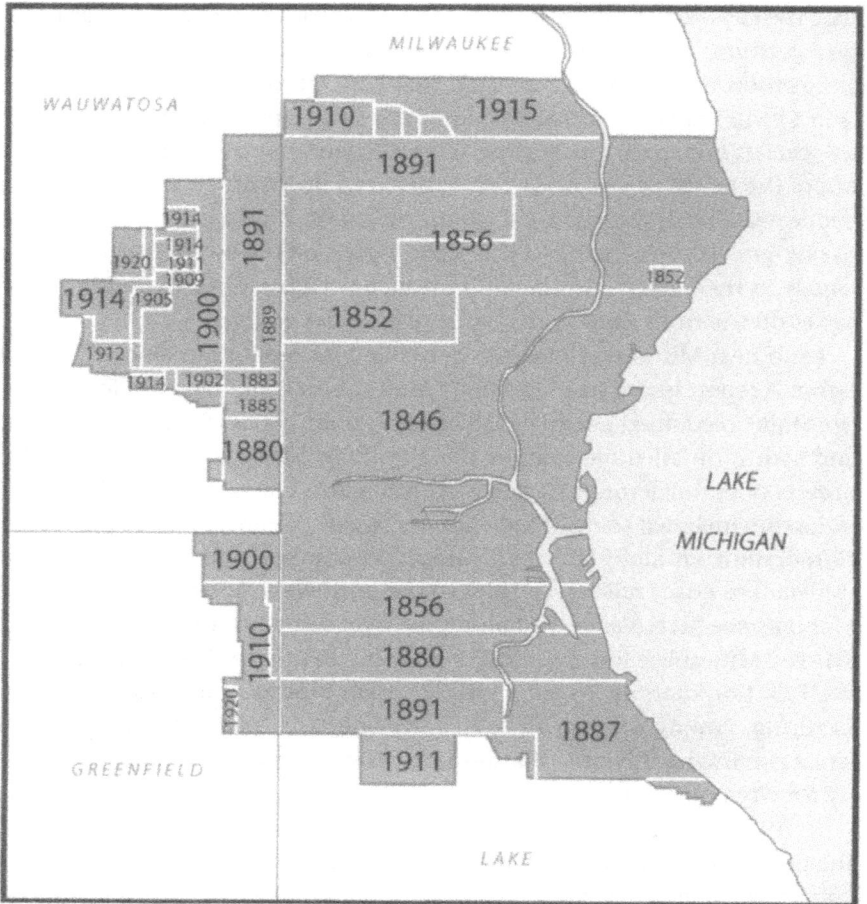

Annexations by the City of Milwaukee, 1846–1920. © Mapcraft

These initial rejections did not deter Milwaukee officials. Support for annexation was increasing as the postwar housing shortage persisted, and city officials hoped to use public opinion to their advantage. Since polite solicitations had fallen on deaf ears, the city next tried public embarrassment. A petition was circulated urging the Wisconsin state legislature to pass a law easing annexation procedures. Endorsed by the Wisconsin Federation of Labor, it represented the first frontal assault in Milwaukee's annexation efforts. Located prominently on the front page of the petition was a large map showing Milwaukee's borders and subsequent growth from 1846 through 1920. Forty-one black dots, one for each large manufacturer just outside Milwaukee, demonstrated local industry's rejections. The petition reminded voters that wherever they saw black dots "you will observe that the advance of the city has halted to that point." Since property owners' permission was needed to annex, "the corporate property interests that dominate these sparsely settled industrial districts can hold the fort as long as they will." The petition also appealed to Milwaukee citizens' wallets, reminding them of the valuable tax revenue that would be lost as long as "the blockade of Milwaukee" continued. "Big corporate property owners" were to blame; they were "largely responsible for the stagnation and lack of uniformity of the City's recent growth." Big business had not only hampered the city's growth; it had compromised the public welfare. The petition was also misleading in its implication that Milwaukee only sought to annex adjacent industries. It promised, "This is no radical proposal to annex the cities and residential suburbs of Milwaukee County that have civic reasons for wishing to prolong their independence." In just a few years, anxious annexation leaders would call for complete governmental unification and come to ridicule the "civic reasons" for suburban independence. In the meantime, the "machine shop of the world's" first opponents were many of its own shops.[19]

While annexation officials struggled with expanding the city to include nearby industry, they managed to connect Milwaukee to its planners' ambitious Garden Homes community. Planners had chosen a twenty-nine-acre site north of Milwaukee's present borders in the unincorporated Town of Milwaukee, and by 1921, construction of the Garden Homes had commenced. While construction took place, annexation officials carved out a strip of land, 120 feet wide and 600 feet long, that linked the city-owned Garden Homes site to Milwaukee's northern border. A local farmer, Fred Zwefifel, who owned the strip of land that forged the link, challenged the annexation in state courts, but the Wisconsin Supreme Court ruled in 1924 that since the Garden Homes site made up the majority of land under the annexation, the city had the legal right to sign for its own land. The cooperative project was thus safely within Milwaukee borders.[20]

The Garden Homes project represented far more than relief from the postwar housing shortage; it also was a physical manifestation of the cooperative commonwealth, a concept largely invented by English planner Ebenezer Howard in his influential book *Garden Cities of Tomorrow*. Howard, in turn, was "profoundly influenced" by Henry George's writings on urban inequality, and called for new worker communities to be built outside central cities, both to bring workers closer to nature and to insulate them from George's "unearned increment" via collective ownership. Howard's ideas became internationally popular, and they resulted in the construction of the English Garden City of Letchworth, designed by Raymond Unwin, an

English planner and Howard associate. William Schuchardt, both a member of the BPLC and chair of Hoan's Housing Commission, was the architect of the Milwaukee Garden Homes. Schuchardt had spent six months in Europe in 1911 studying model Garden Cities such as Letchworth and had ever since been a committed advocate of the garden community concept. He included a report on "co-partnership housing" in the Milwaukee Building Inspector's annual report of 1920, outlining the benefits of garden style communities and noting that "nowhere in Milwaukee are there such charming localities as Port Sunlight, Bourneville, Letchworth."[21] Advocacy of co-operative ownership in Milwaukee was not limited to Schuchardt. Hoan and Whitnall had been charter board members of the Commonwealth Mutual Savings Bank of Milwaukee, a cooperative bank aimed specifically at helping working-class residents of Milwaukee. In 1923, Hoan served as chairman of the Cooperative League of America's Committee on Co-operative Housing.

In short, men who were committed to restructuring America's urban form and economic structure created the Garden Homes. In this context, the project's cooperative structure was indispensable. Each prospective tenant signed a lease and agreed to subscribe to common stock in the Garden Homes Corporation equal to the value of the home. Tenants could pay a fraction of the cost up front and slowly amortize the lease by monthly rent payments. Full title of all properties remained in the hands of the Garden Homes Corporation. The lots on which the new homes were constructed were 60 by 100 feet, considerably larger than most of the 30 to 40-foot-wide lots that dominated Milwaukee's landscape. Curvilinear streets with names such as Letchworth and Port Sunlight Way further identified the project with Garden City principles. In the center of the project, a 200 x 500-foot lot was reserved for a park. By any measure, the Garden Homes was a pleasant community.[22]

Despite the efforts of planners to link the project to Ebenezer Howard and Raymond Unwin's renowned communities, the Garden Homes was neither a Garden City nor a cooperative enclave for long. Howard and Unwin called for planned industrial districts to be included in their communities, with residents' homes in clusters near where they worked.[23] The Garden Homes was about ten blocks east of the north-south Milwaukee Road railway corridor, which rapidly filled up with manufacturing plants in the 1920s. However, planned districts of the kind Howard deemed central to the Garden City ideal proved to be beyond the scope of the project, as was a town center or retail district of any kind. Lacking these crucial elements, the Garden Homes instead grew into another of Milwaukee's increasingly numerous bedroom communities. The project did not remain a coopera-

Garden Homes, Rear View—The Garden Homes remained a distinctive residential community on Milwaukee's north years after it was built, but the project's cooperative structure did not survive the real estate boom of the 1920s. Courtesy of the Historic Photo Collection / Milwaukee Public Library

tive venture for long either. As the 1920s progressed and a real estate boom continued, residents began to agitate for the right to buy out the Garden Homes Corporation to gain individual title to their properties. Under pressure from the vast majority of tenants, the Garden Homes Board of Directors eventually acquiesced. In 1925, the board persuaded the state legislature to amend the original cooperative bill to allow tenants to own their homes. Once the bill passed and the land was assessed, residents quickly cashed in. By 1927, all of the Garden Homes property had been sold off. Whitnall lamented that residents never realized the project's "true purpose of cooperative action," but the project proved successful in other ways.[24] It demonstrated the willingness, albeit halting at first, of private builders to work with municipal government in planning communities on the fringes of Milwaukee. The Garden Homes also confirmed public appetites for carefully planned communities, especially those that were away from the urban

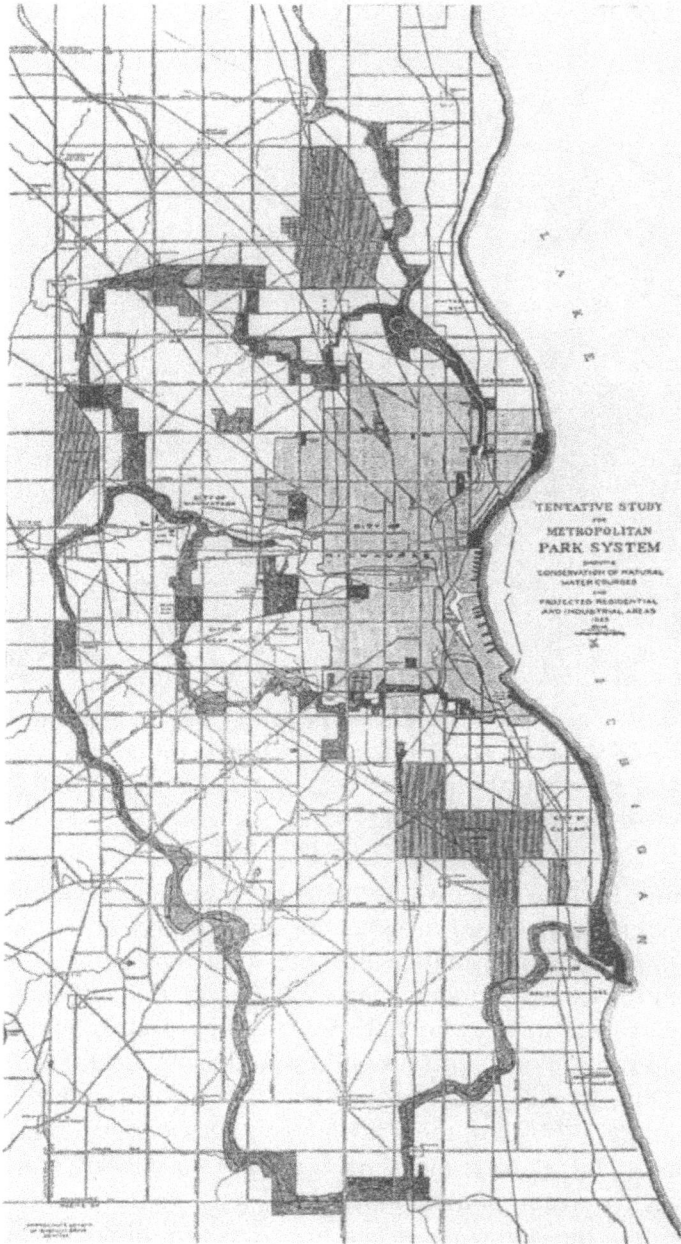

Parkway Plans for Milwaukee County—Largely conceived by Charles Whitnall, the Milwaukee County Parkway System was designed as both a conservationist scheme as well as a magnet to spread out Milwaukee's population. Courtesy of the Milwaukee Public Library core. Milwaukee's public and private officials, in turn, continued in other ways to accommodate those appetites.

Charles Whitnall's most famous contribution to Milwaukee, its system of parkways, was born from his desires to reduce congestion and decentralize the urban population. Whitnall had long called for an increase in parklands to bring city residences closer to nature. Using his twin positions on both the city BPLC and the Milwaukee County Parks and Regional Planning Commissions, Whitnall had pushed for a system of parkways for Milwaukee throughout the 1910s. After World War I, with a sympathetic Mayor Hoan in office and widespread civic concern over Milwaukee's crowded conditions, the parkways gained greater political attention. In 1923, Albert Woller and Herman Tucker, two Socialist state assemblymen representing districts in Milwaukee, introduced in the Wisconsin legislature bills enabling both the city and county to acquire lands along the county's waterways for a comprehensive system of parks. From the parkways' inception, Whitnall perceived their development as a key qualitative salvo against the evils of congestion. In 1923, trying to drum up state support for the parkway legislation, Whitnall reminded the legislature, "Milwaukee is one of the most congested cities in the country. The parkways will provide nature's own beauty spots and will help conserve the natural beauty of the county."[25] That same year, Whitnall released his plan for Milwaukee County's parkways. Eighty-four miles of "parked driveways" would follow the natural contours of the county's lakeshore, rivers, and creeks.

Stream banks would be reforested, certain wetlands preserved, and large parks would be constructed at varying ends along the parkways. According to Milwaukee historian John Gurda, "Whitnall's highway and park maps became, with very little revision, the official guides for all local land use planning."[26] By 1925, all three governmental units had enthusiastically signed off on the parkway plans, and city and county officials spent much of the 1920s slowly acquiring the land necessary to their development.[27]

While the conservationist features of Whitnall's plans were obvious, Milwaukee's parkways were also intended to be a catalyst for decentralization. Whitnall himself repeated this theme countless times in 1923 and 1924 when he was trying to gain support in Milwaukee's Common Council, County Board, and the state legislature to adopt his plans. Parks and parkways would not only provide natural "breathing space" to city residents; they were to be the spine of a decentralized metropolis. Land surrounding the parkways would transform into "residential suburbs," housing people who escaped the grime of the inner city.[28] Equally important, Whitnall had now become a strong believer in the future predominance of the automobile, and he also envisioned his parkway system as a keystone in the city's transportation future. The automobile, Whitnall increasingly proclaimed, was one of the greatest innovations in American history and could become a great gift to planners. At a lecture in Los Angeles, Whitnall expounded on the auto's ability to reduce congestion: "The automobile has taught people that they can live beyond the city's confines with all the coveted city conveniences and do so with less cost and greater benefit to themselves and their children. The auto has done for decentralization in a short period of time what many decades of teaching could not have done."[29] Milwaukee's parkways, as principal auto thoroughfares in addition to pleasant spaces, would thus have multiple positive uses.

Whitnall's parkway system was broadly popular. Both Socialists and their opponents in the Common Council supported them, as did all of Milwaukee's major newspapers, the Association of Commerce, and the Milwaukee Real Estate Board. It soon became apparent that Milwaukee's parkways meant different things to different groups of people. Socialists viewed parkways as a public equalizer. The *Milwaukee Leader*, the city's Socialist daily newspaper, mused, "The parkway will bring the people, without distinction of class or station, closer to nature."[30] Emil Seidel, Milwaukee's first Socialist mayor, returned to local government as an alderman in 1932 and envisioned the Lincoln Creek Park area that ran through his district to become "the best working class section in the city."[31] Other local newspapers seized on the parkways' promotional capabilities; the *Milwaukee Journal* compared them to J. C. Nichols's Country Club Plaza in Kansas City as a signifier of civic greatness.[32] For realtors, parkways meant economic opportunity. Speculators bought up land, not only in the path of the parkways themselves, but near the county's creeks and rivers, in anticipation of their potential desirability as residential communities. In suburban Wauwatosa, an upper-middle-class bedroom community west of Milwaukee, locals predicted that when the Honey Creek Parkway was completed, "an increase in valuation is certain to come."[33] In fact, the parkways promised to be such a boon to Milwaukee's real estate community that subdividers even occasionally donated land—free of charge—located in the path of parkways. The expected increase in the property values of the nearby land apparently drove this benevolence.[34]

In hindsight, the hopes of Whitnall and other Socialists that the parkways would become the spine of a semirural working-class utopia appear naïve. Communities that grew near the parkways in later decades, especially the 1950s, were middle-class in character, and housing was not within the economic reach of lower income families. Parkways also often acted as geographical barriers, with poorer neighborhoods on one side and wealthier suburbs on the other. Furthermore, as the Milwaukee region became politically fragmented and suburbanized, city and county officials found themselves limited in how they could regulate land use decisions and thus affect the character of the communities that were to grow. None of this seemed apparent when Whitnall's parkways were nascent. Milwaukee was busy finding solutions to urban congestion and the postwar housing shortage, and parkways appeared promising in their ability to achieve decentralization. Furthermore, Hoan, Whitnall, and other reformers were hopeful that other initiatives befitting a vigorous local government would provide more immediate relief.

As yet another way of ensuring orderly residential growth on the periphery, the BPLC ordered that new subdivisions on the city's edges (including those located within one and one-half miles from the city limit) could only be platted with its prior approval. New subdivisions that failed to meet their standards were summarily rejected. In 1924, the BPLC released a platting guide to more effectively communicate its community ideals to Milwaukee's builders and speculators. The platting guide required uniform setbacks of homes, encouraged curvilinear streets, and justified the placement of small parks within larger subdivisions as a way not only to ensure higher-quality neighborhoods but to allow realtors and home owners a greater appreciation on the value of their communities. In a sense, the BPLC's platting guide represented a convergence of the interests of city planners and the local real estate industry. The Milwaukee Real Estate Board, the city's largest organization of home builders, had strongly endorsed the zoning ordinance, hoping it would raise property values throughout the region.[35] Now, as Milwaukee's planners looked outside of Milwaukee's urban spaces for room to grow, planners consulted the Real Estate Board before releasing the platting guide, and most builders had little trouble in meeting platting requirements. As Gardner Rogers, who replaced Roland Stoelting as the BPLC's planning engineer in 1923, enthusiastically stated, "Cooperation between the engineers, realtors, and public land commission is becoming so complete that an approved subdivision is an assurance to the prospective purchaser that the lots are adequate for property development."[36] Whitnall was also encouraged by the quality of peripheral growth in Milwaukee. In the BPLC's annual report of 1926, he wrote, "There is no doubt but what the outlying districts, with their convenient and practical platting layouts hold a far better future for the prosperity for those who engage in business than the older and more congested areas of the city."[37] In effect, public regulations of vacant land provided private speculators with a "seal of approval." Builders gained assurance of the legality of plats registered with the BPLC. Home buyers could take comfort in knowing that they were moving into neighborhoods that technical experts in both private and public spheres had approved. This cooperation with the BPLC helped make the city's realtors vocal supporters of annexation as well.

Hoping to continue the synergy between private real estate and public regulators over an even greater area, in 1924 Whitnall helped the Milwaukee County Regional Planning Department establish one of America's first countywide zoning ordinances. The ordinance was applicable only to all unincorporated townships in Milwaukee County, but in the 1920s that constituted over 70 percent of the county's total land area. County zoning reflected the same principles of decentralization as those of Milwaukee, even stipulating minimum lot sizes of sixty feet in width—some 50 percent wider than in the city—by the 1930s. The only material difference in countywide zoning was the inclusion of agricultural land as a "use district." Every affected township in Milwaukee County approved the county zoning ordinance, save for Oak Creek and Franklin, two largely rural communities well to the south of Milwaukee's urban growth in the 1920s.[38]

The mechanics of exercising land use controls and the platting of subdivisions at or beyond the edges of Milwaukee were relatively easy to execute. As Whitnall enthusiastically told the *Leader* in 1926, "in practically every instance sub-dividers have given this board (BPLC) their hearty cooperation."[39] Within the city, however, regulating land use proved to be far more difficult. Developers of individual lots held for "in-fill" development often planned structures that were in conflict with the zoning ordinance. Milwaukee's land use regulations became controversial. Further complicating matters was the highly contested nature of local politics within Milwaukee. A Socialist (Hoan) controlled the office of mayor, but the Common Council remained largely in the hands of the so-called Nonpartisans between 1920 and 1940. The 1912 election law had made it illegal for any candidate for municipal office to run under an official party banner.[40] "Nonpartisans" were in fact primarily Democrats who kept politics in Milwaukee as fiercely partisan as they had been before the election reforms. Determined to undermine Hoan's administration—including the BPLC, whose members Hoan could appoint—the Nonpartisans made the strict regulations of the zoning ordinance a major point of contention almost from the moment they approved it. In 1921, a group of Nonpartisan council members tried to insert an amendment permitting the construction of residences in use districts zoned for industry. The *Milwaukee Journal* ridiculed the amendment: "Are the nonpartisan aldermen looking to tear down one of the few constructive achievements of recent years and hand the Socialists just the kind of political thunder they are looking for?"[41] While this initial foray failed, Nonpartisans vigorously opposed other stipulations in the zoning ordinance throughout the 1920s.

A key Nonpartisan ally was William Harper, Milwaukee's building inspector from 1915 to 1928 and a leftover appointee of Gerhard Bading, who had served as mayor of Milwaukee from 1912 to 1916, between Seidel's and Hoan's Socialist administrations. Harper's office was responsible for enforcing the zoning ordinance, and it quickly became a thorn in the side of Hoan and Whitnall. Milwaukee's city charter allowed Hoan to replace the building inspector only with the majority vote of the Common Council. In 1919 and 1923, when Harper's position came up for reappointment, Hoan reluctantly extended Harper's term. Hoan knew that the Nonpartisan-dominated Common Council would reject any replacement and he especially came to regret Harper's appointment after the zoning ordinance was enacted.[42] Harper frequently sided with the Nonpartisan majority of the Common Council in arguing that the zoning ordinance was stifling economic development in Milwaukee because its building requirements were so strict.

Foremost among these regulations were two stipulations on area usage. First, sections of the city where apartments could legally be constructed could house no more than fifty families per acre. Second, in districts zoned for local businesses, storefront apartments could house no more than twenty families per acre. In effect, this made the building of large apartment buildings illegal in most sections of the city and greatly restricted the ability of developers to construct apartments above storefronts. Throughout most of the 1920s, the Common Council attempted to remove the family-per-acre restriction from the zoning ordinance. In 1926, Harper claimed that during the previous year builders in the city had over $18 million worth of projects that were on permanent hold because their plans did not fit the requirements of the zoning ordinance. To convince any cynic who claimed he may have been "bluffing," Harper listed the property owner and address in the *Milwaukee News* to further embarrass the Hoan administration and to call attention to the allegedly draconian conditions of the zoning ordinance.[43] Many of the construction projects on hold were "storefront apartments" that exceeded the family-per-acre restrictions. Harper claimed that these restrictions on apartments were making rents in Milwaukee $10 to $15 per month higher because they created an artificial demand on housing within the city. "Zoning must be reasonable, not radical," Harper warned the Common Council in his 1926 annual report.[44] Builders whose plans were restricted by the ordinance also came to Harper's and the Common Council's side. In 1925, G. E. Bernecker, a local developer who wanted to build a six-story apartment with fifty-eight units in a district where only twenty were legal, circulated a petition to the Common Council to remove the family-per-acre restrictions, calling them obsolete. Bernecker told the *Milwaukee Journal* that he wanted to bypass the BPLC and deal directly with the Common Council because the former had ignored his complaints for several years. Whitnall furiously responded that men like Bernecker did not understand the concept of zoning. Hoan even wrote a letter to Bernecker informing him that Harper, as building inspector, had no legal right to alter the zoning ordinance. Bernecker's recalcitrance, nevertheless, was not an isolated incident. The Milwaukee Real Estate Board, while sympathetic to the BPLC's zoning ordinance in principle, also began calling for the removal of the family-per-acre restrictions by 1926.[45]

The BPLC ardently defended the family-per-acre restrictions of the zoning ordinance throughout the 1920s, often countering that zoning in Milwaukee was intended to prevent exploitative real estate practices. Stoelting, the BPLC planning engineer until 1923, claimed that the intent of the family-per-acre restriction was to reduce congestion. The family-per-acre provisions, Stoelting claimed, eliminated the practice of speculators who sought to maximize profits by erecting large apartment buildings on property located in secondary business districts, thus creating overcrowding while diluting the ability of zoning to segregate the functions of the city. To Stoelting, "The general welfare of the community is of far more importance than the desire of a few individuals to obtain returns on artificial inflation of property values."[46] Whitnall also vigorously safeguarded the family-per-acre restriction throughout the 1920s, claiming that it was the intention of the zoning ordinance to eliminate apartments over storefronts except in cases where the owner resided.[47] The principles of decentralization dictated the opposite: "If any change is made, we want to lessen the number of families to the acre."[48] In fact, Whitnall's vigor in regulating city building in Milwaukee turned the matter of zoning enforcement into a personal crusade. He frequently traveled the city in search of buildings in varying states of noncompliance with the zoning ordinance, snapping photographs and sending them directly to the Common Council. The photographs revealed widespread evasion of the ordinance. Some buildings contained thirty apartments where only six were allowed, others covered 70 percent of the total area of a lot where only 60 percent was allowed, still others were used as places of business in areas zoned strictly for residences.[49] Whitnall placed the blame for these types of violations squarely on the lap of Harper, who was increasingly perceived as a pawn of the Common Council in their efforts to undermine Hoan's vision of city planning for Milwaukee. Hoan shared these frustrations as well, telling those angry with Harper, "Only the Socialists have been willing to stand with me in the past in naming a new man."[50]

In a December 1926 submission to Hoan and the city attorney, the BPLC charged that Harper had neglected his official duty to enforce the zoning ordinance and had knowingly violated the family-per-acre restrictions on several occasions. With public pressure against Harper increasing, Hoan was finally able to appoint his own building inspector a year later. As a compromise, he chose Leon Gurda, a Nonpartisan who as a resident of the Polish South Side was popular with a crucial constituency of the Hoan administration. Equally important for Hoan, Gurda supported strict enforcement of both the zoning ordinance and the city's building code, and quickly became one of the most zealous and committed public servants in the city. In 1928, the reenergized building inspector's department enacted a new building code enforcement program. Ultimately designed to demolish every structure in the city deemed "unfit for habitation," the code enabled the city to demolish thousands of buildings in the late 1920s and early 1930s. Gurda later became nationally renowned and, like other public officials from the Hoan era, remained at his post well past World War II.[51]

Harper had been forced out, much to the Socialists' delight. However, in the short term, Nonpartisan opponents of the family-per-acre restriction also won the day. In 1927, under pressure from local builders and the Common Council, the BPLC voted, over Whitnall's objections, to eliminate the family-per-acre restrictions of the zoning ordinance. In effect, this allowed larger apartments to be constructed in local business districts. The Common Council also enacted its own revenge in 1929 and 1931. During these two years, the council amended the zoning ordinance yet again. First it converted ten blocks of Milwaukee's principal thoroughfare, Wisconsin (formerly Grand) Avenue, and then eight blocks of Kilbourn Avenue (both west of downtown), from a residential district (in which apartments of any type were illegal to construct) to a local business district. With the family-per-acre restriction rendered null and void, larger apartments could now be constructed on eighteen key blocks of Milwaukee's West Side. The six remaining Socialists in the Common Council opposed both amendments and Hoan vetoed them as well, but Nonpartisans in the Common Council—having won a number of seats in the 1928 aldermanic elections—overrode Hoan's veto each time.[52]

In the late nineteenth century, West Wisconsin (then Grand) Avenue was one of Milwaukee's premier residential areas, home to Captain Frederick Pabst, John Plankinton, Robert Johnston, and Henry Harnischfeger, among other local elites. In the early twentieth century, wealthier families had begun to move east to Prospect Avenue or further west to upscale neighborhoods like the Hegemann-designed Washington Highlands and Washington Heights. Property owners on Wisconsin Avenue thus began to subdivide the larger homes into apartments and rooming houses, finally calling for the area to be rezoned to allow for the construction of larger apartment buildings. With rezoning in effect, the Near West Side of Milwaukee was in danger of becoming a neighborhood of apartments, which Whitnall equated with a "slum district" due to the very type of the structures. In this case, Milwaukee was in the ironic situation in which a Socialist administration was seeking to maintain the somewhat wealthy character of an elite residential neighborhood while local property owners were calling for rezoning to make—in effect—the housing in the Near West Side more affordable. As Whitnall lamented, "Grand Avenue has been needlessly ruined as an avenue of homes."[53] Zoning (and rezoning) had quickly emerged as a potent political issue in Milwaukee.

Other cities witnessed similar neighborhood transformations during this time period. Historian Max Page has revealed that Manhattan's Fifth Avenue—New York City's premier address—also lost its residential character to the unrelenting demands of the market, in which the highest and best uses of land yielded a process of "creative destruction."[54] Demolition, in turn, had emerged as a key part of urban history well before postwar urban renewal. Milwaukee's Wisconsin Avenue was thus not unique. After the amendment of the zoning ordinance, the transition of the street accelerated dramatically, as previously subdivided mansions were demolished and replaced by hotels, apartments, and filling stations.[55] However, the urban real estate market did not operate the same in every city. As Page points out, Fifth Avenue remained a "premier address" even after most of its mansions were demolished.[56] Milwaukee's Grand Avenue, however, lacked national identity, and was not a target for preservation. In this case, public officials like Whitnall actually battled private actors and "the market" in attempting to preserve a street's bucolic character. West Wisconsin Avenue did not remain a premier residential street. As apartments replaced Victorians, the Near West Side neighborhood began a long, slow decline and lakefront neighborhoods on the East Side replaced West Wisconsin Avenue as Milwaukee's preeminent addresses. In this case, politics determined redevelopment just as strongly as the private market did. Most of Hoan's vetoes of zoning ordinance changes held up in the Common Council until 1928, when Nonpartisans won enough aldermanic seats to override Hoan's frequent vetoes.[57]

While zoning ordinances grew in vogue in American cities during the 1920s, amendments to them quickly became common as individual developers sought to attain land uses that achieved maximum profitability. In Los Angeles, Marc Weiss notes, the City Planning Commission spent over 80 percent of its time reviewing applications for zoning changes from builders, with the great majority of them granted.[58] In Chicago, planning historian Mel Scott estimated that from 1923 to 1938, the city's zoning ordinance was amended over 13,000 times, prompting the President of the American Society of Planning Officials to scoff that the changes added up to "nothing more than 13,000 zoning violations."[59] With dogmatic planners like Whitnall on hand, these figures were far lower in Milwaukee; in fact, city planning officials often pointed with pride at the relatively lower number of zoning amendments in their city compared with national averages. Zoning nonetheless still took up much of the BPLC's time. In 1929, of the over 1,100 matters that were referred to Milwaukee's planning arm, 615 regarded zoning.[60] In addition, for all of its commitment to the universal application of land use controls, Milwaukee's Board of Public Land Commissioners was not at all immune to pressure from local builders. In 1927, for example, the BPLC approved forty-eight of the fifty-six proposed zoning amendments.[61] Other developers found more creative and illegal means to weaken zoning's power. Upon taking over as building inspector, Leon Gurda discovered that after purchasing and subdividing land into the required 40 by 120–foot lots, developers would sell only parts of each lot. The BPLC, having approved a plat with three 40-foot lots, would then be unaware that builders had constructed four homes on 30-foot lots.[62] These types of violations were exceptions, however. Larger lots had become more desirable in the 1920s. More importantly, local builders and land speculators shared a mostly amenable relationship with the city's planning officials, no doubt due to their active participation in implementing land use guidelines such as platting. Developers who evaded Milwaukee's land use regulations in effect broke the rules that the private sector had played a large role in creating.

Zoning battles were also matters of politics. Socialist defenders of the original zoning ordinance, led by Mayor Hoan, sought to decrease population densities and eliminate the "unearned increment" of inflated urban land values through stringent land use controls. Peripheral growth in the form of single-family homes was ingrained in Socialist reform efforts. The fact that Milwaukee's real estate community benefited from decentralization was incidental to officials like Hoan and Whitnall, though support from developers was and would remain crucial. Ideally, land use regulations would curb the tendency of realtors to realize the "unearned increment" of higher land values by maximizing the number of tenants. In Milwaukee's older neighborhoods, zoning proved the most controversial. Nonpartisan opponents of Hoan in the Common Council, with the complicity of a building inspector of the same political stripe, whittled away at the zoning ordinance in the 1920s, seemingly limiting its ability to encourage decentralization within the inner city.

Zoning controversies were not the only source of frustration to Milwaukee's planners in the 1920s; the snail's pace of the Civic Center was another. Having voted by referendum to endorse Alfred Clas and BPLC's plan to group public buildings together and place the civic center west of the Milwaukee River, Milwaukeeans now had to decide if they wanted to fund the land acquisition and construction phase of the project. The measure came on a referendum ballot in April 1925, asking city residents to vote up or down a bond issue for $20 million. The high expenditure would not only include acquisition of existing buildings, demolition of them, and construction of the government structures, it also would widen Cedar and Biddle streets (now called Kilbourn Avenue) to seventy-five feet. Though Milwaukee planners tended to emphasize decentralization, they also clearly understood the civic center as an important civic project. Whitnall had started to include the civic center in his highway discussions, noting that the newly widened street could link to other arterials in his county road plan. In this sense, the civic center was a part of his broader metropolitan vision. Schuchardt, still on the BPLC as a citizen board member, also was a vigorous advocate of the bond issue. Milwaukee voters, however, balked at the huge costs and voted against the 1925 bond issue, further delaying the project.[63] Local newspapers, eager to cheerlead a civic project, began to fear Milwaukee was falling behind its neighbors. A *Milwaukee Journal* editorial the following year warned readers that while local officials struggled to push the civic center, "Meanwhile Chicago builds Wacker Drive, costing $20,000,000, straightens the Chicago River, costing $7,000,000, makes parks, opens playgrounds. Detroit lays out 200-foot streets. Cleveland builds a $5,000,000 auditorium."[64] The civic center's delays, combined with the increasingly mundane work required of the BPLC in the 1920s, cost the city the services of William Schuchardt, who resigned from the BPLC in 1925, citing the citizens' refusal to pay the cost of city planning. Milwaukee, Schuchardt noted in his resignation letter to Hoan, did not have a single, comprehensive master plan and never would unless planners could stop focusing on plats, zoning amendments, and the details of the civic center.[65] Schuchardt eventually moved to Los Angeles, California, and landed on that city's Planning Commission in 1928. The Whitnall family connection—Gordon was the secretary of the Los Angeles City Planning Commission in the 1920s—probably helped Schuchardt.

In the long term, however, it was not the slow pace of the civic center or the political difficulties of zoning that had began to subvert planned decentralization. The civic center, while important to planners, was only one small component in Whitnall and his cohorts' broader vision. While zoning was an endless source of personal frustration to Whitnall and Hoan in the 1920s, Milwaukee's strict guidelines went relatively unchallenged when compared to those of many other American cities. Instead, it was annexation, so crucial to make decentralization workable, that politically complicated the planned city. Milwaukee's planners had no choice but to surrender annexation duties to a new city department; the groundwork required technical knowledge of the sort that planners were unfamiliar with. Whitnall, who in the wake of his parkway plans had clearly become Milwaukee's most eminent planner, never lost sight of decentralization as his primary goal. However, his dual status as both county and city planner rendered him silent on annexation controversies; his plans transcended borders. Hoan and city annexation officials did not have the same luxury. Whitnall used his position as county planner to midwife projects that were well outside city borders. Regionalism was not an abstraction for city officials, even if they bought into the concept. If Hoan wanted to address Milwaukee's postwar housing shortage via annexation, he had to find ways to convince outlying areas that city status benefited them. Hoan's first attempt to induce industries encircling the city had failed; other strategies were needed. In 1924, George Altpeter, Milwaukee's first annexation director, hatched a plan to annex several plants north of the city near Green Bay Road. Several industries nearby, most prominently Nordberg Manufacturing, had rejected Milwaukee's overtures. Slightly to the east, the city had acquired land that was being developed as Lincoln Park, to be included in the growing system of parkways. Altpeter drew up a petition on a parcel of land that included the recalcitrant plants, but also included enough city-owned parkland to allow Milwaukee to be the majority property holder.[66] The city of Milwaukee was therefore the signer of the annexation petition and the Nordberg plant was trapped. Nordberg, however, legally contested the annexation on a different technicality: that the Chicago and Northwestern Railroad Company, along whose tracks the plants sat, had improperly claimed to represent Nordberg in annexation discussions with Milwaukee without approval. The case eventually went to the Wisconsin Supreme Court, which ruled in favor of Nordberg, knocking out the annexation.[67]

The Nordberg lawsuit yielded several patterns that became familiar throughout the 1920s and again in the late 1940s and 1950s, when the city resumed annexation with similar motivations. First, most large manufacturers opposed Milwaukee's expansion, believing they could exert greater control over their affairs through smaller village and township governments. This particular type of conflict rarely made large headlines; the petition campaign that decried the "Blockade of Milwaukee" was never repeated. Annexation lawsuits like the Nordberg case were complex and usually resolved by minor legal technicalities that did not make for good press. Furthermore, Milwaukee's top public officials, especially Mayor Hoan and later Frank Zeidler, gained virtually nothing by publicly belittling the city's industrial leaders who spent much of their own time in the public eye complaining of high local taxes. As a result, city leaders turned their invective toward their residential neighbors, especially unincorporated towns whose own governments struggled to handle the functional demands of urbanization.

A second pattern that became apparent was the litigious nature of annexations. In the 1920s alone, twelve lawsuits were filed against the city of Milwaukee. Most of the lawsuits contested not the annexations themselves, but various interpretations of existing state laws. State courts constantly debated the legalities of annexation and added another layer of state involvement in the city-suburban conflicts that began to plague the region. Just as important, the attorneys who fought Milwaukee in the courts emerged as familiar foes to city officials. They came to personify the anti-city bias that Hoan and later Zeidler believed was endemic in both regional and state politics. Equally significant, lawyers who represented the outlying towns began informally sharing information about their numerous legal battles with the city. Out of these gatherings emerged the Milwaukee County League of Suburban Municipalities (LSM), a group that sought to "fight the central city" and to provide suburban governments a voice in legislative affairs.[68] The League exercised little power in the 1920s and 1930s, essentially remaining an informal club of lawyers. It nevertheless had vast symbolic importance. For the first time "suburban interests" coalesced strictly around the crucible of antiurban politics. Annexation Director Arthur Werba, who replaced Altpeter in 1925, began calling the LSM the "The Iron Ring" (a name he probably borrowed from Public Works Commissioner R. E. Stoelting, who used it to describe manufacturers who refused annexation).[69] The term came to exemplify not the attorneys themselves but the suburbs they represented. The LSM remained organized throughout the interwar period and kept up its assault on Milwaukee's expansion well into the 1950s.

City officials quickly learned that in order to break down opposition to annexation, they needed to tout its positive benefits to fringe communities. More specifically, because property owners had a voice in the annexation process, it had to be clear that Milwaukee's growth benefited this constituency. Since realtors had the greatest stake in seeing vacant land beyond the city developed, it was paramount for the city to work with the real estate community in seeing annexation through. During the 1920s, planners from the BPLC sought technical advice from developers in establishing

minimum platting guidelines. Many developers, in turn, strongly supported Whitnall's system of parkways as a crucial way to increase property values. Confident that a program of annexation would yield similar benefits,
developers in large part came to favor annexation. As one real estate official
proclaimed after touring a vast expanse of farmlands just outside city borders on the northwest, "This is a fine illustration of the reason why I have
faith in the future of Milwaukee."[70]

Milwaukee realtors signed off on annexation for one reason above all
others: the promise of municipal service to newly annexed areas. In the
early twentieth century, "municipal service" increasingly meant water and
sewage extension to developers. Prior to 1910, water and sewer lines had
been installed unevenly across the city with poorer inner city districts consistently ignored. Historian Kate Foss-Mollan has noted that before 1910,
inner city wards lacked political influence and as a result were chronically
underserved by public works commissioners who, under Mayor David Rose,
maintained a "proprietary attitude" toward service provisions such as water.[71] Rose preferred to use water extensions as a revenue stream to cultivate
an ever-expanding network of political patronage. As a result, city commissioners were more willing to sell water to bedroom communities like
East Milwaukee (which became the Village of Shorewood in 1917) while
ignoring inner city neighborhoods like the Polish South Side. When the
reform-minded Socialists swept into city hall in 1910, they did so in part
on the promise of providing water to all city residents, and set about the
task of reorganizing Milwaukee's inefficient infrastructure. When Hoan
assumed office in 1916, he carried on these efforts. Professional staffs of
chemists, engineers, and other technical experts helped make Milwaukee's
public works a model and made "sewer socialism" a lasting legacy of the
city's efficient government.[72] They also made annexation far more promising to developers who had invested in land surrounding the city. For this
reason, the Milwaukee Real Estate Board supported the city annexation efforts throughout the 1920s, again for very different reasons than Hoan and
other policy makers had in mind.

Service provision across the board was a democratic idea, but it also
meshed with the increasingly frantic need to reduce Milwaukee's population density and facilitate planned decentralization. As with other elements
of this policy, local developers accepted annexation not in the spirit it was
intended, but because property values would be increased. Milwaukee's annexation officials understood this dilemma. Hoan's vigorous support of annexation never waned, but the machinations of expansion were obviously
out of his hands as well. The task of annexing fell to a separate department,

and the city's army of annexation solicitors had to convince property owners of the concrete benefits in joining Milwaukee. For annexation to work, officials had to promote its monetary benefits. Accordingly, George Altpeter and Arthur Werba, the city's two annexation directors during the 1920s, became the public mouthpieces of Milwaukee's physical growth. Werba, who took over for Altpeter as annexation director in 1925, especially made annexation a municipal crusade, but one that relied on acerbic public rhetoric backed quietly by millions of dollars in public subsidies to finance growth on the periphery.

From 1919 to 1932, Milwaukee grew from 25 to 44 square miles. During that time, the city laid 296 miles of water mains at a cost of $13 million and spent $14 million to lay 393 miles of sewer lines.[73] These figures were points of pride to annexation officials such as Werba, who noted at the end of the decade that Milwaukee's total valuation had increased by $325 million during the 1920s and half of that increase came from construction in newly annexed territory. Reflecting the Socialists' desire to attain complete fiscal solvency, the city paid for over half of the cost of all public improvements in cash. The city also set up an amortization fund to wipe out all bonded indebtedness. This accomplishment moved Werba to boast, "No other city in Wisconsin and perhaps no other city in the United States can show, dollar for dollar, as high a return of municipal services for the taxes collected."[74] Ironically, this same record of municipal achievement made annexation extremely controversial during the 1920s. The quality of Milwaukee's service provision stood as the city's trump card in facilitating annexation petitions. The most obvious measure to demonstrate the city's efficient public works was to compare them with those of the neighboring towns of Milwaukee County where annexations had occurred. Werba's characterizations of town government were—partially by necessity—not kind. He frequently pointed out that public works projects, especially the paving and grading of streets and provision of water and sewer extensions, were slow to develop in towns, but in areas annexed by Milwaukee, improvements came quickly. Annexation's "magic wand" corrected this: city government had ready means to pave streets, collect garbage, and create efficient and pleasant communities. Furthermore, Werba constantly asserted that only Milwaukee was capable of bringing these services to the towns. Meanwhile, developers, caught up in the national real estate boom of the 1920s, claimed that annexation wrought property value increases in excess of 100 percent.[75]

For the communities that bordered or were located near Milwaukee, annexation raised difficult questions as to the future shape of urban growth. Further complicating both the city and its surrounding communities' desti-

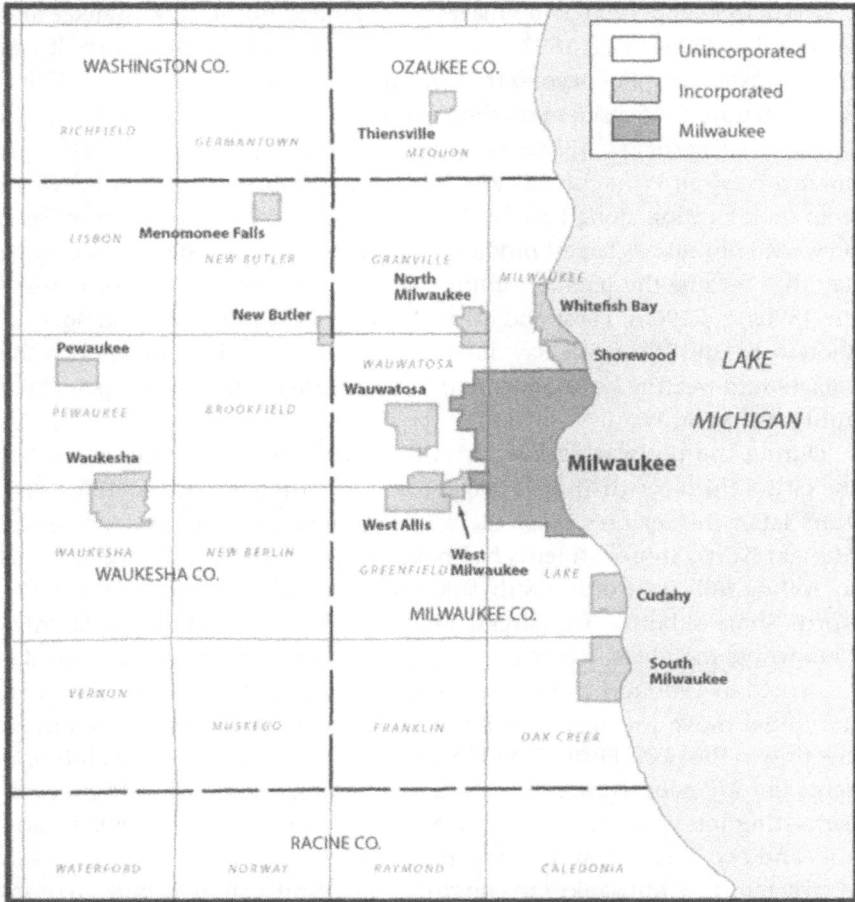

Municipalities of the Milwaukee Region, 1920. © Mapcraft

nies were the geographic dimensions that Milwaukee County had already taken on prior to 1920. Stretching north and east along the coast of Lake Michigan were the region's wealthiest communities. In the late nineteenth century, Milwaukee's most prominent families had started to congregate on the high ground east of the central business district on·the Milwaukee River and, as the city grew more crowded, slowly moved north along Prospect Avenue up the lake. Here, landowners platted large lots to maintain the bucolic character of the "Gold Coast," often leaving the land completely vacant until it was assured that the proper residences were built. As wealthier neighborhoods filled in, they extended beyond the city's northern border at Edgewood Avenue.

Between 1890 and 1900, two villages incorporated north of Milwaukee and along Lake Michigan. In 1892, the village of Whitefish Bay was born. It was actually over two miles beyond the city limits, at least in part because Whitefish Bay's initial 316 residents desired to establish a separate school district. In 1900, the village of East Milwaukee (which became Shorewood in 1917) incorporated between Whitefish Bay and Milwaukee. Both communities benefited from their location along Lake Michigan. Frederick Pabst, the owner of Pabst Brewery, Milwaukee's largest producer of beer, built a large estate in Whitefish Bay that became the premier summer resort for Milwaukee's upper crust in the 1890s and 1900s. Pabst and other elites were the primary landholders in Shorewood and Whitefish Bay and they collectively helped to develop the villages into wealthy bedroom communities that remained lightly populated until after World War I.[76]

During the postwar decade, as middle-class residents increasingly left the city, a third North Shore village, Fox Point, incorporated in 1926. Five years later, the region's most exclusive community came into existence. Affluent North Shore residents had begun to purchase large estates on gently rolling hills west of the Milwaukee River, near but not adjacent to the North Shore suburbs. The largest estate was that of Milwaukee Country Club whose members, seeking to preserve the community's prestigious status, voted in 1930 to incorporate into the Village of River Hills. Ironically, the initial move for incorporation occurred at the country club's annual meeting in the posh Pfister Hotel in downtown Milwaukee. River Hills residents quickly adopted the most stringent zoning ordinance in the region, permitting lots of no less than five acres in 85 percent of the village, and one- and two-acre lots in the remaining territory.[77]

Any effort by Milwaukee to convince these North Shore suburbs to consolidate was complicated by public works contracts that had been made by the Rose administration in the 1900s. Shorewood received Milwaukee water at inflated costs and even agreed to pay for the laying of water mains through the village. By the 1920s, Shorewood also started to sell Whitefish Bay water it purchased from Milwaukee.[78] Thus both villages already received city water and were extremely doubtful that they would benefit from consolidation with the city. Furthermore, the North Shore suburbs had already begun to zone their own land to prevent low-income groups from joining them; Shorewood—the wealthiest village in the state by assessed valuation—even banned all apartment buildings for a time in the early 1920s.[79] North Shore residents were primarily commuters as well, since virtually no industry existed in these communities. In addition to working in the city, North Shore suburbanites frequently owned property in Milwaukee, giving them a stake in urban policies initiated in the city. Nevertheless, annexation did not interest most North Shore residents. The village president of Whitefish Bay, Frank Klode, admitted during a public debate on annexation, "I sleep in Whitefish Bay, but most of my investments on which I pay taxes are in Milwaukee. That's the situation with most of the Whitefish Bay residents, and we are more solicitous of Milwaukee's end of the deal than of the suburbs. If you can convince me that annexation of Whitefish Bay and Fox Point will benefit Milwaukee, I'll change my attitude and go out and boost for it."[80] Werba's frequent public promises of the improved public works that annexation or consolidation with Milwaukee would produce yielded scant interest in the North Shore.

Located west of the city, along the Menomonee River, was Wauwatosa, Milwaukee's oldest residential suburb. Originally settled by Yankee New Englanders in 1833, Wauwatosa had, as early as 1866, proclaimed itself as "the most attractive suburb of Milwaukee."[81] The original village was the site of a commuter railroad stop, and residents officially incorporated in 1892 to break free from the Town of Wauwatosa. Though collectively less wealthy than Shorewood and Whitefish Bay, Wauwatosa's population grew more quickly thanks to its location near both the industries of the Menomonee Valley and the Milwaukee Road, which branched north from the river and ran along 31st Street, only two miles from the village's eastern border. By 1920, Wauwatosa's population reached 5,818 residents and this number more than doubled by 1926, surpassing 13,500.[82]

Five industrial suburbs surrounded Milwaukee to the north, west, and south, each with separate and distinct histories, each long in existence by the 1920s. North Milwaukee grew alongside a stop on the Chicago, Milwaukee, and St. Paul Railroad in the 1880s and incorporated as a village in 1897. Several industries located in North Milwaukee, most prominently the American Bicycle Company, which in the early twentieth century employed over 1,000 workers. South and west of the city were two industrial satellites, West Milwaukee and Allis, both created in part as tax havens for industries. West Milwaukee, incorporated in 1906, had attracted so many industries that it levied no property taxes at all throughout the first half of the twentieth century. West Allis, previously an unincorporated village, grew alongside the Chicago and Northwestern Railroad tracks and incorporated as a city in 1906, shortly after Edward Allis decided to move his massive machine manufacturing plant there. By the 1920s, the Allis plant was the largest in the region, employing over 5,500 workers and propelling West Allis's population past 23,000 by the middle of the 1920s. Finally, well to the south of Milwaukee were two more industrial communities,

Cudahy and South Milwaukee. Like West Allis, both were dominated by one primary industry, Cudahy becoming a village in 1906 after Patrick Cudahy located his meatpacking plant there and South Milwaukee in 1892 after Bucyrus-Erie, a maker of steam shovels, built a large plant. Because Milwaukee's South Side had developed more slowly, both communities remained well beyond the city's urban expansion and were therefore not prominently involved in the annexation controversies of the decade.[83]

In many important ways, these eight communities differed greatly from each other. Whitefish Bay, Shorewood, and Wauwatosa were white-collar suburbs, residential in character. By intent, none of these three communities had industries of any note. With the 1920s real estate boom, all became appealing locations for white-collar commuters who worked in the city. A local newspaper dubbed Wauwatosa "Milwaukee's Bedroom," noting that Wauwatosa officials did not at all mind the designation "for it gives them a chance to brag about the furnishings of the bedroom."[84] By 1926, Shorewood and Wauwatosa led all Milwaukee County suburbs in the percentage of residents who commuted to Milwaukee each day. In contrast, industrial communities like Cudahy and South Milwaukee, well to the south of the city, functioned as more self-contained places where residents worked in factories located in the communities where they lived. In 1926, only 162 residents of South Milwaukee and 413 from Cudahy commuted each day to Milwaukee. West Allis, home to the giant Allis-Chalmers plant, the region's largest employer by the 1920s, actually employed a large share of Milwaukee residents who commuted from the city to this suburb each day. The suburbs also differed politically from each other, with North Shore suburbs overwhelmingly Republican or Progressive and industrial villages and cities to the south and west equally Democratic in voting habits. Predominantly working-class West Allis even flirted with socialism during the Depression, electing Marvin V. Baxter as mayor in 1932.[85]

Despite the very real differences that existed between the incorporated suburbs of Milwaukee County, they shared one important characteristic. With the exception of Fox Point, each incorporated municipality in Milwaukee County had existed as a separate political entity before 1920 and in most cases since the nineteenth century. With long-established separate identities, they saw little reason to allow Milwaukee to swallow them up. The city's aggressive annexation campaign, accompanied by increased calls for some form of metropolitan governance, threatened each suburb, regardless of type, in the same way. Faced with what many perceived to be a threat to their very existence, the suburbs fought back. Wauwatosa, watching as Milwaukee's solicitors slowly pushed the city's boundaries westward, began to annex some land on its own, especially along Blue Mound Road, located to Wauwatosa's south. Shorewood's village trustees acted with less rational means. In 1921, the village's official bulletin instructed residents to notify local police if they heard of any annexation petitions being floated. Milwaukee could not legally annex any land in incorporated communities, but the threat seemed too great for the suburbs to ignore.[86]

Milwaukee's expansion was easier to achieve but no less controversial in the more rural towns that ringed the city. In Wisconsin, "towns" are unincorporated communities (referred to as "townships" in most of the Midwest), often laid out by the original territorial surveyors. Towns were large in land size, usually thirty-six square miles, and were agricultural in nature for most of their histories. Five towns—Milwaukee, Granville, Wauwatosa, Greenfield, and Lake—bordered the city of Milwaukee to the north, west, and south. Each had existed since before the Civil War. While none had absorbed a great share of the region's middle and upper classes, in varying degrees they all

CHART 2-2	Population of Incorporated Cities and Villages in Milwaukee County, 1920 and 1927

	Population, 1920	Population, 1927
City of Milwaukee	457,147	536,400
City of West Allis	13,765	28,102
City of Wauwatosa	5,818	18,000
City of Cudahy	6,725	11,000
City of South Milwaukee	7,598	10,000
Village of Shorewood	2,650	9,239
Village of North Milwaukee	3,047	6,500
Village of West Milwaukee	2,101	3,500
Village of Whitefish Bay	882	3,500

Source: Arthur Werba, "Annexation Activities of the City of Milwaukee," 1927, Folder 1, Box 9, City Club of Milwaukee Records, MARC, GML.

CHART 2-3 | Suburban Employment in Milwaukee, Incorporated Villages and Cities, 1926

	Population, 1926 in Milwaukee	*Persons Employed*	*% Employed*
Shorewood	9,000	1,970	22%
Wauwatosa	13,500	2,075	15%
West Allis	23,150	2,860	12%
Whitefish Bay	3,500	271	8%
North Milwaukee	5,500	394	7%
Cudahy	10,441	413	2%

Source: Milwaukee Transportation Survey, McClellan and Junkersfeld, Inc. 1926, MPL.

grew substantially in population in the early twentieth century as city residents spilled across political boundaries. The expanding South Side Polish and German enclaves moved south into the neighboring Town of Lake. The sturdy bungalows that dominated the northern half of the Town of Lake were very different from the palatial luxury of the North Shore and the solid prosperity of Wauwatosa, but were a definite step up for the working-class Polish Americans who sought escape from the crowded South Side wards.[87] A similar pattern of growth took hold in the Northwest Side, where the Towns of Granville and Wauwatosa began filling up with German Americans who worked in nearby industries on the Milwaukee Road railway corridor along 31st Street. Meanwhile city annexation officials scrambled to keep up with urban growth on the periphery. There, unincorporated towns did not require a community-wide referendum to be dissolved into Milwaukee, as did the incorporated villages and cities. Instead, provided the town land bordered Milwaukee, city annexation officials could pick and choose neighborhoods, carving out pieces of land where a majority of property owners gave sanction for annexation.

Milwaukee's annexation policies threatened these towns' existence in more immediate ways than the incorporated suburbs. Any parcel of land that Werba's army of solicitors carved from the towns was merely subject to a majority vote of the landholders within it. After the Common Council's vote whether to accept or reject the parcel—a virtual rubber stamp in favor of expansion—annexation became complete. Therefore, as Milwaukee's land size gradually rose in the 1920s, each town encountered a curious problem: as towns attracted more residents, their physical size, and in some cases populations, began to shrink. Since city annexation solicitors first went after the ring of factories that surrounded Milwaukee and were mostly located in the unincorporated towns, valuable tax revenue also disappeared. Because of the modest housing values in most of the towns, any loss of industry gravely threatened public revenues. "If our manufacturers are left with us," an anti-Milwaukee pamphlet warned Lake residents, the town could survive, but "the city of Milwaukee WANTS THEM."[88]

As separate but unincorporated political entities, town governments only rarely benefited from Milwaukee policy. Instead the county serviced the towns, regulating land uses and providing police protection. Water service was uneven as well. Most town residents made use of wells; Milwaukee remained loath to provide city water and sewage prior to annexation since these provisions remained the primary motivation for land speculators and residents to join the city. Furthermore, large amounts of land in each town remained dedicated to agricultural use, giving town governments more decidedly rural characteristics that remained at odds with urbanization. Yet farmers often financially benefited from urban expansion. In a report to the Common Council in 1926, Werba observed that many farmers saw their property values rise dramatically as residential decentralization progressed, but they often resisted annexation out of fear of paying city taxes on their farmland.[89]

CHART 2-4	Population of Unincorporated Towns Bordering Milwaukee, 1920 and 1927

	Population, 1920	Population, 1927 (est.)
Town of Wauwatosa	15,082	10,500
Town of Lake	8,876	7,500
Town of Greenfield	6,293	7,500
Town of Milwaukee	2,606	3,800
Town of Granville	2,875	3,300

Source: Arthur Werba, "Annexation Activities of the City of Milwaukee," 1927, Folder 1, Box 9, City Club of Milwaukee Records, MARC, GML.

Urbanization had created rapid growth across the county, but economic development within the region remained irregular. Each town's residents generally were far less wealthy than the white-collar bedroom suburbs of the North Shore. Furthermore, town government was far less sophisticated; town boards "governed" loosely, meeting sporadically to approve budgets and discuss matters facing the community. This informal manner of governance increasingly drew the scorn of metropolitan advocates. Werba reserved his most venomous attacks for the town governments. Of the Town of Granville, which bordered Milwaukee on the north and west, Werba proclaimed, "Their streets are mudholes and ruts; pools of stagnant water befoul the air and breed insects; refuse is dumped wherever convenient; the whole district seems completely neglected and sadly in need of attention."[90] Werba's cantankerous remarks as to the poor quality of town roads and other infrastructure belied the fact that these public improvements were unimportant to many of the town's rural residents. "Suburban residents are in reality Milwaukeeans. They depend on Milwaukee for their livelihood," Werba told a local newspaper in 1929.[91] However, defining "suburban residents" was far more complicated than city officials believed. Farmers in Milwaukee County may well have benefited from urban expansion in terms of land appreciation, but they did not consider themselves "Milwaukeeans" in any meaningful sense. A popular anti-annexation pamphlet in the Town of Lake urged residents, "Don't pay for your neighbor's house," implying that Milwaukee sought to swallow up Lake and milk the town's revenues. "Real estate agents in the Town of Lake," the pamphlet charged, "know that if Lake is annexed to Milwaukee the assessed valuation of the town's property will be increased without improvements."[92]

Urbanization trapped towns between a rural past and an uncertain suburban or urban future. Annexation impelled town residents to make important decisions about the future shape of their communities. Some sought greater municipal autonomy. In 1926, the two towns located most directly in the path of the city's annexation efforts—the Town of Lake to the south and the Town of Milwaukee to the north—both attempted to incorporate into independent municipalities. Both movements for incorporation into independent cities were purely defensive, designed as ways to protect the towns' tax bases from Milwaukee's annexationists. The Town of Lake's referendum, set for a vote on September 18, would have created a city about half the size of Milwaukee. The Town of Milwaukee, north of the city, had already watched the births of Shorewood and Whitefish Bay eat away large chunks of land. In the 1920s, as Milwaukee's annexation program commenced, the rapidly developing Chicago and Northwestern Rail corridor, which ran north along the Milwaukee River, became a primary city target. Determined to protect this valuable tax revenue, a group of town residents attempted to incorporate the Town of Milwaukee into a fourth-class city, with a referendum for incorporation into a city scheduled for October 15.

The incorporation efforts of both towns alarmed Milwaukee officials. The city's entire expansion program was in danger of derailment. "If they win, we're through," warned a city official after hearing of Lake's referendum.[93] Milwaukee officials planned to "influence the vote" through a counteroffensive of propaganda in the weeks leading up to the Lake referendum. Within both towns, a "Voters and Taxpayers League" was hastily organized to combat the two towns' transformation into cities. The main targets were Lake's farmers, most of whom lived in the town's still rural southern sections. "Please remember," the league reminded them, "you are not voting for annexation to the city of Milwaukee."[94] Lake simply could not develop as a city as quickly as Milwaukee; consequently, farmers' property values would plunge. If Lake remained a town instead, land would only "be gradually sub-divided into the city of Milwaukee."[95] Alderman Paul Gauer, a Socialist whose South Side district bordered Lake, warned Lake's farmers of impending bankruptcy if they had to pay for the public improvements the new city would fund. Many Lake residents agreed. A few weeks before the referendum, Agnes Tomkiewicz, a property owner in Lake, sought a court-ordered injunction to prevent the vote, arguing that over 9,000 acres of Lake's total 10,500 acres of territory constituted farmland and hardly fit the definition of a "city."[96] For their part, advocates of incorporation painted opponents of the proposed City of Lake as pawns of both Milwaukee and the real estate interests that city officials seemed beholden to. The "Voters and Taxpayers League" drew the most heat when it was discovered that an employee of a real estate firm on Milwaukee's South Side actually headed the league. Lake's attorney cited this evidence to halt the injunction and the referendum remained scheduled for September 18.[97]

Milwaukee's newspapers joined in the fight against incorporation. A *Milwaukee Journal* editorial asked how a community with one-eightieth the property valuation of Milwaukee but one-half the amount of land could build "city necessities" for itself.[98] The editorial also questioned the motives of the opponents of annexation. Echoing Werba, the *Journal* hinted that town government officials merely sought to hold on to their jobs, which would presumably be lost if the towns continued to shrink in size or disappear entirely. "This much seems certain," stated an editorial shortly before the Town of Milwaukee referendum, "city government is designed for real cities, places densely populated with many people living closely together.

It is not designed for agricultural communities of thinly settled areas."[99] Both referendums failed by wide margins. On September 18, Lake's incorporation was defeated by a vote of 1,417 to 733.[100] A month later, Town of Milwaukee residents voted down incorporation by a similar margin. The city's annexation program was again safe, but defeat of this effort required unprecedented intervention into the affairs of its neighbors. Several aldermen had spoken at public meetings, occasionally accompanied by Werba and even Hoan. The "Voters and Taxpayers League" pamphlets that had surfaced in the Town of Lake curiously emerged in the Town of Milwaukee as well, again alarming farmers of the economic peril that was certain to ensue once the town became a city.[101] Nevertheless, Milwaukee's annexation program had survived a major challenge.

As Milwaukee's land size increased with every annexation, city borders drew closer not only with unincorporated towns on the periphery, but also with the region's long-established incorporated villages, which warily watched the encroaching city draw nearer. By the late 1920s, Milwaukee's northern borders touched Whitefish Bay and Shorewood, and Werba, Hoan, and other officials began trying to persuade the North Shore suburbs to consolidate their governments with the city. Consolidation was only possible if a referendum was held in the village or city in question and a majority of residents voted in favor of it. In Whitefish Bay, by 1928 Werba managed to organize enough initial support for consolidation that some residents formed the Whitefish Bay Annexation Association (WBAA). The WBAA tried to appeal to its residents' sense of regionalism. WBAA pamphlets asserted that residents were not villagers but citizens of a metropolis, and that most people of Whitefish Bay had business contacts throughout the region and especially in Milwaukee. "We are all Milwaukeeans," the WBAA argued in 1928. "We need suburbs, but only in the sense that we need home sites beyond the present boundaries. The goal is to get them to extend the boundaries, not migrate over them."[102] However, foes of consolidation within the affluent village vastly outnumbered the WBAA. Represented by the Whitefish Bay Citizens Committee, they turned Milwaukee's well-known problems of congestion against the city. A pamphlet that circulated late in 1928 highlighted the Citizens Committee's scare tactics. It strongly implied that consolidation with Milwaukee meant pleasant residential neighborhoods would devolve into tenement slums and schools would quickly become overcrowded. Other residents echoed these concerns. A recently arrived homeowner scoffed at the WBAA, claiming that if Whitefish Bay became a part of the city it would become "a place of apartment houses and cheap tenements."[103] In fact, policy makers specifically designed Milwaukee's annexation to reduce the congestion that suburbanites so greatly feared, a point city officials repeatedly made throughout the 1920s. The WBAA also tried to address these fears, assuring residents that the village would remain zoned single-family residential, but to no avail. "Milwaukee zoning turmoil is quite convincing," an opponent of annexation pointed out, apparently referring to Hoan's increasingly difficult attempts to thwart zoning amendments.[104] At a series of mass meetings held to discuss consolidation in 1928 and 1929, hundreds of village residents voiced their overwhelming opposition to the city and no consolidation referendum was ever held.[105]

Only one incorporated community, North Milwaukee, consolidated with the city in the 1920s, but not before encountering significant opposition. The economically modest industrial village, lacking the wealth of the North Shore suburbs, struggled to provide residents with adequate public works. In 1922, Milwaukee annexation solicitors persuaded the village to hold a consolidation referendum, which passed by a wide margin. Nevertheless village trustees, charged with officially voting consolidation into effect, balked for a time, ignoring the results of the referendum. For six years, residents repeatedly elected trustees who promised to join with the city, only to see those promises ignored by men "who had no desire to lose that office by consolidation." The *North Milwaukee Post,* the local newspaper, also repeatedly fought consolidation, presumably afraid their own existence would be usurped once the village became another city neighborhood. Infuriated, local residents published their own newspaper, the *North Milwaukee Annexationist,* which listed a long line of grievances residents held against their local government. The village had reached its bonded debt capacity (which the city of Milwaukee promised to assume), residents frequently were overcharged for water services, and property was taxed at 99 percent of its full value, a far higher rate than even in Milwaukee. The paper made class differences explicit as well, castigating the North Shore suburbs as "Gold Coast" elites whose snobbery was evident by their desire to "remain aloof from the big city."[106] Finally, in 1928, residents succeeded in sweeping into office a group of trustees who swore *in writing* to legislate themselves out of existence by passing an ordinance calling for yet another referendum. North Milwaukee residents ratified the measure by a two-to-one margin. City of Milwaukee residents concurrently voted for consolidation by a ten-to-one majority. In early 1929, after six torturous years, North Milwaukee finally consolidated with the city.[107]

As the 1920s ended, Milwaukee officials confidently promoted their metropolitan planning accomplishments, and linked annexation to the planning and housing concerns that had gripped reformers in the previous

HERE'S WHAT THE OPPOSITION HAS TO SAY

The following is a reprint of an anonymous circular issued by anti-annexationists of Whitefish Bay.

Read it carefully; analyze its tone, the logic of its arguments, the fabric of its "facts." Do you seriously believe that your governmental interests, and the welfare of your homes, will be wisely protected by minds that reason, think and write as these have done? Do you think that consolidation with Milwaukee can possibly be as dangerous as a village government if it should be influenced or controlled by such reasoning as this?

DO YOU LOVE YOUR WHITEFISH BAY?
DO YOU LOVE YOUR HOME?

If you do — then read this:

Milwaukee wants to annex Whitefish Bay — Milwaukee with its terrific tax burden now wants to shift the load to the suburbs — wants you to carry the tremendous load.

Milwaukee, with its 100 school barracks, with 3,500 school children attending school in them, wants you to be annexed. Do you want barracks?

Milwaukee, with its chlorinated drinking water, that contains all the putrid sewage of Manitowoc, Sheboygan, Port Washington and many other lake cities, wants you — your children and their children to drink that unhealthy mess the rest of their lives. No matter how much chlorine is put into the water it is still sewage!

There are a number of big selfish interests, that want to control Whitefish Bay. They work sometimes openly — but mostly under cover. It is your duty — your interest to stop them in their tracks — NOW!

Half the illness in Whitefish Bay is caused by drinking chlorine. Next time you don't feel well drink some more chlorinated water and call the doctor.

Let's preserve the reputation our splendid village has, as a place of peaceful and quiet residence. Let's not be disturbed over the "Big city" idea.

Remember, the selfish interests work night and day — for their interest — not yours.

MEET TONIGHT — BASEMENT WHITEFISH BAY
SCHOOL.

BE THERE EARLY — BUT BE THERE!

CITIZENS' COMMITTEE.

Suburban Anti-Annexation Pamphlet—Opponents of Milwaukee's efforts to annex land or consolidate with neighboring suburbs often went to great rhetorical lengths to convince residents to fight the city. Courtesy of Wisconsin Historical Society two decades. In 1929, Werba authored a report titled "Making Milwaukee Mightier" that detailed the city's progress and future prospects for expansion as well as comparing Milwaukee's experience with other American cities'. Nearly a decade of battles with town and suburban governments had sharpened Werba's tone. The future consolidation of all governments in Milwaukee County, he predicted, was inevitable, only blocked by selfish suburbs: "Milwaukee cannot continue to enjoy the prosperity made possible by its marvelous expansion in recent years if its growth is to be hampered by its suburban satellites."[108] In the report, Werba contrasted Milwaukee's gradual, piece-by-piece annexation with that of other American cities, noting that Detroit and Baltimore, for example, had added far more square miles of territory, but that Milwaukee's method enabled the city "to expand according to a definite plan."[109] Mayor Hoan echoed Werba's confident tone a year later in 1930, in an article Hoan authored for *The American City*, titled "How Milwaukee is Solving the Housing Problem." In it, Hoan expressly linked annexation to the city's congestion problems. Hoan outlined the building of the Garden Homes as the first "relief measure" Milwaukee took up to address its overcrowded housing conditions, and then noted that the city had added sixteen square miles of land, on which "thousands of new homes were built under modernized zoning and building restrictions, forming beautiful new residential districts, adding 150 million dollars in assessed valuation of the city and providing employment for thousands of workers." He lastly pointed with pride at Building Inspector Leon Gurda's initiation of condemnation and demolition proceedings on hundreds of homes in the city's inner core. All three initiatives had addressed congestion. Hoan concluded; "Thus by promoting and financing a cooperative housing project, by developing newly-annexed districts, and by systematically razing old and insanitary [sic] buildings, Milwaukee is in large measure coping with the housing problem."[110] While Hoan and Werba publicized Milwaukee's planned decentralization, city planners pointed to its transportation innovations. In 1930, City Planning Engineer Charles Bennett also authored an article for *The American City* that emphasized the collective efforts planners had made in Milwaukee since 1915. Bennett mentioned the civic center project, but focused more attention on roadways, including five photographs of street-widening projects and Whitnall's parkway scheme.[111]

Implicit in all three articles was the notion that decentralization was part of a broader conception for governance, and that the "mole work" of planners and annexation officials, much of what this chapter has outlined, was in fact connected to a broader civic design. Taken individually, there was nothing innovative in circulating annexation petitions, platting new streets and widening old ones, and upholding or amending a zoning ordinance. Collectively, however, these efforts all had grown out of a planning mentality that sought to transcend industrial urbanization by looking away from the crowded urban core to achieve decentralization. Milwaukee's city government did not exclusively conduct these efforts; Whitnall operated on behalf of Milwaukee County and city and his plans usually extended well beyond city boundaries. However, the urban problems that invited such actions had originated in Milwaukee, and thus decentralization's design was principally a city-driven exercise. Annexation had thrust Milwaukee officials into the region's suburban and rural fringe, and residents outside of city borders made decentralization a hotly contested exercise in growth politics.

Equally ominous, interest in low-cost housing waned in the 1920s. The American planning profession remained largely disinterested in housing, in part due to the initial split between Olmsted's and Marsh's groups and in part due to the technical demands of the profession itself. American real estate developers and home builders also had little incentive to make affordable housing a priority. The skyrocketing property values of the 1920s gave the private sector even less incentive to experiment with cooperatives. Even in a city like Milwaukee, where planners and politicians were earnestly concerned with affordable housing, low-income housing remained in short supply. The Garden Homes was supposed to demonstrate that given the proper attention and financial investment, alternative communities could thrive in the private market and make decentralization humane and orderly. Instead, the private market never emulated the project, and was utterly unresponsive to cooperative housing. Local real estate officials responded far more enthusiastically to planned decentralization when it involved technical advice, and in Milwaukee, realtors worked closely with the BPLC on platting standards and the parkways. But rather than *adopt* the zoning ordinance in its intended spirit—to condition the market to develop better communities for the expanding city—the private market had *adapted* the zoning ordinance to fit its own needs. The result was a housing market chronically short on low-cost shelter throughout the 1920s, despite the success of annexation and the relatively strict adherence to zoning. From 1921 to 1932, Building Inspector Gurda estimated that only 15 percent of the newly built housing was in a rent bracket for "low-wage" earners. By the middle of the Great Depression, low-wage earners made up 66 percent of the population of Milwaukee.[112] During that decade, as the next chapter will demonstrate, Milwaukee retained and even enhanced its status as a city rich in unique planning initiatives, but it also began to fail to achieve the components necessary to make its metropolitan visions political realities.

Planning, Metropolitics, and the Depression

The confidence of Milwaukee's policy makers at the close of the 1920s ended with the onset of the Great Depression. As the economy of the United States atrophied, the crisis narrative that so frequently framed urban reformers' views on cities returned. The evidence was impossible to miss. Across the country, unemployment skyrocketed, the GDP plummeted, and homebuilding ground to a virtual halt. Choked with scores of suddenly tax-delinquent properties, municipal government coffers emptied out. For relief, cities looked increasingly to Washington, D.C., especially in the wake of Franklin Roosevelt's election to the presidency. A variety of interest groups—including progressive and radical housing advocates, organized labor, and city governments—began pressuring the federal government to intervene in America's suddenly dormant real estate market. Roosevelt's administration viewed cities as both political entities that could generate votes and as places where the economic impact of the Depression was the most severe. For their part, city leaders hoped to attract New Deal dollars to address unemployment, attack the continuing problem of slums, and in some cases, maintain patronage. Partly thanks to New Deal mandates to build public housing and partly due to the continued efforts of reform-oriented groups such as the RPAA, America's planning profession took a renewed interest in urban housing problems. Milwaukee avoided major fiscal crisis thanks to some remarkably creative fiscal policies, and the city earned a misleading reputation as a place where the Depression took less of a toll on its inhabitants. Thus while the Great Depression had an undeniable and well-documented impact on the economies of both rural and urban America, it also presented an opportunity to permanently alter federal housing policy, and possibly with it, the built environment of metropolitan America.[1]

The Great Depression also dramatically altered the direction of metropolitan planning in Milwaukee. The city's annexation program came to a stop, a budget victim of the economic downturn. In lieu of physical expansion, Milwaukee officials, helped greatly by a variety of civic groups, stepped up efforts to achieve metropolitan government via consolidation. In the midst of economic crisis in 1934, Milwaukee County residents debated —and eventually defeated at the polls—city-county consolidation. During the 1930s, the Wisconsin state government defeated a watered-down version of city-county consolidation as well. Thwarted at the county and state levels, Milwaukee city officials temporarily curtailed annexation and metropolitan government. But if progress toward metropolitan government in Milwaukee slowed, planning still transcended municipal borders. Charles Whitnall helped lead efforts to consolidate city and county parks commissions, convinced that park planning was best executed on a broader scale. City officials, again deeply concerned about Milwaukee's housing conditions, managed to win New Deal federal funds to plan and build Milwaukee's first low-income housing project, Parklawn, although not without serious disagreement over the location of the project. Federal intervention into the American housing market also benefited the Milwaukee region in the planning and construction of Greendale, one of three United States Resettlement Administration suburban "greenbelt" towns built during the Depression. The greenbelt towns drew heavily from the English Garden City movement, and American regionalist planning ideas illuminated in the Regional Planning Association of America's showcase projects. Planners like Whitnall, William Schuchardt, and Werner Hegemann had long embraced many of the same planning principles for Milwaukee, which the new greenbelt town seemed to fulfill. Greendale eventually became a community that admiring city officials aggressively sought to control and replicate. In the 1930s, its gestation and construction demonstrated that decentralization remained very much alive in design, if not political execution.

As agonizing as the Depression was to virtually every economic sector in America, perhaps nowhere was the pain felt so strongly as in real estate. The construction industry, which had boomed like no other in the 1920s, collapsed after the market shocks of 1929. As the Depression deepened and real estate values kept plummeting, housing construction in Milwaukee ground to a near complete halt. By 1933, total housing construction across the city amounted to fifty-seven units. Home-building remained stagnant throughout the 1930s. From 1929 to 1938, the total number of housing units constructed in the city failed to surpass the number of homes built in the single year before the stock market collapse (1928). Because the city's population growth rate slowed but still increased, families again resorted to the expediency of doubling up. By 1936, housing inspector Leon Gurda estimated that the city's housing shortage had reached over 5,700 units.[2]

Mayor Hoan responded to the housing crisis of the early 1930s the same way he had fifteen years earlier: by appointing a housing commission. In 1933, he chose fifteen civic leaders to conduct a survey of housing conditions in the city and recommend solutions. Like Hoan's previous commission, the group consisted mainly of individuals who were at least sympathetic to public support for housing. City building inspector Leon Gurda sat on the commission, as did Charles Bennett, who had served as the Milwaukee Board of Public Land Commissioner's (BPLC) City Planning Engineer since 1926, and who was gradually assuming many of Charles Whitnall's duties, though the 74-year-old Whitnall still retained his seat on the BPLC. Other key members included Eugene Warnimont, who served as supervisor of the Milwaukee County Board, and Edmund Hoben, a young architect from the BPLC staff who served as the commission's secretary. Frank Harder, now president of the BPLC, chaired the commission, which initially met in Hoan's offices on January 24, 1933.[3] Nine months later, the commission issued a report to the Milwaukee Common Council. Its contents reflected a different kind of housing problem. The 1918 commission challenged the ability of capitalism to provide housing befitting ideal communities; the 1933 commission existed when home-building of any type, regardless of class or quality, had virtually ceased to exist. Furthermore, thirteen years of city-suburban conflicts over growth clearly framed Milwaukee's housing problem in a different way, as the commission's 1933 report opened by observing: "The whole conception of a city as an economically or politically feasible unit of government must give way to a conception of the metropolitan area as a unit of government if the effect of changing patterns of city growth are not to prove economically disastrous as we now know it." Milwaukee, the report continued, was currently "thrown into a competition with its suburbs," and in the absence of winning the competition, it would be forced to either consolidate with its suburban competitors or face the prospect of "permanent bankruptcy." The report also subtly challenged previous views on decentralization, observing that "with people climbing over each other from the center toward the outskirts" the central city was being left "semi-depopulated, not needed for business, and unfit for decent housing."[4]

The Commission's analysis of demographics, however, was slightly misleading, because the city of Milwaukee's population continued to climb in the 1930s, growing from 574,249 to 587,472 people during the decade. Future reports by city officials would demonstrate that overcrowding in the inner core neighborhoods remained a problem. Nevertheless, for the first time, it was now apparent that the city would not experience growth evenly, and that outlying suburbs were attracting residents at higher rates. Efforts to consolidate Milwaukee and its suburbs were beyond the scope of the housing commission—and would become a countywide endeavor by 1934—but the implications of suburbanization were clear nonetheless.

Hoan formed his housing commission just as Franklin Roosevelt assumed the American presidency and began to launch his multitude of federal programs that collectively made up the New Deal. American cities, where Roosevelt had gained some of his largest voting majorities, benefited greatly from the federal dollars, which poured in to provide employment for laid-off workers. Plans for public improvements that the Depression had idled came back to life, and the more specific and detailed ones often stood the best chance of receiving significant federal funds. Whitnall's Milwaukee County parkway plans especially benefited from the Civil Works Administration (CWA) and its later incarnation, the Works Progress Administration (WPA). Over 8,000 people eventually worked on the Milwaukee County Parks in a variety of tasks. Managerial workers helped convert tax-delinquent land into several small neighborhood parks, and laborers built swimming pools and bathhouses, dredged creeks, and planted trees, grass, and shrubs in old and new parks across the county. By 1936, county officials estimated that the development of the park system was well ahead of schedule, thanks almost wholly to federal aid.[5]

The collapse of the American real estate industry in the 1930s also drew the federal government more directly into the housing market. In 1932, President Herbert Hoover, in the midst of the growing housing crisis, chartered the Reconstruction Finance Corporation (RFC). The RFC's primary role was to extend credit to American banks, railroad companies, and other businesses suffering from ill effects of the Depression. However, public housing advocates in New York City, represented by New York Senator Robert Wagner, managed to include a provision for the RFC to provide funds for limited-dividend companies to build low-income housing projects and engage in slum clearance. The limited-dividend companies were slow to develop, but the federal mandate to intervene in the urban housing market grew when Democratic Party nominee Roosevelt routed Hoover in the 1932 election, and launched his New Deal. In 1933, during his famous first "Hundred Days," President Roosevelt signed the National Industrial Recovery Act (NIRA) into law. The act included a federal appropriation of $3.3 billion for public works, a provision of which included grants to local governments to provide for the construction of low-cost housing and slum clearance projects. Such projects fell under the purview of the Housing Division of the Public Works Administration, a creature of NIRA headed by Harold Ickes. The PWA's Housing Division invited submissions of private *and* public housing projects to be eligible for funding; but as of October of that year, only seven housing projects had received PWA money. Milwaukee, however, was well positioned to take advantage of PWA funds. Hoan's housing commission came into existence a full six months in advance of the PWA Housing Division's creation. By the fall of 1933, Hoan's housing commission was ready with a report, recommending that the city take advantage of federally sponsored public housing funds the Roosevelt administration had made available through the PWA. The commission chose the long-beleaguered Sixth Ward, where a high number of demolitions had taken place, as the initial site for the housing project, to be dubbed Parklawn. Hoan, always fiscally conscious, eventually came to disagree with the commission's findings, believing that while the Sixth Ward needed new housing, a large-scale project was more feasible on vacant land northwest of the city. Despite the initial disagreement over location, Hoan's housing commission remained in the running for PWA funds, but since the commission was only advisory and not a permanent, legal entity, confusion existed as to Milwaukee's eligibility. The BPLC had recently hired Edmund Hoben, a planner who was specifically charged with overseeing housing, and he continued to lobby Washington, D.C., to fund the low-cost community in the Sixth Ward.[6]

Even with the slow initial pace of disbursement of PWA funds, the Franklin Roosevelt presidency offered renewed hope to American city planners and housing advocates. Roosevelt's uncle, Frederic Delano, a businessman with a deep interest in planning, had been instrumental in helping launch Daniel Burnham's famed Chicago Plan of 1909, and had become involved in the Regional Plan of New York. While some members of the Regional Planning Association of America (RPAA) had criticized the Regional Plan of New York for not taking dispersal seriously enough, they welcomed Roosevelt's interest in cities and his occasional advocacy for industrial dispersal.[7] Housing advocates had begun to split over the utility of public housing—which was forlorn for most of the booming 1920s—and the extent of state involvement necessary to provide low-cost housing to poor city residents. In 1929 Lawrence Veiller, one of New York City's first notable tenement reformers, passionately told a conference of housing advocates in

Philadelphia that slum clearance remained in the public interest, but that government rehousing of displaced families was un-American and socialistic. Other housing reformers disagreed. Edith Elmer Wood, a member of the RPAA, believed that government loans to low-income urban dwellers were necessary, and if such loans proved insufficient, deeper government involvement, though not desirable, was also possibly needed. By 1931, Wood had published *Recent Trends in American Housing,* and in it she noted that interest in both slum clearance and direct government action was high enough, and the housing crisis serious enough, that public housing had perhaps become necessary. The deepening mortgage crisis and the collapse of the real estate industry in the early 1930s further heightened reformers' interest in housing beyond slums. New voices sought to include low-cost housing in a broader set of planning ideals that could recalibrate or even replace the existing American homebuilding industry.[8]

Foremost among these reformers was Catherine Bauer, a young journalist who had taken a deep interest in city planning and affordable housing through her close relationship with Lewis Mumford, whom she first met in 1929, and her subsequent membership in the RPAA. Bauer first gained national recognition within planning circles by winning an essay contest on architecture sponsored by *Fortune* magazine, and later helped Mumford conduct research in Europe for a series of articles for *Fortune* comparing "modern housing" programs in Europe and the United States. Bauer's frequent trips to Europe convinced her, not unlike earlier social progressives, that cities could not afford to tackle the issue of housing in isolation from the broader region. She expounded upon this idea in her seminal book *Modern Housing,* which was published in 1934. Bauer had grown convinced that truly well-planned and durable new housing in cities was best built on a basis of use and not speculation. In Europe, she noted, that frequently meant government itself built new housing, and cooperatives and other nonprofit groups also heavily involved themselves in the housing industry. America's dismal record of public or cooperative involvement in housing meant that housing had to be, as historian Gail Radford has noted, "a political issue and not a technical one, and certainly not an area of life where gradual improvement could be expected to occur naturally in a capitalistic society."[9] Bauer's *Modern Housing,* in many ways a call to radicalism, was not universally acclaimed, but it effectively synthesized regionalist trends in city planning with new architectural designs in housing, and proved remarkably timely, since it appeared in print just when America's real estate industry was at ebb tide and the federal government appeared willing to experiment with public housing.

Bauer spent three days in Milwaukee during the summer of 1933, with two different purposes. First, to help her research *Modern Housing,* she wanted to broaden her exposure to different built landscapes by visiting American cities that were away from the East Coast.[10] Secondly, she briefly worked as a consultant to Clarence Stein's architecture firm, which was studying possible locations for the new federal housing projects. Bauer's observations about Milwaukee—written to Stein during July of 1933—reflected the older question over whether Milwaukee did, in fact, have slum districts. She noted that Milwaukee had "less of a depression look" than any other American city she had seen. "The whole city," she wrote Stein, "is duplex—mostly duplex 'bungalows.'" The volume and width of "highways" in the Milwaukee region also staggered Bauer, as they made even New Jersey pale in comparison. Bauer found Milwaukee's endless rows of bungalows compact and "ugly," but also remarkably well kept, better than in any other city in the country. A staggering proportion of Milwaukeeans seemed to own cars, and any housing project would have to "plan on garages in practically every dwelling."[11] Bauer also noticed that since there were very few row houses in the city, and those that did exist were in poor neighborhoods, it would be difficult to convince Milwaukee's planners of the utility and cost benefits to constructing row dwellings. Bauer mentioned regret at missing Whitnall, who was out of town during her time in Milwaukee. A brief visit with Charles Bennett, the BPLC's planning engineer, convinced Bauer that in spite of his progressive credentials in broader matters of planning, Bennett had "simply not the faintest notion of what good group housing could be." Milwaukee's bungalows, aesthetically distasteful to Bauer, were "perfectly all right" to Bennett. Bauer's visit to Milwaukee was not a public event; she humorously noted that officials she talked to (such as Bennett) were puzzled as to why she was there in the first place.[12] However, her brief visit does demonstrate the disconnect among reformers over how to define "slums." The older disagreement over whether slums were strict products of building type (tenement apartments, which were almost nonexistent in Milwaukee) or other factors, such as population density and poverty, remained alive in Milwaukee. Bauer came away from her visit to Milwaukee generally impressed with the city, and had familiarized herself with the city's officials. She remained aware of projects and ideas radiating out of Milwaukee after World War II.

While Bauer and other reformers worked to bring housing and planning back together again, leaders in some American cities had never considered them apart from one another. One such place was Cincinnati, where Robert Fairbanks has noted that many civic groups who had pushed for low-cost housing reform also supported the Queen City's early city planning efforts. Like Milwaukee, Cincinnati planners originally believed that "slums" near or adjacent to downtown would gradually and organically be replaced by commercial and industrial buildings. However, by the late 1920s, Cincinnati's planners changed their minds about slums, convinced that they would not go away through natural urban change, and they began devising more elaborate slum clearance plans.[13] Milwaukee's planners generally displayed more willingness to involve the state directly in the housing market, but shared similar notions about slums by the late 1920s, convinced that vigorous slum clearance, if combined with planned extension of city boundaries, could augment decentralization.

The primary executor of what local officials considered "slum clearance" in Milwaukee was its Building Inspector, Gurda. Upon taking over the building inspector's office in 1928, Gurda dramatically stepped up the city's efforts to remove dilapidated residential structures from Milwaukee's built landscape. In the early 1920s, in conjunction with its planned civic center, the city had made plans to widen Kilbourn Avenue in the downtown area and clear buildings along it. Kilbourn Avenue was at the heart of an impoverished neighborhood consisting of Eastern Europeans and a growing number of African Americans, all of whom would be displaced by the civic center. Land acquisition for the center had moved very slowly during most of the 1920s; city administrators were reluctant to pay inflated prices for the site. Gurda's demolition program at the time commanded scant attention when it commenced in 1928, at the height of the real estate boom. But city officials had accelerated it with the bust of the early 1930s, with ironic success. Gurda utilized the state of Wisconsin's liberal condemnation law to impel property owners to raze hundreds of buildings. Under these laws any structure that deteriorated to the point where renovations surpassed half of the property's assessed value could be officially condemned. Property owners were thus forced by law to raze the building themselves. If they resisted, the building inspector's office forcibly demolished the condemned structure.[14] Gurda's knowledge of the building code was so deep that as of 1932, the city had not rescinded a single condemnation and had only lost one case in the courts. Thus from 1928 through 1934, a staggering total of 2,570 buildings in Milwaukee were condemned and razed by either the city or coerced property owners.[15]

During the early 1930s, city officials were extremely proud of Gurda's efforts. The demolition of structures along Kilbourn Avenue had sped forward, making way for the new boulevard and progress toward the new civic center. More broadly, this demolition was connected to urban expansion; as annexation progressed and vacant land opened up, residents of the crowd-

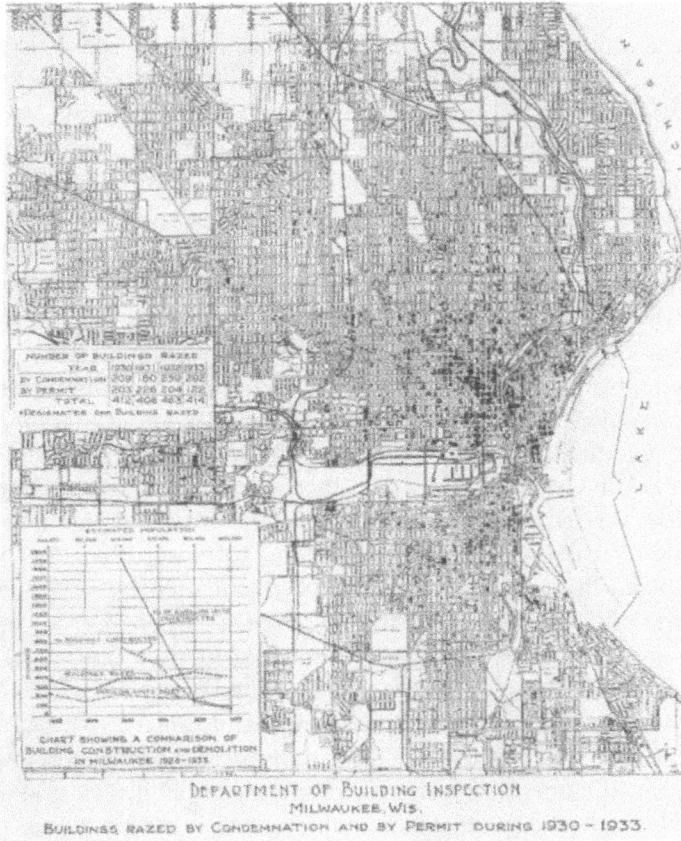

Map of Demolitions, City of Milwaukee 1930–1933—Though policy makers eventually grew ambivalent about its outcomes, Milwaukee's demolition program gained national attention during the Great Depression and was featured in a publication of the National Association of Housing Officials. Courtesy of Milwaukee City Archives / Milwaukee Public Library

ed inner core could find "elbow room" on the urban fringe. Hoan made explicit mention of this broader design in his 1930 article in *The American City*. The extra sixteen square miles of annexed land acted as a safety valve for city residents who sought to move from the "crowded tenements" of the urban core. Gurda's demolition program was also remaking the inner city. Hoan envisioned demolition, annexation, and state intervention in housing as components of a general plan, and that collectively, these efforts all meant that Milwaukee was "coping" with the housing problem.[16] With national attention to slum clearance growing in the early 1930s, Milwaukee policy makers promoted Gurda's efforts in housing circles as well. In his June 1931 edition of *Housing*, a periodical dedicated to tenement reform, Lawrence Veiller issued a "national call" for cities to engage in progressive slum clearance activities. Charles Bennett, Milwaukee chief planning engineer, wrote to Veiller, calling attention to Gurda, whom Bennett called "a crusader if there ever was one."[17] It was largely through Gurda's efforts that the city had razed hundreds of dilapidated structures. Veiller was impressed, but insisted that Milwaukee's program did not constitute "slum clearance." Gurda wrote back, insisting that while Milwaukee lacked multi-story tenements, it had no shortage of slum-like blocks, and it was his duty to remove all unfit structures from the city's landscape. While neither party could agree on a working definition of slum clearance, Veiller praised Gurda's efforts as another example of how the "best governed city in the United States" sought housing reform.[18]

Gurda's slum clearance efforts also increased Milwaukee's already strong presence in the national movement to push for more permanent federal involvement in public housing efforts, and to ensure that city planners were involved in such projects. A prototype for such initiatives emerged in the state of Ohio and in the city of Cleveland, where a local city councilman named Ernest Bohn, deeply interested in slum clearance, helped persuade the Ohio state legislature (where he had previously served) to pass a public housing law that made cities there eligible to receive PWA housing-project funds. Cleveland became an early leader in Depression-era public housing, but the energetic Bohn sought to make public housing a movement that involved city officials from around the country. Other progressive-minded reform groups joined Bohn. Chief among them was the Public Administration Clearing House, a three-year-old organization founded by Louis Brownlow, who had previously worked as a government official in Washington, D.C., and had more recently worked with the RPAA–led City Housing Corporation in developing satellite communities such as Radburn, New Jersey, in the late 1920s. Brownlow's Clearing House invited planners and local officials who were concerned with housing to meet in Chicago, Illinois, on November 25, 1931. Over twenty officials attended and at the meeting announced the formation of the National Association of Housing Officials (NAHO), whose purpose was to promote the cause of low-rent housing across the country. NAHO was not the first nationally based public housing organization in the country—Bauer and other more labor-oriented reformers had already created the National Public Housing Conference earlier in 1933—but its makeup of public officials signaled that the movement for public housing was making serious political headway. NAHO immediately set to work developing standards and best practices for local housing agencies. A year later in 1934, to continue the public relations battle, NAHO organized an international "commission" of renowned housing and planning experts to embark on a tour of fourteen American cities. At each stop, commission members met with the local press, city and civic leaders, and other pro-housing groups. Bohn and Brownlow were tour members, as was Henry Wright, an RPAA member who had helped design several Garden City–inspired satellite communities, including Sunnyside, Queens, and Radburn. An aging Raymond Unwin, original collaborator with Ebenezer Howard on the English Garden City prototypes, also took part in the NAHO tour, as did German official Ernest Kahn. The tour amplified American awareness of public housing, and NAHO began to collaborate with a wider sphere of housing groups to build momentum toward a permanent federal housing law.[19]

Milwaukee officials played a significant role in NAHO's formation and early activities. The links between planners and housing advocates that NAHO fostered were well established in Hoan's administration, as was the determination to use the state to intervene in the failing urban housing market. Hoan sent four BPLC officials—Whitnall, Bennett, Hoben, and Harder—to the Chicago meeting that created NAHO in 1933, the largest delegation any city sent (surely in part due to the ease of travel to the neighboring Windy City).[20] The NAHO–sponsored tour of housing officials also visited Milwaukee for three days in September of 1934. When NAHO began compiling data on best practices for cities to replicate in the realm of slum clearance, it relied heavily on Milwaukee Building Inspector Gurda's expertise. In March of 1934, the Work Division of the Federal Emergency Relief Administration (FERA), a New Deal agency that sought to create national standards for demolition, sponsored a "Conference of the Demolition of Worthless Buildings." Federal officials hoped demolition efforts would complement the Public Works Administration's (PWA) plans to build public housing in cities across America. Because Milwaukee had already undertaken aggressive demolition, Gurda's efforts were a highlight at the conference, and he was selected to chair a FERA committee on surveys planning and preliminary work.[21] After the conference, NAHO published *Demolition of Unsafe and Insanitary [sic] Housing,* a manual for cities to use to learn best practices in slum clearance. Milwaukee's demolition efforts received a lion's share of the report's attention; the conference had made Gurda a nationally known crusader in the demolition of unsafe buildings.[22]

Milwaukee officials also played eager hosts to the NAHO–sponsored international commission of housing experts in September of 1934. Planners in Milwaukee deeply admired English Garden City planning, and had eagerly embraced German innovations in land use controls; thus the presence of Unwin and Kahn was especially thrilling. The NAHO junket spent three full days in Milwaukee, and met with a dizzying array of public and private officials. Hoan kicked off the visit in his office with a private conference with the guests. A frequent Hoan ally in planning matters, the City Club of Milwaukee, hosted a public luncheon and a dinner banquet for the guests. On the second day, Whitnall led the visitors on an all-day trip throughout his burgeoning parkway system in Milwaukee County. Impressed with the scale and location of the park system, Henry Wright agreed with Whitnall and Hoan that the parks could act as a magnet to eventually draw inner city residents to the fringe, as slum clearance worked in concert with fringe development. On the final day of the NAHO visit, the full BPLC board and staff met with Wright and his cohorts, as did the Milwaukee Common Council.[23] Local press covered the visit in great detail, even featuring Unwin's style of dress, which was "so quaintly old-fashioned that he might be a character out of Dickens."[24] Unwin, in turn, was impressed with the care planners had taken to prepare the city's outskirts for development. Milwaukee had spent "more than it needed" on the trunk highways outside of the city, but it had also made public housing developments on the fringe of town more feasible.[25] Hoan agreed with Unwin that new public housing funded through the PWA belonged on the fringe, where costs were lower, and he used the visit as public leverage for his preferred location. "Indecision and procrastination" in Washington had, Hoan told a local reporter, endangered the chances of Milwaukee's landing a public housing project. Furthermore, the Garden Homes had been constructed on "cheap land on the outskirts," which had helped the project remain fiscally solvent. "Clearing buildings off high-priced land and providing low cost housing can't be done," Hoan insisted.[26]

The NAHO visit to Milwaukee heightened national awareness of the city's efforts to mesh planning and housing, and it played a part in the broader efforts to urge the federal government to commit more deeply to low-cost housing. Nationally, many other planners adopted the same stance as Mayor Hoan, that Ickes's firm support of slum clearance too often slowed the ability of government to build larger volumes of low-cost housing. Wright, one of the participants on the NAHO tour, was one of these critics, as was Lewis Mumford, who was slowly growing disillusioned with the New Deal's seeming unwillingness to challenge capitalism more directly. In Milwaukee, Hoan's criticism of the PWA's Housing Division during the visit was not a coincidence of timing. Edmund Hoben, who had worked on staff for the BPLC for several years in the early 1930s, had recently hired on with the PWA's Housing Division, and he gave Hoan inside information as to the delays in funding the Milwaukee project. PWA officials, especially Colonel Horatio Hackett, believed that the Sixth Ward location (preferred by Hoan's housing commission) was not "slummy enough." On the flip side, the second site on the northwest fringe (preferred by Hoan) was on vacant land and thus was not directly contributing to slum clearance. Ickes, Hoben wrote Hoan, was "insisting on slum clearance and kidding himself to think that low rentals can be produced in conjunction with such activity." Hoben's letter also reflects similar criticisms made of Ickes's managerial techniques in the 1930s by other officials, warning Hoan that Ickes used investigators from other offices outside of the PWA Housing Division to "sleuth" and "spy" on cities. While Ickes clearly wanted to ensure waste and corruption did not taint his federal agency's activities, he created distrust among many planners who worked with the PWA. Hoben himself begged Hoan to destroy the letter that outlined these bureaucratic problems.[27]

Debate over a location for Milwaukee's first federally funded housing project finally ended in 1935, when the PWA announced it would build on the site located on vacant land on the city's Northwest Side. City officials still intended to build a future project at the racially mixed Sixth Ward site. But Milwaukee's first federal housing project, dubbed Parklawn, was five miles northwest of downtown. The site was forty acres, and it bordered the Lincoln Creek Parkway, part of Whitnall's broader countywide system. Sixty-two buildings, all low-rise duplexes with multiple units, were to contain 518 housing units. Construction got underway in 1935, and Parklawn officially opened in 1937. Officials received over 5,000 applications to live in the project, demonstrating yet again that the shortage of decent, low-cost housing in Milwaukee was not an abstraction.[28]

Hamstrung by federal regulations largely drawn up by Ickes, city officials were forced to admit African American families only at rates that reflected Milwaukee's racial demographics as a whole. Since African Americans remained a tiny minority, constituting 1.3 percent of Milwaukee's population, only six black families received the opportunity to live in Parklawn. Like the Garden Homes, Parklawn was only a temporary solution to the housing problem, funded as an emergency work relief project. Certain PWA planners (such as Hoben) frowned on public housing sites for the inner core of cities because they envisioned cluster developments on the urban fringe as preferable to replacing the older low-income slums with new low-income housing that would keep poor residents locked up in the inner city. Hoan agreed with this planning method, which largely reflected the ideological underpinnings that had first inspired professional planning in Milwaukee. Well-intended though this goal may have been, it also meant that the

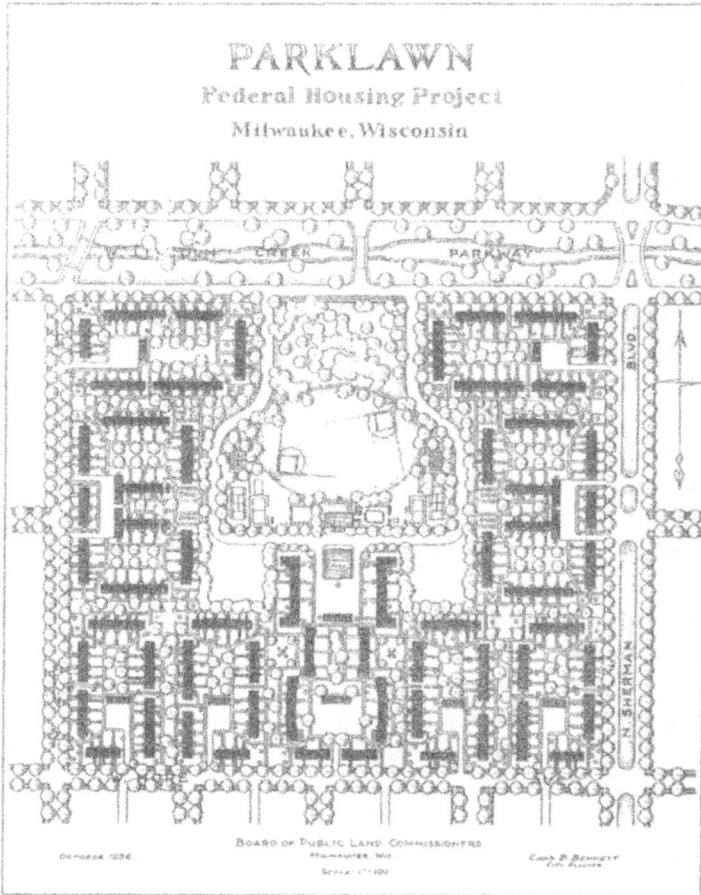

Plans for Parklawn—Parklawn was Milwaukee's sole PWA-funded low-income public housing project. Courtesy of Wisconsin Historical Society

small but growing population of African Americans in Milwaukee were not helped by the city's first low-income housing project and yet were among the most hurt by Gurda's demolition program. Hoan did support the Sixth Ward site as a potential second PWA project, but the higher cost of land in the long built-up neighborhood remained a major obstacle.[29]

While new federal urban housing policies had a major impact on the city of Milwaukee, the county of Milwaukee benefited from a new suburban initiative that originated in President Roosevelt's Resettlement Administration as well: the construction of greenbelt communities. In April of 1935,

President Roosevelt signed an executive order that authorized resettlement of poorer families from rural areas to planned satellite communities located outside of major American cities. Original plans called for over sixty satellite communities, but such an ambitious volume of projects soon proved not feasible. The director of the Resettlement Administration, and the man who had persuaded Roosevelt of the resettlement idea, was Rexford Tugwell, a former professor at Columbia University who was one of the more leftist advisors in Roosevelt's famed "Brain Trust," and a deep admirer of Garden City planning ideas. Tugwell quickly enlisted the advice of a variety of housing and planning reformers familiar with planned communities. He decided to pursue a smaller number of "showcase" projects, with the hopes that concentrating resources in fewer communities would yield more innovative designs. In the summer of 1935, Tugwell appointed a former Columbia colleague, economist Warren Vinton, to head a group of researchers who determined the location for the projects. By August of 1935, Vinton's Research Division had whittled the list of potential sites down to twelve cities.[30]

Milwaukee was one of the finalists, and in the summer of 1935, efforts were already underway in the region to find suitable land for the project. Milwaukee had earned a "reputation for metropolitan planning," as one pair of historians of the greenbelt program there have noted.[31] The Garden Homes, the county parkways, and the exuberance so many local planners displayed toward decentralization all made Milwaukee a strong candidate for one of the greenbelt towns. Moreover, before they even knew of the greenbelt program, planners in Milwaukee had already introduced new community schemes that they hoped would catch federal attention. One such plan was created by BPLC planning engineer Charles Bennett, and released to *The American City* magazine in 1930. After it sat gathering dust in a city government office during the early years of the Depression, Bennett reintroduced it to local media in February of 1933.[32] Bennett admired the planned community of Radburn, New Jersey, which was under construction in the early 1930s to considerable national acclaim. Radburn's two principal designers, Clarence Stein and Henry Wright, had taken Ebenezer Howard's Garden City model and applied it to the automobile age. Homes at Radburn faced away from the street, and cul-de-sacs ensured that streets would serve only the residents, not through traffic. Bennett tried to combine these ideas in his "model village," originally suggested to be located at the far northern end of Milwaukee County, near a railroad line where industry might locate in the future, but well north of the build-out of Milwaukee. Bennett's model village, like Radburn's, would accommodate the automobile, yet would also provide each house access to greenspace. Each road in Bennett's village was to run parallel with long strips of "park mall." At 60 feet wide by 100 feet deep, residential lots were considerably larger than both nineteenth-century home sites and the forty-foot-wide lots stipulated in the Milwaukee zoning ordinance. Echoing one of Radburn's key innovations, houses would not face the street, but instead would be turned around to face the park strips. In terms of site planning, Radburn echoed scholar Clarence Perry's "neighborhood unit," which envisioned residential nodes as self-contained entities, with schools and community facilities in the center, and commercial spaces on intersections.[33] The neighborhood unit also was contained entirely within arterial streets, meaning that residents of the community would have minimal through traffic on their streets. Bennett's village was situated between two major east-west arterials, Good Hope Road to the south and Brown Deer Road to the north. At the center of Bennett's village were several short circular streets, where apartment buildings, a community center, and some commercial buildings were to be centered. Bennett told the *Milwaukee Journal* that his village was the answer to a recent call made by First Lady Eleanor Roosevelt and industrialist Henry Ford that urban populations needed to decentralize into satellite villages, and that industry too needed to disperse. The model village site also abutted the Chicago and Northwestern Railroad and thus could be near new industrial plants. To ensure his village was effectively cushioned from the nearby industrial sites, Bennett also separated it from the railroad with a greenbelt that ran between the two spaces. With the city in no condition to finance a large-scale community, Bennett instead hoped that a private developer would come forward to build his prototype. But its timing—released when real estate activity was at an all-time low—was poor, and Bennett's community plan sat on the shelves of the BPLC, mostly ignored. A second abortive effort in building an experimental community on the urban fringe came from Whitnall, who hoped to set up cooperative "garden homesteads" outside the city. Whitnall worked with some federal officials in scouting sites in rural Milwaukee County, but his project never made it out of the initial planning stages.[34]

While Bennett's and Whitnall's efforts may have been ill-timed for the private sector, they did prove crucial in another way. The massive scale of the greenbelt projects complicated site selection in many cities. But in Milwaukee, federal officials found several sites that matched the scale of the greenbelt towns, most of which had already been scouted by Bennett and Whitnall for their own projects. Vinton and his researchers visited Milwaukee in the summer of 1935, and they (at first) secretly began looking for potential locations for a greenbelt community. When local officials learned of the federal interest in the greenbelt town, they eagerly began showing

Vinton potential sites for the project. The eventual favored site was one of Whitnall's proposed garden homesteads, eight miles southwest of the city, dotted with dairy farms along gently rolling hills. An additional benefit to the site that became Greendale, Wisconsin, was that it was located on the opposite side of Milwaukee from Parklawn, which was about to begin construction. The PWA, an entirely separate federal agency, controlled Parklawn, and any hint of competition with that project was better avoided if the greenbelt community was located in a separate area of Milwaukee County. With the site successfully chosen, federal agents spent the fall of 1935 buying out local farmers, and by early 1936, they had assembled the 3,410-acre site. Federal officials tried to keep the land acquisition for Greendale a secret, but by December of 1935, local media in Milwaukee began reporting on the proposed "Tugwelltown." The *Milwaukee Journal* initially reported on the land acquisition proceedings, predicting it was part of larger "pet visions" by Eleanor Roosevelt and Tugwell to move "low income city families in low cost houses on little farms."[35] As more details of the project slowly leaked out in early 1936, *Journal* coverage was generally favorable, framing Greendale as a positive step in employment relief, since thousands of workers would conceivably be employed in the planning, design, and construction.[36]

In the meantime, federal administrators were busy selecting planners for the greenbelt projects. The chief planner for the greenbelt towns was Frederick Bigger, a longtime planning official from Pittsburgh, Pennsylvania. Bigger had earned a reputation as someone who blended technical expertise and political realism with visionary ideas; he had spent years fighting for comprehensive planning in Pittsburgh, and he had also been a member of the RPAA in the 1920s and thus was deeply familiar with the community planning ideas that Stein, Mumford, and Wright propagated.[37] Bigger selected town planners for each separate federal project. To design Greendale, he hired architects Jacob Crane and Elbert Peets. Both men had experience in large-scale community planning. Crane had studied planning under John Nolen at Harvard, and worked as a planning consultant in Chicago in the 1920s. Peets, also a graduate of Harvard's Architecture and City Planning program, had local ties to Milwaukee, where he had hired on with Werner Hegemann and helped design Kohler, the company town north of the city, and the Washington Highlands neighborhood in suburban Wauwatosa.

In the design of Greendale, Crane and Peets sought to reconcile traditional and contemporary town layouts. Peets was responsible for the principal design of Greendale, and his plan for the community blended modern housing concepts with more traditional village layouts. Deep admirers of American colonial villages, Peets and Greendale architect Walter Thomas centered their community around a town square whose public and commercial buildings looked like twentieth-century facsimiles of Williamsburg, Virginia. Peets hoped that his design would yield a "close-knit" community, to "form a neighborhood in which the group feeling and group activities will be increased in the amount and in quality."[38] The inspiration for this emphasis on public life was, as Greendale historians Arnold Alanen and Joseph Eden have written, "far in the Euro-American past" well before the Industrial Revolution.[39] Peets himself wrote in 1938, "In its origin, Greendale would be classified as a colony town."[40] Howard's Garden City—both progressive in its acceptance of industrial growth and mindful of village tradition—was the second obvious model for Greendale's attempt to recover traditional occidental community life. The original Peets design reserved 2,000 acres, over 60 percent of the site's total acreage, for a permanent greenbelt. Howard's insistence that his Garden City residents were isolated from the harsh environs of the modern industrial landscape clearly resonated with Peets and his fellow greenbelt community planners. The reservation of greenspace also enabled planners to link Greendale to Whitnall's county park system via the Root River, which ran near the village center. Resettlement officials eventually deeded several hundred acres of land to Milwaukee County to link the community to the county parks. The contrived conservation also allowed Greendale to replicate colonial towns, which were, as Peets explained, "compact groups of housing in the midst of green country."[41] The greenbelt towns, however, just as certainly departed from Garden City principles in their conspicuous lack of industry. Peets reserved a small amount of land in his plans for light industry, theoretically to provide supplemental employment for female residents. But in principle, Peets noted, greenbelt towns were meant to "house people who already had employment." Greendale was to be "a workman's dormitory town," not a self-sufficient Garden City.[42] For Greendale's homes, Peets tried to avoid imposing his own tastes on the residents. He spent a considerable amount of time touring working-class neighborhoods in Milwaukee, and neighboring industrial suburbs such as West Allis. The endless rows of detached duplexes and bungalows were "often ugly" to Peets (much as they were to Catherine Bauer), but the pride owners took in them made it clear that the single-family detached home was Milwaukee's architectural folkway. Peets honored that vernacular architecture by providing Greendale with over 270 detached single-family homes, far more than in the other two greenbelt towns.[43]

Despite the careful attention Peets and his planners gave to custom, they also applied a variety of modern planning ideas to Greendale as well. Chief among them were the principles Stein and Wright had displayed at Radburn,

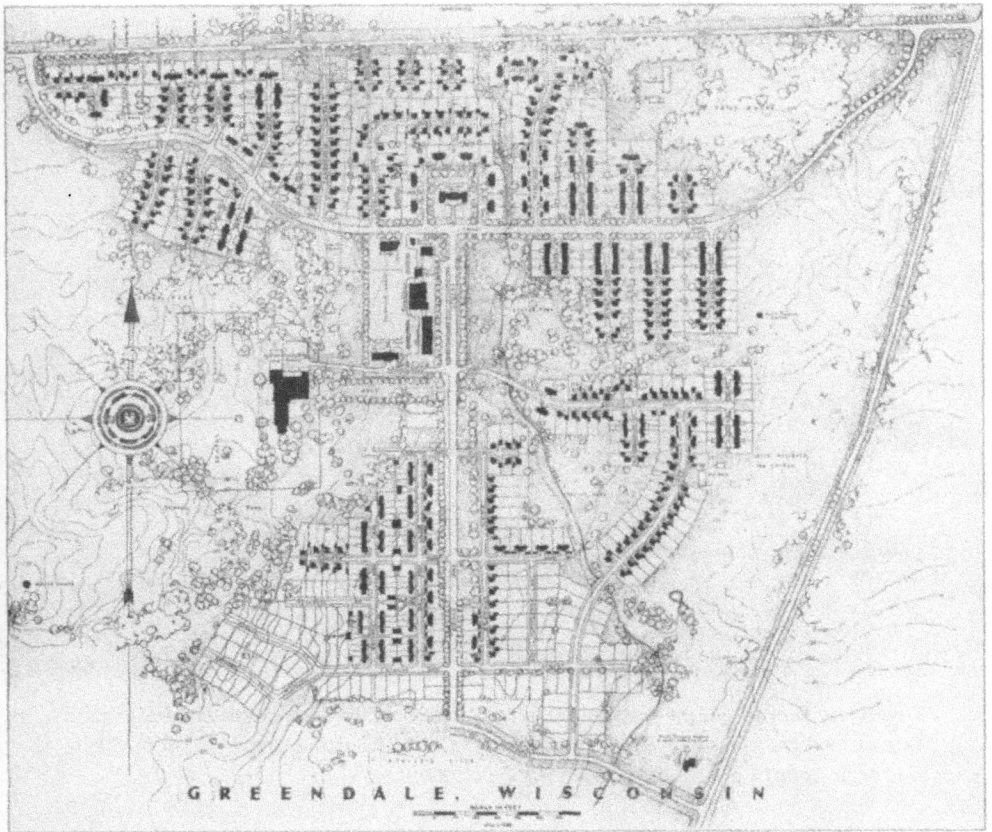

Plans for Greendale—Greendale's site plan was inspired by colonial era towns, but the planners also accommodated the automobile in their design for the community. Elbert Peets Papers, #2772. Courtesy of the Division of Rare and Manuscript Collections, Cornell University Library

New Jersey, regarding the relationship of pedestrians and homes to the automobile. Radburn's "Superblocks" redirected through traffic away from residential streets, which protected pedestrians from cars. The interior of Radburn's superblocks was another radical departure from traditional city building; rear alleys and garages were gone and in their place was common greenspace. Houses at Radburn fronted not the concrete of the street but the rear greenspace, creating a direct and immediate link to home and nature. Pedestrian paths carried walkers to the rear greenspace and, once again, away from the streets. Stein summed up the road plans by noting

Greendale Homes—Many original homes in Greendale were intentionally designed to face away from the street. Elbert Peets Papers, #2772. Courtesy of the Division of Rare and Manuscript Collections, Cornell University Library

that traditionally roadways "dominated" communities, but at Radburn they "served."[44] Like many contemporary planners, Peets admired Radburn, and he benefited from Stein, who served as a consultant for the Resettlement Administration in the greenbelt towns. Some components of Radburn thus smoothly worked into Greendale. Through traffic was entirely separate from residential traffic; cul-de-sacs further separated homes and people from cars. Many of the homes in Greendale also fronted away from the street, but unlike Radburn, rear greenspace was not communal. The pedestrian underpasses of Radburn also did not manifest at Greendale, which was hamstrung by a limited federal budget. The Radburn prototype, however, clearly helped Peets resolve the problem of accommodating automobiles without being overwhelmed by them. Greendale's location, well to the southwest of Milwaukee's urban build-out, nullified streetcar or other transit connections to downtown, and made the community dependent on the automobile. Peets and Crane largely ignored the possibility of mass transit in their site planning. During construction, an interurban spur line was built to link Greendale with the regional Milwaukee network, but the line was temporary, built only for construction workers. The only consistent alternative to cars for Greendale residents was buses, but the long commutes to Milwaukee's far-flung industries made them an unattractive option. The lack of decent mass transit was less of a problem, however, for two reasons. First, Greendale was essentially a middle-income community, and thus most residents could afford cars. Secondly, a disproportionate number of Milwaukee County residents already owned cars, living where the automobile had caught on quite strongly, and planners had openly embraced it throughout the 1920s.[45]

Construction on Greendale began in April of 1936. Originally, federal officials estimated that the project would employ as many as 5,000 relief workers, but at its peak, Greendale employed closer to 2,000 individuals, mostly compensated through WPA allotments. Nearly a year later, the town was half-finished, and a beaming Mayor Hoan led over 200 members of the Milwaukee Real Estate Board through Greendale, insisting to them he cared less about whether private or public sectors built housing than he did over whether any housing was built at all. In 1938, the first residents moved into Greendale, and over the next few years, the project's 572 units filled up completely. The federal government appointed a resident manager to handle day-to-day administrative affairs within Greendale. Eventually, Greendale incorporated into a village, giving the community municipal independence and a greater degree of home rule. The village government took on the same basic structure as other incorporated villages in Milwaukee County, with a village board of elected officials meeting monthly to discuss local matters. The federal government maintained ownership of the village, however, setting rents and coexisting somewhat uneasily with the village board. The awkward tension between local control and federal authority aside, Greendale took its place as Milwaukee's newest suburb at the close of the 1930s.[46]

Greendale and the two other greenbelt communities completed during the New Deal—Greenhills, near Cincinnati, and Greenbelt, near Washington, D.C.—have received a great deal of attention from scholars of planning and housing. Compared to the amorphous suburban development that dominated American metropolitan landscapes after World War II, the greenbelt communities stand out all the more. If federal officials hoped the three communities would be examples that private developers would copy, they eventually were mistaken. Historians usually situate the greenbelt towns within the broader timeline of America's infrequent large-scale community planning history. "The history of the greenbelt towns is the story of a road not taken," historian Joe Arnold wrote, observing that American real estate and construction industries ignored them after the 1930s.[47] This is undoubtedly true and well documented. Nevertheless, Greendale still represented somewhat of a culmination of the efforts of planners in Milwaukee, even though they did not pilot the project. Greendale planner Jacob Crane, speaking to the American City Planning Institute at its annual meeting in Milwaukee in 1936, said that Milwaukee was selected for the greenbelt project in part because the region had "reached a higher degree of maturity in its community life than most metropolitan regions, a situation definitively reflected in the relatively high level of responsibility in that state, county, and municipal governments, and reflected also in the Milwaukee city and county planning work." Greendale, Crane said, was but one "element in Milwaukee regional planning" and its planners recognized "the inexorable logic of land use in suburban territories."[48] Crane further expounded on this new logic in a 1937 article he coauthored with Resettlement Administration official John Lansill for *The American City* that invoked European planning principles in the formation of Greendale. The "suburban ring" of land around Milwaukee, they wrote, was so vast that speculators who platted lots in it would often find them left vacant. The vast majority of this land that ringed cities, Lansill and Crane wrote, "should be reserved for parks, forests, and farms."[49] American cities could control the process of suburbanization by copying European locales such as Stockholm, Sweden, and Berlin, Germany, which publicly controlled thousands of acres of vacant land in their respective suburban rings. Greendale, the authors argued, was the kind of community that municipalities themselves should build. If American cities took similar steps in acquiring peripheral land and planning greenbelt communities, the United States "would unquestionably go a long way toward the solution of problems of housing, land utilization, highway development, recreation, public and private finance, and community life in the great metropolitan regions."[50] Crane and Lansill's article clearly meshed with the principles that social progressive planners had explicated in the 1910s. Benjamin Marsh and his congestion reformers viewed zoning in this light, as did Whitnall and his Milwaukee colleagues. The Garden Homes was a modest example of the same principle: state control of peripheral land to maximize community life. In the absence of mass public purchases of land, Whitnall and Hoan envisioned annexation of vacant land, combined with zoning enforcement, as a mechanism that could achieve the same ends Crane and Lansill called for. More importantly, Crane and Lansill's "metropolitan reserve" principles for Greendale, with their focus on mass building of communities instead of piecemeal land subdivision and municipally controlled decentralization, informed future leaders of the city. A young local engineer named Frank Zeidler, also a Socialist in political orientation, worked for the Resettlement Administration as a surveyor at Greendale, and came away from his experience convinced it was the correct mode of community building. Zeidler later framed his own sense of urbanism on the same decentralization principles that planned and built Greendale when he became mayor of Milwaukee in the late 1940s.[51] The New Deal experiment at Greendale thus gave Milwaukee planners their most cohesive and concrete example of suburbanization. If the city of Milwaukee could maintain momentum in its physical expansion via annexation, such communities could remain within the grasp of similar planning initiatives in the future.

Local officials could point with pride to the fact that in the midst of the Great Depression, planned decentralization had made headway with help from the federal government. Parklawn provided the city with 518 low-cost units. Greendale resulted in another 572 units, and although the homes there were outside the grasp of poorer city residents, the greenbelt town had a profound impact on a future generation of policy makers. But in the late 1930s, as both projects completed construction, neither dented Milwaukee's still massive housing shortage. In 1936 and again in 1938, Leon Gurda issued the city's two most comprehensive surveys of its demolition program and continued housing problems to date. Both reports laid out in stark detail the damage wrought by the Depression. From 1910 through 1929, builders constructed an average of 2,664 housing units per year. Yearly homebuilding had then collapsed to 647 per annum from 1930 through 1937, and those figures included Parklawn's 518 units. By 1938, demolition had displaced 1,377 families throughout the 1930s, and it dwarfed Parklawn's ability to absorb the city's ill-housed. At the beginning of the decade, Hoan linked demolition to annexation and new homebuilding on the periphery, but the private sector remained dormant in the 1930s, in no condition to address the lack of decent housing. Milwaukee County's tax-delinquency rate had skyrocketed during the 1930s; 23,517 properties had foreclosed from 1930 to 1937, a higher rate than in many metropolitan regions in the United States. In his 1938 report, Gurda remained unwavering in his faith that demolition still exerted "a positive influence on the problem of housing," but he also recognized that it had exacerbated overcrowding in the city's poorest neighborhoods. Landlords gained from the housing crunch, further subdividing existing buildings. A total of 1,761 "new" units had been carved out of existing structures. Since the zoning ordinance stipulations drastically limited the number of families per unit, new ordinance violators multiplied. The city could easily have investigated the zoning offenders, but as Gurda put it, "I do not believe in spying" during such dark economic times.[52]

With the supply of new housing constricted by the Depression, demolition also unintentionally acted as an inflationary device on the price of shelter. As unsafe as condemned structures were, they usually offered cheap rents. One of the first questions residents often asked the building inspector's office upon demolition was where else they could find shelter for under $10 per month. "We can't tell them," admitted Gurda in 1937.[53] African Americans suffered the effects of demolition disproportionately, since the vast majority of black residents lived in the Sixth Ward, where a large share of demolitions took place. Gurda remained hopeful that a second public housing project to complement Parklawn in the Sixth Ward could eventually be built and that enlightened racial attitudes would open up decent housing for blacks, but both solutions were well beyond his grasp. "The Negro housing problem is urgent," Gurda warned in 1936, "We cannot any longer permit the shunting of families from one dilapidated shack to another, only to move out again because of the numerous condemnations of buildings in the section of the city they occupy."[54] Local African American leaders also resisted demolition. In 1938, NAACP representatives William Kelly and James Dorsey testified to the Common Council that demolition was exacerbating an already problematic housing shortage in the Sixth Ward.[55] Literally uprooted, Milwaukee's poorest residents again began to double up in nearby duplexes or rooming houses, further straining the inner city housing supply.

Thus while the Depression may have renewed Milwaukee's reputation for efficient city government, the city's demolition efforts were ill timed and perpetuated the housing crisis. A map of Milwaukee on the second page of the NAHO demolition manual revealed the vast majority of razed buildings to be in the wards surrounding downtown. The city's zoning ordinance had already rezoned much of the inner city for commercial and light industrial use, making it clear that Milwaukee's planners preferred demolition to rehabilitation. Consequently, of the more than 1,600 structures condemned between 1928 and 1932, only 151 were repaired in lieu of condemnation. Without a concerted effort to provide low-income housing, the city's demolition program threatened to make the housing crunch far worse for Milwaukee's low-income residents, who often simply could not afford the spacious new single-family bungalows that had sprouted up in row after row on the urban fringe. Already by 1935, city officials estimated that over 23,000 city residents were without decent housing. The Depression had constricted new building so much that razing actually *exceeded* construction within the city from 1932 through 1934.[56]

Gurda displayed remarkable alacrity in his role as chief enforcer of Milwaukee's building code, but he also understood that without a large-scale

CHART 3-1	Foreclosure Rates, Selected Counties in United States, 1932–1937

	Foreclosures	*Population*	*Foreclosures per 1,000 Persons*
Milwaukee County, Wisc.	23,517	725,263	32.4
Shelby County (Memphis), Tenn.	9,033	306,482	29.5
Wayne County (Detroit), Mich.	53,504	1,888,946	28.3
Los Angeles County, Calif.	53,761	2,208,492	24.3
Dade County (Miami), Fla.	3,121	142,955	21.8
Hennepin County (Minneapolis), Minn.	10,5045	17,785	20.3
Cuyahoga County (Cleveland), Ohio	20,396	1,201,455	17.0
Cook County (Chicago), Ill.	66,689	3,982,123	16.7
Jefferson County (Louisville), Ky.	5,873	355,350	16.5
Erie County (Buffalo), N.Y.	11,619	762,408	15.2
Polk County (Des Moines), Iowa	2,557	172,837	14.8
King County (Seattle), Wash.	6,760	463,394	14.6
Allegheny County (Pittsburgh), Pa.	15,710	1,374,410	11.4
Orleans Parish (New Orleans), La.	4,787	458,762	10.4
Marion County (Indianapolis), In.	3,564	422,666	8.4
Providence County, R.I.	2,911	540,016	5.4

Source: Leon Gurda, "Report on Housing to the Milwaukee Common Council," May 9, 1938, File 72, Box 2, Hoan Papers, MCHS.

program of affordable housing initiated by either public or private means, conditions in many city neighborhoods would not improve. Like many other city officials during Hoan's tenure, Gurda envisioned the building inspector's role as part of larger city planning efforts from both public and private sectors. In his 1938 report to the Common Council on housing conditions in the city, Gurda observed: "We in Milwaukee have attempted to solve this problem of slum clearance by demolishing worthless buildings on a larger scale than any other city, and believe that slum reconstruction can wait until owners of properties in these areas realize that they must cooperate with the government in this matter."[57]

Private real estate interests, however, displayed scant interest in following suit. The PWA direct building program ended, and the 1937 Housing Act stipulated that all federally supported low-income housing projects now needed to be funneled through local housing authorities. As the 1930s progressed and housing became a political issue at both federal and local levels, private sector cooperation in the realm of public housing grew in importance. In 1937, the Milwaukee Real Estate Board firmly opposed public housing and, helped by Nonpartisan aldermen in the Common Council, prevented the city from forming a housing authority, which federal guidelines now stipulated was necessary to gain further public housing funds.[58]

At the same time officials addressed Milwaukee's Depression era housing problems, they began to see cracks in the veneer of their ambitious annexation program. As the Depression deepened in the early 1930s and public expenditures constricted, Hoan and the Common Council reluctantly disbanded the city's annexation department. Milwaukee's boundaries froze at forty-four square miles, as the economic alarms of the Depression replaced the rhetoric of growth. The real estate boom of the 1920s ended emphatically. On and just beyond the city's edges, thousands of lots that speculators had eagerly platted during the 1920s sat idle. Unable to pay property taxes, many bankrupt speculators turned their deeds over to the city. In a clear sign of the times, employees of the annexation department, including Werba, transferred to the city's real estate office, where they compiled lists of tax-delinquent properties.[59] With annexation cut off by the Depression, civic attention turned instead to city-county consolidation. Early in 1934, desperate for ways to cut the costs of government, the city and county of Milwaukee separately formed fifteen-member committees to study the feasibility of consolidating certain functions of city and county governments that duplicated one another. To keep costs down and further propel government consolidation, the city and county agreed to merge their two committees into the Joint Committee on Consolidation in Milwaukee County (JCCMC). The joint committee undertook a series of investigations into the feasibility of merging city and county governmental functions with an eye toward complete political unification.

The idea of consolidation was by no means a new one. In 1870, a bill introduced in the Wisconsin state legislature would have merged the city and county of Milwaukee into a single government, but was voted down. State legislators renewed their interest in consolidation after World War I. In 1925, they formed an interim committee to study the viability of consolidation. While agreeing that some form of consolidation was desirable, the committee nonetheless conceded that political will was lacking, and advised against complete city-county consolidation. Werba's 1929 report on the progress of annexation also reluctantly concluded that suburban governments were far too hostile, even though he also confidently predicted the inevitability of metropolitan unification.[60]

The fiscal urgencies of the Depression, however, began to change that perception. The JCCMC's findings of the county and city governments observed what many different groups had believed for a long time, that the present organization of government in the region was illogical and in need of reform. The city directory included suburban addresses. Private charities operated on a regional basis. Patrons from across the region visited city museums and other cultural attractions. Milwaukee department stores like Schuster's and Gimbel's delivered goods to residents across the county. Over 1,300 suburban children attended city schools. Labor unions organized across political boundaries. The Milwaukee Fire Department serviced several outlying towns and villages. It followed, the JCCMC observed, that political units should operate on this same regional basis. The city's effort to unify the metropolis through annexation had been limited through "obstruction" of suburban officials. With the Depression threatening the economic health of the region, now was the time to "wipe out the political boundaries of governments within Milwaukee County."[61]

Nationally, realtors often shared the belief that municipal reform was necessary. In 1930, Judge Arthur Lacy, chairman of the Property Owners' Division of the National Association of Real Estate Boards (NAREB), characterized town governments as "obsolete," offering a needless duplication of services that did nothing more than raise the cost of government.[62] Local real estate officials who remained key allies in annexation efforts shared these opinions. The Milwaukee Real Estate Board, NAREB's local branch, deemed Milwaukee County's unincorporated town governments to be a "barrier to obtaining the maximum development of this area as one municipality, which it is in fact."[63] Werba had frequently pointed out town board members' clumsy attempts to thwart the city's annexation progress, seemingly oblivious to the benefits of being absorbed into a larger political entity. Occasionally, towns proved Werba correct in resorting to raffish obstruction. In 1931, a truck driver from the Town of Lake, Milwaukee's neighbor to the south, drunkenly interrupted a public meeting regarding annexation, taking the stage and haranguing Werba, who was in the middle of a speech. After being thrown out, the man confessed that town officials fed him whiskey at a Lake establishment and then encouraged him to break up the meeting.[64] Episodes such as this were rare, but they fed into an increasing impulse that town government was nothing more than a relic of the past. Local newspapers in Milwaukee ridiculed the "ox-cart governments" of the towns that stood in the way of metropolitan expansion.[65]

For the next nine months, a well-organized coalition of local groups pushed hard for Milwaukee County residents to vote for city-county unification. In the summer of 1934, an eclectic variety of organizations formed the Citizens' Association on Consolidation in Milwaukee County (CACMC). The CACMC encompassed twenty-three civic groups, including the City Club, the Milwaukee Real Estate Board, the Association of Commerce, the Milwaukee County League of Women Voters, the Wisconsin Chapter of the American Institute of Architects, the Lawyers Club, and a variety of neighborhood business organizations.[66] The city's newspapers also supported the JCCMC in a series of editorials urging citizens of the region to consider the city-county merger as a logical step in enhancing fiscal viability. In January of 1934, the *Milwaukee Journal* editorialized that "many local government units should be wholly wiped out" while not specifying which municipalities were savable and which were not.[67] The Milwaukee Real Estate Board had for a long time supported consolidation, characterizing the region's present setup as "a barrier to the maximum development" of the county.[68] Milwaukee's Socialist politicians, concentrated mostly in the city and wary of losing votes in an enlarged political entity that would have included more conservative suburbs, were divided over the merits of consolidation. Alderman and president of the Common Council, Paul Gauer, a Socialist, favored consolidation in principle, and helped persuade the Common Council to voice its approval over the objections of a small Socialist minority led by alderman Carl Dietz, who instead called for the city to "secede" from Milwaukee County to protect its public utilities and secure home rule. Over these objections, the Socialist Party of Milwaukee County, observing that complete consolidation "has been repeatedly urged as a part of our local platforms," also strongly favored political unification.[69]

On November 6, 1934, 104,708 Milwaukee County residents voted in favor of consolidation with only 40,319 opposed. Local newspapers trumpeted the results as a complete victory for consolidation forces, but the total returns were illusionary. Of the seventeen towns, villages, and cities in the county, in only three—Milwaukee and the working-class suburbs of West Allis and Cudahy—had a majority of residents voted in favor of consolidation. Of the 109,770 votes counted in the city of Milwaukee, 90,022 favored consolidation and only 19,748 opposed. The vast majority of residents in the outlying suburbs and rural towns had voted to oppose consolidation. West Allis officials, embarrassed by their residents' apparent enthusiasm for consolidation, resubmitted the referendum to their residents, changing the question to read: "Do you believe that the City of West Allis should by consolidation (annexation) join the city of Milwaukee and thus become a ward or part of a ward of the City of Milwaukee?" With consolidation now presented as another arm of the larger city's annexation efforts, West Allis residents overwhelmingly voted "no" in the second referendum.[70]

The state legislature retained the legal right to consolidate Milwaukee County. However, the voting results had revealed that complete city-county consolidation was far too politically divisive to risk. In 1935 and 1937, the Wisconsin legislature debated a variety of consolidation bills, but never voted on a complete merger of local governments within Milwaukee County. Consolidation opponents, with the help of heavy lobbying by county suburbs, defeated a far more watered-down bill in 1937 that would have allowed city aldermen to represent Milwaukee on the county board (and thus increase Milwaukee's representation there). The League of Suburban Municipalities, first organized in the 1920s to fight annexation, renamed itself the "Milwaukee County League of Municipalities" and lobbied the state government to turn its back to governmental consolidation. The Wisconsin assembly defeated the alderman-supervisor merger bill by a fifty-seven to thirty-two margin in February of 1937.[71] Any small chance of continuing the consolidation fight ended two months later, when the Milwaukee County board voted to pull its support from the Joint Committee on Consolidation, citing "citizen apathy" as the primary reason.[72]

In the absence of metropolitanism, the city and county achieved some functional consolidation. In 1936, Milwaukee city and county governments agreed to merge their parks commissions. The park merger was far less publicly controversial than the city-county consolidation movement, thanks in large part to Whitnall's parkway blueprints, which seemed to benefit city and suburbs evenly.[73] Construction on the parkways accelerated during the Depression, greatly helped by an infusion of New Deal money that allowed thousands of Works Progress Administration workers to continue its development.[74] The relatively smooth park board consolidation, however, did reveal a small but growing rift between county and city planning officials. An aging Whitnall, who served on both city and county park boards, had grown increasingly frustrated with the pace of city efforts to execute his parkways and his accompanying arterial roadway plans. "The county has been making

CHART 3-2	1934 Consolidation Referendum Results by Municipality, Milwaukee County

Question—"Do you favor effecting, by such county board or legislative action or amendment to the state constitution as may be necessary, consolidation of municipal services and governments in Milwaukee County?"

	Yes	*No*	*Total*
City of Milwaukee	90,022	19,748	109,770
City of Wauwatosa	2,769	3,947	6,716
City of West Allis	4,211	2,500	6,711
Village of Shorewood	1,146	3,185	4,331
City of South Milwaukee	727	2,306	3,033
Village of Whitefish Bay	1,108	1,273	2,381
Town of Lake	750	1,482	2,232
Village of Cudahy	1,041	989	2,030
Town of Greenfield	710	816	1,526
Town of Wauwatosa	680	729	1,413
Village of West Milwaukee	652	691	1,343
Town of Granville	506	825	1,331
Town of Milwaukee	149	513	662
Town of Franklin	83	496	579
Town of Oak Creek	83	461	544
Village of Fox Point	42	224	266
Village of River Hills	29	134	163

Source: Referendum Results, City of Milwaukee, November 6, 1934, Folder 3, Box 9, City Club of Milwaukee Records, 1909–1975. Milwaukee Manuscript Collection AS and Milwaukee Micro Collection 69. WHS, MARC.

steady progress," Whitnall told the Milwaukee Board of Estimates in 1936, "but the city is not benefited from the county's growing efficiency for the reason that the city does not maintain a cooperative basis." Whitnall, never patient when local politics got in the way of his ideas, increasingly found his county government work more rewarding in the 1930s. He favored park consolidation solely because "the welfare of the new city crystallizing over the regions beyond our present city, will depend upon the recognition of the human value of Wisconsin's natural landscape."[75]

The failure of complete city-county consolidation in the 1930s and the subsequent piecemeal consolidation of city and county park commissions is the first example of how metropolitan visions often fell victim to selective regionalism in twentieth-century Milwaukee. The planning ideals of Whitnall and other Milwaukee reformers usually transcended municipal borders. Far too often, reformers such as Whitnall and growth proponents such as Werba tried to enact change as if those borders did not exist. Metropolitan government returned to the political agenda of Milwaukee officials after World War II, motivated by a remarkably similar set of planning ideas, but retarded by similar failures to transcend the growing political rift between the city and its suburbs.

An increasingly embattled Daniel Hoan watched as the last remaining Socialist aldermen were slowly voted out of office in the 1930s, limiting his ability to enact new policies. In 1940, Hoan encountered the most serious mayoral challenge of his career. Carl Zeidler, a handsome, outgoing young politician, ran against Hoan on a platform of little substance. Zeidler's political experience consisted of a stint as assistant city attorney under Hoan, but he won popularity as Milwaukee's "No. 1 Extrovert." Zeidler, famous more for his singing voice than his policies, made vague promises to achieve a "clean sweep" of city government, but offered no concrete policy initiatives. Nevertheless, the ebullient Zeidler cast a stark contrast to an aging Daniel Hoan. Milwaukee voters took note, delivering Zeidler a stunning victory in 1940. Twenty-four years of Socialist governance had ended.[76]

Hoan left office with an impressive record of municipal governance. City planning had firmly embedded itself in the bureaucratic fabric. Charles Whitnall had become the city's most vocal opponent of urban congestion and proponent of planned decentralization to alleviate overcrowding. His system of parkways gained near universal popularity, and due in large part to his efforts, the BPLC impelled local realtors to work with the city in its physical expansion. Under Hoan's aegis, city reformers attacked the housing shortage with creativity, building the first municipally funded cooperative housing project in any large American city. Committed public servants like Arthur Werba and Leon Gurda carried out city policies with great energy, earning respect for "sewer socialism" across the country.

Nevertheless, most of the policies of the Hoan administration were long-term in design and controversial when implemented across a metropolitan terrain. Planned decentralization had yielded a city-suburban rift with no resolution in sight; even as the Depression thwarted annexation, the attempted city-county consolidation divided the region on municipal boundary lines. More ominously, the web of independent towns, villages, and cities that surrounded Milwaukee had found common ground in confronting annexation. A "suburban" consciousness, exemplified by new organizations like the League of Suburban Municipalities, would only grow stronger in the following decades. As Milwaukee emerged from World War II, the region's political boundaries would change at ever-quicker rates and correspond more closely with the uneven development that distanced the city and its multiplying suburbs along sociopolitical lines. But before that occurred, a new generation of city leaders emerged and they refused to let go of the metropolitan visions first conceived by social progressives in Milwaukee.

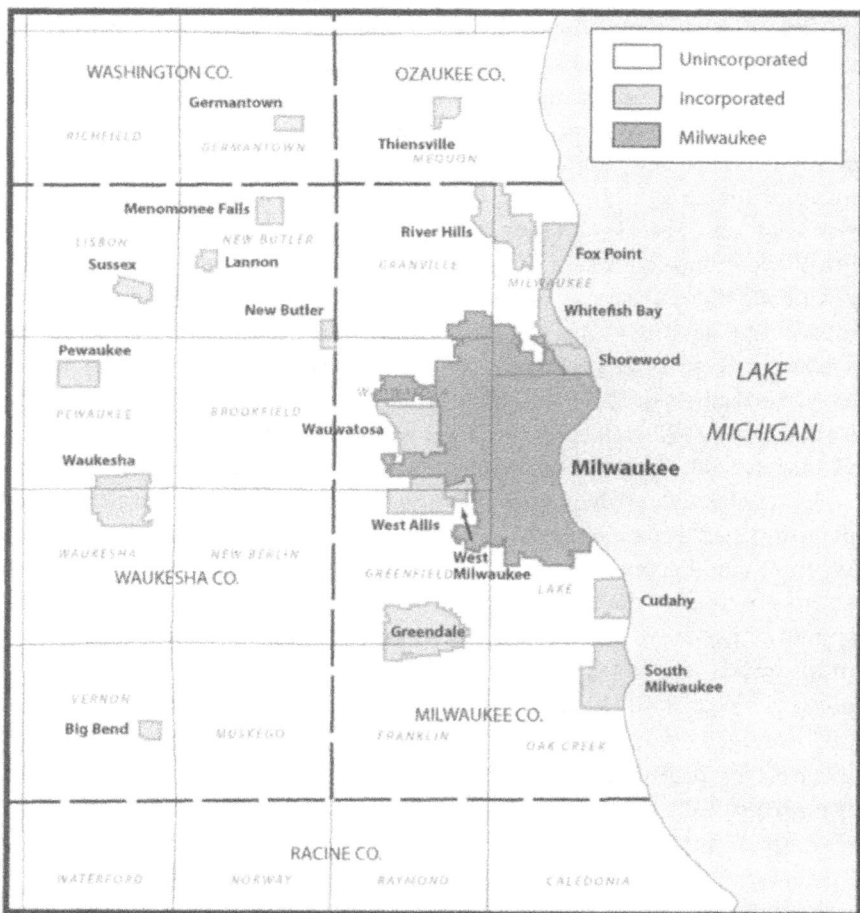

Municipalities of the Milwaukee Region, 1940. © Mapcraft,

4 Diverging Visions

"The ins and outs of the Milwaukee boundary line are like the maze of trenches in a war zone. In one spot the city won a victory and sent out a big 'salient' into 'enemy' territory. At another point the growing city bumped into a Maginot Line or Siegfried Wall. The growth of the city has literally been a 'war.' Instead of guns and bullets, the war in democratic America has been fought with petitions, lawsuits, injunctions, public meetings, referenda, and a whole bag of tricks by smart lawyers."

—*Milwaukee Journal,* February 4, 1940

This hyperbolic description of Milwaukee's border conflicts is perhaps more interesting because the city had disbanded its Department of Annexation eight years before and there had not been any major "battles" over growth in quite some time. Nevertheless, the *Journal* article reflected a sentiment that the region's future growth patterns were anything but resolved. "When the time comes, Milwaukee will be ready to expand again," it promised.[1] Indeed, the Depression and World War II, while obviously important events in the city's history, merely served to delay the region's own local "war" over political control of its growth.

It has become common to portray the post-1945 era in American history as a unique time period—separate and distinctive from the past—that brought sweeping changes to the United States.[2] This type of periodization extends to urban history, where the postwar era ushers in increased federal attention to the plight of American cities, insufficient public housing policy, racial strife, suburbanization, and ill-conceived urban renewal in rapid succession. Less apparent in this story are the alternatives to the policies that failed. Milwaukee's postwar experience differs noticeably from those of many of its urban counterparts because its policy makers clung to older strategies to plan and reshape the city—namely annexation and community planning—that had survived the interwar period. While social progressive planning ideas continued into the postwar era, they now stood alongside—and not in concert with—two sets of organized voices. The first consisted of private sector leaders and civic elites who called attention to downtown's advanced age, and the second consisted of suburbanites who for a multitude of reasons resisted annexation and metropolitan planning. During and immediately after World War II, these groups wrestled with issues such as housing, redevelopment, industrial growth, and metropolitan government. Events in Milwaukee in the late 1940s demonstrate that urban history after World War II does not break nearly so cleanly with the past. Many of the city's problems in 1945 differed little from those in the previous three decades. Public housing had first taken shape with the Hoan administration's support of the Garden Homes cooperative and reemerged on Milwaukee's political agenda during the Depression. During the 1940s, Milwaukeeans continued to debate its utility, scale, and location. Suburbanization continued to directly threaten metropolitan planning and government in the 1940s as it had during the 1920s. Milwaukee had even undergone a form of "urban renewal," although the specific term was not used, in planners' attempts to rezone the inner city for commercial and light industrial use. Officials had eliminated thousands of blighted structures—mostly homes—from Milwaukee's built environment during the Depression. City policy makers viewed demolition as a much-needed type of "slum clearance," albeit one that needed to be augmented by quality low-income housing.

In Milwaukee, public policy theory and social progressive planning ideas bridged the world wars, and the motivations that inspired practitioners of municipal socialism survived Daniel Hoan's political demise in 1940. Charles Whitnall's belief in planned decentralization had embedded itself in the metropolitan fabric with the development of Milwaukee County's parkway system. With Whitnall's support, a unique form of city planning that paid homage to a variety of innovative land use principles had emerged in Milwaukee. Other actors, both within and outside of Milwaukee's planning community, had continued these policies in the 1930s. Whitnall remained on Milwaukee's Board of Public Land Commissioners

(BPLC) through 1945 and stayed on the Milwaukee County Parks Commission until 1948. Although age limited his activity, Whitnall continued to advocate for planned decentralization, telling a local newspaper in 1940 that Milwaukee's workingmen could never thrive in the "debilitating" and congested environment of the inner city. He also remained a champion of cooperative housing projects, although his ideas increasingly fell on deaf ears during World War II. Whitnall never stopped envisioning Milwaukee as a city that would diffuse its residents further into the countryside.[3]

Whitnall's dreams for a decentralized metropolis had always been incompatible with the congested landscape of large cities on the East Coast. Instead, the rapidly growing city of Los Angeles served as a more applicable paradigm for Milwaukee. The familial connections between Charles and his son Gordon Whitnall cemented the relationship between Milwaukee and Los Angeles. Father and son remained kindred spirits in the advocacy of planned decentralization on a regional basis. Both Whitnalls increasingly embraced the automobile as key to their regions' metropolitan futures.[4] Gordon Whitnall was one of the chief architects of the Arroyo Seco Freeway, which connected Los Angeles to the city of Pasadena, one of the nation's first limited access freeways. Charles made many trips west to visit Gordon, even lecturing on city planning for a week at the University of Southern California in 1934.[5] He often returned to the Midwest and called for Milwaukee to copy Los Angeles in embracing horizontal expansion. The Whitnalls' professional relationship preceded a veritable exodus of many of Milwaukee's chief city planners from the 1920s to the booming western city. Charles Bennett had served as the BPLC's city planning engineer from 1926 through the decade of the 1930s. His "model village" plan had indirectly helped Milwaukee house one of the three New Deal greenbelt towns, but no private developer ever replicated Bennett's idea. In 1941, Bennett moved to Los Angeles and assumed the role of chief city planner there.[6] To Bennett, the two cities were united by ideas, but separated by results. The innate caution of Milwaukeeans had worn on him. At his farewell dinner, Bennett expressed his frustration with the slow pace of change in Milwaukee, hoping that "someday Milwaukee would come out of its shell and do things."[7] William Schuchardt, a kindred spirit to Whitnall in many planning matters and architect of the Garden Homes, eventually joined Bennett in Los Angeles in the 1940s. After attending a conference on city planning in Los Angeles in 1950, a BPLC planner reported to city officials that his visit to the West Coast was made more enjoyable since he could visit with six former Milwaukee BPLC officials who now worked in Los Angeles.[8]

While an older generation of Milwaukee's city planners moved west, other local officials who had key roles in city planning in the 1940s and 1950s remained committed to Whitnall's planning principles. Chief among these new planners was Elmer Krieger, a native Milwaukeean, who served as staff member of the BPLC in the 1920s and 1930s, and then temporarily assumed Bennett's position when the latter moved to Los Angeles. Krieger had grown interested in planning as a boy growing up in the city, but learned of the stark differences in rural and urban landscapes. His family spent summers at a country lake—"two months of barefooted freedom" as Krieger once recalled—and the trip back to the city depressed the young boy, who peered at the heavily industrialized Menomonee Valley through his train window and wondered how people could allow their environment to be built in such a stultifying way.[9] The unwanted construction of a bakery next to a beautiful home in Krieger's neighborhood further infuriated the youngster at his built environment. These childhood remembrances of urban problems drove Krieger into planning, where he earned degrees in the young academic discipline from the University of Wisconsin. During that time he worked for the BPLC, first as a playground designer and later as a junior planner. In the 1930s Krieger became impressed by the European "land reserve" concept—direct acquisitions of outlying land by cities themselves—that Greendale planners Jacob Crane and John Lansill had written of. Another major influence on Krieger, "the fountainhead of most of our ideas," as he once admitted, was Whitnall, whose local reputation blossomed just when Krieger first worked at the BPLC.[10]

While Milwaukee's community of city planners remained somewhat ideologically consistent through the 1940s, no public consensus existed as to the question of housing, which remained one of the city's most pressing concerns throughout the decade. The Depression had dramatically undercut Milwaukee builders' ability to construct new housing, and only one public housing project, Parklawn, had picked up the slack within the confines of the city. Hoan had continually failed to establish a municipal housing authority whose charge would have been the redevelopment of blighted inner city neighborhoods and the construction of new housing projects. In 1938, an administrator of the United States Housing Authority questioned why Milwaukee was the only large city east of the Mississippi River without a housing authority. Despite the national attention, common council members—wary of public housing—steadfastly opposed creating a housing authority during Hoan's last years in office, making the issue one of Hoan's biggest political defeats. However, Mayor Hoan's departure from city hall in 1940 did not remove public housing from the municipal agenda.[11]

After World War II began and industrial employment perked back up, perceptions of public housing altered. The housing shortage deepened as the city's population grew more rapidly. Because the wartime shortage affected a greater number of middle- and working-class families, the stigma of "public housing" temporarily subsided as it became associated with housing workers in defense industries as a way of contributing to the war effort. Eric Fure-Slocum has demonstrated that, both during and after the war, public housing was the most politically viable when it was successfully connected to good citizenship. This meant that many civic leaders were far more likely to support housing for war workers or, after the war, public housing for war veterans. Indeed, after World War II, the city of Milwaukee built far more housing units for war veterans than it would for low-income families. In the short term, wartime urgencies won out. Local housing and labor organizations formed the Joint Action Committee for Better Housing (JACBH) in 1943, first to push for the creation of a housing authority, and also to urge the Common Council to renew the dormant Sixth Ward public housing project. The mayors of Milwaukee in the early 1940s, far more conservative than Hoan about public housing, first seemed unwilling to support the project. Carl Zeidler, who defeated Hoan in 1940, said virtually nothing about pubic housing, and as long as the city remained without a housing authority, there was little he could do. Then, in 1942 Zeidler suddenly decided to join the war effort, enlisting in the Navy. Zeidler's ship was lost at sea, his body never recovered. To fill out his term, Common Council president John Bohn assumed mayoral duties. Bohn, a conservative Democrat by party and originally a realtor by trade, at first was equally disinterested in public housing. However, with the war emergency continuing to constrict housing, and facing the possibility that the city would fail to qualify for federal funds for housing war veterans, Bohn eventually lent his support to create a housing authority. In 1944, the Common Council finally gave its support to the creation of a housing authority. The new body's creation encouraged housing activists in the city, and, again led by the JACBH, they pushed local government to build its next public housing project in the Sixth Ward. Plans for Hillside Terrace, as the project came to be known, initially called for the project to house African American war workers, but delays eventually caused the project to become open to any low-income civilian. At only 232 units and on a site of only eight and a half acres, Hillside Terrace contained less than half the housing units as Parklawn with double the population density. The costs of acquiring additional property and clearing the land had minimized the size of the project. Its location, in the heart of the African American Sixth Ward, did not pose any challenge to the city's existing racial geography. Hillside Terrace was the only low-income project built in Milwaukee by a non-Socialist mayor before 1960. Not incidentally, Hillside was the only low-income project built in the inner core of the city before 1960 as well. Thus the existence of a housing authority and the construction of a project did not exemplify local consensus as to the importance of decent housing for all. The type, location, and volume of housing would continue to divide the region well past the war.[12]

World War II had conflicting effects on American cities. On one hand, it virtually wiped away unemployment and industrial decline. Factories that lay idle or greatly reduced their production during the Depression years became reinvigorated with defense contracts. As employment increased, American cities regained their economic vitality. Milwaukee's industries increased hiring across the board and began to expand production once again. From 1940 to 1943, industrial employment in Milwaukee County shot up from 110,000 to over 200,000 workers.[13] However, the near-full employment of the war years masked a more deeply rooted economic problem that most American cities faced in the wake of the Depression. With construction limited in the 1930s, the physical condition of central business districts in most American cities had grown increasingly drab. Private real estate interests had grown so concerned over downtowns that their largest lobbying body, the National Association of Real Estate Boards (NAREB) created the Urban Land Institute (ULI) to address these concerns. Across the country, private land interests in cities created affiliate organizations. With building activity in the United States remaining slow during the war, civic officials had perhaps more time to take stock and issue new studies of the economic health of cities and their downtowns. Such examinations revealed that across America, the central business district was in serious need of attention.

In 1940, for example, the Urban Land Institute sponsored studies of thirteen different downtowns across America.[14] Milwaukee's downtown was the subject of one of the studies. Business leaders, eager for help, had recently formed the Downtown Association, made up of prominent inner city property owners and businesses, to draw attention to the urban core. The Milwaukee Downtown Association joined with the Milwaukee Real Estate Board in supporting the ULI study, which was completed in 1941, under the banner "Proposals for Downtown Milwaukee." It confirmed business leaders' fears that downtown Milwaukee was in trouble. New construction in the central business district had plummeted during the 1930s; the city had only issued 78 building permits over the whole decade. Even worse, land values had showed a precipitous decline as well, dropping from over $279 million in 1930 to just over $192 million by 1939.[15]

The report blamed numerous developments for downtown's decline. City planners bore some of this responsibility. Milwaukee's "ineffective zoning" (established in 1920) had made all of downtown a "commercial and light manufacturing" district, which belied the fact that over 13,000 people lived within the confines of the central business district.[16] Planners' assumption that land uses downtown would gradually change had proven inaccurate, although it is highly unlikely that Whitnall—who rarely had positive remarks for downtowns—would have cared deeply either way. But the result of downtown zoning was clear; no new residential structures had been built downtown for at least a decade. Equally troubling in the report was its assertion that "the central business district is virtually surrounded by blight," strongly hinting that only massive reinvestment in the central city could turn this trend around.[17]

The question of suburban growth was more perplexing to the authors of the report. A survey of local business and civic leaders yielded mostly agreement that annexation of "suburban areas that are dependent upon the city for their major income" was a desirable goal. However, the city-suburban conflict ran so deep that one anonymous suburban Whitefish Bay individual who favored annexation warned, "I have given an answer that would automatically excommunicate me from the village of Whitefish Bay."[18] The Downtown Association also collectively opposed annexation, believing it had taken away attention from the needs of the central business district. Thus while acknowledging that suburbanization was a problem, business leaders viewed downtown in its own context and refused to enter into the city-suburban stalemate.

The Urban Land Institute report revealed vast differences in how public and private interests viewed urban growth. For over two decades, Socialist municipal leaders had focused attention on horizontal expansion through annexation, improved housing conditions, and more democratic reforms such as municipal ownership of public utilities. Business leaders in the private market supported some of these initiatives individually. Their innate devotion to market trends, however, made it almost impossible to swallow more socialistic ideas like cooperative housing or Whitnall's frequent attacks on the "unearned increment" of inflated urban land values. To the Downtown Association the city's main problem was simpler: that very "increment" was lacking, and as long as land valuation in the downtown area continued to stagnate or decline, redevelopment was necessary. This difference was primarily ideological. Large urban real estate interests, industrial

CHART 4-1	Assessed Valuations, Milwaukee Central Business District, 1930–1939

Year	Assessed Values	% of 1930
1930	$279,140,040	100
1931	$265,694,125	95
1932	$243,046,530	87
1933	$217,926,640	78
1934	$221,875,850	79
1935	$217,520,630	78
1936	$213,797,410	77
1937	$213,284,410	76
1938	$205,532,590	74
1939	$192,427,760	69

Source: "Proposals for Downtown Milwaukee," The Urban Land Institute, 1941, MPL, p. 33.

leaders, and retail concerns reacted primarily to the concerns of the market. They acted as part of what historian Sam Bass Warner identified as the "private city," which defined urban places' primary raison d'être as enablers of the individual search for wealth. Thus individuals of the "private city" structured their concerns with urban problems around the logic of the marketplace.[19] Municipal Socialists, however, never bought into this conception of cities. Daniel Hoan, Charles Whitnall, and, later, Frank Zeidler, who served as mayor from 1948 to 1960, each embraced the idea of a polity in which government interference in the local economy was palatable, whether it was in the form of cooperative or public housing, public ownership of transportation and utilities, or even an eventual shift away from "profit" in land values. Zeidler probably summed up the Socialists' ideological differences with the concept of the private city best in his memoirs when he wrote that most people viewed cities as a place to "make money more easily than somewhere else," which meant business leaders were bound to exercise tremendous influence on mayors. In contrast to this model, Zeidler saw a different urban model in which "the purpose of a city is solely to advance human progress. The primary purpose of a city should be to help as many of its inhabitants as possible . . . even to the point of being substantially taxed."[20] Though never as eloquent as Zeidler, Hoan often governed from this perspective.

Interestingly, these two vastly different models for urban governance had rarely clashed during Hoan's tenure in the 1920s and 1930s. While many businesses certainly resented the presence of municipal socialism in their city and actively campaigned against Hoan, no major political struggles pitted these two different ideologies against each other. Hoan governed through the Red Scare of the early 1920s politically unscathed. Later, Mayor Zeidler would win his largest reelection margin in 1952, in the midst of McCarthyism. There are several reasons for this lack of conflict. First, as historians Eric Fure-Slocum, Richard Pifer, and others have already pointed out, the city's most polarizing political battles occurred outside the realm of traditional city hall politics.[21] Milwaukee's large and often militant working class had indeed wrestled with industrial capitalism for decades and helped create the political culture that elected men like Hoan in the first place. Second, many local entrepreneurs realized that Socialist plans—despite their egalitarian and democratic intentions—promised to benefit private interests. Thus, Charles Whitnall's countywide system of parkways was quite popular throughout Milwaukee's real estate community. Third, urban business leaders and real estate interests did not dismiss government interference in the marketplace out of turn, if it served to benefit them. The more downtown land values continued their decline, the greater interest grew in federally sponsored slum clearance and redevelopment. Both the Downtown Association and the Milwaukee Real Estate Board readily welcomed increased federal presence in the urban economy, but only in a way that enabled the market and did not actively compete with it. As the secretary of the board explained to a group of African American residents of the Sixth Ward in 1945, it was "the American way" for private enterprise to rebuild cities.[22] Accordingly, slum clearance and redevelopment held more promise than low-income public housing projects.

Equally important and often lost in the apparent mutual exclusivity of free enterprise and socialism, however, is the fact that business leaders and municipal Socialists did not openly and vocally clash because the issue of urban growth often transcended political ideologies. Place (and eventually class), not politics, began to shape growth battles. Virtually every public official in Milwaukee, regardless of political stripe, firmly supported Hoan's annexation program in the 1920s and consolidation in the 1930s. In the late 1940s and 1950s, when the Zeidler administration resumed annexation and planned satellite communities with an even greater vigor, the political consensus within city hall on Milwaukee's physical expansion largely remained. As Milwaukee grew in size and city officials stepped up their calls for government unification, the issue of urban growth took on spatial dimensions. Residents of unincorporated towns were divided over annexation. Incorporated municipalities almost always opposed metropolitan consolidation, whether they were middle-class commuter suburbs like Wauwatosa or blue-collar industrial cities like West Allis.

The spatial dimensions of urban growth faded into the background during World War II, as the region's attention, like most of the nation's, remained firmly committed to the war. But they never entirely departed from the scene either. Peripheral growth continued during the 1940s, albeit at a pace still slower than in the booming 1920s. The Depression had taken Milwaukee's Annexation Department as a fiscal casualty, and the immediate result was that the city's population grew at dramatically reduced rates during the Depression. Neighboring towns continued to attract families who moved out of the city. During World War II, local officials made several studies of the region's continued trend of decentralization.[23] The BPLC made a study of population changes within Milwaukee by census tract that revealed inner city neighborhoods had been consistently declining in population from 1920 through 1940 and beyond. Another study released in 1945 revealed that during World War II, seven wards in the city drew precisely *zero* dollars' worth of building activity.[24]

These trends complicated reformers' perceptions of the urban core since it was widely recognized by social progressives that close-in neighborhoods like the Sixth Ward were overcrowded, despite the district's population losses. However, it did reinforce city leaders' understanding that people of means were leaving the inner city for the incorporated villages and cities, and unincorporated towns, on the urban fringe.

To answer why families left the city, the Milwaukee County Regional Planning Department conducted a comprehensive and revealing study of the county's unincorporated towns during World War II, and released it in 1946. Richard Dewey, the primary author of the report, set out to examine why people had moved "from the built-up urban areas to the fringe" to help future planners better discern "what constitutes a good community layout." To that end, county officials distributed over 12,000 questionnaires to residents throughout the unincorporated towns of Milwaukee County. After the construction lull of the Depression, such towns were beginning to attract city residents again. Responses to the questionnaire numbered over 4,000, providing regional officials with the clearest picture yet of the nature of residential decentralization.

The study revealed several important patterns to Milwaukee's peripheral expansion. First of all, the peopling of upper-class suburban areas represented a gradual shift, not a Horatio Alger "leapfrog" from the urban core to the choicest communities on the periphery. For instance, the North Shore village of Fox Point, a bedroom suburb, received its principal sources of migration from other suburbs, namely the white-collar communities of Wauwatosa and Shorewood. River Hills, rapidly becoming the most elite suburb in the region, drew its migrants from the wealthiest sections of Milwaukee's East Side and the upper-class North Shore suburbs of Shorewood, Whitefish Bay, and Fox Point. Leaving behind a wealthy community for an even more elite place was not usually a tale of dramatic upward mobility, but instead reflected class-based residential patterns.[25]

Even more important to the authors of the survey were the motivations of the thousands of new residents in the modest unincorporated towns outside of Milwaukee. The most common answers to the question of why one moved out of the city was that the new communities were "best for children," followed by "less congestion," "cleaner," and "larger lot." Only 11 percent of the thousands of respondents stated that "lower taxes" were the key reason for leaving the city, giving the "pull" of the rural fringe a decided edge over the "push" of abandoning the city. When people were asked about their attitude toward their current lot sizes, over half of all residents on lots with widths of forty feet believed their lots were too small. Where lot sizes were larger, residents' attitudes toward them grew more positive. The impulse to live in less congested spaces, long suspected by planners such as Whitnall, seemed borne out.[26]

Balancing desires to attain more space was the still powerful draw of community life, and Greendale seemed to personify its best qualities. The survey revealed that residents desired churches, parks, movie theaters, and schools as well as some form of adequate mass transit to be within walking distance. Interestingly, suburbia seemed to embody communitarian principles more than the large center city. Over 80 percent of the survey's respondents stated they found "more of a community spirit in their new neighborhood as opposed to their old ones." Clarence Stein captured this enthusiasm in a glowing article in *The American City* written to celebrate the tenth anniversary of Greendale. "Strangers who read my description in praise of Greendale may think I am writing about Utopia," Stein summed up, "But those who live there know that Greendale is not a phantom, but a fact. It is a living, growing reality."[27] Just as Elbert Peets and Jacob Crane had intended, residents of Greendale felt the community idyll more strongly than those in any other Milwaukee suburb. In the county survey, over

97 percent of Greendale's respondents reported that a "more neighborly spirit" existed here than in the city. Residents of Greendale gave so many unsolicited positive comments that Dewey, the report's primary author, was moved to characterize the village as nearer to "the ideal community for the average American" as any he had ever seen.[28]

The language used in Dewey's report in designating place also reveals how local planners perceived the metropolitan region's communities. Milwaukee, clearly, was the "city" and its neighborhoods constituted "urban" places. Incorporated villages and cities, such as Whitefish Bay and West Allis, were—just as obviously—called "suburbs." The subjects of the study who had moved to Milwaukee County's unincorporated towns, however, did not fit either designation of place. Dewey characterized the unincorporated towns as "rural" areas. Eugene Howard, who was the director of the Milwaukee County Regional Planning Department and wrote the introduction to the study, noted that Milwaukee County's towns were "largely in a state of flux," gradually urbanizing as the residents spilled beyond Milwaukee's boundaries.[29] The "rural" designation given to the towns reveals a political interpretation of the meaning of the word "suburb." At least according to county officials, the only true "suburbs" were incorporated entities, which in Wisconsin meant villages or cities. Unincorporated towns thus occupied a curious position, not suburban but no longer rural, independently governed but vulnerable to annexation. This sharpened the differences in metropolitan political status. Communities did not become "suburbs" until they incorporated, which, not inconsequently, ended the city's chances of annexation. A city-suburban-rural distinction of this type was not usual, and residents of Milwaukee County's unincorporated towns, especially those adjacent to the city such as Lake and Granville, may well have rejected the "rural" status the report foisted upon them. However, it does reveal suburbanization's political dimension. The mere act of moving away from the urban core was not in and of itself "suburbanization," but instead "residential decentralization," a demographic pattern that had yet to take a political shape.

Dewey's report also revealed what many city officials in Milwaukee had believed for some time: that many people who moved out of Milwaukee were not seeking escape from high city taxes, but instead simply sought better housing in particular and a better quality of life in general. Eugene Howard, Director of the Milwaukee County Regional Planning Department, agreed with Dewey's conclusions in a presentation to a postwar planning group in 1947, noting, "In the early 1920s, so-called forty-foot lots were accepted; in the 1930s, fifty-foot lots were considered a minimum standard."[30] Howard promised not to approve any plats less than 7,200 square feet in the unincorporated lands of Milwaukee County. "The crowding of buildings in the older sections of our communities is one of the greatest causes of blight," Howard noted.[31] Dewey's report had demonstrated that public appetites dictated larger lots as well. The region's local media took notice. "It's Elbow Room, not High Taxes, that Lures City Folk to Rural Lots" chimed a *Milwaukee Journal* headline upon the Dewey report's release in 1946.[32] The report did not make specific planning recommendations to county officials but its sympathy toward large-scale community planning was obvious, hinting at future policies. Just two years later, city officials would begin one of the most ambitious community development programs in the United States.

While county officials were examining residential decentralization, city planners were now under fire for failing to coordinate postwar master planning in a timely manner. For all of the innovations planners in Milwaukee had wrought, they had never completed a comprehensive plan for the city. In the Progressive Era, comprehensive plans such as Daniel Burnham's famed Chicago Plan were often associated with conventional City Beautiful efforts to attain civic greatness. Most of the major planning initiatives undertaken in Milwaukee during the 1910s, 1920s, and 1930s, such as the Garden Homes, the county parkways, zoning, and even annexation, did not involve conformity to a specific master plan. In the wake of the Depression, private entities began actively advocating for the BPLC to create such a plan to coordinate postwar economic growth. During the war, local business leaders created another organization in direct response to downtown's perceived decline. In 1944, Richard Herzfeld, the president of the Boston Store, one of the city's largest downtown department stores, retained a research firm to conduct population projections to gauge future demographics of the city. Herzfeld was shocked to discover that the firm predicted that Milwaukee's population would be in outright decline by 1960. Alarmed by this report, which echoed similarly ominous statistics revealed by the Downtown Association and the BPLC, Herzfeld contacted Irwin Maier, the president of the *Milwaukee Journal,* about the possibility of forming an association of business executives to revitalize the city.[33] At a luncheon in 1945, they formed the 1948 Corporation, ostensibly a "non-partisan, non-political, non-sectional" group who sought civic improvements that were to be underway by the year of the state of Wisconsin's hundredth anniversary celebration in 1948. The corporation held its first meeting on November 30, 1945, quickly adopting a platform that promoted civic improvements. The corporation called for the BPLC to draw up a master plan of the city, for the city or county to build a new stadium and a new museum, and for a new network of limited access freeways to connect downtown to key outlying areas such as Mitchell Field, the city's airport.[34]

Some elements of the plan, such as the museum, were to fill out Alfred Clas's Civic Center, which remained half-fulfilled in the 1940s, much to the embarrassment of city boosters. To pay for the civic improvements, the 1948 Corporation called for the city to reverse over twenty years of fiscal policy and go back into debt by issuing millions of dollars in bonds. While debt elimination was initially a pet Socialist project conceived under the Hoan administration, his Nonpartisan opponents in the Common Council grew to embrace it as well. Mayor John Bohn, who served from 1942 to 1948, had been a longtime Common Council representative and had clashed repeatedly with Hoan during the 1920s and 1930s. As mayor, Bohn came to agree about the importance of staying out of debt, in 1946 publicly announcing his refusal to go into debt without a public referendum.[35] In his annual message to the Common Council that year, Bohn warned, "Our revenues are not sufficient to meet this extreme burden without increasing the load on the owners of property."[36] Other business and civic groups disagreed. Joining the 1948 Corporation in pushing for the city to go back into debt was the Downtown Association, whose members clearly stood to gain from enhancements to the civic center. The civic groups managed to bring the debt issue to a public referendum in 1947, asking city residents if Milwaukee should issue bonds to support the public improvements laid out by the 1948 Corporation.[37]

The 1948 Corporation also joined the growing chorus of civic groups who believed that Milwaukee needed a "master plan" to guide its development. Technical responsibility for such a plan lay with the BPLC; in 1941, the Wisconsin state legislature had broadened the functions of municipal planning bodies, entrusting each with the task of creating master plans. In the wake of the state mandate, civic groups impatiently waited for the city to produce a new plan. Alvin Bromm had replaced Charles Bennett in 1941 as the BPLC's highest-ranking paid staff member, and in the early 1940s, Bromm struggled to balance the heightened demands placed on his staff. To address these concerns, in 1943 the Common Council voted to reorganize the BPLC, adding eleven new staff members, in part to help rush the master plan to completion. Whitnall, by now also in favor of a master plan, resigned his position on the BPLC that year, partly due to age, but also because he believed that planners in Milwaukee were still preoccupied with the tedium of zoning amendments, easements, and other "mole work" that interfered with broader planning initiatives.[38] Much to the chagrin of civic boosters, in 1944 Bromm announced that the master plan was still months away from completion. Pressure on Bromm intensified; the war seemed to be coming to a close, and the city was apparently unprepared to address its postwar needs. The Milwaukee Real Estate Board joined the clamor for a master plan in 1944, warning the *Milwaukee Journal* that the downtown study the Urban Land Institute had made "was not meant to gather dust."[39]

Finally, in 1946, the BPLC again reorganized itself. Bromm remained the commission's planning director, but his second in command, Krieger, was now solely in charge of finishing the master plan. Krieger managed to complete the plan in January of 1947, releasing it to the media just a few months before Milwaukee residents voted for the city to go back into debt to fund public improvements. Krieger's fifty-page "Master Plan for the City of Milwaukee" reflected both the new civic groups' push to renew downtown and older Whitnall/Hoan visions of planned decentralization and peripheral expansion. It recommended, for example, several additional public buildings to the Civic Center, including a new museum and a remodeled public library, and the construction of a new baseball stadium on Milwaukee's west side, all ideas first called for by the 1948 Corporation. The master plan also called for a new zoning ordinance that added more use districts, something that the Downtown Association had first called attention to in 1941. Yet Krieger, in many ways a Whitnall disciple, also noted that in the 1920s Milwaukee was "overly congested" and needed room for expansion. With physical growth stalled by the Depression, postwar Milwaukee now faced "a situation similar to the one in 1920."[40] He thus recommended, once again, annexation as a temporary substitute until the "ideal" of metropolitan government was achieved. In Krieger's conclusion, he repeated his recommendation of annexation, to be continued "until or unless the duplicating taxing units within Milwaukee County are consolidated."[41]

Krieger's master plan was generally well received in the local press. A representative of the Downtown Association responded favorably to the recommendation for rezoning. City Club secretary Leo Tiefenhalter rejoiced that the plan had finally arrived. The Milwaukee Association of Commerce called the plan "very interesting."[42] As a meaningful and influential guide to future city growth, however, Krieger's plan barely registers. First, Krieger purposely never released it to the Common Council for official adoption, fearing that if he did, the plan would be locked in place and thus almost impossible to adjust to future changes in the city. Flexibility meant the plan must stay politically unencumbered, but it also meant that future officials were never legally or even politically obligated to implement it. Secondly, the master plan arrived a year before another major political shift within the city: Frank Zeidler's mayoral election. Zeidler admired Krieger's work, and in fact elevated Krieger to executive secretary of the BPLC, entrusting him with several key community projects. But many of these new schemes, such as satellite cities, were not present in Krieger's master plan. Finally, Krieger had limited his plan to public projects, and included almost no commentary on general urban form. He made no attempt to explicate a grand downtown vision, nor did he specifically call for major redevelopment projects that involved public takeover of privately owned land. The master plan was more a politically expedient response to civic pressure than it was a grand statement for major urban change; Krieger actually implied this in his initial release of the plan to BPLC members, noting that the master plan's delay "has been a serious handicap in the relations of the Commission and staff with the public."[43] The most meaningful area of recommended state intervention was in the echoing of annexation and metropolitan government, both of which Mayor Zeidler passionately embraced in the ensuing decade.

In the short term, Krieger's master plan, released two months before the debt referendum and generally favorable to debt proponents, may have helped nudge city residents' votes in favor of bonded indebtedness. The local press uncritically supported a "yes" vote. A now locally famous story in a 1947 issue of the *Milwaukee Journal* referred to Milwaukee as "Dear Lady Thrift," a shabby and old city whose leaders routinely lacked the vision to see through civic projects that might enhance its stature. Frugality in city hall had begotten public indifference toward metropolitan mediocrity, and the most obvious and ominous result was "possibly the least pretentious business district in all of urban America." Blitzed by media boosters, and by publicity from the 1948 Corporation, city residents voted in favor of the improvements in April of 1947 by a 57 percent to 43 percent margin.[44]

Opposing the 1948 Corporation's push to have Milwaukee go back into debt were some working-class organizations and the South Division Civic Association, whose members lived primarily in the working-class Polish American South Side. Also joining these groups, who called themselves the "Keep Milwaukee Debt Free Committee," was what was left of Milwaukee's Socialist Party, which had dwindled in numbers throughout the late 1930s. By 1947, the most prominent Socialist in Milwaukee was Frank Zeidler, a member of the Milwaukee School Board. Frank's older brother was Carl Zeidler, who had become a martyred hero in the city after he lost his life serving in World War II while mayor, a familial advantage that Frank leveraged to great use in the late 1940s. Zeidler gained civic attention with his eloquent defense of the city's "pay-as-you-go" policy, and his willingness to call attention to the suburban dimensions of the debate. The 1948 Corporation members, it was later discovered, lived mostly outside the central city, a fact that Zeidler and his cohorts made a point of mentioning. Even in the wake of the referendum's defeat, Zeidler announced he was running for mayor in the 1948 election. Bohn, now eighty years old, had decided to retire rather than run again, and Zeidler jostled with no less than fifteen candidates in Milwaukee's nonpartisan open primary, finally defeating Henry Reuss in the runoff election in April of 1948.

In electing Frank Zeidler, city residents had turned to a man whose planning tendencies and growth policies openly replicated those of his Socialist predecessors. Raised on Milwaukee's West Side, Zeidler first became attracted to socialism through reading heavily on the subject at local libraries as an adolescent. In 1932, the twenty-two-year-old Zeidler joined the Socialist Party and became engrossed in the writings of Norman Thomas and Henry Laidler. An engineer by education, Zeidler briefly worked for the Resettlement Administration as a surveyor at Greendale. The experience left an indelible impression on Zeidler; planned greenbelt communities, he believed, were the best way to foster decentralization. Zeidler had served as local Socialist Party secretary from 1937 to 1941 and also became an avowed admirer of Daniel Hoan.[45] After a quixotic run for governor of Wisconsin in 1942 failed, Zeidler served on the Milwaukee School Board until his election as mayor. Less fiery and more cerebral than Hoan, Zeidler brought a highly developed concept of urbanism—both political and technical—to the office of mayor upon his election in 1948. Much like Whitnall, Zeidler believed that congestion debilitated the poorest residents of cities, and he often used the same combination of hyperbole and biologically informed urbanism as Whitnall did in his speeches and writings. In 1951, speaking before the National Association of Housing Officials, Zeidler framed decentralization in terms remarkably similar to his predecessors': "Man was not meant to pass his days in that most ugly of our modern contrivances—the modern city. The blush of dawn, the glory of the sunset, the rustle of golden autumn leaves, the cleanness of the fresh snow, are lost to our modern children. . . . Instead they know the policeman's whistle, the fireman's siren, the grinding noise of traffic, the false world of cheap entertainment."[46] Zeidler also shared Whitnall's conviction that land use controls could stem overcrowding, if managed properly. As mayor, Zeidler even opposed the rezoning of Prospect Avenue to construct high-rise apartments along Milwaukee's north shore because such buildings resulted in high densities, again channeling Whitnall in explaining to a local architect: "I cannot concur in the idea that it is good architecture to crowd people on ever more smaller areas of land."[47] By the end of his three terms as mayor, Zeidler believed

Frank Zeidler—The last
Socialist mayor of the
twentieth century, Zeidler
served in that capacity
from Milwaukee from 1948
through 1960. Courtesy
of the Historic Photo
Collection / Milwaukee
Public Library

that one of urban redevelopment's most deleterious features in American cities was the predominance of upper-income "residential skyscrapers" as well as high-rise low-income public housing.[48]

Zeidler's notorious clashes with Milwaukee's suburbs, which grew more bitter with each passing year, belied his understanding and even acceptance of residential decentralization. Precisely because he opposed congestion in principle, Zeidler understood the allure of suburbia to an increasing number of Americans in the postwar era. Fringe communities, dotted with detached single-family homes on wider lots, were to Zeidler a logical extension of the human desire to attain more "elbow room." "The hunger of most people to own their own home is easily demonstrated anywhere in the world," Zeidler observed after he stepped down as mayor.[49] Homeownership in less congested spaces, so important to Americans, was not antithetical to Zeidler's unique brand of socialism.

Zeidler's distinctiveness as a planning-minded mayor, however, lay in his ardent belief that growth on the fringe should be carefully managed and planned by cities in *advance* of development to attain both maximum efficiency of land use and preservation of nature. Zeidler's previous work on Greendale made him committed to avoiding unplanned and haphazard growth; he also wrote glowingly of English Garden City communities Letchworth and Welwyn. A policy of decentralization would not yield urban sprawl if communities were planned with "compactness but not overcrowding."[50] Large-scale planned communities could achieve this metropolitan balance. Because this type of community building required so much land and yielded extremely high costs of infrastructure, it was often beyond the means of most real estate developers. However, cities were equipped with professional planners and public works engineers and, therefore, appeared to be naturally suited to engage in this type of community development. Krieger, the chief planner for the BPLC throughout Zeidler's twelve years in office, shared a similar mentality, preferring to channel growth to the urban fringes to create complete satellite communities, with a balance of residence and industry, and to maintain greenbelts to separate various land uses.

Zeidler also inherited the older social progressive conviction that planning and housing should be intertwined. Decent, well-planned housing was meant for all residents, rich or poor, white or black. For those that could not afford single-family homes, public housing—also to be constructed on the periphery of cities—was to provide the same modicum of comfort to lower-income groups. "Elbow room" was not, to Zeidler, a privilege of the financially fortunate but instead a fundamental right of all urban citizens. If the city were to rid itself of blight at the center, which was clearly a growing concern to civic elites, then an adequate balance of replacement housing on the fringe would have to complement slum clearance. Zeidler often sounded like any other postwar mayor in attacking "blight," calling for slum clearance and increased federal assistance, and even advocating the development of expressways. The difference in rhetoric was, as Eric Fure-Slocum recently wrote, "unlike the growth proponents who understood efficiency as an economic measure, Zeidler saw efficiency as an issue of governance and politics."[51]

Zeidler's mayoral campaign hinted that he intended to put these principles back into practice. Zeidler ran for mayor in 1948 with the support of the Municipal Enterprise Committee (MEC), a group of liberals who hoped to continue the policies of the Hoan administration. In December of 1947, the MEC released its campaign platform. The first major reform was a "unified program of city-wide planning" that called for the Milwaukee planning department to be "directly attached to the mayor's office." The second plank, which addressed housing, even more directly reflected the planning impulses of Whitnall and Hoan, as it called for 10,000 "low-rent dwelling units" to be built by the city by 1953, and held that new public housing belonged in Milwaukee's outskirts, "until congestion is relieved in inner areas." The MEC platform also included a plank titled "Planning for Political Development," which called for women to play a larger role in local government, and favored "consolidation of county-wide functions under county government," a hint that Zeidler, if elected, would pursue some form of metropolitan government.[52]

Housing was the most pressing issue for Milwaukee in the late 1940s, and Zeidler and the MEC were not the only civic leaders who linked it to Milwaukee's peripheral expansion. There were more pragmatic motivations to extend Milwaukee horizontally. The housing shortage remained chronic and the end of war made it seem ever more acute. Homebuilding had yet to recover from the Great Depression. Only $14 million worth of new construction was undertaken in 1940, $18 million less than a decade before. Even with the drop in construction, during the Depression the city's building inspection department was grossly understaffed. In 1939, only one-third of the required number of inspections was made. Milwaukee thus emerged from World War II with an aging housing stock in desperate need of augmentation.

During the 1940s, real estate developers had begun to purchase and subdivide vacant land near Milwaukee's borders with the expectations that the city would annex it. Well aware that the city could install water and sewage extensions at far lower rates than it could dig private wells or install septic tanks, local real estate interests once again became vocal proponents of annexation, often threatening to delay new housing starts altogether if their land was not made a part of Milwaukee.[53] The city's budget supervisor, George Saffran, noted that by the end of World War II, "the city was being criticized by practically everyone for holding up the development of the metropolitan area."[54] For example, in 1947, eight different builders promised to announce construction of over 1,100 new housing units upon annexation of their lands into the city and the infrastructure improvements that would follow. A year later, Tilton Industries, one of the city's largest builders, announced plans for eighty single-family ranch homes on land just beyond Milwaukee's borders at the northwest fringe. John Tilton, president of the company, said that the homes would not be built until the city annexed the land and connected the subdivision with the city's water and sewer system. During that same year, another developer suggested to Zeidler that the city institute a moratorium on all nonresidential building activities to concentrate construction solely on housing.[55] Citizens virtually deluged Zeidler and the city housing authority with requests for decent housing. Upon Zeidler's election in 1948, Werba informed him that there were virtually no vacant lots left in the city that were ready for development.[56]

The city's housing shortage and the subsequent pressure by the building industry was the primary reason the Milwaukee Common Council voted to reestablish the Department of Annexation and Abstracting in 1946. In a nod to continuity, Arthur Werba, who had served as annexation director during most of Milwaukee's expansion in the 1920s, was chosen to head up the reborn department. Werba's previous experience earned him a reputation for aggressiveness in seeing annexation through. Catherine Bauer, the nationally renowned housing advocate who shared many of the planning ideas that Zeidler later tried to implement, once wrote that Werba literally "eats, drinks, and sleeps annexation."[57] Starting in 1946, Werba resumed his task with a vigor that was to make him infamous throughout the Milwaukee region, especially in the unincorporated townships that bordered the city to the north, west, and south. Krieger, the BPLC's chief city planner, initially served as secretary for the annexation department, to better coordinate annexation with long-range planning. When officials estimated that Milwaukee needed anywhere from 10,000 to 30,000 new residential lots to accommodate demand, it appeared that private industry would account for the vast majority of new housing starts.[58]

But annexation's purpose was far different to many city officials in Zeidler's administration. Peripheral growth would do more than merely provide new space for real estate development. Annexation could be the primary means to attain the politically unified and spatially decentralized metropolis that had been dreamed of for forty years. In 1929, Werba had written of the "inevitability" of the consolidation of all governing units of Milwaukee County.[59] Krieger also believed that annexation had always been the primary tool to properly decentralize Milwaukee and was already an advocate of some form of metropolitan consolidation, as evidenced in his suggestions on the 1947 Master Plan. Zeidler periodically restated this same goal throughout his years in office: Milwaukee had essentially no choice but to "grow or die."[60] If urban "renewal" was to have any lasting value, large-scale annexations and political unification held the key to Milwaukee's future growth, and would allow for planned dispersal to become a city-led exercise.

Annexation was equally important to alleviate the city's lack of industrial land available for expansion. Milwaukee emerged from World War II with a vibrant industrial sector that had little room for expansion within the city. The war had reinvigorated local industry. In 1939, there was over five million square feet of vacant factory space in the city; by early 1946, there was practically none. Milwaukee had reached its actual industrial capacity. In 1948, only 15 percent of the total acreage of land zoned for industrial use was actually available for development. Much of this property was not located close enough to rail lines or major arterials, making it poorly situated and thus considered unattractive by businesses. The spatial crunch that threatened Milwaukee's manufacturing capacity also made it difficult to attract new industry from other regions. Statewide, industrial expansion seemed to be bypassing Milwaukee for smaller towns in Wisconsin, such as Hartford, Wausau, and Stoughton. New plants in these towns faced less competition and as a result could often pay lower wages. In Milwaukee, these conditions did not exist. The Milwaukee Association of Commerce (MAC) had recently embarked on a program to attract defense-related industries to the region. With little to no land available in the city under its present size, any new industries the MAC attracted would be located in the suburbs. Thus, in the immediate aftermath of World War II, stimulating industrial expansion was not as important as ensuring that it occur within Milwaukee's boundaries.[61]

Attracting and maintaining industry was also an important function of municipal financing. In 1947, the Wisconsin state legislature forbade local governments to impose income taxes on residents, ensuring property taxes would remain the most reliable revenue for the state's cities and villages. Upon his arrival in office in 1948, Zeidler appointed a group of civic leaders to examine ways to raise revenues in Milwaukee. The Commission on the Economic Study of Milwaukee's ensuing 120-page report, completed during the same year, concluded that while Milwaukee's industrial workers enjoyed relatively high wages, the city's lack of usable industrial space meant future expansion would occur outside city limits. Because industry yielded a disproportionate amount of property tax revenues to municipalities, providing for its expansion was a matter of fiscal survival for cities like Milwaukee. Moreover, the study commission recognized that the most popular model for plant expansions was low-density, single-story buildings, with enough open space to provide parking for workers who used automobiles as well as vacant land for future expansion. A local industrial real estate agent confirmed this in 1949 when he estimated that a 35,000-square-foot production space—a relatively small amount of floor space—needed at least two-and-a-half acres of land for both building and parking. Another industrial agent warned that "the lack of industrial property in this area is keeping new plants from coming in and old plants from expanding."[62] Industry in the postwar era almost always required more space than the older, multi-storied plants had in the past. Accommodating this new industrial model would, therefore, require far more open land than ever before. With this in mind, Zeidler's Economic Study Commission, too, recommended an aggressive annexation policy to facilitate industrial expansion.[63]

In Werba, Milwaukee had the same person who had overseen annexation during the Hoan era twenty years prior. When the Annexation Department ceased operations in 1932, its entire staff, Werba included, shifted duties to the collection of delinquent taxes. During the Depression and war years, Werba had been able to keep his staff largely intact. When the city reestablished its Department of Abstracting and Annexation in 1946, to quote an observer, "there was a core of experienced annexation personnel who had only to change their job classification titles, hire one new annexation solicitor and one new stenographer and re-open their annexation files to again be in the 'annexation business.'"[64] Now, two years after World War II, Werba—and the city—had another chance. "It's the 1920s all over again," he told a local newspaper in 1947, predicting renewed conflict between city and suburbs.[65] The stakes had risen, however. Whatever the causes of inner city decay may have been, the problem was real enough to city officials to move the Common Council to resolve in 1949 that without annexation of vacant land, Milwaukee would simply "die" as a city.[66]

Milwaukee's initial foray into post–World War II urban "renewal" deviates from common narratives of postwar urban governance. The story of how city leaders focused energy on saving downtowns and redeveloping decaying inner core neighborhoods is well known. The series of failures that make up much of postwar urban history—segregated public housing, freeways that accelerated suburbanization, shortsighted renewal plans—are equally notorious, and they certainly exacerbated urban problems at least as often as they solved them. Urban "renewal" also usually encompassed postwar "growth coalitions" that matched city mayors with business elites, forming new power regimes that parlayed increased federal dollars to pet projects.[67] What unites many of these narratives of postwar urbanism is the concentration of attention on center cities, where downtowns were remade and where racial clashes occurred with growing frequency. The postwar urban renewal narrative remains powerful and valid. Certain cities did engage in successful redevelopment of their downtowns, often termed "renaissances." Pittsburgh and Chicago became paradigms for countless other mayors to replicate as each attempted to initiate "renaissances" of their own.[68] Local media lavished attention on showcase civic projects often because they at least produced tangible results. To be sure, historians do examine growth coalition alternatives, usually cast as a mixture of progressive housing advocates, left-wing union activists, and a growing civil rights movement that pushed for racial parity in the form of open housing and the elimination of job discrimination. But recent scholars of the postwar city readily acknowledge that growth coalition alternatives failed to one degree or another.[69] Because of this, urban policy makers who did not solely favor economic development in the downtowns as the best solution to improve cities seemed to have had a shrinking array of political options after 1945.

Growth coalitions undermined other urban policy alternatives after 1945, and they also usually failed on their own terms to renew cities. Work is still very much underway to correct many of these failures. Chicago recently demolished the infamous Robert Taylor Homes, and Pittsburgh still desires to redevelop its Lower Hill District, which was virtually destroyed during the city's first "renaissance." Because American cities are still trying to wipe away the imprint of urban renewal on their landscapes, historical inquiry into the postwar era often leads to a type of teleology. The policies of city officials and civic leaders to "renew" urban America after World War II—well informed or not—*did* precede an urban crisis that marginalized the national presence of American cities, especially those of the industrial Midwest. Accordingly, historians of cities such as Detroit, Cleveland, Milwaukee, Chicago, Pittsburgh, and St. Louis often engage in a search for "symptoms" of urban decline, which are not hard to find. Some historians refer to the "urban crisis" of the 1960s, others focus on the rapid suburbanization of the 1950s and 1960s that sucked resources from central cities, and still others reach back before World War II to find cities of the North growing at slower rates than the Sunbelt.[70] The narrative of "decline" thus remains powerfully embedded in understandings of postwar urbanism. Somewhat lost in this real story of failure, however, are roads not taken and intentions never seen through. Robert Fogelson's excellent history of American downtowns from 1870 to 1950 titles a chapter on the 1940s "The Specter of Decentralization."[71] From the perspective of downtown business interests, in Milwaukee and elsewhere, decentralization presented a very real threat to livelihoods; it became incumbent upon such interests to adopt a language of "blight" to spur increased government intervention in development of the urban core. But to Zeidler and other officials in his administration, decentralization was not a specter to be feared but a process that the city could control and that could work to its advantage.

Milwaukee participated in "urban renewal" after World War II as vigorously as any city in America, but initially with far different goals and intentions than historians usually attribute to postwar governance. Rebuilding the central city was a concern of local businessmen and other civic leaders.[72] The downtown-centered vision, however, was countered by the Zeidler administration, which largely clung to the social progressive planning principles of Milwaukee's earlier generation of planners and reformers. Metropolitanism could be achieved not solely by remaking the urban core but by city-directed community building, physical expansion and, ultimately, political unification of municipalities in the region. After World War II, Milwaukee embarked on an annexation program that was, as in the 1920s, specifically designed to take in vacant lands that would allow Milwaukee room for horizontal expansion. An urban redevelopment policy emerged that treated the "center" and the "periphery" in harmony; as the inner core was remade, the fringe would be built to provide "elbow room" for Milwaukee to decentralize its population and industry. At the edge of urban development, satellite communities—possibly even municipally owned—would be built to alleviate civil defense concerns and provide replacement housing for those displaced by inner city urban renewal projects. Decentralization was to represent not directionless sprawl but instead "self-sustaining" suburbs fashioned from older models of community growth, namely, Ebenezer Howard's Garden Cities, the greenbelt towns of the New Deal, and Milwaukee's own Garden Homes. In essence, by stripping itself of some of its more urban qualities, especially the high population densities that had been anathema to its planners for so long, Milwaukee could be effectively renewed. This story of postwar planning in Milwaukee was thus in no small part an attempt by city officials to turn Charles Whitnall's, Daniel Hoan's, and other social progressives' dream of a decentralized metropolis into a political reality by combining annexation with a balanced urban renewal program that regarded the periphery and the center with equal attention. Richard Perrin, director of the Milwaukee Housing Authority, explained the Milwaukee model the most succinctly in a speech to the National Housing Conference in 1951. Urban renewal, said Perrin, had three components. First, public housing on the urban fringe would serve as "relocation housing for low-income families" in advance of slum clearance. Owner-occupied single-family homes, again on the fringe, served the middle class. Finally, "new community-type development" would accommodate both low- and moderate-income groups while also providing space for industrial expansion. In sum, Perrin told the conference: "If the core of the city is to be rebuilt according to a sound and logical plan, then it is equally important that the expanding periphery of the city be developed on an equally well-ordered basis."[73]

Milwaukee officials' attempts to reverse urban decline reflected Perrin's "three-tiered" approach to redevelopment. An ambitious public housing program was announced and commenced, with the goal to provide most of the new housing on Milwaukee's fringes. Milwaukee sought to provide middle-income housing—mainly to war veterans—by purchasing and developing hundreds of acres of vacant land in Greendale, the nearby greenbelt town. And finally, Milwaukee would try to purchase open land and develop a satellite city of its own, some fifteen miles north and west in neighboring Waukesha County. All of these policies were initiated in the context of the burgeoning Cold War, thus giving credence to decentralization as an adequate measure for cities against possible nuclear attack. Milwaukee officials only minimally succeeded in their program of planned dispersal, building far less public housing than they desired, and failed to develop Greendale or its "satellite city" in the open spaces northwest of the city.

The failure of these initial policies, a subject that will make up the remainder of this book, does not mean they lacked impact. Milwaukee's municipal leaders were not at all passive with respect to the forces that threatened cities in the aftermath of the war. When city officials expressed concern that Milwaukee would lose population to outlying areas but also regarded the city's population density in 1945 of 14,090 people per square mile as socially and functionally undesirable, they were not presenting mutually exclusive fears. Rather, they were demonstrating that decentralization encompassed many of the dimensions of urban change and that transforming the city under the principles of dispersal could *benefit* Milwaukee if planned and administered appropriately. Postwar government in Milwaukee was "pro-growth" only if we understand the term at its most literal; Milwaukee had to physically increase its size in order to survive as a healthy and thriving city. Thus a very different picture of urban "renewal" becomes apparent: Milwaukee was to engage in the planned dispersal of people, housing, and industry while expanding its borders.

The election of Zeidler in 1948 thus ushered in a new era in Milwaukee's political history, as a variety of civic actors sought to reshape the city. Business leaders, newly concerned with economic decline downtown, coalesced around the 1948 Corporation and, deciding that the organization needed a permanent place on the civic scene, changed its name to the Greater Milwaukee Committee. Voters, heavily influenced by a barrage of publicity from the corporation, agreed that Milwaukee needed to issue bonds and go into debt to finance the baseball stadium, museum, and other public improvements. However, a year later, they also voted Frank Zeidler into office, a politician who had not only campaigned against going into debt, but who was a Socialist whose political philosophies consciously replicated those of Daniel Hoan. In terms of planning, Zeidler recalled that one of the chief motivations for annexation was that city officials in his administration were "imbued" with Charles Whitnall's planning ideas that sought to reduce congestion.[74]

As these new actors emerged on the scene, older ones departed. In 1949, Charles Whitnall died at the age of eighty-nine, ending over forty years of public service. But visions of a decentralized metropolis did not end with the death of Whitnall. Nor were they marginalized by an increased national focus on physically aging downtowns, and the rise of urban redevelopment projects that sought to rebuild the central city, and slow or reverse decentralization. If anything, the end of World War II brought a renewed vigor to planning for decentralization that would strengthen Milwaukee by dramatically expanding its boundaries. In the war's wake came a national discourse on the best way to rebuild cities in the United States, and the stakes seemed to be rising. Impending federal legislation promised to make more capital available for urban redevelopment than ever before. The Cold War suddenly made densely populated cities appear vulnerable to possible nuclear attack. The return of hundreds of thousands of veterans from the war placed housing construction at an unprecedented premium. Planned decentralization, Milwaukee's unique policy response to the postwar era, had direct antecedents in the visions of the city's original generation of Socialists and planners in the early twentieth century. As the next chapter demonstrates, new forces emerged to animate old policies: most prominently, nuclear-age fears of wholesale atomic destruction. But they only reinforced the will of public officials to make Milwaukee mightier through a program of community building unmatched in scale and vision across the United States.

The Rise and Fall
of the Satellite City

The Zeidler vision for metropolitan Milwaukee did not materially differ from the dreams of Charles Whitnall and Daniel Hoan, but a new motivation for urban dispersal, civil defense, suddenly emerged in the aftermath of World War II, and it colored two ambitious projects launched in Zeidler's first term as mayor. Scholars have begun to make sense of civil defense in the context of postwar urbanism, and its role as yet another enabler of modern day sprawl.[1] In the midst of the Cold War, city planners and other national and local government officials made civil defense an integral part of the postwar urban planning discourse. Federal agencies encouraged low-density development on the periphery of cities to lessen vulnerability to nuclear attack. As one scholar has noted, this encouragement was given legal sanction in the 1954 Housing Act, when the Housing and Home Finance Agency was charged with "facilitating progress in the reduction of vulnerability of congested areas to enemy attack."[2] Federal policy regarding civil defense, in effect, contributed to metropolitan sprawl.

Federal agencies were concerned about the possibility of atomic attacks on American cities almost from the moment bombs were dropped on Hiroshima and Nagasaki. A year after the war, the federal government produced a document titled *The United States Strategic Bombing Survey* that examined the amount of damage wrought in the two Japanese cities. The study asked the question "'What if the target of the bomb had been an American city?'" The answers were unnerving, as the survey predictably concluded that "the overwhelming bulk of the buildings in American cities could not stand up

against an atomic bomb bursting a mile or a mile and a half from them."
And even though Japanese cities were, on the whole, more densely populated than American cities, by day Manhattan contained more than double the number of people per square mile than Nagasaki. The only way to
counter such devastation was "a reshaping and partial dispersal of national
centers of activity."[3]

The Strategic Bombing Survey was the first document to address what
became a puzzling new problem for city planners and other government officials. How vulnerable were American cities to nuclear attack? What kinds
of efforts should cities make to prepare for attack? To answer these questions, cities began to rely on the expertise of certain city planners, atomic
scientists, and ex-military officials, all of whom rather expediently became
civil defense "experts" in World War II's aftermath.

Tracy Augur emerged as the planner with the most impressive civil defense credentials. Augur was an early member of the Regional Planning Association of America (RPAA), a chief town planner of the Tennessee Valley
Authority in the 1930s, and president of the American Institute of Planners in the 1940s. After the war, Augur grew deeply concerned with urban
problems in a nuclear age and wrote extensively about regional planning's
relationship to civil defense in a series of articles in the *Bulletin of the Atomic
Scientist*. By 1949, with the Soviet Union firmly behind the Iron Curtain, Augur noted that any hope that war could be avoided "through international
agreement" seemed remote. Worse yet, the target area that cities presented
had been growing continuously through amorphous urban expansion. To reduce the target area, Augur called for a planned dispersal that would allow the
United States "to achieve a pattern of dispersed small cities located singly [sic],
in small clusters, and in large metropolitan agglomerations that will give it the
advantages of a highly developed urban civilization."[4] Augur's new community patterns meshed well with the National Security Resources Board's (NSRB)
conclusions about civil defense and planning. The NSRB, charged with civil
defense as a provision of the National Security Act of 1947, concluded a year
later that the ideal form for the new metropolitan landscape was resettlement
clusters well outside of central cities and far apart from each other: "areas of
industry concentration less than five miles, or urban concentrations of less
than 50,000 people, separated by about ten miles of relatively open country."[5]
The similarities between Augur's and the NSRB's civil defense–inspired decentralization and Ebenezer Howard's older Garden Cities were clear, and provided a quality-of-life justification for this new regional form that underpinned
the nuclear emergency. The need to manage future urban growth to make
living and working conditions "tolerable" meshed neatly with the demands

of the nuclear age. As Augur noted in a 1949 commentary, "A metropolitan area that is well organized in terms of the amenities of modern urban living and the efficient conduct of modern business will also be an area of decreased vulnerability to atomic bombs and to other weapons of mass destruction."[6] To Augur, the nuclear bomb had instantly made the American city obsolete in its current form and logic dictated that it be replaced: "We do not hesitate to scrap an obsolete factory and rebuild it on new lines if it is failing to keep pace with the demands of national production; why should not the same course be applied to American cities?"[7]

In addition to planners like Augur, atomic scientists also quickly came to believe that permanent decentralization of urban areas was the best preventive measure against nuclear attack. The most prominent advocate of decentralization in this discipline was Ralph Eugene Lapp, a nuclear scientist who worked on the Manhattan Project during the war. Toward the war's end, however, Lapp grew so scared of the atomic bomb's destructive potential that he joined dozens of other scientists in signing the Szilard Petition, which urged President Harry S. Truman, in vain, not to use nuclear weapons against Japan.[8] After the war, Lapp's fears of the continued misuse of nuclear power grew as the Cold War quickly became tense. Like Augur, he became especially concerned with the bomb's destructive power on American cities. In a 1949 book called *Must We Hide?* Lapp compared the nuclear age with the industrial revolution in its potential for forcing social change, particularly for cities. Lapp's solution for safety paralleled Augur's, and he called for an immediate federal policy to reduce congestion. To Lapp, lessening nuclear vulnerability was a serious military concern; accordingly, under his model American cities were to be decentralized through the existing $15 billion defense budget.

Lapp also was gravely concerned about the proper dimensions that replanned cities should take that would maximize safety. He formulated three new urban models that he deemed adequate for civil defense. Lapp's "rodlike city" was essentially an elongated ribbon, with the business district stretched along a few streets running parallel to each other over a span of ten miles. The "rodlike city's" residential and industrial districts were to be located at least two miles from the business district, separated from each other by parks, museums, golf courses, and green space, all of which were to act in part as fire breaks. Highways would connect the business district with the periphery at varying points along the rod. The second model Lapp suggested was the "doughnut city," which was circular, but with only an airport at the center and businesses, residences, and green spaces situated in loops surrounding the airport. In this model, industry was to be located even beyond the "doughnut," in outlying areas connected to highways. Finally, Lapp's "satellite city" was also circular, with the central business district in the core built around a park, and residents and industry again located on the periphery, separated from the business district by parks, cultural institutions, and open spaces, with highways radiating out of the center circle to connect to the outlying districts.[9]

Lapp's models were not revolutionary. The industrial suburb borrowed heavily from Howard's Garden City, and the greenbelts that separated use districts from one another were offshoots of both Howard and the New Deal greenbelt towns. Other city planners had called for smaller, compact cities that were efficiently organized in varying degrees and forms, including Milwaukee's chief planner in the 1930s, Charles Bennett. It is also difficult to gauge what influence Lapp had on American city planners on a national level because the cost of implementing even small parts of the plan would obviously have been astronomical. However, Lapp was not a lone voice in calling for a new urban form that made proper civil defense provisions. In a 1948 issue of the *Bulletin of Atomic Scientists,* Jacob Marshak, Edward Teller, and Lawrence R. Klein argued that "ribbon" or "linear" cities were ideal urban forms because they presented no obvious target to a nuclear bomb. Recognizing that "complete dispersal" was impossible because of the nature of the American economy and dense clusters were the most vulnerable urban formation, Marshak, Teller, and Klein believed that ribbon developments provided an adequate compromise between the two.[10]

The feasibility of using civil defense as a catalyst to regional planning was vexing to city officials, and it was perhaps more expedient to laugh off ambitious regional designs as being ignorant of how cities actually existed. Even if Augur was correct—that cities *were* obsolete in the nuclear age—wishing them out of existence was by mere common sense impossible. Robert Moses, the famed New York City parks commissioner, reflected this belief that dispersion along the lines that Augur and Lapp advocated was naïve, writing in 1949, "Even if dispersion for military reasons were logical, most people would still regard it as fantastic, absurd, and contemptible. . . . Those who think we should scrap plans and substitute a revolutionary program of total reconstruction and dispersion are just a little bit mad."[11] "Replacing" an entire city, let alone New York, was of course impossible. However, guiding future horizontal growth according to these civil defense principles seemed more achievable in the context of the postwar years. The national housing shortage, the lack of industrial space within cities for expansion, and the apparent social problems that accompanied congestion all could be addressed if cities were dispersed. New cities, whether they were to be

formed as satellites, rods, ribbons, or doughnuts, would provide more con-
veniently spaced new housing and room for industrial expansion. Though
still relatively compact, the new urban form would be far less congested
than the industrial city.

To Milwaukee officials, planned dispersion was a viable option that fit
neatly within the context of the Zeidler administration's postwar plans.
City officials thus vigorously pursued planned dispersion in the Zeidler
administration's early years because urban civil defense dovetailed with
Zeidler's own sensibilities about the American city. Like his Socialist predecessors, Zeidler believed that on its own terms congestion bred a poorer
quality of life. Even without the threat of nuclear attack, acute shortages
of land for new homes and industry already threatened to squeeze cities
into obsolescence. Civil defense was thus only another reason for Milwaukee to engage in a planned decentralization that would make the metropolis
not only more humane and efficient, but safer from nuclear attack as well.
Even if urban renewal as dispersal was not popular with the general public, it
could be justified by the principles of civil defense. Zeidler made civil defense
public policy almost immediately upon taking office in 1948. In June of that
year, he formed the Civil Defense Disaster Relief Committee, which agreed
that local planning had to be coordinated with state and federal civil defense
efforts. In 1951, the position of civil defense director was made permanent.
And in 1952, to more fully coordinate defense planning, the Milwaukee
Common Council created a separate Department of Civil Defense.[12]

Throughout the postwar era, Milwaukee prepared itself for nuclear holo-
caust as best it could. When the city issued 100,000 civil defense questionnaires to its public schools, 66 percent of the recipients replied.[13] Emergency
rescue trucks, nicknamed "Calamity Janes," were built.[14] In 1960, the city
received a $200,000 federal grant for the construction of a fallout shelter in
its new public museum.[15] Over 3,600 block wardens were appointed to work
in conjunction with the Milwaukee police.[16] In 1955 alone, public activity
related to civil defense in Milwaukee was staggering. That year, every family
in Milwaukee received evacuation guides. The civil defense speaker's bureau
gave 198 talks to varying organizations and groups regarding civil defense.
Approximately 10,000 people attended the sessions. Radio and television
time donated to the Civil Defense Department amounted to roughly 2,149
separate time units. A total of 24,403 people in the Milwaukee area watched
255 showings of civil defense films. A civil defense newsletter was published
and sent out to over 9,000 "volunteers" each month.[17]

Because civil defense was so publicly prominent in Milwaukee in the
postwar era, city officials were able to connect its importance to the trajec-

tory of Milwaukee's urban transformation as well. Zeidler became an important enough civil defense expert in his own right to merit an invitation by the federal government to witness the detonation of an atomic bomb in Nevada in 1952. The chilling experience moved him to say, "No one who has not seen this phenomenon can appreciate its beauty and horrifying power."[18] Zeidler also regularly communicated with civil defense experts, most prominently Lapp, whose book he much admired and distributed to Krieger and Deputy Civil Defense Director George Parkinson.[19] Upon reading *Must We Hide?* Krieger wrote Zeidler that he was confident that Lapp's study "provides a compelling argument in support of Milwaukee's past and present approach to city planning." "The aim of our zoning ordinance," Krieger wrote, "seeks to spread the city horizontally rather than vertically," as did the city's annexation policy.[20] Administrative assistant John Kugler also agreed that Milwaukee's plans were in concert with Lapp's, but worried that Milwaukee did not have the suitable parks and green spaces that separated residential, business, and industrial districts as firebreaks in the event of nuclear attack.[21] Civil defense consultant George Parkinson, an officer in the Naval Reserve, also concluded that planned dispersal fit into civil defense principles. By reaching outward rather than upward, Milwaukee would keep pace with urban growth while providing the measure of safety civil defense and planning that experts dictated.

Milwaukee's first opportunity to engage in planned dispersal came about almost by accident. At the end of World War II, the federal government began to make plans to sell off the three greenbelt towns it had developed in Maryland, Ohio, and Wisconsin during the Depression. Greendale, located ten miles south and west of Milwaukee, contained 572 housing units, but preliminary plans had called for over 3,000 units in the village's 3,400 acres. In 1945, Elbert Peets, one of Greendale's original planners, finished a government-sponsored plan to add 3,000 more housing units in neighborhood clusters surrounding the original village. According to Greendale historians Arnold Alannin and Joseph Eden, Peets's plan "became the model for all subsequent public and private planning in the village."[22] Peets's greatest wish in planning for Greendale's addition was to preserve the Garden City principles that had made it so appealing a place to live. Even though the 1945 plan was formulated without any guarantee of construction, with the housing shortage growing more severe by the day, Greendale's open land seemed as conducive to development as any in the region.

When the federal government announced its intentions to sell off the three greenbelt towns after the war, surprisingly few groups showed interest in buying and developing them. One significant exception came from

Milwaukee and Greendale. A group of veterans concerned about the lack of housing formulated a plan to purchase Greendale from the federal government upon passage of legislation that enabled the sales to commence. With the purchase of Greendale, the open land around the original town could be developed as housing for veterans of the war in accordance with Peets's plans of 1945. Arthur Marcus, a Greendale resident, became the federal government's first serious bidder. Marcus had served in the merchant marine during World War II and subsequently became a national advocate for veterans housing. Marcus served on the American Legion's National Housing Committee, and he saw in Greendale an opportunity to build the housing units that thousands of veterans needed in the aftermath of the war. To properly bid for Greendale, Marcus organized the American Legion Community Development Corporation (ALCDC) and, in October of 1948, the national convention of the American Legion approved of Marcus's plan.[23]

Seeking adequate funding, Marcus canvassed local civic officials in both Greendale and Milwaukee and quickly found newly elected mayor Zeidler to be receptive. Zeidler, who had worked on Greendale in the 1930s, greatly admired its Garden City principles. With Milwaukee's housing shortage growing more acute by the day, Zeidler, like Marcus, saw in the potential purchase of Greendale the opportunity to build much-needed new housing for veterans. More importantly, Zeidler was an advocate of public housing, broadly defined, not only for low-income dwellers, but for working- and middle-class families as well. The Milwaukee region's own history informed Zeidler's planning preference. Greendale, while federally funded, was essentially a middle-income village. An even older development, the Garden Homes, had initially been devised as a cooperative venture. Zeidler clearly wanted to replicate either or both models to address Milwaukee's postwar housing problems. In August 1948, Zeidler invited ex-mayor Daniel Hoan to his office to learn firsthand of Hoan's experience in developing the Garden Homes project in the 1920s. At this meeting, Hoan advised Zeidler to "eliminate the middle man" by having the city act as its own general contractor to mitigate construction costs.[24] Zeidler liked this idea enough to ask Perrin, director of the Milwaukee Housing Authority, to have his agency give it attention. But the real opportunity for public enterprise in housing had arrived with Greendale's situation. The ALCDC's invitation to Milwaukee provided the first chance for the city to gain greater control in planning on the periphery, if not as general contractor then at least as a possible investor.

Wisconsin state law already permitted Milwaukee to buy stock in building companies provided that construction took place within three miles of city limits.[25] Most but not all of Greendale's 3,400 acres were within these boundaries. Confident of the project's legalities, Zeidler publicly announced his support of the ALCDC's efforts on October 15, 1948, alluding to the housing shortage by saying that "the city is interested from the point of view of encouraging any groups, based on the principle of self-help, to put up homes."[26] Next, Zeidler turned to the Common Council, which proved equally impressed by the ALCDC's plan. On December 7, 1948, they voted to approve the purchase of all of the preferred stock of the ALCDC, at a sum of $300,000. Because the city of Milwaukee had invested so heavily in the corporation, it received substantial representation on the ALCDC's Board of Directors, with Zeidler, three aldermen, two city attorneys, and the city comptroller joining three Greendale residents and an American Legion official on the board. Marcus, one of the three Greendale residents on the board, was elected the ALCDC's president.[27]

Marcus and other ALCDC officials spent much of the winter of 1948 and 1949 in Washington, D.C., trying to convince the federal government to make Greendale more affordable by passing a new law that ended competitive bidding for the greenbelt towns and replaced it with direct negotiations. Zeidler and Alderman Milton McGuire testified before the Senate Committee on Banking and Currency in February 1949, arguing that Milwaukee's community development efforts were solid solutions to the present housing shortage. The ALCDC was also greatly helped by Wisconsin Senator Joseph McCarthy and Representative Clement Zablocki, whose district included Greendale. McCarthy, especially, was enthusiastic to the ALCDC because of its ties to the American Legion and its promise of housing for war veterans. Congress acquiesced by passing a new bill that eliminated competitive bidding and allowed for direct negotiations between federal housing officials and potential purchasers. President Harry S. Truman signed the new law on May 19, 1949. With all legal hurdles now cleared and a favorable status in Congress, the ALCDC seemed perfectly positioned to complete the sale. Further approval of the sale was provided, unsolicited, by the Greendale Village Board, which voted its support of the ALCDC on May 3, 1949. A perfect opportunity to develop the fringe had fallen into Milwaukee's lap.[28]

Once the sale was complete, as primary stockholder in the ALCDC Milwaukee could theoretically petition *itself* for annexation and give its entire expansion program an enormous jump start. More pointedly, to Zeidler and other Milwaukee officials, the development of Greendale was not merely a way to construct a large amount of homes for veterans, but one early step in the broader execution of planned dispersal. Greendale's Garden City scale represented a desirable urban form that could be repeated in other vacant areas near the city. In February 1949, Zeidler told Greendale Village President Walter Kroening that Milwaukee was considering another "townsite development" to the northwest.[29] Krieger, who had taken over as Executive Secretary of the BPLC and was now the city's chief planner, was enlisted to provide both Kroening and the federal government with a brief explanation of Milwaukee's broader community development program. Krieger wrote that urban redevelopment in the city's core "cannot be carried out without community development programs." Milwaukee was ready to engage in such projects "but its ultimate success begins with the public ownership of adequate, properly located acreage." Krieger's memo also highlighted the crucial role that annexation had to play in ensuring that fringe developments remain under Milwaukee's jurisdiction. He noted that since annexation activities had resumed in 1946, physical expansion had occurred as "at best a piecemeal approach." Ideally, annexation could be guided to "concentrate the provision of improvement in one area, such as a 1,000 to 2,000 acre community development project."[30] The city would save money by enabling public works to focus improvements on a few clusters, rather than small scattered sites across the fringe. Public ownership is was a key distinction; new satellite cities were not only to be zoned and annexed by the city, but *owned* by it in some form as well. Krieger's memo thus both evoked the older land reserve idea that Greendale's planners had explicated, and reflected continuity with the city's own tradition of social progressive planning. Greendale, in this context, was only one component of Milwaukee's eventual decentralization. In May of 1949, Krieger officially recommended to Zeidler that the ALCDC commence with its sale, and that upon its sale, Milwaukee immediately "dissolve" the village and annex it. Even with this recommendation, Krieger told Zeidler that vacant land on the city's Northwest Side was even more ideal for a satellite city. "Greendale" Krieger wrote, "is not an immediate answer but serves rather as a long pull project."[31]

The Greendale scheme, however, proved to be beyond Milwaukee's grasp. Behind the failure of the ALCDC were suburban residents who feared annexation to the central city and desired local control over development, a type of group that would become all too familiar to Milwaukee. Both Zeidler and the Milwaukee Common Council had supported the financing of the ALCDC under the assumption that eventually Greendale would be dissolved and folded into Milwaukee.[32] Werba, the city's Director of Annexation, began trying to annex land to Milwaukee's south to allow the city to border Greendale, thus making the consolidation legal. When Milwaukee's intentions became public in the summer of 1949, support for the ALCDC among Greendale residents dropped considerably. *The Greendale Review*, the village's local newspaper, vigorously opposed the sale to the ALCDC in part because it promised annexation. In an open letter to Zeidler on July 22, the paper asked: "Do you think that a for moment the city of Milwaukee will colonize (annex) Greendale using the same despotic methods employed by the British in the Revolutionary War days?"[33] When a rival group of veterans called the Greendale Veterans Cooperative Housing Association (GVCHA) put forth their own plan for the village's purchase, the village board voted to hold a referendum to allow citizens to choose between the two plans. In the weeks leading up to the referendum, the *Review* kept fanning the flames, warning residents, "Back the GVCHA and you will have your homes and security. If you don't back it—Goodbye homes!"[34] With these fearful warnings still echoing, village residents voted against the ALCDC's plan by the overwhelming margin of 621 to 98.[35] In the village board elections that following spring, every pro-ALCDC candidate up for reelection was swept out of office.[36] Even though these votes were not direct statements on annexation, the message was clear: the ALCDC may have been the handpicked favorite of the federal government and Milwaukee, but Greendale residents had little use for the group.

The failed purchase of Greendale was not narrowly based on opposition to annexation, but driven by an expressed desire of suburban residents to control their own destiny. Even before the summer of 1949, the ALCDC had done an extremely poor job of informing Greendale residents of its plans and intentions. When the initial ALCDC delegation left for Washington in December 1948 to garner congressional support, they did so without informing the village board. The board responded with an angry telegram to President Truman and five Wisconsin congressmen, informing them that "the village of Greendale board of trustees, who represent the residents, have never been consulted by said legion group and therefore speak entirely without our or the resident's [sic] authority."[37] Even when the village board eventually did vote its support of the ALCDC plan, it did so at a special session at which no one from the general public was allowed to speak and over the dissenting votes of three board members.[38] Greendale's village attorney stated at the meeting that he had no real idea of what the ALCDC's plan entailed. Greendale residents also expressed bitterness that their future was being decided arbitrarily. ALCDC President Marcus testified before Congress that village residents would have to absorb anywhere from

30–60 percent rent increases to make the project viable; the *Review* responded by inviting Marcus to lay out exactly what type of increases the ALCDC intended to levy. Marcus never acceded, much to the paper's chagrin.[39] A public meeting of Greendale residents on July 17 revealed still more anger at the ALCDC's perceived paternalism, with one resident complaining that Marcus and the ALCDC had falsely implied to Congress that a majority of residents supported the veterans' group.[40]

Desires of local control motivated Greendale residents to instead support the second veterans' group, the Greendale Veterans Cooperative Housing Association (GVCHA). The *Review* periodically reminded its readers that this group, unlike the ALCDC, was made up entirely of village residents. Support for the GVCHA was strong, even though the group did not possess adequate funds to execute the purchase of the village. Because of this, Congress refused to enter into negotiations with the GVCHA. But even faced with this reality, the forces of local control proved strong. In the spring of 1950, Greendale residents voted onto the village board a majority of officials who expressed support of the GVCHA.

Zeidler tried to convince Greendale residents that Milwaukee had the best of intentions, assuring the village manager in writing that whatever development did take place in Greendale would be in line with Charles Whitnall's Garden City principles.[41] But by advocating expansion, city officials had placed themselves in a position that they would find themselves in time and again throughout the postwar era. Suburban residents saw the city's planned decentralization in one-dimensional terms. Expansion was contingent upon acquiescence of residents in areas to be annexed; Milwaukee officials all too often assumed that residents on the outskirts supported the city's expansion. When Werba began to explore the feasibility of annexation of Greendale, he observed to the Common Council on July 15, 1949, "As is usually the case, the opposition appears to radiate from a minority of village officials and employees."[42] Just one month later, Greendale residents proved him wrong by overwhelmingly voting down the ALCDC.

Technically, even with Greendale residents officially opposed to the ALCDC, the federal government could award the purchase to the embattled group. The village-wide referendum in Greendale had no legal underpinning. But in the vote's wake, the project was in serious peril of appearing undemocratic. Further complicating matters, Arthur Marcus suddenly died, and when the city of Milwaukee began to demand increased representation on the ALCDC board and the legion resisted, it became clear that the project had faltered. The ALCDC dissolved in 1951, and Milwaukee officials had to take the group to court to recoup the city's $300,000 investment. Other public housing projects for war veterans were completed, and all were located several miles away from the central business district, as city officials intended. However, when 4,000 people applied to live in the 578 units finished by 1949, it was obvious that the housing shortage remained severe.

For his part, Zeidler eventually demonstrated that he was in fact concerned with preserving Greendale's Garden City heritage and not simply usurping the apparent will of village residents. Later in the 1950s, he managed to convince a group of Milwaukee civic leaders to form a consortium to buy the land surrounding the original village and develop it according to Peets's original plans. Greendale's greenbelt heritage was maintained, but Milwaukee had failed in its initial attempt to control growth on the periphery.[43]

Greendale by no means reflected Milwaukee's only effort to gain control of decentralization. At the same time the village purchase was being attempted, city officials were planning an even larger community development project northwest of the city. Here, the goal of Zeidler, Krieger, and Werba was to create a comprehensive "satellite city" that would have homes, parks, industry, and retail, which would provide public and private housing for a variety of income groups. This "Northwest Community" would prove to be one of the most ambitious development projects attempted by any city in the postwar era. Like Greendale, it was ultimately defeated, not by poor administration or management, but by recalcitrant suburban and rural residents.

Zeidler and many of Milwaukee's city planners had envisioned development of a complete community almost from the moment he was elected. Once again, the initial conception of a large-scale planned community harkened back to planning endeavors first explicated in the Hoan administration. In the late 1920s and early 1930s, Charles Bennett introduced plans for a "model village" that had borrowed from Ebenezer Howard's Garden City, Milwaukee's own Garden Homes, and the RPAA–inspired New Jersey suburb of Radburn. Bennett had believed the ideal location for his planned community was northwest of the city, in the unincorporated Town of Granville, where land was relatively cheap. The model village idea never took off, ill-timed by the collapse in the housing industry during the Depression, but it indirectly helped the region land the Greendale project. Now, in 1948, with the war over, the economy recovering, the housing shortage still acute, and another Socialist in office, the broader idea of a city-initiated planned community regained traction. That year, city planners decided that vacant areas northwest of the city were the best-suited for such a development. It was in its northwest side where Milwaukee previously had enjoyed the most progress in its annexation program. Most of the city's major railroads ran to the northwest as well; thus land here would be better suited for industrial expansion.

On December 11, 1948, Zeidler and Alvin Bromm of the BPLC publicly announced Milwaukee's intentions to develop one or two "huge communities" on the northwest side. Zeidler endorsed the project, telling local press, "It is my hope that the city will not do things in driblets next year but start something on a more massive, community-sized scale."[44] The project called for the city to annex and improve an as yet unidentified parcel of land on the northwest side by building streets, lights, and water and sewer extensions, as well as creating stringent zoning requirements to segregate potential industrial, residential, commercial, and recreational areas. In another important variation to mere annexation, the city of Milwaukee was also to purchase the vacant land and either sell it off to developers or set up long-term leases.

To better coordinate planning the new "satellite city" (as these planned communities came to be known among officials) between varying city departments, Zeidler asked Krieger to arrange a committee consisting of three aldermen, Werba, another city planner, and a local builder to look for proper sites. Zeidler also enlisted the Milwaukee Common Council to provide money to allow the city to begin negotiations for purchase of the vacant land. The council followed through on April 11, 1949, approving an initial sum of $25,000 that provided initial start-up money to help find adequate locations for the planned community. Local press heartily approved of Milwaukee's initial plans; the *Milwaukee Journal* noted after the council appropriation that no large-scale housing starts had begun in Milwaukee, in part because no single developer owned enough land to commence such a project. In any case, Milwaukee was acting the part of "general contractor," as Hoan had earlier advised Zeidler.[45]

The satellite city project quickly gained national attention. In 1949, Congress was debating and eventually signing into law the National Housing Act. While Congress deliberated on the finer points of the law, cities began scrambling to make local projects conducive to the legislation's stipulations. For Zeidler and Milwaukee officials, the key component of the Housing Act was the "vacant land provision" inserted in Title I. The provision permitted cities to obtain loans to purchase open land, provided housing was constructed in a timely manner. For Milwaukee officials, it meant that federal money might have been available to help acquire land to establish the satellite city. While the Housing Act was being debated in Congress, Zeidler filed a brief to Alabama Senator John Sparkman, who sat on the Banking and Currency Committee that was debating the bill, explaining

Milwaukee's community development ideas. Zeidler's brief arrived too late to put into the official Congressional Record, but Sparkman assured Zeidler that it was helpful. Other prominent officials—including Catherine Bauer—later credited Zeidler with helping to win the inclusion of the vacant lands provision into the housing act.[46]

The Regional Planning Association of New York also expressed interest to Zeidler in Milwaukee's satellite city. Zeidler enlisted Krieger to outline Milwaukee's plan, and he explained that, first and foremost, "the City of Milwaukee is interested in effecting city-county consolidation," but in its absence, the "next best bet" to unify the metropolis was large-scale projects like Greendale and the "northwest community." Krieger also explained that satellite cities complemented city officials' conception of urban renewal as planned dispersal: "Planning must simultaneously attack on two fronts: it must plan for the old, built-up sections, and for the new, unimproved sections. But planning development in the newer sections is cheaper and usually more effective than in the older sections, and in general can provide large numbers of living units in a desirable environment at the most economical cost."[47] Zeidler also helped draw national attention to the satellite city idea, outlining Milwaukee's plans to the National Housing Conference and the U.S. Conference of Mayors. Again, Zeidler's explanation of the push for satellite communities was firmly in the context of urban renewal; as he wrote, "I first broached the idea of building satellite communities to the City of Milwaukee as a means to overcoming the housing shortage and of meeting the slum clearance problem."[48] Satellite cities could "fundamentally attack the problem of blight in the city" by rehousing thousands of families who were to be potentially displaced by urban renewal.

Outside of Milwaukee, the Zeidler administration's satellite city resonated most strongly with Catherine Bauer. After her New Deal work to push for public housing, Bauer had married and settled in academia, teaching at the University of California-Berkeley and then at Harvard. Bauer remained a passionate advocate for public housing, and in the late 1940s had joined the growing and disparate chorus in pushing for the National Housing Act. Bauer visited Milwaukee in December 1949, now fully excited at the news of Milwaukee's push to build satellite cities.[49] Bauer essentially repeated this to Zeidler, later writing him, "From my viewpoint at least, your scheme to purchase and annex the site for a satellite community, to include industry as well as private and public housing, is the most progressive and significant move being made in the whole field of city planning and housing in America today."[50] Like Zeidler, Bauer had long viewed public housing in broad terms, not solely to be a warehouse for America's indigent but instead to serve as a well-planned alternative to the speculative private sector. She was suspicious that the 1949 Housing Act was too favorable to slum clearance and private sector–subsidized redevelopment. Bauer, however, shared Zeidler's hope that the vacant land provision in Title I of the act could be utilized toward the ends proposed in Milwaukee. These hopes became apparent in a speech to the National Housing Conference during the summer of 1950, when Bauer told her audience of fellow housers, "Milwaukee's scheme for a complete and balanced community as a first step toward central redevelopment, seem to me at least to hold the *key* to successful use of the tools of the housing act, in the immediate future."[51]

Milwaukee officials had made it obvious that satellite community development comprised a key part of urban renewal. However, the heightening of the Cold War made civil defense an equally compelling justification to develop satellite cities. After learning of the development of the hydrogen bomb in 1950, Krieger assured Zeidler, "We ought to spread out anyhow, H-bomb or no H-Bomb."[52] For their part, civil defense officials in Milwaukee, already favorable to decentralization in the mode that R. E. Lapp and Tracy Augur had envisioned, were heartened that Milwaukee's city planners also had always advocated dispersion for its own sake. Deputy Civil Defense Commissioner George Parkinson acknowledged in a report to Zeidler, "the city of Milwaukee has been very fortunate in having for many years the benefits of city planning of the Milwaukee City Planning Commission," which had advocated decentralization since its early years under Charles Whitnall.[53] Since civil defense seemed to intuitively demand population dispersion, it clearly fitted into Milwaukee's postwar plans.

Civil defense motivated city officials to choose a different and much larger site for their satellite city, one much further into the countryside than the initial two-square-mile plot near 60th and Mill Road. By early 1951, officials favored a location that encompassed approximately ten square miles in neighboring Waukesha County, just beyond the tiny village of Butler. The location had direct antecedents in the Hoan administration's annexation program of the 1920s. Just before the Depression halted annexation in Hoan's tenure, Milwaukee had begun to make inroads to its northwest. In 1930, residents of Butler, an incorporated village in Waukesha County that bordered Milwaukee County to the west, appeared before the BPLC, stating they needed improved water and sewer lines. Ben Fortin, a village trustee, spoke for the residents, stating that Butler was "extremely eager to obtain Milwaukee's conveniences."[54] The BPLC referred the matter to Werba, who faced the daunting task of connecting Milwaukee's western boundary to Butler, which was two-and-a-half miles to the west. Werba immediately began planning to annex a strip of land along Hampton Avenue that would physically connect the city to Butler. The Depression halted annexation, but Werba and much of his staff from the Hoan years had stayed intact during the interim. In 1946, when the city reactivated its Annexation Department and placed Werba back in charge, he annexed a five-mile-long and 330-foot-wide strip of land along Hampton Avenue to access the Chicago and Northwestern Railroad yards at the border of Milwaukee and Waukesha Counties.[55] The village of Butler was located along Hampton Avenue and was now in Werba's path. The "Butler Strip" annexation, as the Hampton Avenue parcel became known, gave Milwaukee access to undeveloped but potentially valuable industrial real estate. It also gave Milwaukee a window to Waukesha County, and it was on land just beyond Butler that the city hoped to build its satellite community.

On January 31, 1951, in a speech before the Milwaukee Press Club, Zeidler gave another public hint of what was to come by announcing that city planners were about to release a more detailed plan for Milwaukee's expansion. Zeidler told the club that, eventually, Milwaukee would develop several satellite cities that would extend into five neighboring counties, and all would be spread out enough from each other to make the region an uninviting nuclear target. This type of planning, Zeidler argued, was proactive and creative; as he told the Press Club, "I believe we must challenge the imagination of the people."[56] The Milwaukee region's imagination was duly challenged the following month when a report on the scope and nature of the satellite city written by Krieger was made public. In it, Krieger acknowledged that the planning staff had worked closely with civil defense officials to shape the new satellite community into a form that would be sufficiently less vulnerable to nuclear attack. The site consisted of 9.6 square miles of what was mostly agricultural land west of Butler. Milwaukee was to purchase the entirety of the designated land and, as in Greendale, subsequently petition itself for annexation. Krieger set aside 4.7 square miles for housing of all types, private and public, large and small lots, single-family homes and low-rise apartments. He estimated that 50–75,000 people could live in population densities roughly comprised of seventeen to twenty-five persons per acre. The contours of existing land use patterns remained in place; industry was only to be located along the Chicago and Northwestern rail line. Curvilinear streets replaced the older urban grid, prompting applause from one local journalist who believed that grid planning "has made Milwaukee and a hundred other cities dangerous, dreary, and expensive."[57] Since the community was to be a "self-sustaining suburb," Krieger reserved 1,000 acres for industry and 120 acres for retail. Krieger also evoked Ebenezer Howard and the New Deal greenbelt towns in reserving some 2,000 acres of land, nearly a third of the site's total, for greenbelts and parks. The greenbelts had double significance in a nuclear age; Lapp had envisioned green space to act as a firebreak in the event of bombing.[58]

Civil defense concerns, in fact, rang throughout the report. Krieger acknowledged, "There will always be cities because of their obvious economic, social, cultural, and educational advantages . . . but our compact, congested cities of today no longer offer protection." If cities were to survive, they could no longer be built as compactly as they had in the past. Instead, "in the long run, planned dispersion is by far the city's most practical, effective, and least expensive defense against air attack."[59] As a local newspaper later put it, the plan would "protect the city by scattering it."[60] Krieger's initial site plans also provided for transportation in varying forms. The northern end of the site bordered the Menomonee River Parkway, part of Whitnall's countywide system, and was also close to a proposed northwest freeway that county officials planned to link to downtown. Krieger hoped that additional transit options could be provided by building commuter rail on existing rail lines, and even hoped interurban service would accompany the new freeway, "to lessen the new community's dependence upon gasoline consumption during time of war."[61]

Another major motivation that Krieger acknowledged in his report was the city's need to "control its destiny," which meant, once again, understanding that political lines were arbitrary in matters of planning. "County limits," Krieger wrote, "remain fixed while the limits of a healthy, growing, and vigorous city are forever expanding." Krieger framed urban expansion in the context of national defense, noting that civil defense principles demanded permission to allow the city "to develop into neighboring counties."[62] Furthermore, Milwaukee was to not only annex but also own the entire site, and either gradually sell off parcels after careful zoning or simply lease the land to homeowners, business, and industry. Large-scale community planning also would enable Milwaukee to end piecemeal annexation, and save millions of dollars in infrastructure by concentrating public improvements in this and potentially other growth clusters.

Later in March of 1951, the Board of Public Land Commissioners voted approval of Krieger's report and made plans to hold public hearings on the satellite city. Werba had told Zeidler several times in the previous three years that the "Butler Strip" annexation, which made the proposed satellite city technically adjacent to Milwaukee, was the key to Milwaukee's entire annexation program. Werba also was confident that the village of Butler, which sat between Milwaukee and its satellite city, would vote to consolidate with the city.[63]

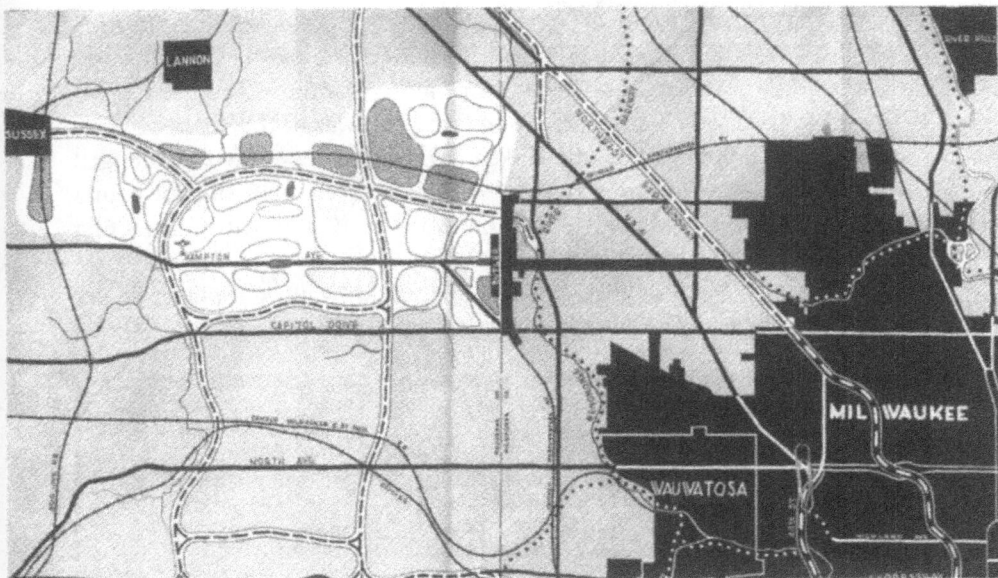

Milwaukee's Proposed Satellite City—In the aftermath of World War II, Milwaukee's planners hoped to build several "satellite cities" well outside of existing city borders. This community was located in present-day Waukesha County and was designed to house between 50,000 and 75,000 residents. Courtesy of Milwaukee City Archives / Milwaukee Public Library

But for the second time, residents of the areas affected by the city's plans vigorously opposed Milwaukee's physical expansion. Butler had grown as an industrial village next to the Chicago and Northwestern Railroad yards in the 1910s and 1920s.[64] The 1940 census counted only 778 residents in the village, but urbanization had proved expensive even to this small number of people. By 1946, residents were again clamoring for infrastructure improvements, especially to the village's water supply. But the costs of a new waterworks for the tiny village were prohibitive. It was estimated that a new water system would cost the village $300,000. Since the entire assessed valuation of Butler was only $500,000, the increased taxes that the waterworks would require were deemed excessive by many residents, and the village began exploring other ways to improve its water and sewage systems without the great costs. The most obvious candidate to help Butler was Milwaukee, which had reestablished its annexation department the same year. The Common Council asked Werba to annex land to allow Milwaukee to border Butler and thus give residents there a chance to consolidate with the city if they voted to do so. Werba immediately predicted that "in nine months Milwaukee will be knocking at the door of Waukesha County," and he delivered by annexing the "Butler Strip" along Hampton Avenue.[65] However, part of the land he annexed along Hampton was in the Town of Wauwatosa, an old opponent of Milwaukee annexation. The town challenged the Butler Strip annexation in the state circuit court in 1948, but the courts upheld the legality of Milwaukee's annexation in 1950.[66] Milwaukee's first satellite city briefly seemed safe and legal.

However, the Town of Wauwatosa surprised Milwaukee officials by appealing the ruling to the state supreme court, and enlisted the help of

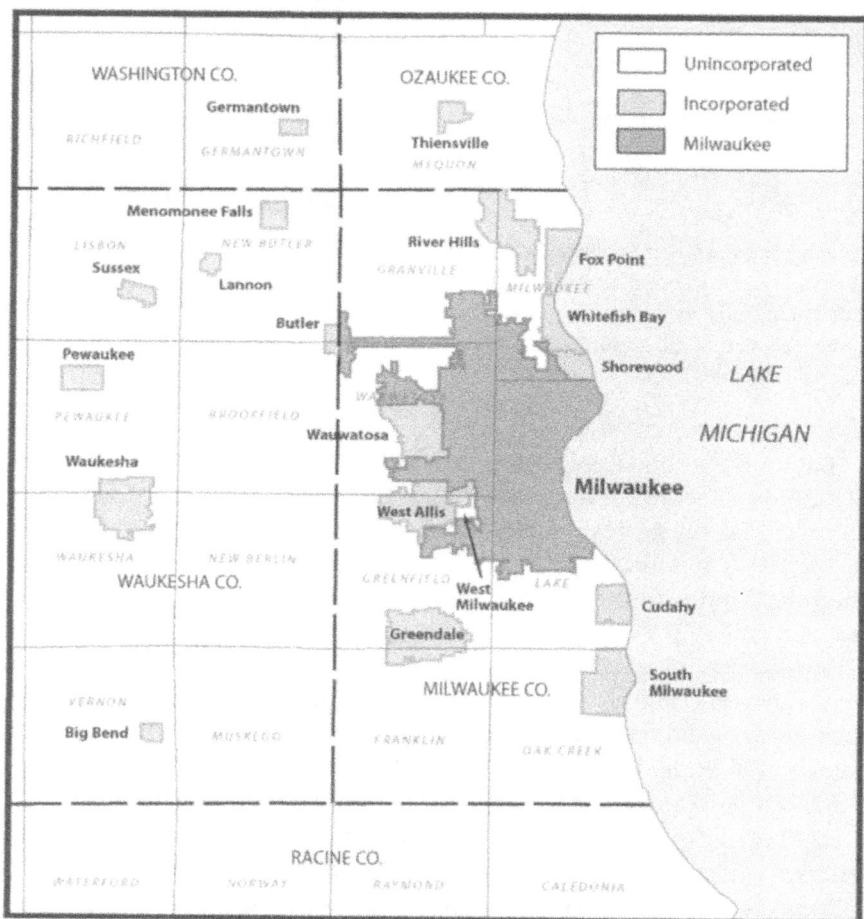

Municipalities of Milwaukee Region, 1950 (with Butler Strip Annexation). © Mapcraft

William Kay and Conrad Dineen, two suburban lawyers who had previously (and successfully) defeated other annexations by Milwaukee. Once it became apparent that Milwaukee officials desired to expand the city and eventually achieve some form of metropolitan government, the case became not only a matter of the legality of annexing land along Hampton Avenue, but one that would greatly determine how the region would develop in the postwar era. As in the 1920s, Milwaukee again appeared as the region's bully, gobbling up land at the expense of innocent residents of the semirural townships. As the court listened to oral arguments in the case of the *Town of Wauwatosa* v. *Milwaukee,* nine local attorneys representing nine different suburbs in Milwaukee County filed briefs on behalf of Wauwatosa. Milwaukee's planned decentralization was again being directly challenged by a unified suburban front.[67]

Opposition to the satellite city had rural sources as well. The site for the satellite city was technically located not in Butler but beyond it to the west, in the towns of Brookfield and Menomonee. Residents here proved as reluctant as their neighboring suburbs to support Milwaukee's expansion. In 1951, most of this part of Waukesha County remained agricultural. Waukesha County had contained so many dairy farms in the nineteenth century that it was locally known as "Cow County USA," and residents here still displayed a healthy agrarian distrust of the large neighboring city. After it became apparent that Milwaukee's expansion plans included Brookfield and Menomonee, residents of the two towns formed a "Property Owners Association" with over 200 members to resist the city. After Krieger's report was released to the public, the association held a public meeting attended by over 250 people to discuss the satellite city. Again, the opposition cloaked their arguments in the context of democratic local control, sounding remarkably similar to city residents who would later fight inner city urban renewal. Sylvester Claas, a farmer in Menomonee and the chair of the association, likened Milwaukee and its "plague of annexation" to a "dictatorship" because, as he said, "you don't have any voice in what happens to you. They take your land and you haven't anything to say about it."[68]

The village board of Butler, once open to Milwaukee's offer to consolidate, also took steps to ensure it would not become a part of the larger city. Werba had warned Butler that if it voted to develop either a water or a storm sewer of its own, the village could not join Milwaukee because the Common Council would be unwilling to incur the considerable debt Butler would take on. With a vote for public improvements now essentially a vote against joining with Milwaukee, village residents, once resistant to internal improvements, made their intentions clear in 1950 by voting to build a $280,000 storm sewer. The Menomonee Town Board also passed a resolution that officially opposed any annexation efforts on the part of Milwaukee and offered to provide whatever financial assistance the town could give to neighboring townships and villages that also fought the city.[69]

The battle over the Butler Strip also reached the state legislature. Assemblyman Leland McParland, who represented the south side industrial suburb of Cudahy and also served as attorney for the Town of Lake, which bordered Milwaukee to the south and was also threatened by annexation, introduced several bills seeking to delay annexation efforts by Milwaukee. McParland explicitly referred to the Butler Strip annexation so many times that assemblymen began to laugh when he would frequently hold up a map showing the annexation. While the state legislature took no action against Milwaukee, the forces of opposition were apparent there as well.[70]

On April 3, 1951, the state Supreme Court dealt Milwaukee's annexation efforts a serious blow when it ruled the Butler Strip annexation to be invalid. Justice Edward Gehl, who wrote the majority opinion in the case, ruled the annexation illegal because no referendum had been held in the annexed areas. In a ruling on another contested annexation to the south of the city, the court awarded 250 acres to the suburb of West Allis. This ruling implied the suburbs had the same rights to post notices of intent to annex as Milwaukee, thus reversing a 53-year-old law that had given Milwaukee the first right to post notices of intent to annex. Thanks to these court decisions, annexation would now become a "right" of any incorporated municipality that wished to pursue it.[71]

The threat to Milwaukee was obvious, and city officials were shocked and dismayed by the rulings. In a statement to the *Milwaukee Sentinel* in the aftermath of the ruling, Zeidler worried: "The city of Milwaukee is caught in a strangling grip. Caught in a similar situation, other American cities are slowly dying."[72] Later, in his memoirs written a year after he left office in 1960, Zeidler recalled that the day the Butler Strip was defeated by the Supreme Court was "a black day" for the city of Milwaukee. Krieger was asked to write an article in the July 1951 issue of *American City* magazine describing the Waukesha County satellite community, but with the Butler Strip annexation rendered null and void by the courts, the article sounded more like a wish than a plan.[73]

The defeat of the Butler Strip and the failed purchase of Greendale were not only severe blows to community planning and the concept of satellite cities. Zeidler, Krieger, Housing Authority Director Richard Perrin, and other city officials had expressly linked decentralization to a "three-tiered" approach to urban renewal, one in which peripheral building was to come in advance of slum clearance in the urban core. The satellite city would have contained a substantial low-income public housing component, a fact that suburban residents were equally well aware of. "Isn't Milwaukee trying to eliminate its slums and move them out here?" asked a resident of Waukesha County whose farm was in the path of the satellite city.[74]

Other factors complicated urban renewal during Zeidler's first term, but foremost among them was the persistent chorus of opposition to low-income public housing that reached a crescendo in 1951. Local realtors and other business groups had earlier opposed public housing as "socialistic," a charge that had more concrete meaning in a city that routinely elected Socialists like Hoan and Zeidler mayor. After World War II, anti–public housing groups were forced to tread more lightly around the ideology of public housing since it was clear that the general public overwhelmingly supported government-built housing for war veterans. In 1948, Milwaukeeans voted affirmative to a referendum that authorized the use of $3.5 million in municipal funds to build three veterans' projects. The Milwaukee Housing Authority built and managed the projects between 1948 and 1953. Two sites on the North Side eventually became the locations for Northlawn and Berryland, and a third on the South Side contained Southlawn. Combined, the three veterans' projects contained over 950 housing units in detached multiple-unit row houses. The wood frame buildings were austere, but were surrounded by considerable yard space. All three project sites were on the urban fringe, well outside of the city's grid extension. Each was also low-density, containing no more than seventeen people per acre, thus fitting neatly with local planning principles. Between 1948 and 1951, the city also built one new public housing project for low-income residents. At 726 units on an 81-acre site, Westlawn, on the far northwest side of Milwaukee, was the largest housing project Milwaukee ever built in terms of both units and site size. The simple vernacular architecture that colored the three veterans' projects also appeared in Westlawn's detached row homes.[75]

Zeidler had run for mayor, in part, on a commitment to provide over 10,000 units of affordable housing to the city of Milwaukee; thus Westlawn, Northlawn, Southlawn, and Berryland were only a small fraction of a larger and more gradual effort. As these initial projects came to completion, however, anti–public housing momentum was back in motion. At the forefront was an umbrella organization of local real estate interests who called themselves the "Affiliated Taxpayers Committee (ATC)." The ATC had been founded in 1938, after the first federal Housing Act of 1937 stipulated that new public housing projects would be built under the auspices of local housing authorities. In the law's wake, the Milwaukee Real Estate Board, the Savings and Loan League, the Building Owners and Managers Association, and the Milwaukee Association of Commerce formed the

ATC as a group dedicated to "promote efficiency in local government."[76] The real reason for the group's existence was to oppose public housing by calling into question the city's need for creating a housing authority. It succeeded in helping delay the creation of such an agency in Milwaukee for six years, until wartime urgencies won out in 1944. The ATC, however, kept up its oppositional rhetoric to public housing. In a 1945 survey the Common Council conducted to gauge the opinions of interested parties over the matter of housing and blight, the ATC argued that public housing benefited "a pitifully small percentage of Milwaukee's citizens" at exorbitant costs. The housing shortage would go away, noted the ATC, if the 1920 zoning ordinance that greatly limited the height of buildings was "relaxed or altered," thus allowing landowners to construct buildings that matched the high property tax assessments they apparently suffered under. The ATC even opposed veterans' housing, which was a mostly unpopular stance that forced the organization to reconsider its strategy in the late 1940s.[77]

The answer came in separating the issue of slum clearance, which businesses supported, from public housing, which they opposed. In early 1951, ATC members created a "Citizens Committee" that succeeded in placing two separate referendum questions on the city's election agenda. The first question pointedly asked voters to write "yes" or "no" to requiring the city to hold a referendum before each future individual housing project began. Theoretically, voters could approve popular veterans projects and vote against low-income projects. The second question asked if "slum clearance housing projects" should be built "irrespective of any other resolution or act." The wording of each referenda was confusing, and on April 3, 1951, voters sent Milwaukee government a mixed message of sorts, with a majority choosing "yes" on the question of slum clearance housing projects and also "yes" on the question of referenda prior to all future housing projects. The votes also confused city officials, who purposely delayed slum clearance in the 1950s, in part because they were unsure of its legalities. What was made clear by the two referenda, however, was that Zeidler's goal of 10,000 affordable units had little chance of succeeding. The three-tiered approach, once again, was complicated; "rehousing" families on the urban periphery was supposed to occur *in advance* of slum clearance. The ATC referenda ended up dictating the opposite; voters approved "slum clearance housing" but also would have to approve all future Westlawns or Waukesha County satellite cities.[78]

Remarkably but not coincidentally, voters participated in the public housing referenda the very same April week in which the Wisconsin Supreme Court shot down the Butler Strip annexation. Collectively, the incidents revealed that regardless of how unique Milwaukee's planning and redevelopment ideas were nationally, they clearly threatened existing boundaries in the region that a great many residents sought to maintain. Those boundaries hardened in the 1950s and as they did, became even more jealously guarded along class, and increasingly racial, lines. Rural and suburban opponents, who did not vote in the public housing referenda but almost certainly would have opposed public housing, cared less for the national exposure the satellite city received and far more for local control over growth. They even dismissed civil defense as an urban guise; as a Butler village official scoffed, "Milwaukee is only exploiting the current war crisis for its own ends."[79] The failed purchase of Greendale, in essence a satellite city half-made, also hinged on a kind of localism that implicitly defied the blessings of planning experts. When Clarence Stein published his tome to the greenbelt community in 1948, he made special mention of Greendale's local governance: "There has been exceptional leadership on the part of one of America's ablest town managers, Walter Kroening."[80] As one of the planners who had inspired the greenbelt program, Stein obviously took great pride in the community he had indirectly helped to develop and that Kroening administered. But ironically, many Greendale residents had come to perceive Kroening as a pawn of the federal government because of his complicity with the ALCDC's abortive purchase of the village. For their part, Milwaukee's officials had proven that they were not ignorant of the forces of decentralization that threatened the city's survival. But planned dispersal had yielded forces of local control that would remain prominent throughout the postwar era. Annexation became the most hotly debated and publicly prominent political issue in the region for the remainder of the 1950s, just as it had been in the 1920s.

Milwaukee's attempts to engage in planned decentralization did not end in April of 1951. But they had been dealt a serious blow. "Vacant lands" for satellite cities were not in fact empty; people who lived there often had very different ideas about the nature and trajectory of urban development. Arthur Werba and others may have still believed that the political unification of the region was "inevitable," as he had written at the close of the 1920s. But in reality, political unity was even less inevitable in 1951 than it had been in 1929. The postwar era would not be defined by planned decentralization, but instead by a race between city and suburbs to control urban growth on the periphery through annexations, consolidations, incorporations, petitions, lawsuits, injunctions, public meetings, referenda, and more devious means. The result would be not planned decentralization and political unity, but a great race for the highest and best uses of land that rapidly balkanized and suburbanized the political landscape of the Milwaukee metropolis.

Municipal Mercantilism

After the Wisconsin Supreme Court nullified Milwaukee's Butler Strip annexation, the region's annexation battles were fought in a different legal context, and large-scale community planning became much harder to implement. To comply with the court's reinterpretation of annexation law, the Wisconsin state legislature moved quickly to amend annexation procedures. By the middle of June 1951, the legislature hammered out new regulations that made the annexation process more publicly competitive than it ever had been. The new law stated that any incorporated municipality that sought annexation needed to post "notices of intent to annex" in at least eight public places (libraries, town halls, fire stations) within the towns where the proposed territory was located. Additionally, at least ten days before annexation petitions could be circulated, municipalities had to publish posting notices in a newspaper of "general circulation" within the county where the land in question was located.[1]

The new annexation laws applied to all cities and villages, regardless of size. Zeidler, most of the Milwaukee Common Council, and other city policy makers remained clear in their beliefs that annexation was absolutely necessary to the city's long-term health, no matter how shrill suburban opposition became. However, the strategy of obtaining massive parcels of land conducive to satellite city building had now failed twice, first with Greendale, then with the Butler Strip. City officials were forced to review their annexation policy in light of these setbacks. The internal reevaluation of annexation policy in 1951 took place alongside broader efforts at bureaucratic reform. Like the earlier generation of Milwaukee Socialists, Mayor Frank Zeidler believed strongly in municipal efficiency and gave great attention, especially during his first mayoral term, to technical experts. This resulted in the creation of a commission of economic experts who were to study the city's revenue sources and recommend policy based on its conclusions. The Commission on the Economic Study of Milwaukee released its report in 1948 just after Zeidler took office. It placed most of the revenue concerns on maximizing property tax returns, reinforcing Milwaukee policy makers' commitment to annexation and industrial development. The 240-page report also called for a detailed study of "the efficiency and methods by which city departments, bureaus, boards, and commissions were being conducted."[2] In reaction to the Commission's recommendations, the Common Council and Mayor Zeidler agreed in 1949 to appoint a team of consultants to monitor the city's government and to ensure that maximum efficiency and economy were being achieved in each department. The Chicago firm of Griffenhagen and Associates won the bidding and set to work on a comprehensive survey of the machinations of city government. To ensure that Griffenhagen's study was given proper attention, Zeidler and the Common Council formed a twelve member-committee to act as liaison between Griffenhagen and the Common Council. The makeup of the administrative survey committee reflected Zeidler's preference for appointing public servants and labor leaders to government commissions instead of business and civic elites. The Greater Milwaukee Committee, the permanent offshoot of the 1948 Corporation that had pushed for the city to reissue public improvement bonds, did not receive a seat on the survey committee, nor did the Milwaukee Real Estate Board. In fact, only two of the twelve seats went to representatives of business: members of the Downtown Association and the Milwaukee Association of Commerce. Instead, the committee consisted of representatives of organized labor (the AFL and CIO), and local public policy think tanks (the City Club, Citizens Governmental Research Bureau, and League of Women Voters). The remaining five seats were reserved for Zeidler, his budget supervisor, and three aldermen.[3]

Initially, the Administrative Survey Committee's task was to ensure that cost-saving measures recommended by the Griffenhagen consultants were executed, and in 1950 and 1951, the city of Milwaukee did manage to save an estimated $250,000 in various bureaucratic reforms.[4] However, after the Wisconsin Supreme Court's nullification of the Butler Strip annexation and subsequent reinterpretation of state annexation laws in April of 1951, the survey committee turned its attention to the problem of annexation. They chose George Saffran, secretary to the committee and budget supervisor of the city of Milwaukee, to prepare a detailed report evaluating Milwaukee's annexation program. Saffran's report, released in 1952, perceived annexation as an increasingly uphill battle, and it revealed a growing divide between the city's annexation and planning officials. The report recalled the success of annexation in the 1920s, and acknowledged the cessation of annexation activities in 1932 as "shortsighted," since Milwaukee's population density had crept back up during the war, forcing city officials to reestablish the Department of Annexation. Since annexation's return in 1946, Milwaukee had gained an additional 7.78 square miles, a scant total that did not keep up with the region's peripheral expansion.[5]

Saffran's report revealed a growing rift in Milwaukee's policy-making circles over the nature of annexation. City planners in the Board of Public Land Commissioners (BPLC), led by chief planner Elmer Krieger, favored taking in huge chunks of land at a time. Krieger made this preference known in a variety of memos and reports, especially amplified in his now in-limbo site plan for the Waukesha County satellite city.[6] Large-scale annexations of the kind attempted with the Butler Strip were clearly more useful to the formation of planned communities. Planners could monitor land uses. Industry, residences, commerce, and public parks could all be included in new land plans from these types of annexations. Any chance the city had of engaging in cooperative housing, or in owning and leasing public land for community development, both of which Zeidler preferred, seemed to lie, at least to BPLC planners, in large-scale annexations. Saffran acknowledged these planning impulses in his report, noting that piecemeal annexation created more "animosity" and resulted in uneven deployment of city services. For the Department of Annexation, however, large-scale annexations were unrealistic and heavy-handed. Assembling massive parcels of land required convincing a dizzying number of property owners to join with Milwaukee, and it was exceedingly rare to find that type of consensus across larger geographical areas. Large annexations also gave suburban officials more ammunition in their characterization of the city as a monster bent on gobbling up as much land as possible. Cantankerous Arthur Werba, the city's lead annexation official, had already threatened to retire on numerous occasions, often due to stress from the negative publicity heaped on him as the region's main lightning rod of annexation.[7] For these reasons, during the remainder of the 1950s, Milwaukee officials did not try such ambitious satellite city planning schemes. Instead, they continued to annex smaller parcels of land, and simultaneously tried to convince neighboring unincorporated towns to merge with the city.

In spite of the increasing difficulty that Milwaukee's annexation program now faced, Mayor Zeidler's administration remained committed to planned decentralization and political unification as the best way to direct future urban growth. In a new report on annexation released in 1952, BPLC planners again registered the conviction that taking in vacant land on the urban periphery went hand-in-hand with inner city redevelopment. The nature of annexation had changed but the underpinning motivations remained. City policy makers remained convinced that residents—regardless of class—increasingly desired single-family homes on larger lots. If there was any doubt of this, studies of the type completed by the Milwaukee County Regional Planning Department in 1946 made this reality quite clear. "It's precisely because city people don't like dirt and congestion that they want their city to grow by expanding into open fields, where there would be room for a better kind of city life," wrote William Norris, a journalist at the *Milwaukee Sentinel* who strongly favored annexation.[8] Even Socialists like Daniel Hoan, Charles Whitnall, and Frank Zeidler accepted lower densities as an article of faith in city-building. The problem was to ensure it took place within a greatly enlarged metropolitan Milwaukee. Throughout the late 1940s and the 1950s, Zeidler never wavered from this goal. Court rulings that struck down annexations altered but did not end Milwaukee's physical expansion. What ultimately halted Milwaukee's postwar horizontal growth in its tracks was the process that eventually eclipsed the metropolitan visions of city leaders and is taken up in the remainder of this chapter: the postwar wave of political incorporations of outlying territories that sealed the city off from expanding its territory. In the fifteen years after World War II, an "iron ring" of suburbs (a term city officials first coined derisively) enclosed Milwaukee. City officials specifically perceived the individual acts of incorporation as "suburbanization," and in political terms, this was accurate enough. Virtually all of the incorporations that occurred adjacent to Milwaukee's borders in the postwar era were intended to stave off annexation. None went uncontested by the city.

Political fragmentation was a national phenomenon that occurred most rapidly in the twentieth century, and it amplified what a growing number of urban scholars term "uneven development." This generally refers to the unequal distribution of economic resources across metropolitan areas in the United States. Numerous studies by sociologists and urban historians tie suburban economic growth to central city stagnation or decline. Usually, they focus on overt practices by private market forces, unchecked or implicitly tolerated by public officials, to ensure that racial segregation and spatial exclusion remained in place. Uneven development thus became economically encoded along familiar lines of race and class. When historians study efforts to increase opportunity and redistribute resources more democratically, they usually place these stories in the larger context of the postwar effort by racial minorities to win political and economic power denied them for generations. These movements often took place in central cities with shrinking resources available to attack the broader economic inequalities that uneven development strengthened. Studies of this type address the socioeconomic problems that uneven development fostered instead of looking at how metropolitan inequality manifested itself in the first place.[9]

The *process* by which the fragmentation of metropolitan America took place is equally important, and it took different forms in different regions. Metropolitan fragmentation is a matter of both degree and kind, tied not only to national policy but also to state laws and local decisions by thousands of individuals. In the Milwaukee region, the bruising annexation wars of the late 1940s and 1950s gave a specific shape to political balkanization. From 1948 to 1960, eleven communities in the Milwaukee region politically incorporated as cities or villages, and all immediately became "suburbs" by their location adjacent to the city of Milwaukee or within the Milwaukee metropolitan area. In virtually all eleven cases, incorporation was a direct reaction to Milwaukee's annexation efforts, which doubled the city's size by the end of the 1950s. Annexation struggles between city and suburb gripped the Milwaukee region during the postwar era. These battles took place at precisely the moment when regional planning and cooperation was perhaps most needed. Milwaukee's private sector civic and business organizations launched efforts to attract industry to the region and promote economic development. These groups' strict subscription to laissez-faire economic conservatism contrasted sharply with Frank Zeidler's liberal/socialist politics, further preventing public-private political cooperation. As meaningful terms, "regionalism" or "metropolitanism" were increasingly abstractions in 1950s Milwaukee.

The structure of fiscal inequality within the metropolitan area deserves more attention. The decisions that contributed to the creation of new suburbs or the consolidation of towns with the city of Milwaukee were tied to an increasingly aggressive pursuit of tax revenues by municipalities in the postwar years. In a key study of metropolitan financing in the Milwaukee region conducted in 1970, Donald Curran, an economist at Cleveland State University, characterized the municipal policies of unincorporated towns and incorporated cities and villages of the region as forms of "municipal mercantilism" that divided the region and politically codified economic inequality.[10] "In the scramble for limited goods" noted Curran, "the success of one locality is at the expense of its neighbor."[11] Curran borrowed the term *municipal mercantilism* from Robert C. Wood's famed study of the New York City region, *1400 Governments*.[12] Wood's term is a useful analytical framework from which to examine Milwaukee's postwar suburbanization. While in hindsight the 1950s often appear to have been an era of limitless economic growth, the picture becomes more complicated when specific metropolitan areas are examined. The industrial Midwest grew at a far slower rate than the South and the West, a fact of which urban leaders of the Midwest were becoming painfully aware. The "rising tide" of America's postwar economy was not lifting all municipal boats to the same levels. Making matters worse, central cities were beginning to feel the fiscal effects of population loss to the periphery, where the number of incorporated suburban municipalities increased dramatically.

The relatively slower growth of the urban Midwest, even in the midst of the booming 1950s, made local leaders redouble their efforts to maximize tax revenues to pay for the costs of public improvements. Urban leaders addressed disinvestment in a variety of ways, with local circumstance dictating each urban development effort. In St. Louis, for example, local elites opted to rebuild vast swaths of the city's urban core to stem decentralization, in part, at least, because the city's borders had been locked in for decades, making physical expansion impossible. Pittsburgh's annexation program had long stalled as well, making central city revitalization the key component of that city's "Renaissance." The city of Detroit flirted briefly with large-scale annexation in the late 1940s, but Michigan state laws thwarted that city's efforts. In contrast, Milwaukee's borders remained fluid in the postwar era, making annexation viable and city-suburban confrontation over growth virtually inevitable, considering the annexation conflicts of the 1950s. These intra-metropolitan conflicts occurred as the urban Midwest first began to truly struggle economically. This made the tax revenues that each municipality so desperately craved finite. Job growth in one locale often meant a corresponding job loss in another community within the Milwaukee region. "Municipal mercantilism," then, consisted of a heated competition between local governments—city and suburban—to capture the maximum amount of tax revenues at minimal costs. In this competition, city and suburban governments sought the "highest and best" land uses to obtain the optimum public wealth.[13]

Both state and local revenue distribution dictated municipal mercantilism. In 1911, the state of Wisconsin levied its first income tax and created a revenue distribution formula that was heavily weighted to return the taxes to the location of origin. The state kept only 10 percent of income taxes it collected, returning 20 percent to the county of origin, and 70 percent to the city, village, or town of origin. In 1947, the state legislature barred its municipalities from levying income taxes of their own, ensuring the state tax would "grow unobstructed."[14] In general, this usually worked to the suburbs' advantage. Because the state distribution formula returned such a high proportion of income taxes to place of residence, rather than location of employment, for example, it favored high-income municipalities where a large number of affluent residents resided. Curran calculated that in Milwaukee County from 1920 to 1970, the suburbs' per-capita shared income tax revenues increased by 1,413 percent, compared to 935 percent for the city of Milwaukee.[15] The state also assessed the value of utility properties, collected the utility property tax and utility sales tax (which were counted together), and distributed the revenues under a formula that favored the municipality where the utility was located. For example, the massive Lakeside electric power plant in the unincorporated Town of Lake, which yielded hundreds of thousands of dollars a year in tax revenues, paid its sales and property tax to the state, which then kept 15 percent of the revenue, returning 20 percent to Milwaukee County and 65 percent to the Town of Lake. The city of Milwaukee, whose residents were by far the Lakeside plant's largest consumer, got almost nothing. Dating back to the 1920s, residents of Lake who lived near the Lakeside Plant repeatedly attempted to incorporate as a separate village, but Milwaukee officials had managed to thwart their efforts in court.[16]

Shared taxes collected by the state of Wisconsin were important sources of public revenue, but local property taxes remained the largest revenue stream for municipalities. As a result, industrial land remained the most highly sought-after commodity by many annexing municipalities, especially Milwaukee, since it yielded the highest land values as well as corporate income tax returns. Industry also demanded comparatively little in public services, especially schools. Incorporated communities with large concentrations of industry, such as the city of West Allis and the village of West Milwaukee, almost always contained high volumes of modest working-class residences. At the close of World War II, communities that were primarily residential in character, with little or no industry, tended to consist almost exclusively of middle- to high-income homes. In varying degrees, each of the North Shore suburbs—Shorewood, Whitefish Bay, Fox Point, and River Hills—had established themselves as premier residential neighborhoods with the subsequent homes that yielded high property tax returns. Wauwatosa, less affluent than the North Shore suburbs but still prosperous, also had long prided itself as a quintessential bedroom suburb, a "city of homes," and virtually no major industrial property was contained within its boundaries. To the south and west, the city of West Allis and the village of West Milwaukee both had long existed as industrial tax havens for local manufacturers. The fiscal largesse created by corporate income taxes and returned from the state allowed West Milwaukee to not levy any property taxes at all, a fact that did not escape Mayor Zeidler's watchful eye. "Those plants could be helping support schools or other services in Milwaukee or West Allis," he noted in 1951.[17]

Methods of increasing public wealth had changed little in the twentieth century, but the historical circumstances under which public wealth was gained had changed. The pressure of the baby boom in the postwar years altered the fiscal realities of municipal governance across the Milwaukee metropolis. As birth rates exploded after 1945, local governments came under tremendous pressure to build new schools to accommodate the sudden influx of children. The public costs of providing education to this postwar generation of children proved startling, especially for communities that housed high densities of modest-income families and thus collected lower proportions of tax revenue. As a 1957 city report noted, "A $12,000, $15,000, or even a $20,000 home does not produce enough in tax revenue to pay for keeping a single child in elementary school."[18] Municipalities thus became ever more determined to secure the most public revenue as possible to offset the rising fiscal costs of service provision. Accordingly, each individual community sought as never before to attain, as Curran put it, "the most profitable land uses and land users" to produce the most revenue and demand as few municipal services as possible.[19]

In the contest to develop the highest and best uses of land, it was clear that some incorporated communities had already major built-in advantages over others. By the middle of the twentieth century, the North Shore suburbs had already established themselves as affluent communities whose expensive housing stock, especially near Lake Michigan, offset the absence of industry. West Milwaukee's residents were overwhelmingly working-class, but the heavy concentration of industry within the village's borders allowed it to levy no property taxes. For this reason, West Milwaukee remained highly appealing to manufacturers.[20]

Conversely, communities that housed large numbers of modest- or low-income families were in more dire fiscal straits. Modest homes on smaller lots did not produce sufficient tax revenue, and higher-density neighborhoods meant there would likely be far more children who would attend school, but without adequate property tax revenue to pay for it. The city of Milwaukee most obviously fit this bill; the quest to annex land was thus strongly motivated by the need to increase the city's property tax revenues. However, other communities felt the fiscal crunch as well. West Allis, whose population had swelled to 42,959 residents by 1950, the seventh highest in the state, was poised to take advantage of the state legislature's liberalization of annexation laws to take in more land, as was Wauwatosa.[21]

Meanwhile, unincorporated towns, vulnerable to annexation, desperately sought to protect their revenue-enhancing assets. In 1951, residents of a large part of the Town of Milwaukee, which had already shrunk in size after the creation of the North Shore villages, voted to incorporate into the city of Glendale.[22] The new city encompassed the growing industrial corridor north and east along both the Milwaukee River and the Chicago and Northwestern railroad line. The birth of the city of Glendale blocked Milwaukee's annexation to the north and east, and essentially placed a fence around some of the most valuable industrial land in the region. "We have seen 3,000 people in the new city of Glendale take millions of dollars of industrial property into their taxing areas to virtually eliminate their residential taxes," Zeidler lamented in the wake of Glendale's incorporation.[23] The same fiscal logic drove residents of the eastern portion of the Town of Lake to incorporate as the village of St. Francis. The inspiration for the new village was the Lakeside power plant, which produced over $300,000 a year in utility tax revenues. In terms of class, Glendale and St. Francis had modest housing stocks; their residents were mostly middle- and working-class, similar to tens of thousands of city of Milwaukee residents. However, the dictates of municipal mercantilism divided people according to political boundary, not class, further exemplifying that, as Curran concluded, "the common needs of the metropolitan area are not only neglected but are directly obstructed."[24]

Perhaps foremost among the "common needs" of the metropolis was continuing the economic growth that the wartime boom had spawned. Influential local civic groups, alarmed by the decline of land values in and around downtown Milwaukee, had taken urban development to heart during the 1940s. The Greater Milwaukee Committee (GMC) strongly pushed for the city to go back into debt, which the city had avoided since the Depression, to finance a variety of public improvements, including a veterans' war memorial and art museum along the lakefront, expansion of the Milwaukee Public Library, and a system of expressways to improve transportation within Milwaukee County. The GMC had already managed to bring the issue of public debt to a citywide referendum in 1947, which pointedly asked Milwaukeeans whether the city should issue bonds again. The debt referendum passed over the objections of many city officials, including Mayor John Bohn, and soon-to-be-mayor Frank Zeidler. While the public improvement program made headway in the 1950s with the construction of Milwaukee County Stadium, the lakefront war memorial, and the construction of a new museum and a library addition, leaders of both the public and private sectors continued to search for other ways to jump-start economic development.

From the beginning of his three terms in office in 1948, Mayor Zeidler favored aggressive annexation of land with industrial potential as the surest way for the city to benefit from industrial expansion. The Butler Strip satellite city proposal, which sought to capture valuable land along the Chicago and Northwestern Railroad, was the most prominent example of the use of annexation as a tool to capture industrial development. However, the new legal environment that placed suburbs on a more equal footing with Milwaukee in matters of annexation, coupled with the new postwar fiscal realities of municipal mercantilism, virtually guaranteed Milwaukee's neighboring communities would just as actively seek out the same potential industrial land uses. Attracting industry yielded the highest tax revenues at the lowest public costs, making it the "highest and best" land use available in the dictates of public finance.

The open competition for industry between Milwaukee and its suburbs greatly complicated the role of the region's oldest and most prominent private sector economic development generator, the Milwaukee Association of Commerce (MAC). Founded in 1861 as the Merchants Association, a consortium of prominent local commercial businesses, the group merged with the Manufacturers Association in 1894 to form the MAC, whose goal throughout most of the twentieth century was to "safeguard and promote the economic advancement and welfare of commercial and civic enterprises in Milwaukee."[25] The MAC was active in local politics, coexisting uneasily with Socialist Mayor Daniel Hoan in promoting annexation and metropolitan political unification during the 1920s and 1930s. By the close of World War II, the MAC had grown into an extremely heterogeneous organization, comprising over 3,000 business and professional firms, many of which were located outside the city of Milwaukee.[26] This made the MAC the most naturally "metropolitan" organization in the region, a potential mediator between the various warring local governments. However, during the years following World War II, the MAC's Board of Directors chose to stay out of the region's endless annexation controversies. Instead the MAC adopted the appearance of a broader group above the fray. They promoted an apolitical image of a "Greater Milwaukee," where politics never interfered with employment harmony and production. By 1964, the MAC even changed its name to reflect its status as a metropolitan organization, reinventing itself as the Metropolitan Milwaukee Association of Commerce.

In reality, the MAC's nonpartisanship was only skin-deep. The association's leaders consistently displayed political conservatism on multiple levels. The MAC's National Affairs Division voted to endorse and oppose a variety of federal legislation. For example, the Board of Directors vocally spoke out against the Wagner Housing Act of 1949, claiming it threatened to "socialize real estate" by taking a large chunk of building away from the private market. The Board endorsed the U.S. House on Un-American

Activities Committee as a way "to bring to light subversive elements in our economy." In 1949, the MAC Board of Directors opposed repeal of the Taft-Hartley Act, opposed the Marshall Plan, opposed any minimum wage over 60 cents an hour, and opposed expansion of Social Security.[27]

In local matters, the MAC remained ostensibly nonpartisan, but proved politically influential in obvious ways. Through the Affiliated Taxpayers' Committee (ATC), which had played the key role in fighting public housing's expansion, the MAC and each of the region's real estate interest associations could support and oppose local measures as they saw fit while appearing to remain outside of local politics. The MAC's relationship with such a partisan group came to rankle some of its leaders by the postwar years. Clifford Randall, an MAC board member and prominent local businessman, repeatedly called for the MAC to break all direct ties to the ATC, recognizing its betrayal of the MAC's political independence. "Officials of city and county government view the attitude and position of the Committee as primarily that of the Association of Commerce," Randall warned in 1950. MAC leadership agreed to withdraw from the ATC, but remained "against public housing at all levels of government."[28]

The MAC's deep conservatism also pervaded its marketing of Milwaukee to the rest of the state of Wisconsin. Historian Elizabeth Fones-Wolf has noted that the 1950s witnessed an unprecedented effort by American businesses to promote capitalism as a way to undermine labor activism and socialism.[29] Milwaukee's businesses proved no exception. In 1952, the MAC's American Opportunity Committee launched its first annual "Business-Agriculture Day," inviting hundreds of farmers from around the state to Milwaukee to tour the city's factories and listen to lectures on economics, to better learn about the interconnectedness between farming and manufacturing. Over 800 farmers and their spouses attended the first "Business-Agriculture Day," about double the number expected.[30] In essence, the MAC–sponsored event counteracted subversive political ideologies by championing laissez-faire capitalism. William A. Mann, chairman of the Opportunity Committee and the event's key organizer, called the event's deeper purpose the purging of "false prophets" who said that Americans needed to abandon the "free enterprise system." The event drew over 1,300 farmers in 1953 and continued for several years. The free enterprise message remained its theme. With similar motivations, in 1956 the MAC took its free enterprise indoctrination to the classroom, holding a "Business Education Day" for local teachers.[31]

On a national level, the MAC assumed the task of attracting industry to Milwaukee to fill vacant plant space used by World War II defense industries. The effort accompanied a broader plan to "stimulate the establishment of main or branch plants in the Milwaukee area" by marketing Milwaukee's industrial prowess to the rest of the nation. In 1946, the MAC produced a brochure titled "Milwaukee Has Everything—for Profitable Industry, for Enjoyable Living!" that characterized Milwaukee as a nearly perfect place to do business. The brochure went to great lengths to play down labor unease, focusing instead on the impressive productivity of Milwaukee's manufacturers. The promotion included implicitly nativist language to describe the region's workforce. Milwaukee County "boasted" the nation's second highest percentage of native whites, the brochure reminded its readers. In 1946 and 1947, the MAC sent over 15,000 copies of "Milwaukee Has Everything . . ." to various businesses around the nation, hoping to attract industry to the region.[32] In the process, the MAC ignored the reality of the region's labor relations. In 1946, thousands of workers struck at the Allis-Chalmers plant in West Allis, and the long strike proved labor militancy had by no means subsided in the region.[33]

Despite (or perhaps because of) the MAC's invention of Milwaukee as a veritable business Garden of Eden, industrial promotion was initially successful after World War II. In 1947, the region gained a clear victory when two manufacturers, the General Electric X-Ray Division and Hotpoint, Inc., a producer of kitchen appliances, announced their intentions to locate a great portion of their manufacturing operations in the Milwaukee region. A year later, the MAC won an even bigger industrial prize with the announcement that General Motors' AC Spark Plug Division intended to purchase a large, multi-story plant on Prospect Avenue in Milwaukee's East Side, where it was to build bombing navigational equipment. The plant would eventually employ over 5,000 workers, a huge economic coup for the city. In 1950, success continued when two more sizeable manufacturers, American Can Company and Continental Can Company, revealed that they intended to build large manufacturing facilities in the Milwaukee area. Each plant would employ over 1,000 workers.[34]

The MAC's initial success in attracting industry to Milwaukee belied deep political divisions in the region. The race to gain the highest and best land uses meant that every new plant attracted to the metropolis was essentially up for grabs. When G.E. X-Ray and Hotpoint decided to locate their new plants in the unincorporated Town of Greenfield, nearby communities engaged in a veritable feeding frenzy to annex the land where the plants would be built. Milwaukee, West Allis, and West Milwaukee each competed over this land. The Town of Greenfield's leaders tried to convince the companies to stand pat and not be annexed away from the town. In 1950, West Milwaukee won the prize, announcing the annexation of a parcel of land that encompassed G.E. X-Ray, Hotpoint, and eight other factories. The village levied no property taxes, and this was no doubt a key advantage in the minds of the annexed companies, who as landowners could sign the annexation petitions.[35] Staying out of the city of Milwaukee was an equally strong motivator. For West Milwaukee, the ten new plants produced sizeable corporate income tax revenue, and as the village's attorney gleefully noted, "They don't have any children to make demands on the school facilities."[36] For their part, Greenfield's town leaders begged the industrial firms to stay. Spurned West Allis officials even sent a delegation to Chicago to try and convince General Electric executives to change their minds, but to no avail. The annexation robbed the Town of Greenfield of over a third of its public revenues, while reminding Milwaukee's city leaders how difficult it would be to attract industry. A further reminder came in 1951, when the Town of Granville sued the city of Milwaukee over an annexation that had brought the American Can Company's new plant into Milwaukee.[37]

The MAC may have acted as a nonpartisan promoter of the entire metropolitan area, but political conflicts within the region clearly complicated the group's efforts. Attracting large new corporations such as G.E. X-Ray and Hotpoint created jobs, but also intensified municipal mercantilism. Both companies displayed an unwillingness to locate within the city of Milwaukee. More ominously, the MAC's vocal support of laissez-faire conservatism put it at loggerheads with Milwaukee's public officials, especially Mayor Zeidler. Neither side found sympathy for the other's politics; both coexisted uneasily at best. Ideologically pitted against the MAC's logic of purely "free enterprise" was Mayor Zeidler's contention that the "purpose of a city is solely to advance human progress. The primary purpose of a city should be to help as many of its inhabitants as possible ... even to the point of being substantially taxed." In its promotional material, the MAC barely acknowledged the city's long and sterling record of municipal efficiency and service delivery. The MAC's Board of Directors remained silent on the matter of annexation, which was a reversal of its vocal support in the 1920s. Through the Affiliated Taxpayer's Committee, other groups obstructed Zeidler's attempts to expand low-income public housing in the city. For his part, Zeidler ignored the city's business leaders "whenever he could," filling his appointive positions with labor leaders, academics, clergy, and other public officials.[38] Across the nation, postwar urban policy may well have been dominated by public-private partnerships, dubbed "growth coalitions."[39] No such consensus existed in Milwaukee during this time. Werba frequently accused uncooperative local industry of "tax dodging." Zeidler recalled in his memoirs that early in his tenure as mayor, when attending a social function sponsored by a group of local industrial leaders, "I was not uncomfortable in their presence, but I could see that these men moved in a stratum of society into which I had never entered."[40] While the MAC continued to push a conservative agenda through a variety of venues, the Zeidler administration battled it out with its neighboring cities, villages, and towns, escalating the city-suburban conflict to ever greater heights.

On July 9, 1951, Wisconsin Governor Walter Kohler signed the state legislature's reworked annexation bill into law, giving incorporated municipalities virtual parity in enacting annexation.[41] In Milwaukee County, the new law almost instantly set off a race to post notices of intent to annex all over the region. The first salvo came not from municipal governments, but from a group determined to save the financially troubled interurban transit line that ran from Milwaukee to the city of Waukesha. Two months after the new annexation bill became a law, five individuals announced that they had posted notices of intent for the city of Milwaukee to annex a whopping thirty-eight-square-mile stretch of territory in the Towns of Greenfield, Wauwatosa, and Franklin in Milwaukee County, and the Towns of New Berlin and Brookfield in Waukesha County. The proposed annexation was conditional on the city of Milwaukee's agreeing to purchase and operate the Milwaukee-Waukesha interurban line, formerly owned by the Milwaukee Rapid Transit and Speedrail Company, which had recently announced the abandonment of all operations and was about to have its assets liquidated. Part of the interurban route was in the path of the proposed new expressway that was to run west from downtown Milwaukee. Robert Crawford, the leader of the transit riders, acknowledged that the sole purpose of the gimmick was to save the rapid transit line. "We do not want annexation unless the rapid transit line will run again," Crawford announced.[42]

The transit riders' request placed Zeidler's administration in a difficult position. On one hand, an opportunity to annex a huge chunk of land had fallen into the city's lap, one that could conceivably open up a new corridor of growth well to the south and west of the city. Conversely, the new annexation meant the city had to assume the great cost of publicly operating what had been a privately run system. Between 1946 and 1951, five different companies had purchased the rapid transit line, hoping to run it at a profit; none had success.[43] The purchase of the interurban was to Mayor Zeidler a "large order" that would require a citywide referendum to be made legal. Circulating annexation petitions in such a massive and unwieldy piece of land would take at least a year and, even if the petitions successfully circulated (a dubious prospect, at best), there was no guarantee the sale of the transit line would go through. Perhaps equally important, political will to save older mass transit systems was already in the process of evaporating. Wisconsin Avenue, downtown Milwaukee's busiest commercial street, had recently been stripped of its trolley tracks, which had been replaced with busses. With older forms of mass transit in the process of being dismantled, saving the region's interurban trains was not a high priority for Milwaukee's policy makers, who had for a long time tied the city's transportation future to the automobile. The success of Charles Whitnall's parkway system had spurred hopes that traffic congestion, an increasingly troubling problem, could be solved by further accommodation of the automobile. In 1946, a committee of Milwaukee County officials released a comprehensive plan of expressways that, once funded, would tie the region together in all directions.[44] City leaders, cognizant of the decaying of downtown Milwaukee, hoped the expressways would improve access both into and out of the city. Zeidler even believed that expressway construction in Milwaukee's inner city could help *eliminate* substandard housing altogether. In 1953, Zeidler told the Common Council "new trafficways [sic] tend to force destruction of decaying buildings and can redevelop entire neighborhoods altogether."[45] Since expressways seemed so important to the city's future, the task of reinvigorating other forms of mass transit was not in the realm of political reality.

Milwaukee officials did not pursue the rapid transit annexation, but its announcement was ill timed because it came on the heels of a pronouncement by the city that it had posted a notice of intent to annex twenty-seven square miles of land in the Town of Granville. If executed, the annexation would swallow up all but four square miles of the town. Werba tried to cushion the blow by stating he had no realistic aims on all of the land in Granville, hoping instead to slowly convince property owners in various parts of the town to join the city. However, both annexation postings fed into suburban mistrust. In the minds of the outlying cities, villages, and towns, once again Milwaukee's expansion amounted to nothing more than municipal hegemony. Sylvester Claas, president of the Towns of Menomonee-Brookfield Advancement Association, who had been instrumental in opposing the satellite city and Butler Strip annexation, scoffed at the newest postings as nothing more than a "bluff" by the city to secure additional land.[46] A resident of the unincorporated community of Hales Corners, located in the Town of Greenfield and now in the path of potential annexation to Milwaukee, noted that his community sought to incorporate as a village specifically due to deep fears of Milwaukee's annexation program. An official of the Town of Greenfield called the rapid transit annexation "an awful crazy scheme."[47] The *Milwaukee Journal*, the city's afternoon newspaper, conducted random telephone checks of residents within the combined areas posted for annexation to Milwaukee and announced that affected residents "hated" the idea of becoming city residents.[48]

The initial postings set off a frenzy of legal activity during the winter of 1951–1952. A group of municipal attorneys who represented a variety of suburbs in Milwaukee County immediately challenged the rapid transit annexation posting's legality in court. The city of West Allis, eager to gain more public revenue, announced that it had posted a notice of intent to annex over thirteen square miles in the Town of Greenfield. Residents of the unincorporated community of Hales Corners, located on territory posted for annexation to Milwaukee, decided to try to incorporate, an action that succeeded after a referendum in January of 1952. Other municipalities jumped into the fray. The city of Wauwatosa posted notices of intent to annex eight square miles in the Town of Wauwatosa. The village of Butler, once in favor of consolidating with Milwaukee, but now a bitter foe of annexation, posted for eight square miles of land on the western edge of Milwaukee County. In early 1952, residents of a northern portion of the shrinking Town of Milwaukee incorporated as the village of Bayside. By June of 1952, Milwaukee and a variety of incorporated suburbs had posted all of Milwaukee County for annexation, save thirteen square miles in the rural Town of Franklin. Many of the postings overlapped, virtually guaranteeing legal conflicts.[49]

The reaction of city officials was predictably steadfast; Mayor Zeidler refused to let up on annexation, even in the spring of 1952 when he was running for reelection, warning, "Milwaukee must and will fight for its right to grow." For their part, the city of Milwaukee's residents gave Zeidler an apparent mandate on the issue of annexation, returning him to a second term by an overwhelming margin. In his second inaugural address to the Common Council, Zeidler made the annexation conflict his top issue, repeating that its best resolution was political unification of the entire metropolis.[50]

The posting race sped up the annexation wars, but the conflict's dimensions were remarkably similar to those of previous city-suburban confrontations. On June 13, 1952, a group of state legislators who represented various parts of Milwaukee County convened a summit of civic leaders, including mayors, municipal attorneys, real estate developers, and other civic officials, to discuss annexation conflicts. Thirty-three individuals attended the all-day meeting. Mayor Zeidler led off the proceedings with a lengthy statement defending Milwaukee's expansion. He warned that the posting race threatened to upset the economic development of the entire region. The problem of physical growth was a metropolitan issue, Zeidler said, but it tore the region apart instead of melding it together.[51] Suburban leaders disagreed. George Schmus, city attorney for West Allis and a vocal opponent of Milwaukee's annexation, believed that resistance to annexation was a matter of political philosophy and that residents outside of Milwaukee

CHART 6-1	Total Square Miles of Land Posted for Notice of Intent to Annex, August 1951– April 1952

Village or City	Amount of Land Posted
City of Milwaukee	76 Square Miles
City of West Allis	28 Square Miles
City of Wauwatosa	12 Square Miles
City of Glendale	Posted Entire Town of Milwaukee
Village of Butler	13 Square Miles
City of Cudahy	2 Square Miles

Source: George Saffran, "Annexation Practices in Milwaukee County: An Administrative Analysis," 1952, MPL.

"preferred to raise their families in smaller, more efficient and responsive communities."[52] The city's plans were "tremendous in scope," said Schmus, claiming (accurately) that an anonymous city official told him Milwaukee wanted to add well over seventy-five square miles of land in the 1950s.[53] Other suburban officials grilled Zeidler on the abortive satellite city plans for Waukesha County, calling the plan "forced annexation." As they had before, local developers remained supporters of annexation; a representative of the Milwaukee Board of Realtors characterized Milwaukee's annexation plans as "proper and right."[54] Town officials registered the greatest alarm. The posting race threatened to "annihilate" town government within the metropolis, noted William Kay, an attorney for the Town of Wauwatosa. The only recourse for towns was to incorporate as cities, but most did not have the population density requirements necessary to do so.[55]

The annexation summit resolved virtually nothing. As Zeidler had noted, the fiscal structure that encouraged municipal mercantilism was at root a problem only the state legislature could address, and it seemed unwilling to do so. Absent any reform at the state level, the annexation wars continued with the same allies rounded up on both sides. The city of Milwaukee's strongest carrot to coax annexation remained cheap water and sewage installations. As before, this placed city officials in a curious partnership with real estate developers in the region. The Milwaukee Real Estate Board had obstructed Zeidler's public housing program at every turn, but remained

committed to annexation because of the money it saved in residential development. "The cost of raw land is the same wherever you go," a developer told the *Milwaukee Journal* in 1949, but to install water pumps, wells,
and septic tanks for a single home in an unincorporated town cost nearly
$1,000. "In the city," the developer noted, water and sewers installations on
a forty-five-foot lot cost about $200, meaning that, "The saving—and ulti-
mate result in a lower priced house—is obvious."[56] Developers saved so much
money from annexation to the city of Milwaukee that they occasionally went
to extraordinary lengths to convince town residents to sign annexation petitions. One resident of a home located in an area posted for annexation to Milwaukee resisted joining the city because he claimed he could not afford the
increased assessments that were to accompany water and sewer installation
once the land around his home was connected to Milwaukee. The development company that sought annexation responded by giving the recalcitrant
resident a "gift" of $435 to cover the increased assessments. Episodes such
as this were rare; many town residents—especially those with more modest
means—saw the benefits of annexation without monetary bribes.[57]

Developers built thousands of modest homes on newly annexed land on
Milwaukee's northwest and south sides in the 1950s, ultimately cushioning
population decline in ensuing decades. However, the public costs of these
improvements were beginning to overwhelm the city's ability to provide
adequate services. Infrastructure improvements of the type that developers
so strongly favored usually cost more than the city assessed its new residents, a fact that did not go unnoticed by aldermen who represented older
districts in the city. Milton McGuire, president of the Common Council and
Zeidler's most vocal critic within the city, warned that the inner wards of the
city could not continue to subsidize development of the periphery through
their property taxes.[58] Another inner city alderman, Mathias Schimenz of
the Fifth Ward, complained that the city was essentially subsidizing the real
estate industry through its inexpensive service provisions. If Milwaukee annexed even 10 percent of the land it had posted for, the alderman claimed,
the city would "go broke."[59] The logic of municipal mercantilism held that
modest homes on relatively small lots, which developers were constructing
in unprecedented numbers in Milwaukee in the postwar era, did not come
close to paying for what they demanded in city services. Supporters of annexation were quite cognizant of this problem. William Norris, a columnist
for the *Milwaukee Sentinel* and for years a strong supporter of annexation,
warned in a column written in the fall of 1952 that the preponderance of
new residential homes threatened to plunge the city into "municipal bankruptcy."[60] The city desperately needed to acquire industry and businesses

to offset its new costs. Suburban municipalities operated under the same apparent fiscal logic, however, almost guaranteeing uneven development in the absence of political unification.

Slowly, almost imperceptibly, class lines began to harden as the annexation wars continued, lines that often were creations of government. Developers did not merely respond to privately created "market forces" in their land planning decisions. The city of Milwaukee's policy of public improvements encouraged developers to build in the smallest lots the 1920 zoning ordinance had allowed, which remained forty-foot frontages in the 1950s. Almost as often, incorporated suburbs feared the encroachment of modest housing as well, driving some communities to annex land on their own to protect home values. "Iron ring" attorneys who represented the suburbs in their numerous conflicts with the city were perhaps more cognizant than anyone else of the need to protect class interests. In 1953, Richard Cutler, village attorney of Fox Point, an upper-middle-class suburb on the North Shore, encouraged the village to annex land bordering to the west. Cutler claimed that prefabricated mass-produced homes were planned for that territory, which he predicted would slice the home values of some village residents by over a third. To prevent this, Fox Point needed to annex the land and institute its own rigid zoning regulations. Suitably alarmed, the village government voted to annex the land to block the building of affordable homes. The annexation ended at the Milwaukee River, where the Indian Creek Parkway had been built according to Charles Whitnall's original plan, providing a natural "barrier."[61]

Milwaukee's policy makers remained confident that the city's sterling record of efficient service delivery and effective governance would sway the people of the Milwaukee region to the benefits of annexation. To city leaders, the anti-annexation culprits were a small but powerful minority and usually consisted of interest groups who had the most to lose if Milwaukee succeeded in political unification. Perhaps at the top of this list were publishers of a variety of small village and town newspapers. It followed that if a town ceased to exist, the newspaper that covered town activities would eventually lose its readership. To that end, suburban publishers actively involved themselves in the annexation conflicts. In the fall of 1951, Phil Nickerson, publisher of the *Tri-Town News*, which covered affairs in the Town of Greenfield, posted 13.5 square miles of land in the Town of Greenfield for annexation to West Allis, strictly to keep Milwaukee from further encroaching upon his town. Political activity of this type made objective reporting in suburban newspapers a hopeless cause. In a *Tri-Town News* editorial that discussed suburban growth a few years later, the newspaper noted that every technological convenience that had existed in the city was now available in the outskirts, meaning that urban places had essentially outlived their usefulness. "Cities are obsolete," the newspaper declared in 1954: "Practically no one lives in the city unless he has to."[62]

The brazen rhetoric emanating from Milwaukee's suburban newspapers illuminates a broader national shift in the function of post–World War II suburbs. Far from simply being empty vessels that white urbanites escaped to, postwar suburbs were often attracting industry and retail in their own rights, and were gradually shedding their reputations as dormitories for city workers. As historian Robert Self has argued of metropolitan Oakland, "Municipal boundaries were not merely arbitrary markers in a hazy metropolitan 'sprawl'" but instead "represented important forms of publicly-controlled space."[63] In this postwar context, Self notes, suburbanization was not solely a matter of white flight, but the creation of "industrial and residential property markets."[64] The East Bay suburbs of California developed along these lines, often promoting their low property taxes to industrial concerns, and using rhetoric remarkably similar to that of Milwaukee County suburbs in describing the threats that neighboring larger central cities posed to their autonomy. Milpitas citizens, for example, referred to neighboring San Jose as an "octopus" that was using annexation to rob smaller communities of their very rights to existence.[65] Suburban officials in Milwaukee also reveled in framing Milwaukee along the same lines. Furthermore, as the 1950s continued, some of Milwaukee's neighbors, aware that they were beginning to win the battle for publicly controlled space, stopped thinking of themselves as "suburbs." The *West Allis Star*, which hammered away at the growing differences between Milwaukee and its suburbs with great frequency during the 1950s, represented this new mindset. As West Allis grew through annexations of its own, the *Star* proclaimed in 1957, "We think that it is high time that West Allis protests rather strongly that it is a sub-urban community. We are not 'sub' anything. We are a prosperous, growing city of 65,000 persons which would not find it difficult to exist without the benign presence of Milwaukee or any other large community at our doorstep."[66]

Alongside suburban newspapers, another sworn enemy of Milwaukee's annexation was the group of suburban attorneys who in the 1920s had formed the League of Suburban Municipalities (LSM) to give Milwaukee County suburbs a unified voice in legislative affairs. During the 1920s, Arthur Werba began calling the LSM the "Iron Ring."[67] By the 1950s, this term's meaning had changed to include all of Milwaukee's suburbs, making for more dramatic newspaper headlines. When suburbs posted notices of intent to annex, the print media chimed in that more "links to the Iron Ring" had formed.[68] However Milwaukee's suburbs differed from one another in

terms of population, land use, and class, the LSM gave them a collective political consciousness. Not only did they legally challenge countless annexations by Milwaukee, the LSM's leaders provided a reliable counterpoint to
Zeidler's and Werba's frequent public attacks. Hyperbolic rhetoric frequently shaped the tone of the metropolitan growth debate. In 1952, Zeidler
claimed that suburban attorney Conrad Dineen was leading a "secessionist"
movement in the region that was no different from what the Confederate
states had done before the Civil War. One attorney referred to the city as an
"octopus," and yet another responded by calling Zeidler an Adolph Hitler
clone: "There is no difference between Milwaukee's methods and Hitler's
methods. Both are based on the same kind of compulsion."[69] The animosity
between Milwaukee and its suburbs was so deep that in a book chronicling
the history of the Town of Greenfield, William Bowman, an attorney who
represented Greenfield in annexation matters, recalled that in the 1950s he
once found bugging devices in his offices. Apparently, Milwaukee officials
had installed the espionage equipment to anticipate the legal moves Bowman planned to make in various court proceedings to settle annexation
conflicts. The bugging devices discovered, Bowman remembered with glee,
he proceeded to "throw off" city officials by speaking one way in his offices
and an entirely different way in the courts, apparently allowing him to win
a variety of legal victories against Milwaukee's befuddled officials.[70]

Beyond rhetoric and posturing, both parties also flexed their political
muscles at the state level of government. By 1959, Milwaukee was spending about $13,000 annually on state lobbying; the suburban league nearly
matched the city, spending $12,800. The frequent petitions from city and
suburbs to Wisconsin's legislature often compelled the body to get involved
in the region's annexation wars, but both groups had different agendas.
The city sought tax reforms to distribute more evenly what the Zeidler administration saw as metropolitan revenues. Representatives of the LSM, cognizant that the present annexation laws had helped set off a growing wave
of political incorporations that weakened Milwaukee's expansion, characterized the annexation conflict as a "family affair" that did not require state
intervention. The LSM did, however, grow increasingly interested in getting
state help in cutting off what remained Milwaukee's greatest advantage in
achieving annexation: municipally controlled water provisions. As suburbs
such as Wauwatosa attempted to annex larger chunks of land, they exceeded
their capacity to provide water to new territory. Milwaukee's water authority
remained the most readily able to furnish the water installations, but the city
steadfastly refused to provide it to any territory outside its borders. Suburbs
with designs on annexation thus sought to use the state legislature to pry

water from the city. Well aware that without the ability to offer efficient and affordable public improvements the city's physical growth would grind to a halt, Milwaukee's leaders jealously guarded the precious commodity.[71]

The final group most opposed to the city of Milwaukee's annexation program consisted of town governments themselves, whose leaders were fully aware that the annexation race was bringing them ever closer to extinction. As in the 1920s, town governments had three options, all of which they explored. They could stand pat and use the courts to resist annexations. They could fully consolidate with the city of Milwaukee, which was by far the least appealing alternative. Or they could allow individual residents and property owners to decide their own political futures, which often led to a town's extinction. For example, when Glendale incorporated as a city, breaking away from the Town of Milwaukee in 1950, it took with it virtually all of the town's valuable industrial real estate. Alarmed residents of the Town of Milwaukee's northeastern corner, fearing being annexed by neighboring suburbs or even the city of Milwaukee, responded by incorporating as the Village of Bayside. A few years later, Fox Point and Glendale had swallowed up what remained of the Town of Milwaukee, forever ending its existence as a political unit. Consequently, town leaders first tried to fight for their survival, using any and all weapons at their disposal. In greatest peril were the Town of Granville, the Town of Wauwatosa, the Town of Greenfield, and the Town of Lake, all of which were adjacent to the city.

Lake, which bordered Milwaukee to its south, had the longest history of conflict with the city, driven mainly by the logic of municipal mercantilism. The Wisconsin Electric Power Company's Lakeside power plant, the largest in the region, produced over $300,000 in tax revenue for Lake residents, keeping property taxes minimal and ensuring Milwaukee would strenuously seek annexation of the plant. Wisconsin Electric officials had no desire whatsoever to become part of the city of Milwaukee. Nevertheless, Werba spent years trying to "trap" the plant by drawing annexation petitions in a way that encompassed enough landowners to trump the utility company's unwillingness. Plans continuously failed, but they further embittered Lake officials toward the city. Town of Lake chairman John Koweleski reveled in calling Milwaukee "The Big Octopus" that extended its tentacles throughout the region, choking off the weaker towns' ability to survive. At Koweleski's side was Lake's town constable, Louis Hibicke, whose methods against the city proved more heavy-handed. In 1947, a group of tavern owners in Lake charged Hibicke with extortion, claiming that when he heard of their intentions to be annexed to Milwaukee, he threatened to suspend their liquor licenses and have them arrested. Hibicke, removed from his position, continued to thunder away at Milwaukee at public meetings, contributing to the perception that the city officials would have to move heaven and earth before they annexed all of Lake.[72]

However, municipal mercantilism's dictates to attain the highest and best uses of land dramatically changed the Town of Lake's attitude toward the city. In July of 1951, residents surrounding the Lakeside power plant "put a fence" around its utility revenues when they voted that month to incorporate as the Village of St. Francis.[73] Overnight, the Town of Lake lost over a third of its tax revenue.[74] "The Town of Lake faces a bleak prospect of rising government costs and lowered revenues—in other words, soaring taxes," predicted the *Milwaukee Sentinel*.[75] Sensing renewed opportunity, Milwaukee's annexation solicitors set about selling the virtues of the city to Lake's residents. The Department of Abstracting and Annexation got a name change in 1952, reinventing itself as the more palatable "Department of Community Development." That year, city officials put together an ostensibly objective report weighing the pluses and minuses of a complete consolidation of Lake with Milwaukee. The report warned Lake's residents that town government was ill-equipped to handle their increasing service demands. Joining the city meant lower taxes since Milwaukee was prepared to assume the town's $1.5 million debt and provide better-funded public schools, more reliable police protection, and "a substantial increase in land values."[76] The enticements worked. In 1953, Lake residents voted over four to one in a referendum to dissolve their town government and consolidate with Milwaukee.[77] Decades of bitter conflict between town and city ended over the fate of a power plant.

Examined strictly as a public asset, the consolidation of the Town of Lake minus its most valuable commodity, the Lakeside plant, added a tremendous new cost to Milwaukee city government. The city had agreed to assume all of Lake's considerable municipal debt. A new aldermanic district was created to represent the entirety of the former town. The town's civil service employees received jobs with the city as a stipulation of the consolidation agreement. While some industry existed along three railroad lines that ran north and south, it was offset by the absorption of 13,000 new, mostly working-class residents, whose service demands outweighed the new property tax revenues gained by the city. Judged by the standards of municipal mercantilism, Milwaukee had not secured a highest and best land use. For the time being, however, the new public costs did not matter. The city had opened up a vast new corridor of potential growth to the south, one that seemed extremely unlikely to be available prior to the incorporation of St. Francis. The Town of Lake's land uses were extremely heterogeneous, reflecting its geography as the last community of substantial residential outflow

Ariel View, Lakeside Power Plant—A vivid illustration of "municipal mercantilism" in action, Milwaukee feuded over control of the Lakeside power plant for years with the Town of Lake, until residents around the plant broke off and formed their own village. Courtesy of Milwaukee County Historical Society

from the city. To the south, past the long lines of modest bungalows that dominated the northern portion of Lake, lie Mitchell Airport, now within city limits, and a series of farms for which the city was forced to create a new agricultural land use classification in its zoning ordinance. The vacant land had great potential for industrial development. The Chicago and Northwest Railroad ran through Lake and southward to the Town of Oak Creek. The region's transportation plans also included a proposed expressway (eventually Interstate 94) that would parallel the rail line, eventually connecting Milwaukee with Chicago ninety miles to the south.[78]

Milwaukee officials were by no means the only ones who recognized the vast development potential south of the city and along expressways. Since the 1940s, manufacturers had begun changing their shipping methods, favoring trucks over freight rail. This was coupled with a desire by industries to move away from multi-storied plants to horizontally organized production sites surrounded by vast expanses of parking that allowed employees to drive to work. Due to the lack of available space, newer plants such as these were almost impossible to build in dense cities. Further encouragement for plant decentralization came from the federal government, where a variety of studies echoed Cold War fears of the nuclear vulnerability of cities. The National Industrial Dispersal Program of the early 1950s urged manufacturers to build all new plants at least ten to fifteen miles outside of "present industrial concentrations" to lessen the damage of nuclear attack.[79]

Whether impelled by the federal government or the logic of plant location and newer shipping techniques, by the 1950s manufacturers were already developing horizontal production systems that required far more space. In a 1960 study of plant location in Milwaukee County that covered 950 different firms, Norbert Stefaniak, a commerce professor at the University of Wisconsin-Milwaukee Extension illustrated industry's new spatial needs. Of the 218 companies in Stefaniak's study that had built plants within ten years of 1960, 76 percent of them stated that they used no rail transportation at all. Furthermore, Stefaniak estimated that two out of every three manufacturing workers in Milwaukee used automobiles to get to and from work, demonstrating the increased need to provide ample parking for the postwar industrial workforce. The future expansion of industry seemed bent toward new production methods that stretched plants out horizontally, increasingly utilized trucks to supplement or replace freight transport, and provided acres of parking for workers. Vacant land near future expressway expansion thus became extremely valuable industrial real estate and was also hotly contested throughout the postwar years.[80]

Recognizing these trends, General Motors' AC Spark Plug Division, which had located its first large plant in the Milwaukee area in the city's crowded East Side, began to seek out vacant land past the urban periphery to expand its regional operations. In 1955, the company settled on a huge tract at the northern edges of the rural Town of Oak Creek, which suddenly bordered Milwaukee in the wake of the Town of Lake's consolidation. Milwaukee officials immediately began making plans to continue annexation to the south, successfully taking in 223 acres of Oak Creek land in 1953.

The Town of Oak Creek differed greatly from other towns adjacent to Milwaukee. While Granville, Greenfield, and Wauwatosa had long absorbed residential outflow from the city, Oak Creek remained rural in the 1950s, with 80 percent of its land dedicated to agricultural use. Approximately 7,000 people lived in a town that encompassed twenty-nine square miles.

The town's rural characteristics greatly limited the options of its residents in preventing annexation. Communities near Milwaukee could incorporate as villages, since their population densities usually met the state requirements for village status. Oak Creek had no chance to seek incorporation under present state laws, which required incorporated cities to have no less than 400 people per square mile. However, with the city knocking at its door, the town's officials began to explore its options.[81]

Once again, the logic of municipal mercantilism infected another town's political future. The Wisconsin Electric Power Company, which operated the Lakeside power plant in St. Francis, made plans for its largest expansion to date, choosing to build a $300 million plant along Lake Michigan at the southern edge of the Town of Oak Creek and promising to increase property tax revenues there by over $300,000 per year. With the new plant under construction, residents first voted to combine the town's eight school districts together to more evenly spread out the utility revenue. With that accomplished, it became obvious that Oak Creek needed to prevent annexation by Milwaukee. Residents besieged town officials to try something, anything, to incorporate the entire town, but the aforementioned state laws made it impossible.[82]

Into the debate stepped Anthony Basile, an attorney who had been persuaded by an old friend from school to work for Oak Creek. Basile convinced town officials that if Oak Creek took its case to the state legislature, where antiurban sentiment had existed for years, perhaps there would be enough sympathy to create a new law that would allow Oak Creek to incorporate. Town officials agreed to the plan. Basile crafted a bill that essentially waived the "urban characteristics" requirement *reserved only* for towns bordering the city of Milwaukee, paving the way for them to incorporate as "fourth-class cities" pending referenda. The town spent over $50,000 lobbying state legislators in Madison to bring the bill to the state floor. The legislature debated the bill in 1955. The "Oak Creek Bill" was more palatable to many legislators because it specifically applied to towns surrounding the city of Milwaukee, but it proved controversial nonetheless. By the narrowest of margins, the Wisconsin state assembly voted to approve it by a vote of 44 to 42. The deciding vote came from an assemblyman from Milwaukee's South Side, who claimed to vote in the affirmative only in the hope that the law would be reconsidered, a technical mistake that eventually allowed the bill to escape the legislature, as it passed through the state senate unchanged. Belatedly, another Milwaukee assemblyman warned the legislature that Oak Creek only wanted to "grab the taxes" of the new Wisconsin Electric Power Plant and moved for reconsideration of the bill, but he was voted down.[83]

With the Oak Creek Bill now sitting on a wary Governor Walter Kohler, Jr.'s desk, Basile again applied his persuasive skills, appealing for Kohler's signature, ironically, on the grounds of regionalism. Basile warned Kohler that General Motors' AC Spark Plug Division intended to build a large new plant in Oak Creek, but the corporation wanted assurances that it could avoid being annexed to Milwaukee. Given that guarantee, the plant's construction would progress. Absent an apparent Oak Creek incorporation, General Motors had no desire to build anywhere else in Milwaukee and would instead expand to Florida or California. While Basile continued to persuade Governor Kohler, desperate Milwaukee officials maneuvered in damage control mode. Joe Lamping, who had replaced the retired Arthur Werba as community development (annexation) director a year earlier in 1954, met with General Motors executives, hoping to convince them instead to build their new facility on land in the former Town of Lake. To protect future expansion should the Oak Creek Bill fail, city officials quickly reposted ten square miles of land in the northern half of Oak Creek for annexation.[84]

An obviously ambivalent Governor Kohler signed the Oak Creek bill, telling the legislature that "I have some reservation about the ultimate effect of signing this bill into law," and assuring them that he was convinced that the bill would be severely tested in the courts.[85] In the meantime, Kohler said, piecemeal annexation, which he felt was at the root of the city and suburban conflicts in the first place, could be halted. Milwaukee officials were horrified. Zeidler, rarely one for hyperbole, believed the Oak Creek Law was "one of the worst developments that has occurred in the history of local government in the United States."[86] The League of Wisconsin Municipalities, which broadly represented all cities and towns in the state, tried to get the legislature to pass a law allowing for Milwaukee to contest the new law in court, but the state senate killed the bill. Meanwhile, Oak Creek town officials quickly moved to give town residents the chance to vote themselves into city status, scheduling a referendum for October 31, 1955. Now in a race against time, Milwaukee's city attorney moved for state courts to issue a restraining order postponing the referendum until the Oak Creek Law could be legally contested in court. The legal maneuvering failed. To avoid having any legal papers served against them, Oak Creek's town officials literally disappeared from sight until the referendum. On October 31, town residents voted 2,107 to 126 for the incorporation of the city of Oak Creek. Running out of legal options, the city next obtained a temporary injunction in a Dane County circuit court, where the state capital of Madison was located, to restrain the results of the referendum, but Oak Creek officials certified the election anyway. Before the state agreed to issue an official certification of Oak Creek as a city, hundreds of town residents gathered together and declared Oak Creek a city. By December, the state issued Oak Creek an official charter, essentially ending the legal conflict for good.[87]

Once again, state legislation had dramatically altered the political development of the Milwaukee region. Metropolitan planning was dying on the vine of rapid fragmentation. "What it does," said Zeidler, referring to the Oak Creek Bill, "is to prevent the city from spreading out horizontally. It means the city must now grow vertically and that will require changes in zoning and the entire concept of planning."[88] The Oak Creek Law gave even the most rural towns the ability to incorporate as "cities" provided that they bordered Milwaukee. Only six years later, every single remaining town that bordered Milwaukee had incorporated, enclosing the iron ring for good and essentially ending annexation. The city did manage to convince the Town of Granville to consolidate with Milwaukee in 1956, and after a lengthy litigation process, the Granville-Milwaukee consolidation was made official in 1962.[89] The twenty-eight square miles of land Milwaukee subsequently absorbed provided the city a much-needed "safety valve" for middle-class residential outflow and played a key role in keeping Milwaukee's rate of population decline far less onerous than those of many cities of the same size, age, and economy. None of this, however, was apparent in 1955, and Zeidler warned to the *Milwaukee Journal* a year later that the Oak Creek Law was another major blow to planned decentralization. Being locked in by the Iron Ring—much more likely after the new law—was bound to lead to higher population densities. Urban renewal, originally contingent upon dispersal in advance of slum clearance, also was going to be far more difficult. Officials had banked on the complete unification of the Milwaukee metropolis; thus the Oak Creek Law was obviously a devastating blow. It demonstrated, yet again, that the logic of municipal mercantilism invited conflict rather than cooperation and made a mockery of "metropolitanization" as a genuine exercise in regional development. With Milwaukee reeling from the Oak Creek Law, Governor Kohler, who had signed a law he was not sure was even constitutional, sought state help, arguing that a commission to study metropolitan problems in Milwaukee County was desperately needed. The Greater Milwaukee Committee (GMC) had long advocated the idea for a metropolitan committee, suggesting it to Kohler on numerous occasions. As perhaps the city's most influential group of civic elites, the GMC remained determined to market the region as a harmonious place. However, the politically fragmenting metropolis belied any accurate perception of political cooperation.[90]

In fact, assessing the economic health of metropolitan Milwaukee as a whole was complicated by intra-metropolitan conflict. The 1950s were a time of general prosperity across the United States, and the region was by no means left behind during the economic boom. However, the annexation wars' yielding of political suburbanization had already taken a toll on the city of Milwaukee. If the contest was about which municipality could create, capture, or maintain the highest and best land uses, Milwaukee was losing the battle, despite dramatically increasing its size. The most valuable industrial territory in Milwaukee County almost always wound up in other hands. Glendale's incorporation had fenced in the industrial corridor along the Chicago and Northwestern Railroad lines above Capitol Drive. West Milwaukee and West Allis had annexed most of the southwest corridor of industry. In 1953, Wauwatosa annexed 8.5 square miles of mostly vacant land to its north and west, giving it ample room for industrial, commercial, and residential expansion. While these suburbs grew, they also increasingly attracted industry away from Milwaukee, an ominous sign demonstrating that well before *deindustrialization* drained jobs from the Milwaukee region, *industrial decentralization* was beginning to remove jobs from the city of Milwaukee itself. By the count of city officials, from 1949 to 1955, eighteen major manufacturers vacated Milwaukee. Of that number, only four left the region entirely, and the other fourteen manufacturers moved to one of Milwaukee's suburbs.[91]

The political conflicts between Milwaukee and its suburbs were not narrowly constricted to legal maneuverings and inflamed rhetoric over physical growth. At no time in the history of American cities was regional cooperation more needed to address the increasing problems that existed within central cities. Despite record manufacturing employment, city officials had been well aware that Milwaukee's ability to prosper hinged upon fostering future industrial development within its boundaries. Political fragmentation made this exceedingly difficult, as did a deep distrust between Mayor Zeidler and Milwaukee's business community. Just as ominously, the city's social problems dramatically grew during the postwar era. Milwaukee's African American population substantially increased in size, and the city's newest residents sought the same opportunities to advance economically that previous generations of urban migrants had largely attained. However, African Americans who moved to Milwaukee during the years following World War II arrived in a city that was at an economic crossroads, beginning to lose ground to the increasingly growing number of suburbs that had emerged as a direct result of the annexation wars. The postwar city's social and racial problems were contested in a fragmented metropolis.[92] This reality gave a specific economic shape to both urban and suburban development, with resources distributed unevenly across newly created political boundaries that divided people by race and class.

Selective Metropolitanism

"Industry finds itself in a position comparable to that of the only
man shipwrecked on an island inhabited only by women."

—*Wisconsin Metropolitan Study Commission, 1959*

While political borders on the metropolitan fringe were hardening, equally dramatic changes were taking place in Milwaukee's urban core. African Americans moved to Milwaukee at far greater rates than ever before, beginning a "Late Great Migration" that tripled the city's black population during the 1950s. The influx of these new residents not only altered the racial makeup of the city, it also subtly shifted the already contentious rhetoric of the metropolitan growth debates. Racial issues moved to the forefront of Milwaukee's politics at precisely the same time that any hopes of equitable regionalism failed. Instead, regional issues became institutionalized on a selective basis that privileged middle- and upper-class suburbs, often at the expense of the city. This chapter explores the intersection of race and metropolitanism, which took place during the final years of Socialist governance for Milwaukee, when one last salvo against fragmentation was made at a different level of government with ultimately familiar results.[1]

In the first half of the twentieth century, Milwaukee's African American population remained minuscule compared to other Midwest cities'. African American migrants from the South were far more likely to settle in Chicago, where black cultural and economic institutions were stronger and longer in establishment, or in Detroit and Cleveland, whose auto and steel industries more readily accommodated unskilled labor. Before World War II in Milwaukee, African Americans occupied only a small and clearly defined section on the northwest end of downtown, living mostly within the confines of the Second and Sixth Wards, two of the oldest sections of the city. Milwaukee's tiny African American population had accordingly existed as a city within a city. The Sixth Ward had long been associated with urban decay, but its population was racially mixed for most of the first half of the twentieth century. Numerous Eastern European immigrant families lived in similarly difficult conditions. Milwaukee's social progressive planners and reformers rarely framed urban problems in racial terms. They were by no means immune to ethnic and racial stereotypes that were common at that time. The city's black population, however, was exceedingly small before World War II—smaller, in fact, than that of virtually any city of its size in the United States.[2]

Despite Milwaukee's comparative lack of racial diversity prior to World War II, public policy decisions too often deleteriously and disproportionately affected the city's black population. The Sixth Ward, where the vast majority of Milwaukee's African Americans lived prior to the war, was one of Milwaukee's most notorious and—by its location adjacent to the central business district's northwest—conspicuous slums. The city's 1920 zoning ordinance, informed largely by planners' abhorrence of congestion, subsequently transformed much of the lower half of the Sixth Ward into a commercial and light industrial "use district." Historian Joe Trotter has noted that this part of the Sixth Ward contained the vast majority of Milwaukee's tiny but growing African American population. Suddenly, homes located in this part of the Sixth Ward were now officially a "nonconforming use," making it more difficult to rehabilitate residences in a section of the city that most needed these types of improvements. During the 1920s, the private sector worked in less subtle ways to segregate the city. In 1924, the Milwaukee Real Estate Board hinted at its intent to racialize the city's geography when it announced intentions to create a "Black Belt" in an unidentified part of the Near Northwest Side (the Sixth Ward) as a way of containing the city's African American population to a well-defined area, ostensibly away from the majority of whites. Milwaukee's African American residents numbered only 1,200 in 1920 and the vast majority already clustered in the Sixth Ward. While the city's black population did not grow substantially until the decades after World War II, the private real estate community was on guard. During the Depression, Milwaukee's housing demolition program eliminated thousands of dilapidated dwellings from the built landscape. A disproportionate number of demolitions occurred in the Sixth and the increasingly African American Second Wards, amplifying the housing shortage in precisely that area where African Americans' concentration was the highest. These policies only reinforced the growing connection between African Americans and "blight" in the city.[3]

Land use control policies in the 1920s and 1930s revealed policy makers' assumptions that inner city residents, regardless of race or ethnicity, would slowly vacate the inner city. Between 1920 and 1940, the population of twenty-five census tracts in Milwaukee's innermost wards did decrease, but during that same time, racial segregation increased as black families replaced ethnic whites in neighborhoods that already had poor housing stock, and long before had earned poor reputations in reform and real estate circles. Between 1920 and 1940, Milwaukee's African American population grew from 2,229 to 8,821 residents, within the confines of a slowly expanding "inner core" on the northwest side of downtown.[4] By the close of World War II, inner city wards remained associated with decay. It became more convenient to associate "blight" with African American residents, even though they still encompassed a tiny fraction of the city's overall population.[5]

After World War II, African Americans left the South for northern cities with increasing frequency, and Milwaukee became a more important destination. During the 1940s, African Americans found opportunity in the city's booming wartime industries, and Milwaukee's black population grew more rapidly, from 8,821 to 21,772 residents. The nearly 13,000 newcomers outnumbered the entire existing black population. During the 1950s, this same statistical trend held true; over 40,000 more new black residents almost doubled the number of existing black Milwaukeeans.

Nationally, Milwaukee still appeared to be a "white" city. As late as 1960, of the twenty-five largest cities in America, Milwaukee still had the third lowest percentage of African Americans. Local boosters probably fed the perception of racial homogeneity by trying to attract industry on the basis of marketing whiteness. But locally, a groundswell of racial fears was increasingly noticeable in the contest over urban growth. When Milwaukee was an overwhelmingly white city, planned decentralization and the sharing of regional resources between city and suburb seemed palatable. Opposition to policies that embraced these ideas had almost no racial overtones; suburban and rural residents framed anger toward annexation and metropolitan government primarily in terms of local control, and secondarily in the exclusionary language of class. After World War Two, when the city's black population grew by over 50,000 residents in twenty years, neighborhoods on

CHART 7-1	Milwaukee's African American Population by Decade, 1910–1960

Year	Black Population	Total Population	Percentage of Total Population
1910	980	373,857	0.26%
1920	2,229	457,147	0.5%
1930	7,501	578,249	1.3%
1940	8,821	587,472	1.5%
1950	21,772	637,392	3.4%
1960	62,458	741,324	8.4%

Source: Milwaukee Metropolitan Area Fact Book: 1940, 1950, 1960. Madison: University of Wisconsin Press

the northwest side began changing demographically, and racial confrontations, long familiar in cities such as Chicago, Philadelphia, Cleveland, and Detroit, now touched an unprecedented number of white Milwaukeeans. Mayor Zeidler's urban policies now seemed to implicitly upset the region's racial status quo in ways that the same planning ideas Hoan launched had not. Zeidler spent a good deal of his first term promoting large-scale community development schemes such as the acquisition of Greendale and the construction of a satellite city in Waukesha County, as well as developing a reliable source of funding for public housing. Now, in the minds of many whites, each plan threatened to bring urban problems to rural or suburban spaces. While the strongest source of opposition to Zeidler's satellite city came from local residents determined to cling to local control, an implicit racial fear of the city existed as well, as one local Waukesha County resident accused Zeidler of trying to "eliminate Milwaukee's slums and move them out here."[6] In 1951, Zeidler's ambitious community development and public housing plans ended somewhat abruptly. City residents rejected a referendum that would have given the city greater latitude in the construction of public housing. Civic organizations such as the Greater Milwaukee Committee (GMC) and the Milwaukee Association of Commerce remained committed to subsidizing the rebuilding of downtown and gave no support to public housing. By 1955, the city had not built a single new public housing unit for five years, but the MAC's leaders continued to grumble about Zeidler's support for "socialized housing."[7]

Zeidler's orientation toward public housing and planned decentraliza-tion, matched with his blunt declaration that blacks "were the last hired in industry" in the city, made him an increasingly attractive target for a growing number of political opponents.[8] Adding to Zeidler's problems by the middle of the decade was the ever-increasing animosity between city and suburbs in Milwaukee County over annexation, which had culminated in the 1955 passage of the Oak Creek Law. A few months later, these twin tensions boiled over in the spring mayoral election of 1956, the most con-tentious in Milwaukee's postwar history.

The 1956 election hinged implicitly on the question of race, but it also revealed the deep political and economic tensions that were by now en-demic to the metropolis. Zeidler's opponent, Milton McGuire, the president of the Common Council, commanded the support not only of white city residents nervous about the influx of African Americans, but also of busi-ness leaders increasingly put off by Zeidler's socialism and suburban resi-dents obviously bitter at the city's annexation program. Zeidler's relatively narrow victory and subsequent last four years in office took place against a backdrop of a state-mandated Metropolitan Study Commission that had been established to herald a new era of metropolitan cooperation. Instead, the MSC failed to achieve political compromise, and in the process indirect-ly revealed that suburban sprawl and uneven development were persistent by-products of the fragmented metropolis.

Several incidents quickly became the flashpoints for racial conflict that surfaced ominously in the early 1950s. To many whites, the most dramatic was the 1952 murder of three white Milwaukeeans by a recently arrived black migrant to Milwaukee. The murder, briefly recounted in historian Jack Dougherty's study of school integration in Milwaukee, spurred the city's law enforcement officials to call for increased police surveillance of the Sixth Ward. More broadly, the murder seemed to exemplify a "migrant crisis."[9] Milwaukee's all-white Common Council believed that the majority of black migrants came to Milwaukee not to access well-paying industrial jobs, but instead to take advantage of the relatively generous county-operated wel-fare that was available to impoverished residents. A month after the murder of the three whites, the County Board began considering lengthening the residency requirements for relief. The Milwaukee Common Council passed a resolution supporting the board's action. Zeidler vetoed the resolution on December 23, recognizing that the new ordinance and the County Board's potential new policy sought explicitly to "prevent migrant people of southern

origin from getting Milwaukee County aid easily." To many of Zeidler's political enemies, the veto confirmed his political vulnerability on the issue of race.
The Milwaukee Real Estate Board, which endorsed Zeidler's annexation plans,
objected to increasing the construction of low-income public housing in the
city, assuming that it, too, attracted "southern migrants." In a letter to Zeidler
written soon after his veto, the board pointedly asked if the county's relief
policies and the city's newest low-income projects, Westlawn and Hillside, had
been an "inducement" to blacks, noting that "more than half the colored tenants in the projects" had lived in Milwaukee for two years or less.[10]

Zeidler's frank observations about the city's racial tensions, his unwillingness to obstruct black migration to the city, and his oft-stated but never
realized policy of planned decentralization infuriated some city and suburban residents. An anonymous resident of the Northwest Side, frustrated
over Zeidler's unwillingness to *discourage* African Americans from coming to
Milwaukee, directly questioned the notion of encouraging poorer migrants
to vacate the urban core, asking Zeidler pointedly: "Why scatter them all
over the city, creating trouble and problems for us?"[11] In reality, virtually no
"scattering" had taken place. Over 98 percent of the city's black population
was confined to the inner core. Yet the recent construction of Westlawn,
the city's newest low-income public housing project that was located on
the Northwest Side on land recently annexed from the Town of Wauwatosa, had frightened suburban whites. Westlawn was the last—and largest—
low-income project the city built before the 1951 referendum halted public
housing expansion. The *Wauwatosa News-Times,* the suburb of Wauwatosa's
newspaper and frequent opponent of annexation, plainly stated in 1953
that while the suburbs "did not hate" Milwaukee, they did fear Zeidler's
policies, particularly the idea of building low-income public housing in formerly rural territory. In implicitly racial terms, the *Times* claimed to "have
listened to stories of good hard-working people who claim that they have,
in good faith, fine residences in the city of Milwaukee only to have their
values come tumbling down because of a Zeidler-inspired housing development erected 'right next door.'"[12] Westlawn's 750 units were racially integrated, but in the early 1950s only 18 percent of its residents were African
American. Nevertheless, suburban residents did occasionally associate annexation to racial integration, further complicating the city's expansion
plans. As the 1956 election approached, they added to the upsurge of ir-
rational rumors within white communities that Zeidler was initiating a plot
to move large numbers of blacks to Milwaukee.

For those who sought to exploit racial fears to deny Zeidler a third term
in 1956, the emergence of conservative Democrat Milton McGuire as a vi-

able mayoral candidate was a virtual godsend. McGuire, who had served as an alderman of the Third Ward since 1936 and as president of the Common Council from 1944 through 1955, had opposed low-income public housing from the start. McGuire's candidacy is easy to see solely in racial terms; he was, after all, a white alderman seeking to unseat a racially "enlightened" mayor in the name of preserving racial homogeneity.[13] The 1956 election was clearly the first in Milwaukee's history in which race occupied center stage. National media took notice; *Time* magazine called readers' attention to "The Shame of Milwaukee" in April, subsequently unearthing Milwaukee's racial tensions to the nation. A "whispering campaign" had Zeidler plastering the South with billboards inviting blacks to Milwaukee. Another rumor hinted that Zeidler's daughter and sister had married black men. Apparently, McGuire's aides called Zeidler a "nigger lover" out of public eye. McGuire himself called the rumors "shameful," and his official campaign platform made no explicit mention of race, but he also promised an audience of landlords that he would keep Milwaukee free of "southern migrants" if elected mayor. McGuire did little else to dissuade people from believing he was, as one resident angrily wrote Zeidler, the "only honest white man" running for mayor.[14]

More difficult for national audiences to see, but vitally important in southeast Wisconsin, were broader political, economic, and spatial conflicts festering within the metropolis that the 1956 election also amplified. For the first time, Zeidler's socialism, always problematic to the region's business and civic elites and some of the local media, withstood a frontal assault from a political opponent. McGuire's campaign may have kept silent over race, but it loudly and frequently attacked Zeidler's socialism as un-American. "Milwaukee needs a mayor who believes in the *American* system of free enterprise," McGuire's campaign literature told Milwaukee residents. Zeidler's long pro-labor record ensured him the support of the city's increasingly powerful unions, but McGuire could and did take aim at the city's paucity of industrial expansion. "Labor is being 'short-changed' in Milwaukee because Milwaukee is not attractive to industry," stated another McGuire pamphlet, adding that "industry is afraid of a city mayor who wants to end the free enterprise system."[15] When the Oak Creek Bill passed in the fall of 1955, McGuire also attempted to exploit this major setback. Under Zeidler, McGuire noted, Milwaukee had annexed new territory, but not nearly enough industrial land, further ensuring that the city's manufacturing sector was crawling toward obsolescence. Finally, McGuire claimed that during Zeidler's tenure, city-suburban relations had degenerated into all-out municipal war. The region badly needed "greater harmony," and that had to begin with a mayor who could get along with Milwaukee's suburbs. McGuire's genteel rhetoric toward the suburbs was perhaps fiscally motivated. By the end of February 1956, McGuire's individual campaign donations from suburban residents outnumbered donations from city residents by nearly a two-to-one margin.[16]

Other assaults on Zeidler's socialism arrived in more ideological terms. Anti-Zeidler opponents also created the "Milwaukee for America Committee," formed to help deliver the city to McGuire, which issued a sixteen-page pamphlet titled "Think Milwaukee Voters!" that outlined in great detail the dangers of socialism. To encourage readers to "think," the committee contrasted its free market rhetoric with a variety of quotes from some of Zeidler's speeches. The pamphlet noted, in closing, that Zeidler's socialist "utopias . . . crashed upon the American reefs of roast beef and apple pie," further warning that "Mr. Zeidler would do well to meditate on these words."[17] The *Milwaukee Sentinel*, long known as the city's more conservative newspaper, also saw salvation in McGuire and became a virtual mouthpiece for his campaign in the spring of 1956. In March, the *Sentinel* ran a series of articles titled "Americanism or Socialism?" practically implying Zeidler was a Soviet insurgent by repeatedly referring to him as a "longtime, dedicated, doctrinaire, Marxian Socialist." McGuire on the other hand was "a man who has thrown down the gauntlet against Mr. Zeidler and his socialism in the name of the American system of free enterprise."[18] The *Sentinel* gravely warned voters that the mayoral election was about "basic principles" that would forever be perverted should Zeidler be reelected. The paper went to extraordinary lengths to cast Zeidler's eight years in office as an utter failure. Apparent success stories appeared in *Sentinel* print spun into tales of urban woe. A forty-six-page memo Zeidler wrote to his advisors on the city's accomplishments and future needs earned the dubious tagline, "Frank Zeidler's Confession of Failure." *Sentinel* columnist William Norris, once a supporter of annexation but now in lockstep with the paper against Zeidler, even criticized the mayor for *refusing to accept a salary raise*. Norris reasoned that the economic sacrifice made Zeidler a "poor teammate," since the members of the Common Council all had voted themselves raises and stood to look selfish as a result.[19]

Local industrial leaders, represented by such groups as the MAC and the Greater Milwaukee Committee, remained silent and nonpartisan during the campaign. Nevertheless, the city's business elites' vitriol toward Zeidler was apparent. The MAC's Board of Directors angrily condemned a Zeidler speech to a student group at the University of Wisconsin-Madison in October of 1955 where he "attacked" America's system of free enterprise.[20]

Zeidler had pointed out with some irony that "free" enterprise was never as laissez-faire as businesses liked to characterize it; corporate welfare existed at all levels of government. The speech came immediately after the signing of the Oak Creek Bill into law, which among other things, had created a virtual tax haven for General Motors' AC Spark Plug Division, a fact that well may have been in the back of Zeidler's mind during the speech. Whatever Zeidler's personal motivations in making his speech, the MAC's leaders considered any harsh words toward "free enterprise" subversive, and they were already planning subtle election year indoctrination of their own. The A. O. Smith Corporation, one of the city's largest employers, had previously required that its 10,000 employees view a video titled "Our Way of Living," which demonstrated the greatness of the American system of free enterprise and the importance of political participation. Recognizing that 1956 was an election year, the MAC decided to distribute "Our Way of Living" to forty other local companies as well.[21] Other businesses actively campaigned against Zeidler in the workplace, explicitly citing his potential reelection as a threat of termination. The owner of a small manufacturing plant on the North Side passed out copies of "Think Milwaukee Voters!" to all of his workers, telling them to pass the chain along to friends. The memo sternly warned employees: "IF YOU DON'T KEEP THIS CHAIN ALIVE [emphasis in original] you will get . . . oh; let's not think of unpleasant things." On the other hand, a vote for McGuire supported "a man who firmly believes in the American free enterprise system."[22]

Intimidation at workplaces failed. Zeidler's supporters strongly came to his defense, with organized labor in the lead. To counter the vicious racial rumors, the Federated Trades Council of Milwaukee wrote letters to unions in ten different southern states asking them to check their territories for billboards from Zeidler welcoming African Americans north to Milwaukee. None were found. The *Milwaukee Labor Press*, the city's local labor newspaper, characterized McGuire's attacks as two-pronged, one openly aiming at Zeidler's socialism, the other tolerating the racist rumors about Zeidler and his family that had enveloped the city. The migration of African Americans, the press noted, was a national phenomenon originally rooted in manufacturers' wartime needs for cheap labor. For his part, Zeidler remained above the fray, calmly framing black migration to Milwaukee in terms of economic opportunity, and calling upon city residents to ignore the rumors and vote their conscience. Only in an interview with an outside newspaper, the *New York Post*, did Zeidler's rhetoric heat up. "We're seeing the rise in Wisconsin of a new American fascism," he said of his political enemies. "These people took over the Republican Party; now they're trying to get Milwaukee." If the effort really did represent a conservative insurgency, it failed in 1956. In the end, a majority of Milwaukee voters looked beyond the overt attacks on Zeidler, delivering him a third term by a margin of 117,912 votes to McGuire's 95,943.[23]

Zeidler had won the bruising reelection by over 20,000 votes, no small accomplishment considering the flood of propaganda he had faced. In fact, the 1956 election made Zeidler something of a national figure in civil rights circles. The *Pittsburgh Courier*, the nation's second largest black newspaper, twice sent a reporter to Milwaukee to feature Zeidler's struggles against the racist rhetoric. Philadelphia Mayor Joseph Clark and Pittsburgh's popular postwar mayor David Lawrence both came to Zeidler's aid, calling him one of America's best mayors.[24] Recent historians of civil rights struggles in Milwaukee have offered a more nuanced assessment of Zeidler's civil rights credentials. Jack Daugherty noted that Zeidler showed far more genuine concern for the plight of African Americans than other political leaders of Milwaukee, but was nevertheless pressured by whites to view the "migrant crisis" within the confines of the inner core. The city's newest residents needed to be "acculturated" to city life by first adjusting their behavioral patterns to be more acceptable to the white majority of the city. Patrick Jones has similarly concluded that Milwaukee public officials "invariably explained away inequality as a problem of 'acculturation.'" Such officials therefore had little use for a growing civil rights insurgency that was beginning to politicize racial inequality more forcefully than ever before.[25]

The problems of race and suburbanization were undeniably matters of degree rather than kind in virtually every large city in America. Municipal leaders who encountered unprecedented racial conflict had few resources to address these problems. Zeidler's racial politics were constricted not only by an apparent racial "moderation" but also by the very real boundaries that hardened in reaction to his planning policies and annexation program and increasingly divided the Milwaukee region by class as well as race. During Zeidler's final term that closed out the 1950s, the Wisconsin state government essentially forced the city and its Milwaukee County suburbs to explore ways to address countywide, or "metropolitan," problems of common concern. As Zeidler repeatedly noted, suburbs were only willing to discuss issues that affected their residents, mainly improving their access to water and sewage facilities, but were utterly unwilling to discuss slum clearance, unequal tax burdens, and other problems which the city disproportionately bore. Absent meaningful metropolitan cooperation, urban problems were guaranteed to remain marginalized in a central city that was losing the economic resources most needed to help its new residents. Zeidler thus acted on a metropolitan stage during his last term as he had done before, advocating on behalf of the city in a suburbanizing metropolis. If the problems of race manifested across political boundaries, as civil rights leaders repeatedly asserted, then solving them meant addressing the very boundaries that divided the region to begin with.

The 1956 election was a flashpoint for not only Zeidler's socialism or the city's increasing racial tensions, but also the city-suburban conflict and Milwaukee's fractured public-private institutional cooperation. Suburban residents whose hatred for Zeidler ran deep could not vote in a city election; they nonetheless financially supported McGuire. Zeidler emphasized suburban support for McGuire; in a public statement made in late February, he warned city residents that McGuire's "slush fund" came mostly from suburban residents, noting that the fund should serve as a warning to Milwaukeeans that "a drive is underway against their independence and self-government and home rule."[26] The erosion of Milwaukee's "independence" was most apparent in the suburbs' obstruction of annexation, but suburban political opposition had manifested in the 1956 election as well. During the decade's last four years, the undermining of the city continued, and the iron ring closed.

Even before the 1956 election, it had become apparent that the region's issues were unsolvable on a strictly local level. In 1954, the Milwaukee County Board voted to create a permanent "Committee of 21" consisting of seven Milwaukee aldermen, seven county supervisors, and seven representatives of suburban governments, to consider "matters of mutual interest to the local governments." The committee met first in December 1954 and throughout 1955, but agreed on virtually nothing. Suburban officials complained that the city only seemed interested in complete metropolitan unification and a Milwaukee alderman confirmed this suspicion. From the start, Zeidler never supported the Committee of 21, arguing that it disproportionately represented suburban interests. Furthermore, Zeidler and other Milwaukee officials were growing increasingly concerned that "metro organizations" were nothing but a front for suburbs to access city water without having to consolidate or voluntarily allow annexation. Milwaukee's ability to provide water to outlying territory had long been the city's strongest annexation weapon, and in the wake of the Oak Creek Law's passage it seemed to be its last significant asset.[27]

The continued bickering between Milwaukee and its suburbs irritated the region's civic organizations most of all. The Greater Milwaukee Committee considered itself an independent arbiter in metropolitan issues and, with both city and suburbs at a stalemate of mutual disgust, sought to fund an independent research firm to examine key issues facing city and suburbs alike. The GMC first tried to force the Committee of 21 to allow it to control the scope and content of the proposed study. Zeidler, always suspicious of suburban bias at the GMC, helped convince the county to reject the proposal. Undeterred, the group appealed to Governor Walter Kohler, Jr., to appoint a "citizens' study commission" to examine metropolitan problems. Governor Kohler, acutely aware of city-suburban animosity, agreed to push for legislation to create a state-funded Metropolitan Study Commission. The legislature eventually agreed, voting in the summer of 1957 to form a commission of fifteen members, appointed by the governor, to examine the "common problems" faced by municipalities in Milwaukee County and to seek solutions. Vernon Thomson, who replaced Kohler as governor in 1957, signed the bill into law that summer. Local media lauded the bill as progressive and foresighted, an example of the civic cooperation that was driving urban renewal in cities across America.[28]

Only on the surface did the creation of the Metropolitan Study Commission (MSC) indicate willingness on the part of Milwaukee and its suburbs to engage in meaningful intergovernmental dialogue. In fact, the arduous process of drafting the bill that established the commission proved once again that suburban interests trumped urban ones in the state legislature. The GMC flexed its political muscles in the state, presenting Governor Kohler with a list of fourteen prominent private citizens from which Kohler chose seven individuals to recommend the legislation that the state government should pursue. Robert Dineen, Vice-President of the Northwestern Mutual Life Insurance Company, and an active GMC member, headed the seven-member delegation. The committee originally proposed to study only the region's water and sewage problems. Infuriated city officials were now more convinced than ever that any "metropolitan" commission would be nothing more than a front for suburbs to gain access to or even take over Milwaukee's water authority. Henry Schmandt and William Standing, authors of a monograph that covered the history of the MSC, concluded that suburban officials supported the Dineen committee and the commission that grew out of it "only because they felt that the primary objective of civic officials at the time was the solution to the water problem. Since they had no control over this function, one which was of real concern to them, they stood to gain from such a study." Acutely aware of the potential of a metropolitan body weighted against Milwaukee, Zeidler warned Kohler prior to the governor's exit that extending water service outside of city boundaries would bring about an "exodus of industry" to the suburbs. Zeidler correctly suspected that his own perspective had "little weight" in the decisions that led to the creation of the MSC; he had no knowledge that GMC members had actually advised the governor on the MSC in the first place.[29]

When the geographical distribution of the MSC's members was first discussed in December 1956, Zeidler requested that the commission members' place of residence be tied to the county's demographics, a proposal which would have ensured the city a majority, since Milwaukee's population still made up the vast majority of Milwaukee County. Absent a demographically fair representation on the MSC, Zeidler warned, the result would be a commission "composed of suburban citizens to study how to parcel out the city of Milwaukee's services."[30] Any trace of "impartiality" would thus cease to exist. The city's pleas fell on deaf ears. The governor, again under advisement of the GMC, had great latitude in commission appointments. The commission had fifteen members, twelve of whom were to be Milwaukee County residents who did not hold elective office of any kind; the remaining three members public officials, one from the city of Milwaukee, one from suburban cities, and one from suburban villages. The geographical makeup of the original fifteen members confirmed the city's fears that Milwaukee's suburbs were usurping political power from the city. When added up, nine of the fifteen members of the MSC resided in Milwaukee County suburbs, compared to six city residents.

The state's bill that created the MSC directed the commission to undertake four main functions. First, the MSC was to "investigate the adequacy, cost, and efficiency of the principal services provided by the various governmental units of Milwaukee County." Next, the commission was to investigate and uncover the "extent" to which the county's municipalities cooperated with each other. Third, the MSC would determine what services could be provided on a local level and a county level. Finally, the MSC would submit written reports to the governor and state legislature detailing its findings, and to offer recommendations for future metropolitan cooperation and coalescence.[31]

As disappointed as Zeidler and other city officials may have been over the MSC's makeup, they still hoped to influence the commission. Fighting to keep ownership and control of Milwaukee's water supply was a necessary rear-guard action, but city officials also tried to use the MSC as a forum to float the long-hoped-for metropolitan solutions that had informed annexation in the first place. Foremost among these was the consolidation of the region, or at least Milwaukee County, into a single metropolitan government. George Parkinson, civil defense director of Milwaukee, represented the city on the MSC. Shortly after the group began its official duties, Parkinson released a "proposal" that sought to make the "record clear" from

Milwaukee's perspective. "I believe metropolitan government is urgently required for the Milwaukee area," Parkinson asserted, calling for the complete consolidation of all governmental units in the county. Parkinson acknowledged that getting the county's suburbs to agree to such a plan would be "difficult, if not impossible." The Milwaukee Common Council agreed, reminding the MSC in a 1959 resolution: "It is the long-standing position of the city of Milwaukee that the entire contiguous urban area of the Milwaukee region should be under one single unit of government, a municipality." The city had laid its cards on the table.[32]

In the past, other civic groups had shared the dream of metropolitan consolidation. The City Club, Milwaukee Real Estate Board, and Milwaukee Association of Commerce had each reacted positively to the possibility of consolidation during the Depression, which coincidentally was the most recent time when the Wisconsin state legislature had closely looked at metropolitan cooperation. By the late 1950s, these same groups seemed amenable at least to the spirit in which the MSC was intended to operate. The MAC, always eager to play down city-suburban squabbles, gave its public support to studying metropolitan problems, and one of its directors, Ebner Luetzow, was chosen to serve on the MSC. However, when Luetzow asked the MAC's Board of Directors to donate funds to support the MSC's studies (which received only a paltry $30,000 from the state budget) the board rejected the request.[33] The City Club, on the other hand, strenuously supported some form of metropolitan government in Milwaukee County, consistent with its previous support of consolidation during the Depression. Leo Tiefenthaler, the longtime secretary of the City Club, appeared before the state legislature during the debate of the MSC bill in December of 1956 and encouraged the state to expand its study of metropolitan problems beyond the provision of water. "The Milwaukee metropolitan area is one economic unit," Tiefenthaler reminded the state. He appealed for consolidation on the well-worn merits of civic greatness, echoing the famous Daniel Burnham phrase: "Make no little plans; they have no magic to stir men's blood . . . remember that a logical diagram once recorded will not die."[34] However, the City Club's membership and impact in local politics had been long on the wane; groups like the Greater Milwaukee Committee had far greater influence over civic affairs. For its part, the GMC seemed less interested in genuine political unification; perhaps more important was creating the *perception* of municipal cooperation. Well aware that other American cities had tackled urban problems with public-private partnerships that were "metropolitan" in makeup, the GMC considered city-suburban bickering as a nuisance that obstructed economic development and prevented Milwaukee from rebuilding its downtown, a process that was well underway in many peer cities. The GMC did not necessarily care to equalize growth across the region's fragmented boundaries.

Ultimately, appeals to civic greatness fell on deaf suburban ears. Political fragmentation had in fact multiplied the Milwaukee region's "economic units," as interrelated as they may have seemed to objective observers. While Milwaukee's suburbs remained different from each other in a myriad of ways, their stance against the city, once again, gave them common ground. Almost uniformly, Milwaukee County's suburbs envisioned the MSC less as a mediator between their conflicts with the city than as a conduit through which to clarify their municipal independence once and for all. In fact, at the same time, Milwaukee officials called on the MSC to pursue metropolitan government; the city of West Allis Common Council in a resolution that same year asserted that the region's suburbs "had attained municipal government close to their people, responsive to their people, important to their people, and participated in by their people."[35] This municipal pride had, if anything, only grown during the annexation wars, and it precluded the MSC from reaching any meaningful level of intergovernmental cooperation. With economic growth healthy in most of the region's suburbs, these communities had less incentive to pursue consolidation or even recognize that Milwaukee's problems were of regional concern. The *West Allis Star* put it bluntly: "We don't have any 'metropolitan problems,' except perhaps one—**to get the metrocrats to leave us alone!**" (emphasis in original).[36]

In fact, from 1956 to 1961, at the very time of the creation and term of the MSC, four towns bordering Milwaukee (Franklin, Greenfield, New Berlin, and Mequon) took advantage of the provisions of the Oak Creek Law and incorporated as fourth-class cities. Unlike past incorporations of relatively intact and self-contained communities, the four newest suburbs were huge in physical size and short on people. In 1956, the year the Town of Franklin, located southwest of Milwaukee, incorporated as a "city," it recorded a population density of only roughly four people per acre. Mequon's 8,543 residents were scattered over an area of land larger in size than the entire city of San Francisco. Upon hearing of Mequon's birth in 1959, a Milwaukee city official observed that it heralded a closing of "the ring of suburbs around the city of Milwaukee." The four newest suburbs totaled 122.4 square miles, or 20 percent more than Milwaukee's land size, with 689,000 fewer residents.[37]

Rapid suburbanization had also increased the demands on local government. As the MSC's Land Use and Zoning Committee observed in 1959:

"The dream of country living far from the smoke, noise, and dirt of the older industrial areas has become clouded by increasingly troublesome demands for new school buildings, better sanitation, and more of the services which city expatriates had become accustomed to in the older urban areas."[38] Put more bluntly, suburbanites wanted the municipal services of the city without having to reside there. By the late 1950s, this primarily meant gaining access to the Milwaukee water system, which pumped cheap and plentiful water from Lake Michigan to city residents. Suburban communities had sought access to city water for decades and some, especially on the North Shore, were able to purchase water from the city by contractual agreements long in effect.[39] City policy makers, cognizant of the fact that water was Milwaukee's chief weapon in compelling outlying areas to be annexed, had for years steadfastly refused to sell city water to other new suburbs. Thus municipalities such as Wauwatosa were forced to dig wells; and some developers of subdivisions outside the city dug private wells of their own. By the end of 1957, with suburban development mushrooming, there were over 20,000 private wells in the region, by one estimate. Many suburbs also used septic tanks instead of sanitary sewers. The threat of seepage into private wells was real enough that the MSC's Metropolitan Functions Committee made its primary focus the study of problems posed by private wells and septic tanks to the public health of Milwaukee County. In a report released in 1958, the committee acknowledged that water contamination, especially in areas where the soil contained clay, posed a potential threat to public health. However, the Metropolitan Functions Committee decided not to publicly identify subdivisions that did have contaminated wells. As Ebner Luetzow, the committee chairman and MAC Board Member, worried: "Such action might have an adverse effect on real estate values in those areas."[40] Nevertheless, the Wisconsin State Board of Health was already working to educate suburban residents about the dangers of water contamination, and suburban governments used the public health threat as an excuse to zone larger lots, which mitigated the volume of seepage.

Suburban governments were already hard at work using the public health issues of water supply to their advantage. The suburbs had sought access to city water for decades, and rapid postwar suburban expansion made the water issue more crucial than ever. This was more particularly obvious in the city of Wauwatosa. After annexing over eight square miles of land in 1953, Wauwatosa repeatedly applied to the city of Milwaukee's water authority, seeking permission to purchase city water to facilitate its development. Milwaukee steadfastly rejected each application. As Zeidler wryly noted in 1958, Wauwatosa's water shortage was its own fault and the huge annexation had given it a case of "municipal indigestion."[41] Having been thwarted by Milwaukee, Wauwatosa's leaders turned to the state's Public Service Commission (PSC), the governor-appointed authority that regulated public utilities within Wisconsin. The LSM, now officially called "The Municipal League of Milwaukee County," backed Wauwatosa, calling the provision of water "not a governmental function, but a proprietary, or private" endeavor.[42] In April 1958, the PSC ruled in favor of Wauwatosa, forcing the city to sell its water to every piece of land in the burgeoning suburb. A dismayed Zeidler suspected political motivations behind the decision, recognizing that the PSC was filled with appointees of Republican Governor Thomson. It had ruled in favor of an overwhelmingly Republican suburb and against an equally Democratic Milwaukee.[43]

The PSC's ruling made the functions of the MSC almost completely irrelevant to suburban municipalities and the city of Milwaukee, for different reasons. Since city water had been wrested away, no other problems of "metropolitan concern" preoccupied suburban leaders, as they would repeat time and again. For city leaders, metropolitan government's last gasp had ended. The precedent of the PSC's ruling was bound to compel it to furnish water to other, equally thirsty, suburbs. From the city's vantage point, suburban influence at the state level had been overwhelming throughout the 1950s. The PSC's decision had completed a dubious political trifecta. Through its judiciary branch, the state had ended the development of satellite cities by repealing the Butler Strip annexation. Through its legislative branch, the state had accelerated suburbanization through the passage of the Oak Creek Law. At least indirectly through its executive branch, the state had now taken away Milwaukee's water authority. The city thus had little reason to cooperate with the MSC, a body whose makeup had been created without its input in the first place. Any faith in the MSC's ability to solve metropolitan problems had ended, and it was apparent that the study commission's creation came at the end of an era of city-suburban conflict, not the beginning of an era of metropolitan cooperation.

In this political climate, the Metropolitan Study Commission carried out its duties. Each potentially meaningful reform the MSC introduced for discussion was perceived as a slight to one side or the other. The MSC's first president, Charles Lobb, suggested that metropolitan consolidation was at the very least a matter that deserved consideration. Suburban reaction to Lobb's remarks was predictably hostile, further undermining the MSC's already limited legitimacy. In 1958, the MSC decided to survey each municipality in Milwaukee County to determine what types of "metropolitan cooperation" the municipalities were willing to accept. Save for support of a "metropolitan" water authority, each suburb uniformly rejected practically any type of metropolitan cooperation. The county's newest incorporated municipalities adopted the rhetoric of suburban independence as assuredly as their forerunners. The newly minted city of Franklin accused Milwaukee of "political warfare."[44] Hales Corners and St. Francis, both incorporated in the 1950s, invoked the rights of home rule in their respective resolutions rejecting "metropolitan cooperation."[45]

One year later, in 1959, hoping to hinder unplanned or poorly managed sprawl, the MSC began to explore ways to merge the county's planning departments into a regional body that would have broad powers in regulating land use. Suburban governments in Milwaukee County had virtually no professional planners on their staffs, often relying instead on nonprofessionals in their local government to handle land use planning. For example, in 1959, the city of Milwaukee budgeted $175,000.00 for its Planning Division of the BPLC and Milwaukee County's other eighteen municipalities budgeted a *combined total* of only $32,000.00 for planning. The MSC assumed that there was a clear need for a regional planning authority, one that would have regulatory power. However, city and suburbs alike refused to cede their zoning powers. When queried by the MSC about countywide planning, every single municipality in Milwaukee County, including the city of Milwaukee, rejected the idea.[46]

With the regulatory muscle of a regional planning agency having been uniformly dismissed, the MSC tried to compel the city and suburbs to agree to an advisory body that would tackle issues of "metropolitan impact." At a public meeting of the MSC's Land Use and Zoning Committee, the commissioners asked representatives of each municipality to name specific common problems of "metropolitan impact." No one present managed to name a single issue. Zeidler again stated that any metropolitan planning agency should be only one function of a metropolitan government that had broad powers. An uneasy consensus of sorts was reached over the scope of land planning. Since development was spilling outside of Milwaukee County and into Waukesha and Ozaukee Counties to the west and north, it was agreed that an advisory land use planning body that served these counties (and perhaps Washington County to the northwest) would be useful. However, any regional planning agency would have only advisory powers; suburban and city governments remained unwilling to give up their autonomy. The eventual result of these preliminary discussions was the Southeast Wisconsin Regional Planning Commission (SEWRPC), established by state legislation and an executive order by Governor Thomson in 1960. After the United States Congress passed the Federal Aid Highway Act in 1962, which compelled local governments to cooperate with each other more fully in highway planning, SEWRPC's primary function became coordinating the region's nascent expressway system. However, SEWRPC's land use planning authority was in an advisory capacity only; local governments could utilize its technical assistance yet still veto any of the commission's recommendations. The reality of the politically fragmented metropolis meant that regional planning in Milwaukee was essentially stillborn. SEWRPC was unable to restrain suburban sprawl; from 1950 to 1990, the land consumption rate in metropolitan Milwaukee was eight times the rate of population growth, as compared with a national ratio of three to one.[47]

The MSC's Land Use and Zoning Committee may have failed to convince city and suburbs alike to cooperate in matters of planning, but its studies did reveal that intra-metropolitan competition for economic growth remained a by-product of municipal fragmentation. In a broad report that studied land use patterns in Milwaukee County, released in 1959, the Land Use and Zoning Committee reached several conclusions about the results of each municipality's quest to capture maximum tax revenues at minimal costs. The most obvious was that newer suburbs tended to zone larger residential lots, both to ensure that local schools could absorb the sudden influx of students and to attract individuals of "higher income levels." In the competition for public wealth, newer suburbs had awakened to the "shocking recognition" that most homes did not yield enough tax revenue to pay for the services demanded by their residents. New suburbs thus ignored Milwaukee's tradition of "medium density housing." The Land Use Committee noted bluntly that some of the suburbs "use the zoning power in an attempt to prevent the construction of less expensive homes." The city of Franklin, anticipating the fiscal strain of growth, decided to zone for minimum lots of a half-acre and forced developers to pay for water and sewer installations, costs that were usually passed on to consumers. The city of Mequon, north of Milwaukee in Ozaukee County, also required a minimum of half-acre lots. Greenfield and Oak Creek considered similar restrictions, and the city of Brookfield in Waukesha County required minimum lot frontages of 100 feet. These public land use policies virtually guaranteed the upper middle class—and therefore white—character of many postwar suburbs well before they were fully populated, further intertwining suburbanization with class, race, and uneven development. The MSC could illuminate these problems, but the deep freeze in city-suburban relations precluded meaningful land use reform.[48]

Zoning larger lots could ensure that more affluent middle-class residents would populate newer suburbs, but did not guarantee that local taxes would stay low unless nonresidential sources of revenue were secured. This usually meant creating space for industrial development. As the Land Use and Zoning Committee noted, continued competition for industry between many municipalities had "intensified the disunity and fragmentation of the natural metropolitan unit."[49] Local industrial concerns had long complained of high local and state taxes, which they claimed put them in an unfair competitive position in comparison with other regions of the country. The Milwaukee Association of Commerce's Industries Division was perhaps the most vocal proponent of this position.[50] The frequent complaints had long annoyed Mayor Zeidler, who was obviously preoccupied with keeping industry within city limits. However, even Wisconsin's Republican governor, Vernon Thomson, had had enough by 1957. At a speech to a junior chamber of commerce group that year, Thomson claimed that the state's "worst enemy" in industrial development was the state's own industrialists, who invariably called attention to the poor business climate within Wisconsin. The rhetoric did not stand up to the MSC's Land Use and Zoning Committee's observations about industry, which enjoyed an enviable position in the growing battle within metropolitan Milwaukee between city and suburbs to attract industrial development. In this battle, the committee wryly noted, "Industry finds itself in a position comparable to that of the only man shipwrecked on an island inhabited only by women. While a few of the so-called 'luxury suburbs' are completely self-sufficient and express no present interest in wooing industry, the majority are becoming increasingly dissatisfied with the state of residential 'single-blessedness,' and the competition for the security of an 'industrial daddy' is growing ever keener."[51]

Of the four municipalities that incorporated after the passage of the Oak Creek Law, three (Oak Creek, Franklin, and Brown Deer) had zoned a considerable amount of land for heavy commercial and industrial purposes. However, postwar suburbanization transformed the character of older suburban communities as well. Nowhere was this more evident than in Wauwatosa, one of the region's oldest and most self-consciously residential suburbs. As the village grew in the late nineteenth and early twentieth centuries, its boosters began to market Wauwatosa as the quintessential dormitory suburb, a place where middle-class families could escape the chaotic bustle of an industrial urban landscape. The village reclassified as a city in 1897, but clung to its suburban residential character, proudly dubbing itself the "City of Homes."[52]

The twin strains of municipal mercantilism and Milwaukee's annexation compelled Wauwatosa officials to pursue their own physical expansion in the early 1950s more aggressively. In 1953, Wauwatosa annexed an 8.5-square-mile tract of land to its north and west, virtually tripling its size.

CHART 7-2 | Milwaukee County Suburbs, Industrial Zoning, 1958

Municipality & Year of Incorporation	Area zoned for Industrial Purposes	Area in Industrial Use
Village of Brown Deer (1956)	966.40 acres	137.51 acres
Village of Bayside	0 acres	0 acres
Village of Fox Point	0 acres	0 acres
City of Cudahy	1,152.75 acres	300.08 acres
City of Franklin	335.40 acres	156.95 acres
City of Glendale	774.04 acres	324.49 acres
Village of Greendale	82.58 acres	49.40 acres
City of Greenfield	0 acres	9.79 acres
City of Oak Creek	1,533.69 acres	748.74 acres
Village of Hales Corners	37.86 acres	7.53 acres
Village of Shorewood	30.14 acres	23.90 acres
City of St. Francis	456.23 acres	166.42 acres
City of South Milwaukee	432.30 acres	186.97 acres
Village of River Hills	0 acres	0 acres
City of Wauwatosa	943.68 acres	581.27 acres
City of West Allis	1,566.92 acres	608.84 acres
Village of Whitefish Bay	0 acres	0 acres
Village of West Milwaukee	514.09 acres	378.34 acres

Source: Land Use and Zoning Committee Folder, Box 2, Metropolitan Study Commission Collection, Wisconsin Series 1720, MARC, GML.

Much of the newly acquired land lay next to railway lines and a future expressway extension, making its commercial and industrial uses self-evident. Wauwatosa officials—with the approval of a committee of citizens from the newly annexed land—zoned much of the new land for commercial and industrial purposes; large local manufacturers quickly moved in. In the early

1950s, the Briggs and Stratton Corporation purchased 85 acres of land in Wauwatosa and built a new plant that eventually covered over 1.5 million square feet and employed several thousand workers. Briggs and Stratton also began gradually phasing out work from its two older plants in the city of Milwaukee, vacating its offices in its facility on Milwaukee's north side in 1967 and ending production there entirely by 1974. Briggs also moved its employment offices to Wauwatosa in the 1960s.[53]

Shortly thereafter, Stroh Die-Casting and S-B Manufacturing built large installations in Wauwatosa. In 1957, the Harley Davidson Corporation built a production facility in Wauwatosa that initially employed 600 workers. J.C. Penney built a massive distribution center in 1962, eventually covering two million square feet. Wauwatosa was also the site of the construction of the region's largest indoor shopping mall, Mayfair, rushed to completion in 1957. The PSC's decision to force Milwaukee to connect Wauwatosa to its water system was heralded at a "historic" day by the city bulletin, one that would allow economic development to continue unabated well into the future.[54]

Wauwatosa had won numerous revenue plums through its expansion and in the process had transformed itself. No longer a bedroom community, Wauwatosa had grown into an economically diverse city, a change that its officials now readily embraced. The new industries allowed Wauwatosa to assess property taxes at only 38 percent of the land's full value, keeping taxes low, virtually a raison d'être for postwar suburbs. Wauwatosa's annual bulletins of the late 1950s featured numerous photographs of the new structures. Industry was no longer an aesthetically dubious stepchild; a caption under a photo of the Stroh Die-Casting plant proudly noted the plant to be "typical of many of the architecturally beautiful manufacturing plants in our city." Wauwatosa's status as a city of homes had ended, and its moniker eventually changed with the character of the community. By 1965, the annual bulletin had reinvented Wauwatosa as the "City of Homes, Industry, and Commerce."[55]

The functional transformation of suburbia was not separate from the plight of cities. It had been widely understood that Milwaukee and its suburbs were at political loggerheads, dating back well before the 1950s. What became increasingly clear, however, was the postwar upward mobility that was increasingly personified by the suburbs. "It all adds up to a revolution in community development—a revolution being felt on the edges of city after city across the nation," observed the *Milwaukee Journal* in a series of articles that ran in 1957 addressing the suburban "strangling of Milwaukee."[56] Older incorporated communities of the region had been peopled by a variety of classes. North Shore suburbs were wealthy. Wauwatosa was middle-class. Cudahy, South Milwaukee, West Milwaukee, and West Allis were industrial satellites and working-class in character. Postwar suburbs, by conscious intention, existed specifically as nodes of new or growing middle-class wealth. "Joe Suburb lives in Brookfield, Bayside, or Franklin . . . he's making more money than he ever did before," noted the *Journal*.[57] The "dream" of the region's new, large communities was also unprecedented: "a rural atmosphere mixed with sprawling industrial plants."[58] The upward mobility metaphor was now a suburban symbol.

Scholars of American cities remain divided over the significance of the closing of the 1950s. John Gurda, Milwaukee's redoubtable historian, inter-

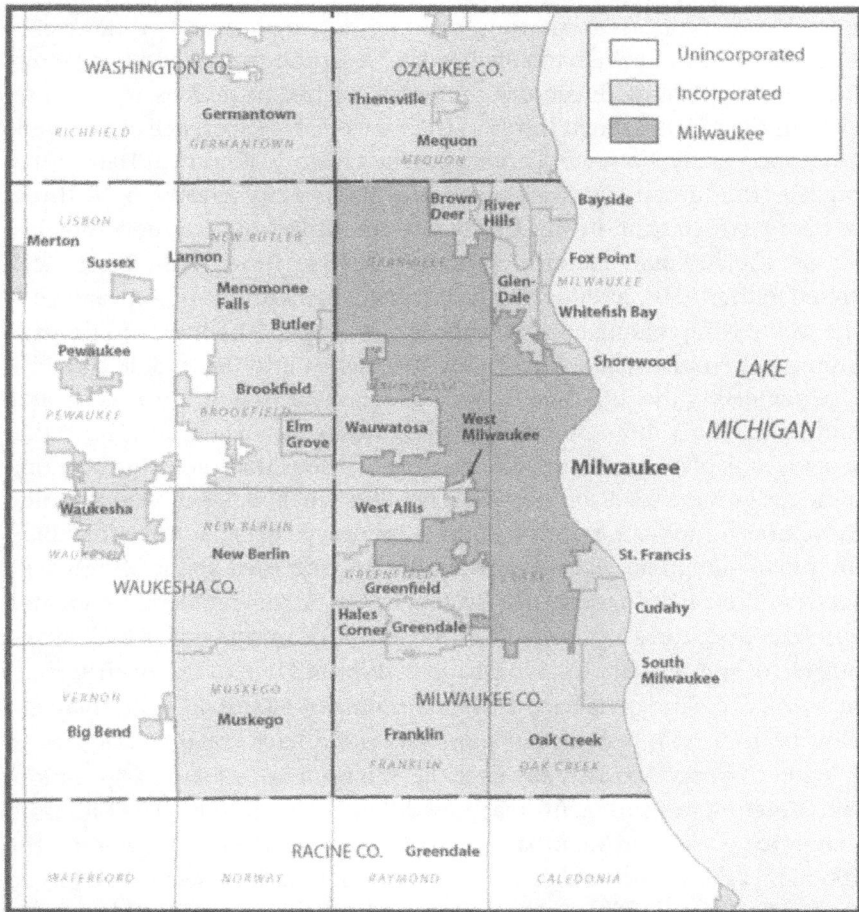

Municipalities of the Milwaukee Region after the Annexation Wars (1970)

preted that era as a time when Milwaukee was "at a pinnacle, a civic summit that seems all the more imposing in hindsight." Gurda pointed to the 1960 U.S. census, which counted Milwaukee's population at an all-time high of 741,324 residents, along with the recent completion of a variety of civic projects including a new art museum and veterans' memorial on Lake Michigan, and a new baseball stadium that lured the Braves away from Boston. Anthony Orum's study of city-building in Milwaukee, on the other hand, noted: "The decline happened rather swiftly after the war." Orum focused on the closing of the ring of incorporated suburbs, which sealed off Milwaukee's growth, as well as the flight of industry from the region to the Sunbelt.[59]

Opinions about the civic condition of other American cities in the 1950s are equally divergent. Writing of American cities more generally, Michael Johns's *Moment of Grace* portrays bustling downtowns and working-class neighborhoods in a "remarkable heyday," a period that would not be replicated in the twentieth century. "America reached its peak as an urban society in the 1950s," stated Johns in the very opening sentence of the book. More specifically, however, Thomas Sugrue's history of postwar Detroit that predates the "urban crisis" of the 1960s portrays a city already in the throes of deindustrialization in the 1950s. The city of Detroit, Sugrue wrote, lost almost 130,000 manufacturing jobs from 1948 to 1967. These losses accelerated in the 1950s, interlocking racial inequality with the disappearance of the well-paying manufacturing work in city neighborhoods that European immigrant families had used to buoy themselves into the middle class.[60]

Undeniably, the 1950s were, very generally, a time of great economic growth in the United States. However, when just where and how that growth took place is examined, it becomes obvious that the rising economic tide gave suburbs disproportional benefits when weighed against cities. Even more ominously, political boundaries proved to be far more than lines on a map. Suburban leaders were simply unconcerned about Milwaukee's social and economic problems. By the 1950s "urban problems" conflated with race and, since a minuscule number of African Americans had moved outside of the central city, suburbanites did not have to use overtly racist methods to defend or develop their communities. Suburban policy may not have been racist in intent, but nonetheless did have racial consequences. A vigorous debate exists today over the extent of Milwaukee's segregation, with different measurements reaching different conclusions. The Mumford Center for Urban and Suburban Research has concluded that, based on the 2000 U.S. census, Milwaukee is the second most racially segregated city in the United States. A recent study conducted at the University of Wisconsin-Milwaukee's Employment and Training Institute insists the Mumford Center's methodology is flawed and that the city is not nearly as segregated as had been previously believed.[61] The *Milwaukee Journal-Sentinel,* which has observed, "Perhaps no label associated with Milwaukee is more derogatory than 'hypersegregated,'" eagerly publicized the UW-Milwaukee study.[62]

No such confusion should exist, however, when the Milwaukee metropolitan area is examined as a whole. By any measurement, the metropolitan area is hypersegregated by race and class, with less than 2 percent of African Americans in the metropolitan area residing in the suburbs. Even the authors of the UW-Milwaukee study that played down segregation within the city acknowledged in their findings: "Except in Brown Deer and a small number of other scattered blocks, almost no black-white integrated blocks were located in the suburbs or rural communities of the Milwaukee area."[63] Black exclusion from suburbia was not an unfortunate coincidence, and neither was the overdevelopment of the suburbs and the underdevelopment of the city; all are consequences of political fragmentation, and the suburban development policies pursued as direct results of that fragmentation. The parameters of inequality within metropolitan Milwaukee were well established before the emergence of the more tumultuous civil rights movement in the 1960s.

Zeidler chose not to run for a fourth term as mayor in 1960. Worn out by the racial tensions and intragovernmental conflicts of the 1950s, Zeidler passed the city's reins to Henry Maier, who defeated Congressman Henry Reuss in the 1960 election. Maier assumed political leadership just as American cities, including Milwaukee, were at a crossroads. On one hand, Milwaukee seemed to have fared better demographically than other industrial cities of similar size. Annexation gave Milwaukee a luxury that very few other Midwest and northern cities enjoyed: a reserve of land that caught some of the rapid postwar residential outflow. While St. Louis, Cleveland, Pittsburgh, and Cincinnati all lost residents in the 1950s, Milwaukee's population increased from 637,392 residents in 1950 to an all-time peak of 741,324 in 1960. Annexation had virtually doubled Milwaukee's size.

On the other hand, the very same civic ambition that made Milwaukee a regional anomaly after World War II also propelled the city into a series of conflicts with burgeoning suburbs. The result was a fragmented metropolis and one ill prepared to address the divisions created by political balkanization. Annexation provided "elbow room" for growth, but it did not prevent the city's industrial base from eroding. Nor was annexation sufficient to allow for the satellite city projects in Greendale and Waukesha County that two generations of Milwaukee policy makers tried to develop in reaction to the city's rapid urbanization. Instead, the northwest side of Milwaukee, where most of the annexations took place, became, as Mayor Zeidler later recalled, merely "subdivisions, neat and clean, but without special character and with the dulling sameness of amorphous growth of an urban area."[64] The legacy of annexation is thus mixed; in a regional context Milwaukee was relatively healthy compared to its less fortunate urban counterparts.

Maier quickly distanced himself from Zeidler's socialist ideas and began building coalitions with the region's business elites. This strategy, coupled with Maier's colorful populist rhetoric, proved politically successful. Maier served a remarkable seven terms in office, from 1960 to 1988, and was rarely challenged for office. He displayed relatively scant interest in public housing, but became a vigorous advocate of urban redevelopment, in 1964 calling for the establishment of a "blight line in Milwaukee." Between 1956 and 1975, the city redeveloped 256 acres of land north, west, and east of downtown. Freeway construction also rapidly progressed; between 1959 and 1971, bulldozers cleared 6,334 housing units and displaced over 20,000 residents, the vast majority of whom lived in Milwaukee's city neighborhoods on the north and south sides. The new roads were a Milwaukee County project, but city leaders supported the initial plans when released by the Milwaukee County Expressway Commission in 1946. By the early 1970s, however, a variety of groups had grown tired of seeing neighborhoods swallowed up. Maier himself argued that freeways had become a "concrete monster, which gulps up huge blocks of housing each year." Urban redevelopment and freeway construction were not mutually exclusive, either. About 10 percent of all of the land the city "redeveloped" went to freeway usage.[65]

Urban renewal exacerbated the region's racial tensions, which became far more acute in the 1960s. Milwaukee's civil rights movement grew along with the city's African American population, which topped 100,000 residents by 1970. Maier gained a reputation for soft-pedaling race, dismissing a Zeidler-appointed study of black neighborhoods as a useless mass of facts and figures. When a key Maier appointee to a new inner city commission commented that poor blacks had "an IQ of nothing" and all looked alike, Maier's administration became a prime target of the city's civil rights leaders. Not incidentally, Maier's popularity rose dramatically in white ethnic neighborhoods on the south side and far northwest side. The mayor increasingly projected an image of "law and order" in the face of racial turnover and increasing poverty. In 1967, a riot broke out along North Third Street and spread to adjoining neighborhoods, killing three people and injuring almost 100 more. Maier acted quickly to quell the disturbance, calling in the National Guard and issuing a mandatory curfew. As a result, his popularity only increased among white residents. The 1968 mayoral election proved to be a landslide for Maier, who won 86 percent of the vote, an all-time record in Milwaukee's history.[66]

Critics of Maier argued that he sidestepped race too frequently. Maier preferred to blame Milwaukee's heightened racial tensions on a variety of issues tangential to city politics, especially a lack of adequate federal funding for antipoverty programs and the "iron ring" of suburbs that whites moved to in ever-greater numbers in the 1960s and 1970s. Civil rights leaders who emerged in Milwaukee during the 1960s, especially Father James Groppi and Alderwoman Vel Phillips (Milwaukee's first African American member of the Common Council), made the passage of a citywide open housing ordinance a top political priority. Maier was, at best, lukewarm toward the open housing idea. Instead, he singled out the region's suburbs for refusing to absorb their share of African Americans, which resulted in "urban apartheid." In his view, no open housing ordinance would work if suburban communities refused to embrace integration along with the city.[67]

Maier's frequent attacks on Milwaukee's suburbs, whatever their true political motive, were not without substance. Racial tensions played out in a fragmented metropolis. The newly incorporated communities that formed the iron ring became, by explicit design, middle-class havens. Suburbs sought to attain the highest and best uses of land at the lowest possible costs of service provision. Anthony Orum dubbed these communities as virtual "barricades behind which the wealthy can take refuge."[68] This process of community-building made scant provisions for lower-income housing. As historian David Freund has recently pointed out, it often couched racial inequality in the ostensibly "color-blind" language of property values.[69] It also made the matter of "open housing" irrelevant. Even if communities adopted nondiscrimination policies toward housing, few blacks could afford to move there anyway. This became apparent in 1969, when the sprawling community of Mequon, which had first incorporated ten years earlier, became the first suburban community to adopt an open housing ordinance. Mequon's strict residential zoning required half-acre lots in much of the community. African Americans did not move there in any significant numbers. By 2000, Mequon's median family income was more than double the national average, but even with open housing long in place, African Americans represented just 2 percent of its nearly 22,000 residents.

Further complicating the problems of race and class in the fragmented metropolis was Milwaukee's industrial decline. Job losses in manufacturing could be felt as early as the 1950s, but decline progressed more rapidly in the 1960s and 1970s. The Milwaukee metropolitan area's total of employed industrial workers dropped from 138,500 in 1950 to 127,800 in 1960. By

1971, the number of employed industrial workers in the four-county metropolitan area was only a little over 110,000. This decline in industrial employment during the 1960s occurred at the same time that globalization began to have real consequences for Milwaukee's industrial companies. Longtime privately held and managed corporations such as Nordberg Manufacturing and Chain Belt, "with no family to continue management," merged in 1970.[70] A new generation of executives took over the helm at the Allen-Bradley Corporation beginning in 1967 and brought with them "a new attitude toward market penetration, acquisitions, and product development." Allen-Bradley established branch plants or acquired subsidiaries in England, Mexico, France, West Germany, and South America. The new executives, lacking the familial ties to community forged by earlier industrialists, found it easier to move operations out of the region. In the 1970s, Allen-Bradley shifted 1,200 production jobs from Milwaukee to El Paso, Texas, and Greensboro, North Carolina, and convinced its Greensboro workers not to form a union. Corporate restructuring immediately preceded the decline in manufacturing that occurred across the region. From 1968 to 1976, seventy-six different Milwaukee area companies, employing a total of 16,000 workers, closed down, reduced operations, or moved out of the region. Once open, the floodgates never closed. In 1970, the ten top employers in the Milwaukee region were either manufacturers or brewers. By 2004, every company from 1970s list had vanished from the top ten, a lineup that did not include a single manufacturer.[71]

The deindustrialization of Milwaukee both transcended political borders and exacerbated the effects of the fragmented metropolis. Suburban communities, especially older industrial satellite communities like West Milwaukee, West Allis, and Cudahy, experienced the impact of industrial decline as strongly as Milwaukee. More broadly, deindustrialization was a global phenomenon. It had multiple causes, most of which seemed well beyond the control of city, state, and even federal policy makers. Virtually no American city emerged from deindustrialization completely unscathed. However, the reality of fragmentation contributed to the uneven effects of deindustrialization. In a study of employment changes in the Milwaukee region from 1979 to 1987, a team of researchers at the University of Wisconsin-Milwaukee led by Sammis White, Jr., discovered that the city of Milwaukee lost over 32,000 manufacturing jobs during that span. Gains in other sectors did not compensate for the industrial decline, as the city also recorded a net loss of over 29,000 jobs across all economic sectors. The four-county (Milwaukee, Waukesha, Ozaukee, and Washington) region's suburbs did lose over 18,000 manufacturing jobs, but made dramatic gains in service and in every other sector. While the city's losses mounted, the suburbs gained a net of over 36,000 jobs.[72]

Milwaukee's economic struggles were not unique. Nor was the political acrimony that characterized the metropolis during the twentieth century. Not every suburb remained economically healthy, either. Regardless, the political lines that divide Milwaukee and its suburbs were not the result of circumstance, accident, or coincidence. People created them for specific reasons. In Milwaukee's case, a remarkable number of suburbs came into existence out of three motivations: to prevent annexation, protect or enhance tax revenues, and preserve local government. This heightened the importance of making new suburbs so residentially exclusive that people became segregated by class. Furthermore, it led suburbs to welcome commercial, office, and industrial development, which increased tax revenue, accelerated suburban sprawl, and only further eroded the central city's revenue base. Milwaukee's leaders often took suburban localism less seriously than perhaps they needed to. They consistently misinterpreted desires for local autonomy as a cabal orchestrated by suburban government officials determined to hold on to their jobs, a small circle of suburban attorneys who made litigating against the city their primary source of legal work, and suburban newspapers that feared that the loss of local government would end their existence. While suburban residents themselves often shared the same fears as their government officials and local media, they also resented what appeared to be a hegemonic city government arbitrarily deciding their political future.

Epilogue

If it can be argued that the built landscape is a physical expression of American values, Milwaukee's conflicted twentieth century hints that its municipal landscape is perhaps the institutional expression of American values. Scholars still grapple with the meaning of "regionalism" in American history, and it is very rare to find cases where it lived up to the dreams of planning reformers. This does not mean regionalism became extinct in the United States, but rather that it has come to serve different ends. In twentieth-century Milwaukee, a unique set of planning policies advocated by an equally distinct group of politicians and planners eventually gave way to selective metropolitanism, in which citizens make discriminatory choices as to what responsibilities should be shared across municipal border and class lines, and what should be handled "locally" or even individually. In this regard, Milwaukee's local problems illuminate national patterns. Americans have proved willing to seek out regional solutions to resource management, water supplies, highways, and even mass transit. But Americans have also proved to be far less willing to treat more complex social problems on a regional basis. Regional solutions are far more seldom offered for poverty, equality of educational opportunity, and revenue sharing. To be sure, "regional cooperation" remains a time-honored political catchphrase that chambers of commerce, public intellectuals, local media, and municipal, county, and state officials all find useful to gain public traction. Perhaps because regionalism is so often a political tool, too frequently in American history, regionalist policies that encourage economic growth or promise to lower taxes are privileged at the expense of ideas that might encourage equity, wealth redistribution, and smart growth land use patterns.

The material circumstance that perhaps ultimately conflicted with Milwaukee's metropolitan visions is the reality of "privatism." Historian Sam Bass Warner has famously asserted that the private search for wealth has driven the process of urbanization.[73] Other historians have refined the notion of "privatism" in critiques of urban policy, correctly noting that city leaders too often responded to the demands of the private market in formulating policy. Implicit in the story of Milwaukee is the search for *public wealth* as a process driven not by abstract planning principles but instead by municipal mercantilism. Public land use decisions, annexation battles, court decisions, and state legislation profoundly affected the nature of urban and suburban development in the Milwaukee region. Acknowledging that the private search for wealth in the modern metropolis helps define the life cycle of cities does not circumscribe the reality of political balkanization as the context in which that search has taken place. In Milwaukee, two generations of politicians challenged both privatism and municipal mercantilism, but the reach of planning visions exceeded the municipal grasp of the city.

Notes

Preface

1. As quoted in William Fulton, "The Garden Suburb and the New Urbanism," in Kermit C. Parsons and David Schuyler, eds. *From Garden City to Green City: The Legacy of Ebenezer Howard* (Baltimore: Johns Hopkins University Press, 2002), 164.

2. James Howard Kunstler, *The Geography of Nowhere: The Rise and Decline of America's Man-Made Landscape* (New York: Touchstone Press, 1993), 10.

3. For a critique of "modernist urbanism," see Emily Talen, *New Urbanism and American Planning: The Conflict of Cultures* (New York and London: Routledge Press, 2005), 50–68. For a more general critique of sprawl and twentieth-century land use policies, see Andres Duany, Elizabeth Plater-Zyberk, and Jeff Speck, *Suburban Nation: The Rise of Sprawl and the Decline of the American Dream* (New York: North Point Press, 2000).

4. John Norquist, *The Wealth of Cities: Revitalizing the Centers of American Life* (Reading, Mass.: Addison & Wesley, 1998), 105.

5. John F. Bauman and Edward K. Muller, *Before Renaissance: Planning in Pittsburgh, 1890–1940* (Pittsburgh: University of Pittsburgh Press, 2006), 7.

6. Susan Marie Wirka, "The City Social Movement: Progressive Women Reformers and Early Social Planning," in Mary Corbin Sies and Christopher Silver, eds., *Planning the Twentieth Century American City* (Baltimore: Johns Hopkins University Press, 1996), 55–76.

7. Another exception to the planning/housing split can be found in Robert Fairbanks, *Making Better Citizens and the Community Development Strategy in Cincinnati, 1890–1960* (Urbana: University of Illinois Press, 1988).

1—City Planning and Social Progressivism

1. The account that this paragraph relies on can be found in Jon A. Peterson, *The Birth of City Planning in the United States, 1840–1917* (Baltimore: Johns Hopkins University Press, 2003), 246–55.

2. The most complete accounts of the early split between the American planning and housing movements are Peterson, *The Birth of City Planning in the United States, 1840–1917*, 246–59; Peter Marcuse, "Housing in Early City Planning," *Journal of Urban History* 6, no. 2 (February 1980): 153–76; and Susan Marie Wirka, "The City Social Movement: Progressive Women Reformers and Early Social Planning," in Mary Corbin

Sies and Christopher Silver, eds., *Planning the Twentieth Century American City* (Baltimore: Johns Hopkins University Press, 1996), 55–76.

3. For an account of the early growth of Milwaukee's economy, see Roger D. Simon, "Foundations for Industrialization, 1835–1880," in Thomas Jablonsky, ed., *Milwaukee Stories* (Milwaukee: Marquette University Press, 2005), 303–27.

4. As quoted in Carl S. Thompson, "The Housing Awakening: Socialists and Slums—Milwaukee," *The Survey*, December 3, 1910, 367.

5. See Judith T. Kenny, "Polish Routes to Americanization: House Form and Landscape on Milwaukee's South Side," in T. Vale and R. Ostergren, eds., *Wisconsin Land and Life* (Madison: University of Wisconsin Press, 1996).

6. Bayard Still, *Milwaukee: The History of a City* (Madison: State Historical Society of Wisconsin, 1948), 389.

7. Letter, Catherine Bauer to Clarence Stein, July 16, 1933, Folder 1, Box 2, Clarence Stein Papers, #3600. Division of Rare and Manuscript Collections, Cornell University Library (CUL).

8. Edith Elmer Wood, "Slums and Blighted Areas of the United States," Housing Division Bulletin No. 1, Federal Emergency Administration of Public Works, 19.

9. The best ethnography of the Polish South Side is Kenny, "Polish Routes to Americanization: House Form and Landscape on Milwaukee's South Side."

10. Peterson, *The Birth of City Planning in the United States*, 21–25. Two excellent studies that link engineers to the rise of city planning are Stanley Schultz, *Constructing Urban Culture: American Cities and City Planning, 1800–1920* (Philadelphia: Temple University Press, 1989); and Clay McShane, *Technology and Reform: Street Railways and the Growth of Milwaukee, 1887–1900* (Madison: State Historical Society of Wisconsin, 1975).

11. Judith Walzer Leavitt, *The Healthiest City: Milwaukee and the Politics of Health Reform* (Princeton, N.J.: Princeton University Press, 1982).

12. On uneven water service provision, see Roger Simon, *The City-Building Process: Housing and Services in New Milwaukee Neighborhoods, 1880–1910* (Philadelphia: The American Philosophical Society, 1996), chap. 4. On the politics of water service in the 1900–1920 period, see Kate Foss-Mollan, *Hard Water: Politics and Water Supply in Milwaukee, 1870–1995* (West Lafayette, Ind.: Purdue University Press, 2001), 80–89. Foss-Mollan argues, unlike Simon, that uneven water service in poorer areas of the city was a political issue, and not merely a choice of working-class residents to avoid special assessments.

13. Frank A. Cassell, "Milwaukee and the Columbian Exposition of 1893," in Thomas Jablonsky, ed., *Milwaukee Stories* (Milwaukee: Marquette University Press, 2005), 89–93.

14. Richard W. E. Perrin, "Resurgent Classicism: Wisconsin Architecture in the Wake of the Columbian Exposition," *Wisconsin Magazine of History*, Winter 1962–1963, 119–23.

15. Still, *Milwaukee: The History of a City*, 388–89.

16. For more on the McMillan Plan, see Howard Gillette Jr., *Between Justice and Beauty: Race, Planning, and the Failure of Urban Policy in Washington, D.C.* (Baltimore: Johns Hopkins University Press, 1995), 88–109, and Peterson, *The Birth of City Planning in the United States, 1840–1917*, 120.

17. Peterson, *The Birth of City Planning in the United States, 1840–1917*, 213.

18. Marvin Christian, "The Milwaukee Park Movement: A History of its Origins and Development," M.A. Thesis, University of Wisconsin-Milwaukee, 1967, 119–20; Diane M. Buck, "Olmsted's Lake Park," in Thomas Jablonsky, ed., *Milwaukee Stories* (Milwaukee: Marquette University Press, 2005), 186–87.

19. Alfred Clas, "Civic Improvement in Milwaukee," address before the Greater Milwaukee Association, December 14, 1916, Legislative Reference Bureau (LRB), 4.

20. Charles Whitnall, Untitled Report, January 1906, 1936 Folder, Whitnall Papers, Milwaukee County Historical Society (MCHS).

21. Florence Schulson, "History of Planning Activity in Milwaukee," 1952, Board of Public Land Commissioners, 1.

22. "First Tentative Report," Metropolitan Park Commission, January 28, 1909, LRB, 18.

23. Frederick Law Olmsted, Jr., and John Nolen, "Report on Civic Center as proposed by the Metropolitan Park Commission," July 27, 1909, LRB, 3–4.

24. "Third Tentative Report," Metropolitan Park Commission, 1910, LRB, 36–37.

25. As quoted in John Gurda, *The Making of Milwaukee* (Milwaukee: Milwaukee County Historical Society, 1999), 266.

26. Milwaukee Citizens Governmental Research Bureau, "Report Made to the Research Clearinghouse of Milwaukee," 1947, Frank P. Zeidler Humanities Room, Milwaukee Public Library (MPL), 2.

27. Alfred Clas, "Civic Improvement in Milwaukee," address before the Greater Milwaukee Association, December 14, 1916, 15.

28. The most complete overview of City Beautiful civic projects is William H. Wilson, *The City Beautiful Movement* (Baltimore: Johns Hopkins University Press, 1994). For Pittsburgh, see Bauman and Muller, *Before Renaissance*, 98–99. For Cleveland, see Ronald R. Weiner, *Lake Effects: A History of Urban Policy Making in Cleveland, 1825–1929* (Columbus: Ohio State University Press, 2005).

29. Gurda, *The Making of Milwaukee*, 203–6; Marvin Wachman, *History of the Social-Democratic Party in Milwaukee, 1897–1910* (Urbana: University of Illinois Press, 1945), 74–75; Sally Miller, "Milwaukee: Of Ethnicity and Labor," in Bruce Stave, ed., *Socialism and the Cities* (Port Washington, N.Y.: Kennikat Press, 1975).

30. Still, *Milwaukee: The History of a City*, 320.

31. For examples of historians framing Milwaukee Socialists as moderates, see Richard W. Judd, *Socialist Cities: Municipal Politics and the Grass Roots of American Socialism* (Albany: State University of New York Press, 1989) 23, 36–40; Sally M. Miller, "Race, Ethnicity, and Gender in Early Twentieth-Century American Socialism," in *Garland Reference Library of Social Science* 880 (New York and London: Garland Publishing, 1996): 59–62; and Still, *Milwaukee: The History of a City*, 320.

32. "No Millennium Yet for Milwaukeeans," *New York Times*, April 7, 1910.

33. Ibid.

34. The most thoroughgoing discussion of Milwaukee Socialists' fiscal policies is Douglas E. Booth, "Municipal Socialism and Government Reform: The Milwaukee Experience, 1910–1940," *Journal of Urban History* 12, no.1 (November 1985): 51–74.

35. As quoted in Wirka, "The City Social Movement: Progressive Women Reformers and Early Social Planning," in *Planning the Twentieth Century American City*, 66. An excellent account of the broadening civic role women seized during the Progressive Era can be found in Daphne Spain, *How Women Saved the City* (Minneapolis: University of Minnesota Press, 2000).

36. Donald Krueckeberg, ed., *The American Planner: Biographies and Recollections* (New York: Routledge Press, 1983), 60.

37. Benjamin Marsh, "Planning in Justice to the Working Population," *Charities and the Commons* (February 1, 1908); Peterson, *The Birth of City Planning*, 238.

38. Ruth Harman and Charlotte Lekachman, "The 'Jacobs House,'" *The Wisconsin Magazine of History* 16, no.3 (March 1933): 262.

39. Elizabeth Jozwiak, "Politics in Play: Socialism, Free Speech, and Social Centers in Milwaukee," *Wisconsin Magazine of History* 86 (Spring 2003): 17.

40. "Milwaukee Social-Democratic City Platform, 1910," in Wachman, *History of the Social-Democratic Party in Milwaukee,* 80.

41. Carl S. Thompson, "The Housing Awakening: Socialists and Slums–Milwaukee," *The Survey*, December 3, 1910, 368.

42. Ibid., 370.

43. Ibid., 373.

44. George Allan England, "Milwaukee's Socialist Government," *American Review of Reviews* (October 1910): 451.

45. "The Point of View of the New York Committee on the Congestion of Population," "Proceedings of the Third National Conference on City Planning," Philadelphia, May 15–17, 1911, 39.

46. Florence Schulson, "A History of Planning Activity in Milwaukee, 1892–1952," 1. See also Emil Seidel, "Defense of the Socialist Regime in Milwaukee," Folder 4, Box 1, Emil Seidel Papers, UWM Manuscript Collection 76. University Manuscript Collection, Area Research Center, Golda Meir Library, University of Wisconsin-Milwaukee (MARC, GML).

47. Gurda, *The Making of Milwaukee*, 268.

48. John L. Thomas, "Holding the Middle Ground," in Robert Fishman, ed., *The American Planning Tradition: Culture and Policy* (Baltimore: Johns Hopkins University Press), 36. For commentary on both Whitnall and his surrounding neighborhood, see Tom Tolan, *Riverwest: A Community History* (Milwaukee: Past Press, 2003), 18–23.

49. "C. B. Whitnall Is President," *Milwaukee Sentinel*, October 4, 1899.

50. For George's influence on English Fabian societies, see Stanley Buder, *Visionaries and Planners: The Garden City Movement and the Modern Community* (New York and Oxford: Oxford University Press, 1990), 14–20.

51. Ibid., 40.

52. "Five Lectures on City Planning: Given by C. B. Whitnall at the Ninth Annual Session of the Institute of Government, University of Southern California, June 14–18, 1937," 1937–1938 Folder, Charles Whitnall Papers, MCHS; Henry George, *Progress and Poverty: An Inquiry into the Cause of Industrial Depressions and of Increase of Want with Increase of Wealth: The Remedy* (Garden City, N.Y.: Doubleday, Page & Co., 1912).

53. Untitled Report by Charles Whitnall, Issued by Milwaukee County Parks Commission, 7–8, 1936 Folder, Charles Whitnall Papers, Milwaukee County Historical Society (MCHS).

54. Ibid., 7.

55. C. B. Whitnall, "Milwaukee City Planning," 1911, LRB, Milwaukee, 11.

56. Ibid., 17.

57. Ibid.

58. Ibid., 6.

59. For more extensive coverage of Gordon Whitnall, see, for example, Greg Hise, *Magnetic Los Angeles: Planning the Twentieth Century Metropolis* (Baltimore: Johns Hopkins University Press, 1999); Jeremiah B. C. Axelrod, "'Keep The "L" Out Of Los Angeles': Race, Discourse, and Urban Modernity in 1920s Southern California," *Journal of Urban History* 34 (2007): 3–37; and Gregg Wassmansdorf, "Public-Private Dialects in the Planning and Development of Los Angeles, 1781–1993," M.A. Thesis, University of Southern California, 1994.

60. "Biography of Gordon Whitnall," Folder 127, Box 32, American Society of Planning Officials Records, #3247. Division of Rare and Manuscript Collections, CUL.

61. Letter, C. B. Whitnall to Gordon Whitnall, September 1941, Gordon and Brysis Whitnall Papers, #2880. Division of Rare and Manuscript Collections, CUL.

62. As quoted in Gurda, *The Making of Milwaukee*, 218.

63. Ibid., 218–20.

64. The similarities between Mumford and Hegemann—especially both men's proclivity to view cities in terms of intellectual engagement—are drawn in Nicholas Dagen Bloom, "Architects, Architecture, and Urbanism," *Journal of Planning History* 7, no. 1 (February 2008): 76. For a penetrating and highly original account of transatlantic so-

cial progressivism, see Daniel T. Rodgers, *Atlantic Crossings: Social Politics in a Progressive Age* (Cambridge, Mass.: Harvard University Press, 1998).

65. Richard E. Fogelsong, *Planning the Capitalist City: The Colonial Era to the 1920s* (Princeton, N.J.: Princeton University Press, 1986), 169.

66. The authoritative work on Hegemann's life is Christine Craeseman Collins, *Werner Hegemann and the Search for Universal Urbanism* (New York: W.W. Norton and Co., 2005), 23–26.

67. Ibid., 116.

68. Werner Hegemann, "City Planning for Milwaukee: What It Means and Why It Must be Secured," 1916, MPL, 8.

69. Ibid., 9.

70. Ibid., 20.

71. Ibid., 22.

72. Collins, *Werner Hegemann and the Search for Universal Urbanism*, 119–26. For another example of Hegemann and Peets's collaboration, see Werner Hegemann and Elbert Peets, *The American Vitruvius: An Architects' Handbook of Civic Art* (New York: Architectural Book Publishing Co., 1922).

73. Melvin G. Holli, *The American Mayor: The Best and Worst Big-City Leaders* (University Park: Penn. State University Press, 1999).

74. For example, see Richard W. Judd, *Socialist Cities: Municipal Politics and the Grass Roots of American Socialism* (Albany: State University of New York Press, 1989), 23, 36–40; Holli, *The American Mayor: The Best and Worst Big-City Leaders,* 67–68, 71. A somewhat different analysis of Hoan's mayoralty, one that emphasizes social experimentation, can be found in Douglas E. Booth, "Municipal Socialism and City Government Reform: The Milwaukee Experience, 1910–1940," *Journal of Urban History* 12, no.1 (November 1985): 51–74.

75. Frederick I. Olson, "The Milwaukee Socialists, 1897–1941," Ph.D. Diss., Harvard University, 1952, 426.

76. "Organizations of Membership to the City Beautiful Committee," Folder 147, Box 6, Hoan Papers, Manuscript Collection #546, Milwaukee County Historical Society (MCHS).

77. "Milwaukee Sewage Commission, Annual Report," Housing Clipping File, LRB.

78. "Congestion Found by Health Commissioner Ruhland in Study of City's Housing Problem," *Milwaukee Sentinel*, January 26, 1916, Housing Clipping File, LRB.

79. "Poor Housing Conditions," *Milwaukee Daily News*, November 23, 1916, Housing Clipping File, LRB.

80. "Housing Conditions in Milwaukee," *Milwaukee Journal*, August 2, 1917, Housing Clipping File, LRB.

81. "Report of the Housing Commission," Folder 455, Box 19, Hoan Papers, MCHS; "First Report on Housing Reforms Made to Mayor," *Milwaukee Sentinel*, December 1, 1918.

82. Edward K. Spann, *Designing Modern America: The Regional Planning Association of America and Its Members* (Columbus: Ohio State University Press, 1996), 6–7. See also Stanley Buder, *Visionaries and Planners: The Garden City Movement and the Modern Community* (New York and Oxford: Oxford University Press, 1990), 165.

83. Letter, Charles Whitaker to William Schuchardt, January 16, 1919, Folder 453, Box 19, Daniel Hoan Papers, MCHS.

84. "Report of the Milwaukee Housing Commission," *Journal of the American Institute of Architects*, February 1919, 79–81.

85. Letter, Clarence Stein to William Schuchardt, March 20, 1919, Folder 449, Box 18, Daniel Hoan Papers, MCHS.

86. "Co-Operative Housing from the Architect's Viewpoint," panelists Charles Whitnall, Clarence Stein, and Agnes D. Warbasse, 4th Cooperative Congress of the Cooperative League of America, New York City, Nov. 7, 1924, Folder 12, Box 6, Clarence Stein Papers, Carl Kroch Library, Cornell University.

87. Letter, John Patrick Hume to Daniel Hoan, December 3, 1918, File 449, Box 18, Hoan Papers, MCHS.

88. "Housing Need Not Serious, Report Says," *Milwaukee Sentinel,* July 11, 1919, Housing Clipping File, LRB.

89. "A. of C. Report Not Completed," *Wisconsin News,* July 11, 1919, Housing Clipping File, LRB.

90. "Statistics vs. Van Scoy on Milwaukee Housing Problems," *Wisconsin News,* July 14, 1919.

91. The most complete overview of the Garden Homes appears in chap. 4 of David Barry Cady, "The Influence of the Garden City Ideal on American Housing and Planning Reform, 1900–1940," Ph.D. Diss., University of Wisconsin-Madison, 1970. Also see Wayne Attoe and Mark Latus, "The First Public Housing: Sewer Socialism's Garden City for Milwaukee," *The Journal of Popular Culture* X, no.1 (Summer 1976): 142–49; and Gail Radford, *Modern Housing for America: Policy Struggles in the New Deal Era* (Chicago: University of Chicago Press, 1996), 49–51.

92. Cady, "The Influence of the Garden City Ideal on American Housing and Planning Reform, 1900–1940," 100; "Garden Homes Housing Project: A Summary," 1934, Legislative Reference Bureau, Milwaukee.

93. Cady, "The Influence of the Garden City Ideal on American Housing and Planning Reform, 1900–1940," 101.

94. M. Christine Boyer, *Dreaming the Rational City: The Myth of American City Planning* (Cambridge, Mass.: MIT Press, 1990), 139–70; Patricia Burgess, *Planning for the Private Interest: Land Use Controls and Residential Patterns in Columbus, Ohio, 1900–1970* (Columbus: Ohio State University Press, 1994).

95. Roy Lubove, *Community Planning in the 1920s: The Contributions of the Regional Planning Association of America* (Pittsburgh: University of Pittsburgh Press, 1963), 15; Rodgers, *Atlantic Crossing,* 197.

96. "Owning an Apartment as a Tenant," *The Survey,* June 29, 1919, 10–11.

97. "Address of Edward M. Bassett On the Subject of Zoning, Milwaukee," June 22, 1920, in "Zoning for Milwaukee," 51, LRB.

98. Letter, Civic Secretary of the City Club of Milwaukee to Russell Griffen, Secretary of the Grand Rapids Citizen's League, December 14, 1922, Folder 9, Box 10, City Club of Milwaukee Records, MARC, GML; "Zoning Ordinance Passes Council," *Milwaukee Sentinel,* November 16, 1920, Zoning Clipping File, LRB.

99. "Zoning for Milwaukee: Tentative Report of the Board of Public Land Commissioners," 1920, LRB 6.

100. Ibid.

101. Ibid., 6.

102. Gurda, *The Making of Milwaukee,* 265.

103. Ibid. See also "Restricted Heights of Buildings," Milwaukee Board of Public Land Commissioners, 1920, MPL.

104. "Proceedings of the Thirteenth National Conference on City Planning," Pittsburgh, 1921, 64.

105. "Zoning for Milwaukee: Tentative Report of the Board of Public Land Commissioners," 1920, LRB.

106. Quoted in Steven Reisser, "Immigrants and House Form in Northeast Milwaukee, 1885–1916," M.A. Thesis, Department of Geography, University of Wisconsin-Milwaukee, 1977, 31.

107. For a colorful and irreverent folk history of the neighborhood, see Robert Wells, *This Is Kilbourntown* (Milwaukee: Times Holding Inc., 1971).

108. *Once a Year,* Milwaukee Press Club, vol. 13, p. 37, MPL.

109. *Milwaukee Sentinel,* January 26, 1916, Housing Clipping File, Legislative Reference Bureau, Milwaukee.

110. In 1919, a St. Paul, Minnesota, business association asked the mayors of fifteen American cities to rank their top three accomplishments. Hoan's reply is listed in a document sent back to him on December 8, 1919, titled "Biggest Things in Several Cities," Letter, Paul N. Myers to Daniel Hoan, December 8, 1919, File 517, Box 21, Daniel Hoan Papers, MCHS.

111. Gurda, *The Making of Milwaukee,* 265.

112. Fogelsong, *Planning the Capitalist City,* especially chap. 6.

2—Decentralization by Design

1. Lewis Mumford, "Regions—To Live In," 151–52; Clarence Stein, "Dinosaur Cities," 134–38; Benton MacKaye, "The New Exploration," 153–57, all in *Survey Graphic* 7, May 1925. See also Lubove, *Community Planning in the 1920s,* 97–101.

2. The phrase "mole work" was first used by William H. Wilson in his "Moles and Skylarks: Coming of Age in Urban America, 1914–1945," in Donald Krueckenberg, ed., *Introduction to Planning History in the United States* (New Brunswick, N.J.: Center for Urban Policy Research, 1983), 88–121. On Sunnyside and Radburn, see Daniel Schaeffer, *Garden Cities for America: The Radburn Experience* (Philadelphia: Temple University Press, 1982). For a good overview of the RPAA, see Lubove, *Community Planning in the 1920s;* and Spann, *Designing Modern America: The Regional Planning Association of America and Its Members.* For the relationship between planners and the automobile, see Mark S. Foster, *From Streetcar to Superhighway: American City Planners and Urban Transportation, 1900–1940* (Philadelphia: Temple University Press, 1981).

3. U.S. Bureau of the Census, "Population of the 100 Largest Urban Populations: 1920," accessed online at http://www.census.gov/population/documentation/ twps0027/tab15.txt Internet. Release date June 15, 1998.

4. Charles Goff, "The Politics of Governmental Integration in Metropolitan Milwaukee," Ph.D. Diss., Northwestern University, 1952, 87. The same concerns are cited in Arnold Fleischmann, "The Politics of Annexation and Urban Development: A Clash of Two Paradigms," Ph.D. Diss., University of Texas at Austin, 1984, 88–92. See also Foss-Mollan, *Hard Water: Politics and Water Supply in Milwaukee,* 122.

5. "Zoning Use Figures," Folder 8, Box 5, City Club of Milwaukee, Records, 1909–1975. Milwaukee Manuscript Collection AS and Milwaukee Micro Collection 69. Wisconsin Historical Society. Milwaukee Area Research Center. Golda Meir Library. University of Wisconsin-Milwaukee (MARC, GML).

6. Committee on Annexation, Notes 1921–1922, Folder 2, Box 5, City Club of Milwaukee, WHS, MARC.

7. Letter, Daniel Hoan to S. B. Way, December 30, 1927, File 32, Box 1, Hoan Papers, MCHS.

8. Letter, Daniel Hoan to Walt Clyde, June 25, 1925, File 26, Box 1, Hoan Papers, MCHS.

9. Goff, "The Politics of Governmental Integration in Metropolitan Milwaukee," 89.

10. Undated Memo, Folder 2, Box 5, City Club of Milwaukee, Records 1909–1975, WHS, MARC.

11. "Annexation for Milwaukee: The Concern of the Entire State," Report to Daniel Hoan, File 26, Box 1, Hoan Papers, MCHS.

12. Ibid. See also Fleischmann, "The Politics of Annexation and Urban Development," 88–95.

13. Goff, "The Politics of Governmental Integration in Metropolitan Milwaukee," 90–91.

14. By the 1950s, some Milwaukee aldermen, especially those in the inner city, began complaining that too much public money was being poured into newly

annexed areas at the expense of decaying inner city neighborhoods. However, this rarely stopped any alderman from supporting annexation.

15. "Annexation for Milwaukee: The Concern of the Entire State," Report to Daniel Hoan, File 26, Box 1, Hoan Papers, MCHS; and "Industries Adjacent to City Limits," Folder 13, Box 5, City Club of Milwaukee, Records 1909–1975, MARC, GML.

16. Open Letter, Daniel Hoan to "Gentlemen," February 7, 1921, File 26, Box 1, Hoan Papers, MCHS.

17. Letter, Evinrude Motor Company to Daniel Hoan, February 11, 1921, File 26, Box 1, Hoan Papers, MCHS.

18. Letter, South Side Malleable Casting Company to Daniel Hoan, February 9, 16, 1921, File 26, Box 1, Hoan Papers, MCHS.

19. "The Blockade of Milwaukee," Folder 2, Box 5, City Club of Milwaukee, Records 1909–1975, MARC, GML.

20. "Garden Homes Annexation Threatened," *Milwaukee Leader,* May 10, 1923, LRB. "City Wins Fight for Annexation," *Milwaukee Journal,* December 9, 1924, LRB.

21. William Schuchardt, "Co-Partnership Housing," Inspector of Buildings, "Buildings Operations, Year 1920," 14, LRB, Milwaukee.

22. Cady, "The Influence of the Garden City Ideal on American Housing and Planning Reform, 1900–1940," 99–107. See also Attoe and Latus, "The First Public Housing: Sewer Socialism's Garden City for Milwaukee," 142–49.

23. Ebenezer Howard, *Garden Cities of Tomorrow* (Cambridge, Mass.: MIT Press, 1965).

24. As quoted in Cady, "The Influence of the Garden City Ideal on American Housing and Planning Reform," 106.

25. "County Parkway Plan Is Pushed by Socialists," *Milwaukee Leader,* May 7, 1923, Parkway Clipping File, LRB.

26. Gurda, *The Making of Milwaukee,* 270.

27. Charles Whitnall, "The First Plans for a Parkway System for Milwaukee County," First Annual Report of the Milwaukee County Regional Planning Department, 1924, MPL; William Schuchardt, "The Milwaukee County Highway and Park Plan," *The American City,* March 1923, 363.

28. "Why a County Parkway System? An Explanation of the Plan, the Purpose, the Method of Land Acquisition, and the Benefits," by the Milwaukee County Park Commission, 1929–1930 Folder, Charles Whitnall Papers, MCHS.

29. "The Planner—What about Him?" Part of Five Lectures on City Planning, 1937 Folder, Charles Whitnall Papers, MCHS.

30. "Friends Point to Advantages of Reclaiming Mud Creek," *Milwaukee Leader,* November 18, 1929, Parkway Clipping File, LRB.

31. "Parkway Is Reward for Ald. Seidel on His 71st Birthday," *Milwaukee Leader,* December 13, 1935, Parkway Clipping File, LRB.

32. "82 Mile River Drive Will Link Parks and Residential Suburbs," *Milwaukee Journal,* May 27, 1923, Parkway Clipping File, LRB.

33. "Proposed Parkway Would Relieve Congestion and Raise Property Value," *Wauwatosa News,* July 26, 1928, Parkway Clipping File, LRB.

34. For example, see "Land Gift to Aid Parkway," *Milwaukee Sentinel,* December 4, 1936, Parkway Clipping File, LRB; and *Milwaukee Sentinel,* September 8, 1928, Land Clipping File, LRB.

35. Milwaukee Board of Public Land Commissioners, "Platting Guide, City of Milwaukee," 1924, MPL; "City Zone Plan Highly Praised," *Milwaukee Journal,* May 7, 1923, City Planning Clipping File, LRB.

36. "Platting Ideal Rises Rapidly around City," *Milwaukee Journal,* September 16, 1923, Land Clipping File, LRB.

37. Milwaukee Board of Public Land Commissioners, Annual Report, 1926, MPL.

38. Eugene A. Howard, "Twenty Three Years of Planning for Milwaukee County,"

Park Commission Folder, Box 1, Milwaukee County Regional Planning Department Files, MCHS; Florence Schulson, "A History of Planning Activity in Milwaukee, 1892–1952," MPL, "County Zoning Law Adopted," *Milwaukee Journal,* October 26, 1927, in Zoning Clipping File, LRB.

39. *Milwaukee Leader,* December 31, 1926, City Planning Clipping File, Legislative Reference Bureau, Milwaukee.

40. For example, see Tim Casey, "The 1912 Non-Partisan Election Law: Reform, Social Democrats, and Reaction," M.A. Thesis, Marquette University, 2000.

41. "Attack on Zoning Law," *Milwaukee Journal,* September 7, 1921, Zoning Clipping File, LRB, Milwaukee.

42. For example, in 1927, Hoan wrote to a Milwaukee resident: "I fear the Common Council will not replace Mr. Harper regardless of the seriousness of the charges for reasons which you may be able to understand. Only the Socialist aldermen have been willing to stand with me in the past on the policy of naming a new man." Letter, Daniel Hoan to Charles L. Lesser, April 28, 1927, File 72, Box 2, Daniel Hoan Papers, MCHS.

43. "$18,711,000 Building Barred by Zoning," *Milwaukee News,* January 9, 1926; "Zoning Bars City Growth, Says Harper," *Milwaukee Sentinel,* May 11, 1926, Zoning Clipping File, LRB, Milwaukee.

44. "Annual Report, Inspector of Buildings," 1926, 1, LRB.

45. "Zone Law Ties Up Huge Sum," *Milwaukee Journal,* November 4, 1925, Zoning Clipping File, LRB; "Report of the City Planning Committee of the Milwaukee Real Estate Board in Re-Amending the Zoning Ordinance of the City of Milwaukee," February 15, 1926, Folder 11, Box 9, City Club of Milwaukee Records, MARC, GML.

46. "Zoning Family Rule Defended," *Milwaukee Journal,* November 23, 1925, Zoning Clipping File, LRB.

47. Letter, Charles Whitnall to Alderman Albert Janicki, January 29, 1926, Folder 11, Box 9, City Club of Milwaukee Records, MARC, GML.

48. "Fights Zoning Law Change," *Milwaukee Journal,* November 5, 1925, Zoning Clipping File, LRB.

49. Letter, Charles Whitnall to Mayor Daniel Hoan and the Milwaukee Common Council, January 29, 1926, File 518, Box 21, Daniel Hoan Papers, MCHS.

50. Letter, Daniel Hoan to Charles L. Lesser, April 28, 1927, File 72, Box 2, Daniel Hoan Papers, MCHS.

51. "Charges Filed against Harper," *Milwaukee Journal,* December 19, 1926, Zoning Clipping File, LRB; Stachowski, "The Political Career of Daniel Webster Hoan," 149; Milwaukee Inspector of Buildings, Annual Report, 1928 LRB.

52. "Zoning Change Veto is Filed," *Milwaukee Sentinel,* October 13, 1929, Zoning Clipping File, LRB; Stachowski, "The Political Career of Daniel Webster Hoan," 149, 154.

53. Letter, Charles Whitnall to Milwaukee Common Council, July 19, 1926, Folder 2, Box 10, City Club of Milwaukee Records, MARC, GML.

54. Max Page, *The Creative Destruction of Manhattan: 1900–1940* (Chicago: University of Chicago Press, 1999), 2–3.

55. John Gurda, *The West End: Merrill Park, Pigsville, Concordia: Milwaukee* (Milwaukee: The Program, 1980).

56. Page, *The Creative Destruction of Manhattan,* 65–67.

57. Stachowski, "The Political Career of Daniel Webster Hoan," 154–55.

58. Marc A. Weiss, *The Rise of the Community Builders: The American Real Estate Industry and Urban Land Planning* (New York: Columbia University Press, 1987), 99.

59. As quoted in Scott, *American City Planning since 1890,* 196. For a thoroughgoing overview of zoning in one city over an extended period of time, see Patricia Burgess, *Planning for the Private Interest: Land Use Controls and Residential Patterns in Columbus, Ohio, 1900–1970* (Columbus: Ohio State University Press, 1994).

60. "Milwaukee Board of Public Land Commissioners, Annual Report, 1929," MPL.

61. "Milwaukee Board of Public Land Commissioners, Annual Report, 1927," MPL.

62. "Building Lots Shaved; Law Deftly Eluded," *Milwaukee Journal,* July 17, 1929.

63. "Electric Pact Beaten while Repeal Wins," *Milwaukee Sentinel,* April 8, 1925.

64. "Milwaukee—The Same Old Delay," *Milwaukee Journal,* October 12, 1926.

65. "May Keep Post for Schuchardt," *Milwaukee Journal,* September 29, 1925.

66. Untitled Annexation Memo, February 11, 1924, Folder 1, Box 9, City Club of Milwaukee, Records 1909–1975, MARC, GML.

67. The case is briefly summarized in Arthur Werba, "Annexation Activities of the City of Milwaukee," 1927, Folder 1, Box 9, City Club of Milwaukee, Records 1909–1975, MARC, GML.

68. As quoted in Henry J. Schmandt and William H. Standing, *The Milwaukee Metropolitan Study Commission* (Bloomington: Indiana University Press, 1965), 39.

69. Anthony Orum, *City Building in America* (Boulder, Colo.: Westview Press, 1995), 79–80.

70. "Annexation for Milwaukee: The Concern of the Entire State," Report to Daniel Hoan, File 26, Box 1, Hoan Papers, MCHS.

71. Kate Foss-Mollan, *Hard Water: Politics and Water Supply in Milwaukee, 1870–1995* (West Lafayette, Ind.: Purdue University Press, 2001), 63–66.

72. Ibid., 80–87. Also see John Gurda, *The Making of Milwaukee* (Milwaukee: Milwaukee County Historical Society, 1999), 261–63.

73. "Milwaukee's Growth and Expenditures for Public Improvements in the Last Ten Years," File 28, Box 1, Hoan Papers, MCHS.

74. Arthur Werba, "Annexation Activities of the City of Milwaukee," 1927, Folder 1, Box 9, City Club of Milwaukee, Records 1909–1975, MARC, GML.

75. For example, see *The North Milwaukee Annexationist,* March 10, 1928. Chas. Davis, a realtor in North Milwaukee, promised in an advertisement that "annexation of North Milwaukee to the city of Milwaukee means 100% increase in value" of all property. Folder 1, Box 9, City Club of Milwaukee, Records 1909–1975, WHS, MARC.

76. See *The City-Building Process* (chapter 5 especially deals with the East Side of Milwaukee); "Metropolitan Milwaukee Fact Book: 1970," Milwaukee Urban Observatory, 455. See also Gurda, *The Making of Milwaukee,* 186–88.

77. "Metropolitan Milwaukee Fact Book: 1970," Milwaukee Urban Observatory, MPL, 367.

78. Foss-Mollan, *Hard Water: Politics and Water Supply in Milwaukee,* 125.

79. "Shorewood Is Richest Village in Wisconsin," *Milwaukee Leader,* May 13, 1922, Suburbs Clipping File, LRB; "Apartments Banned along Gold Coast," *Milwaukee Sentinel,* January 8, 1921, Zoning Clipping File, LRB.

80. *Milwaukee Sentinel,* January 8, 1931, Annexation Clipping File, LRB, Milwaukee, Wisconsin.

81. "Metropolitan Milwaukee Fact Book: 1970," Milwaukee Urban Observatory, MPL, 399.

82. Gurda, *The Making of Milwaukee,* 186–87; McClellan and Junkersfeld, Inc., "Milwaukee Transportation Survey, 1926," 175, MPL.

83. The best study of the early history of all of Milwaukee County's suburbs is Christopher Mark Miller, "Milwaukee's First Suburbs: A Re-Interpretation of Suburban Incorporation in Nineteenth-Century Milwaukee County," Ph.D. Diss., Marquette University, 2007. A similar approach to Chicago, which emphasizes the role of developers, is Ann Durkin Keating: *Building Chicago: Suburban Developers and the Creation of a Divided Metropolis* (Columbus: Ohio State University Press, 1988). See also "Milwaukee Transportation Survey," McClellan and Junkersfeld, Inc., 1926, MPL, 175.

84. "Distinct: That Is Wauwatosa," *Milwaukee Journal,* August 1, 1920, Suburbs Clipping File, LRB.

85. "Milwaukee Transportation Survey," McClellan and Junkersfeld, Inc., 1926,

MPL, 175; "West Allis Has 35 Industrial Plants," *Milwaukee Journal*, December 31, 1921, Suburbs Clipping File, LRB, Milwaukee; Frederick I. Olson, "City Expansion and Suburban Spread: Settlements and Governments in Milwaukee County," in *Trading Post to Metropolis: Milwaukee County's First 150 Years*, ed. Ralph M. Aderman (Milwaukee: Milwaukee County Historical Society, 1987), 50.

86. "Warn Shorewood to Fight Annexation," *Milwaukee Journal*, June 6, 1921, Folder 13, Box 5, City Club of Milwaukee, Records 1909–1975, MARC, GML.

87. For life on the Polish South Side, see Judith Kenny, "Polish Routes to Americanization: House Form and Landscape on Milwaukee's Polish South Side," in Thomas R. Vale and Robert C. Ostergren, eds., *Wisconsin Land and Life* (Madison: University of Wisconsin Press, 1997).

88. "Don't Pay for Your Neighbor's House," Town of Lake Booster Club, Folder 1, Box 9, City Club of Milwaukee, Records 1909–1975, Milwaukee Manuscript Collection AS and Milwaukee Micro Collection 69, MARC, GML.

89. "Annexation since January 1, 1922, to November 1, 1926," Folder 1, Box 9, City Club of Milwaukee, Records 1909–1975, Milwaukee Manuscript Collection AS and Milwaukee Micro Collection 69, MARC, GML.

90. *Milwaukee Journal*, May 30, 1929, Annexation Clipping File, LRB.

91. *Milwaukee Journal*, April 11, 1929, Annexation Clipping File, LRB.

92. "Don't Pay for Your Neighbor's House," Town of Lake Booster Club, Folder 1, Box 9, City Club of Milwaukee, Records 1909–1975. Milwaukee Manuscript Collection AS and Milwaukee Micro Collection 69, MARC, GML.

93. "Incorporation of Town of Lake into a Village," Memo, September 1, 1926, Folder 1, Box 9, City Club of Milwaukee, Records 1909–1975, Milwaukee Manuscript Collection AS and Milwaukee Micro Collection 69, MARC, GML.

94. "To the Farmers Living in the Town of Lake," by the Taxpayers and Voters League of the Town of Lake, Folder 1, Box 9, City Club of Milwaukee, Records 1909–1975, Milwaukee Manuscript Collection AS and Milwaukee Micro Collection 69, MARC, GML.

95. Ibid.

96. "Push Fight against Plan to Incorporate," *Milwaukee Journal*, September 15, 1926; *Milwaukee Sentinel*, September 17, 1926.

97. "Don't Pay for Your Neighbor's House," Town of Lake Booster Club, Folder 1, Box 9, City Club of Milwaukee, Records 1909–1975. Milwaukee Manuscript Collection AS and Milwaukee Micro Collection 69, MARC, GML.

98. "Lake Votes Saturday," *Milwaukee Journal*, September 17, 1926.

99. *Milwaukee Journal*, October 11, 1926.

100. "Lake Gives Up City Ambitions," *Milwaukee Sentinel*, September 20, 1926.

101. "Fight Attempt to Create City," *Milwaukee Journal*, October 13, 1926.

102. "Annexation: Shall Our City and Village Combine? An Argument by the Whitefish Bay Annexation Association," Folder 1, Box 9, City Club of Milwaukee, Records 1909–1975, Milwaukee Manuscript Collection AS and Milwaukee Micro Collection 69, MARC, GML.

103. Pamphlet authored by Whitefish Bay resident Walter S. Smith, File 32, Box 1, Hoan Papers, MCHS.

104. Ibid.

105. Ibid.; "Do You Love Whitefish Bay? Do You Love Your Home?" Pamphlet, File 32, Box 1, Hoan Papers, MCHS; "Bulldozing the Suburbs," *Milwaukee Journal*, January 17, 1928; "Werba Says Klode Backed Annexation," *Milwaukee Leader*, January 11, 1928, Annexation Clipping File, LRB.

106. *North Milwaukee Annexationist*, March 10, 1928, Folder 1, Box 9, City Club of Milwaukee, Records 1909–1975, Milwaukee Manuscript Collection AS and Milwaukee Micro Collection 69, MARC, GML.

107. Joint Committee on City-County Consolidation in Milwaukee County, "Metropolitan Milwaukee: One Trade Area Burdened with 93 Local Governments," 1934, MPL.
108. Arthur Werba, "Making Milwaukee Mightier," 1929, MPL, 50–51.
109. Ibid., 48.
110. Daniel Hoan, "How Milwaukee Is Solving the Housing Problem," *American City,* July 1930. An earlier draft of the same article can be found in Folder 455, Box 19, Daniel Hoan Papers, MCHS. See also "Hoan Writes of City's Method as to Housing," *Milwaukee Leader,* July 12, 1930, Housing Clipping File, LRB.
111. Charles B. Bennett, "Fifteen Years of City Planning Accomplishments in Milwaukee," *The American City,* October 1930, 89–92.
112. *Milwaukee Journal,* February 2, 1936, Housing Clipping File, LRB; Schmitz, "Milwaukee and Its Black Community: 1930–1942," 13.

3—Planning, Metropolitics, and the Depression

1. The most comprehensive general history of America and the Roosevelt presidency is David Kennedy, *Freedom from Fear: The American People in Depression and War, 1929–1945* (New York: Oxford University Press, 1999). An excellent interpretation of the New Deal's housing policies, and planners' involvement in these reforms, is Gail Radford, *Modern Housing for America: Policy Struggles in the New Deal Era* (Chicago and London: University of Chicago Press, 1996).
2. Leon Gurda, "Report on Housing to the Milwaukee Common Council," Milwaukee Building Inspector's Office, May 9, 1938, File 72, Box 2, Hoan Papers, MCHS; "Shortage in Housing Is a Puzzling Issue," *Milwaukee Journal,* February 2, 1936, Housing Clipping File, LRB, Milwaukee.
3. "Mayor's Housing Commission," Folder 1, Box 1, Series 25, City of Milwaukee Department of Building Inspection Records, MPL. See also Minutes of the First Meeting of the Mayor's Commission on Housing, January 24, 1933, Advisory Housing Commission Folder, Box 1, City of Milwaukee Department of Building Inspection Records, MPL.
4. Untitled Report, File 458, Box 19, Daniel Hoan Papers, MCHS. This report is extensively quoted as what the Milwaukee Common Council received in September 1933 in "See Suburbs Gain on City," *Milwaukee Journal,* September 12, 1933, Housing Clipping File, LRB.
5. Gurda, *The Making of Milwaukee,* 284; "Parkway Ring Growing Fast," *Milwaukee Journal,* August 5, 1934, Parkway Clipping File, LRB; "WPA Building New Parkway," *Milwaukee Journal,* January 3, 1936, Parkway Clipping File, LRB; "Parkway's Influence Studied by Realtors," *Milwaukee Sentinel,* October 11, 1936, Parkway Clipping File, LRB.
6. Radford, *Modern Housing for America,* 89–90; Alexander von Hoffman, "The End of the Dream: The Political Struggle of America's Public Housers," *Journal of Planning History* 4 (August 2005): 230–32; Report of Committee Numbers 1–3 of the Mayors Housing Commission, Folder 1, Box 1, Series 25, City of Milwaukee Department of Building Inspection Records, MPL; *Milwaukee Sentinel,* September 5, 1933, Housing Clipping File, LRB.
7. For Delano's involvement in planning, see Carl Smith, *The Plan of Chicago: Daniel Burnham and the Remaking of the American City* (Chicago: University of Chicago Press, 2006), 66–68. The famed disagreement between RPAA members (especially Lewis Mumford) and advocates of the Regional Plan of New York (especially Thomas Adams) is retold in many works, including Schaffer, *Garden Cities for America,* 74–76; and Lubove, *Community Planning in the 1920s,* 119–22.
8. Scott, *American City Planning,* 257–58.
9. Radford, *Modern Housing for America,* 79.
10. Mary Susan Cole, "Catherine Bauer and the Public Housing Movement, 1926–1937," Ph.D. Diss., George Washington University, 1975, 132.

11. Letter, Catherine Bauer to Clarence Stein, July 16, 1933, Folder 1, Box 2, Clarence Stein Papers, #3600, Division of Rare and Manuscript Collections, CUL.

12. Catherine Bauer, "Milwaukee Survey: In Connection with Proposed Housing Development," July 18, 1933, Folder 1, Box 2, Clarence Stein Papers #3600, Division of Rare and Manuscript Collections, CUL.

13. Robert Fairbanks, *Making Better Citizens: Housing Reform and the Community Development Strategy in Cincinnati, 1890–1960* (Urbana and Chicago: University of Illinois Press, 1988), 71–72.

14. Wisconsin's condemnation law mentioned in this narrative is commonly referred to as "The Kline Law," an explanation of which can be found in "Statutes of the State of Wisconsin Relating to the Condemnation of Buildings," File 458, Box 19, Daniel Hoan Papers, MCHS; and "City Is Upheld on Kline Law by High Court," *Milwaukee Journal*, November 11, 1938, Folder 3, Box 23, City Club Papers, MARC, GML.

15. "Report on Housing to the Milwaukee Common Council," by Leon Gurda, Milwaukee Building Inspector, May 9, 1938, File 72, Box 2, Hoan Papers, MCHS.

16. Daniel Hoan, "How Milwaukee Is Solving the Housing Problem," *American City*, July 1934; *Milwaukee Leader*, July 12, 1930, Housing Clipping File, LRB.

17. Letter, Charles Bennett to Lawrence Veiller, October 20, 1931, File 458, Box 19, Daniel Hoan Papers, MCHS.

18. Letter, Veiller to Bennett, October 23, 1931, File 458, Box 19, Daniel Hoan Papers, MCHS.

19. On Bohn and NAHO's formation, see von Hoffman, "The End of the Dream," 232–33; and D. Bradford Hunt, "Was the 1937 Housing Act a Pyrrhic Victory?" *Journal of Planning History* 4 (August 2005): 198–99. For Brownlow's involvement in NAHO, see Scott, *American City Planning*, 320. For the NAHO-sponsored tour, see Rodgers, *Atlantic Crossings*, 464–65.

20. "Officials Attending Meeting of Housing Officials, November 25, 1933," File 451, Box 18, Daniel Hoan Papers, MCHS; Louis Brownlow, "Meeting of Public Housing Officials, November 25, 1933," File 451, Box 18, Daniel Hoan Papers, MCHS.

21. "Conference on the Demolition of Worthless Buildings Held in Washington DC, March 23–24, 1934," Report by Leon Gurda, Folder 2, Box 1, Series 25, City of Milwaukee Department of Building Inspection Records, MPL.

22. "Demolition of Unsafe and Insanitary [sic] Housing: An Outline for a Comprehensive Procedure," National Association of Housing Officials, Folder 2, Box 1, Series 25, City of Milwaukee Department of Building Inspection Records, MPL.

23. Program, "Visiting European and American Housing Experts," File 451, Box 18, Daniel Hoan Papers, MCHS; Charles B. Bennett, "Announcement," File 451, Box 18, Daniel Hoan Papers, MCHS.

24. "Yes, Sir Raymond Unwin Scorns Fashion; Says So Himself!" *Milwaukee Journal*, September 13, 1934.

25. "Praise Given City Housing," *Milwaukee Sentinel*, September 13, 1934.

26. "Mayor to Fight Housing Delay," *Milwaukee Journal*, September 12, 1934.

27. Letter, Edmund Hoben to Daniel Hoan, September 1, 1934, File 458, Box 19, Daniel Hoan Papers, MCHS.

28. "Parklawn: Modern Low Rent Homes for Residents of Milwaukee, Wisconsin," Folder 1, Box 1, Parklawn Collection, MCHS; "New Housing a Social Ideal," *Milwaukee Journal*, July 22, 1935, Housing Clipping File, LRB.

29. Eric Fure-Slocum, "Challenge of the Working-Class City: Recasting Growth Politics and Liberalism, 1937–1952," Ph.D. Diss., University of Iowa, 2001, 171–73; see also "Six Negro Families Get Quarters in Parklawn," *Milwaukee Journal*, September 21, 1937, Housing Clipping File, LRB. For an excellent analysis of the relationship between race and planning, see John F. Bauman, *Public Housing, Race, and Renewal: Urban Planning in Philadelphia, 1920–1974* (Philadelphia: Temple University Press), 22–39.

30. Joseph Arnold, *The New Deal in the Suburbs: A History of the Greenbelt Town Program, 1935–1954* (Columbus: Ohio State University Press, 1971), 30.

31. Arnold R. Alanen and Joseph A. Eden, *Main Street Ready Made: The New Deal Community of Greendale* (Madison: The State Historical Society of Wisconsin Press, 1987), 13.

32. Charles Bennett, "Planning a Residential Neighborhood for Better Living Conditions at Lower Cost," *The American City* (February 1930): 96–97.

33. For the link between Perry's concepts and Radburn, see Schaffer, *Garden Cities for America,* 157–59.

34. "Model Village Laid Out Here," *Milwaukee Journal,* February 7, 1933, Planning Clipping File, LRB. On the Whitnall garden homestead, see Alanen and Eden, *Main Street Ready Made,* 14–15; and "On Wisconsin: More Home Plans," *Milwaukee Journal,* January 14, 1934.

35. "10,000 Acres Optioned for Little Farms," *Milwaukee Journal,* December 4, 1935.

36. "U.S. Housing Projects Will Employ 3,000," *Milwaukee Journal,* April 30, 1935.

37. For an interesting conceptualization of Bigger's career, see John F. Bauman and Edward K. Muller, "The Planning Technician as Urban Visionary: Frederick Bigger and American Planning, 1881–1963," *Journal of Planning History* 1, no. 2 (2002): 124–53.

38. Elbert Peets, "Greendale Final Report," p. 10, Folder 25, Box 1, Elbert Peets Papers, #2772, Division of Rare and Manuscript Collections, CUL.

39. Alanen and Eden, *Main Street Ready Made,* 42.

40. Elbert Peets, "Greendale Final Report," p. 148, Folder 25, Box 1, Elbert Peets Papers, #2772, Division of Rare and Manuscript Collections, CUL.

41. Ibid.

42. Ibid., 11.

43. Alanen and Eden, *Main Street Ready Made,* 43.

44. As quoted in Schaffer, *Garden Cities for America,* 154.

45. Alanen and Eden, *Main Street Ready Made,* 60–61.

46. Ibid., 50.

47. Arnold, *The New Deal in the Suburbs,* 243.

48. Jacob Crane, "Greendale: The General Plan," Paper for American City Planning Institute Meeting, Milwaukee, Wisconsin, October 24, 1936, Suburbs Clipping File, LRB.

49. John S. Lansill and Jacob Crane, "Metropolitan Land Reserves: As Illustrated by Greendale, Wisconsin," *The American City* (July 1937): 57.

50. Ibid., 58.

51. "Biographical Sketch of Honorable Frank P. Zeidler, Mayor of Milwaukee," Folder 7, Box 188, Frank Zeidler Papers, MPL; Frank Zeidler, interview with author, September 13, 2002, Milwaukee.

52. "Statistical Report on Housing," Bureau of Building and Elevator Inspection, 1936, Folder 2, Box 1, City of Milwaukee Department of Building Inspector Records, MPL; "Report on Housing to the Milwaukee Common Council," by Leon Gurda, Milwaukee Building Inspector, May 9, 1938, File 72, Box 2, Hoan Papers, MCHS.

53. "Mr. Gurda and Mr. Taylor Talk about Low Cost Housing," *Milwaukee Sentinel,* October 4, 1937, Housing Clipping File, LRB.

54. "Statistical Report on Housing," Folder 2, Box 1, Series 25, City of Milwaukee Department of Building Inspection Records, MPL.

55. Kenneth Robert Schmitz, "Milwaukee and Its Black Community: 1930–1942," M.A. Thesis, University of Wisconsin-Milwaukee, 1979, p. 13, MPL.

56. "Statistical Report on Housing," Folder 2, Box 1, Series 25, City of Milwaukee Department of Building Inspection Records, MPL; Hoan, Glassberg, and Gurda, "Tell Need for Housing in Milwaukee," *Milwaukee Leader,* October 11, 1937, Housing Clipping File, LRB.

57. Bureau of Building, "Statistical Report on Housing," 1936, Folder 2, Box 1, City of Milwaukee Department of Building Inspector Records, MPL.

58. Fure-Slocum, "Challenge of the Working-Class City," 188–93.

59. Charles Goff, "The Politics of Governmental Integration in Metropolitan Milwaukee," 89; *Milwaukee Board of Public Land Commissioners Annual Review, 1932*, MPL.

60. Schmandt and Standing, *The Milwaukee Metropolitan Study Commission*, 39; "Report of the Interim Committee on City-County Consolidation in Milwaukee County," Folder 1, Box 9, City Club of Milwaukee, Records 1909–1975, Milwaukee Manuscript Collection AS and Milwaukee Micro Collection 69, MARC, GML.

61. "Metropolitan Milwaukee: One Trade Area Burdened with 93 Local Governments," from the Joint Committee on City-County Consolidation in Milwaukee County, MPL; "County Merger Groups United," *Milwaukee Journal*, March 9, 1936.

62. *Milwaukee Journal*, November 16, 1930, in Folder 3, Box 9, City Club of Milwaukee, Records 1909–1975, Milwaukee Manuscript Collection AS and Milwaukee Micro Collection 69, WHS, MARC.

63. "Statement of Milwaukee Real Estate Board," October 30, 1934, Folder 3, Box 9, City Club of Milwaukee, Records 1909–1975, Milwaukee Manuscript Collection AS and Milwaukee Micro Collection 69, MARC, GML.

64. *Milwaukee Journal*, February 6, 1931, in Folder 1, Box 15, City Club of Milwaukee, Records 1909–1975, Milwaukee Manuscript Collection AS and Milwaukee Micro Collection 69, WHS, MARC.

65. For example, see *Milwaukee Journal*, February 6, 1931; December 12, 1932; and "Town of Lake Scandal," *Wisconsin News*, December 26, 1933.

66. Meeting of Citizens' Association on Consolidation in Milwaukee County, August 9, 1934, Folder 3, Box 9, City Club of Milwaukee, Records 1909–1975, Milwaukee Manuscript Collection AS and Milwaukee Micro Collection 69, MARC, GML.

67. "Milwaukee: New Consolidations," *Milwaukee Journal*, January 11, 1934.

68. "Statement of Milwaukee Real Estate Board," October 30, 1934, Folder 3, Box 9, City Club of Milwaukee, Records 1909–1975, Milwaukee Manuscript Collection AS and Milwaukee Micro Collection 69, MARC, GML.

69. "Statement of Socialist Party, Milwaukee County, adopted by the County Central Committee of the Socialist Party," December 26, 1934, File 28, Box 1, Hoan Papers, MCHS.

70. "Referendum Results, City of Milwaukee," November 6, 1934, Folder 3, Box 9, City Club of Milwaukee, Records 1909–1975, Milwaukee Manuscript Collection AS and Milwaukee Micro Collection 69, MARC, GML.

71. "Consolidation Measure Killed by Assembly Vote," *Milwaukee Sentinel*, February 25, 1937, in Folder 5, Box 23, City Club Papers, Milwaukee Manuscript Collection AS and Milwaukee Micro Collection 69, MARC, GML.

72. "Citizens Apathetic, So County Quits Joint Committee on Consolidation," *Milwaukee Journal*, April 16, 1937, in Folder 5, Box 23, City Club Papers, Milwaukee Manuscript Collection AS and Milwaukee Micro Collection 69, MARC, GML.

73. Schmandt and Standing, *The Milwaukee Metropolitan Study Commission*, 57–58.

74. Gurda, *The Making of Milwaukee*, 283–88.

75. Charles Whitnall Untitled Report, Consolidation 1935–1936, Folder 5, Box 23, City Club Papers, Milwaukee Manuscript Collection AS and Milwaukee Micro Collection 69, MARC, GML.

76. Gurda, *The Making of Milwaukee*, 303–5.

4—Diverging Visions

1. *Milwaukee Journal*, February 4, 1940.

2. A challenge to this notion can be found in Joe Heathcott, "The City Quietly Remade: National Programs and Local Agendas in the Movement to Clear the Slums,"

Journal of Urban History 34, no. 2 (2008): 221–42. Another nuanced view of the interwar period, as it relates to planning ideas, can be found in Zane Miller and Bruce Tucker, *Changing Plans for America's Inner Cities: Cincinnati's Over-the-Rhine and Twentieth-Century Urbanism* (Columbus: Ohio State University Press, 1998).

3. Milwaukee County Park Commission Minutes, October 10, 1944, Box 1, File 36, Jerome Dretzka Papers, MCHS.

4. For example, see Charles Whitnall, "Milwaukee's Automobile Problems," 1938, MPL. Gordon Whitnall wrote a section on divided highways in this report. Gordon's generally favorable opinions toward automobiles can also be found in Foster, *From Streetcar to Superhighway,* 88. A recent and more critical examination of the ramifications of supporting decentralization in Los Angeles can be found in Jeremiah B. C. Axelrod, "'Keep the "L" Out of Los Angeles': Race, Discourse, and Urban Modernity in 1920s Southern California," *Journal of Urban History* 34, no. 1 (November 2007): 3–37. See also Robert Fogelson, *The Fragmented Metropolis: Los Angeles, 1850–1930* (Cambridge, Mass.: Harvard University Press, 1967); and Robert Fishman, *Bourgeois Utopias: The Rise and Fall of Suburbia* (New York: Basic Books, 1987), 155–82.

5. "Five Lectures on City Planning: Given by C. B. Whitnall at the Ninth Annual Session of the Institute of Government, University of Southern California, June 14–18, 1937," 1927–1928 Folder, Charles Whitnall Papers, MCHS.

6. Gregg Wassmansdorf, "Public-Private Dialectics in the Planning and Development of Los Angeles, 1781–1993," M.A. Thesis, University of Southern California, 1994.

7. *Milwaukee Journal,* August 15, 1941.

8. Memo from Elmer Krieger to the Members and Employees of the Board of Public Land Commissioners regarding the National Planning Conference in Los Angeles, August 13–17, 1950, Folder 5, Box 190, Zeidler Papers, MPL.

9. Letter, Elmer Krieger to Frank Zeidler, September 30, 1953, Folder 5, Box 190, Zeidler Papers, MPL.

10. Letter, Krieger to Zeidler, September 30, 1953, Folder 5, Box 190, Zeidler Papers, MPL; "Elmer Krieger Helped Shape Milwaukee," *Milwaukee Journal-Sentinel,* June 28, 1996; "Elmer Krieger: Biographical Data," Folder 71, Box 30, American Society of Planning Officials Records, #324, Division of Rare and Manuscript Collections, CUL.

11. Fure-Slocum, "The Challenge of the Working Class City," 182.

12. Fure-Slocum, "The Challenge of the Working Class City," 484–550; Richard Perrin, "Public Housing in Milwaukee," 2nd edition, 1953, p. 29, MPL.

13. Gurda, *The Making of Milwaukee,* 310. An excellent overview of industrial Milwaukee, especially as it applies to workers, is Richard L. Pifer, *A City at War: Milwaukee Labor during World War Two* (Madison: State Historical Society of Wisconsin Press, 2002).

14. Robert M. Fogelson, *Downtown: Its Rise and Fall, 1880–1950* (New Haven, Conn.: Yale University Press, 2001), 238–39. Another excellent recent history of American downtowns is Alison Isenberg, *Downtown America: A History of the Place and the People Who Made It* (Chicago: University of Chicago Press, 2004).

15. Howard Tobin et al., "Proposals for Downtown Milwaukee," The Urban Land Institute, 1941, MPL.

16. Ibid., 60–63.

17. Ibid., 66.

18. Ibid., 70.

19. Sam Bass Warner, *The Private City: Philadelphia in Its Three Periods of Growth* (Philadelphia: University of Pennsylvania Press), 1968.

20. Frank Zeidler, "A Liberal in City Government: My Experience as Mayor of Milwaukee," 61, MPL. Zeidler's memoirs, unpublished when I began this research, have since been edited and published by Milwaukee Publishers LLC (2005) under the same title. For the remainder of the book, all citations from Zeidler's memoirs will be from the unpublished version.

21. Fure-Slocum, "The Challenge of the Working Class City," in Richard Pifer, *A City at War: Milwaukee Labor During World War Two* (Madison: Wisconsin Historical Society Press, 2003).

22. *Milwaukee Journal,* October 15, 1945.

23. For example, see "Report of Richard O. Roll, Director of Real Property Survey on Substandard Housing in Milwaukee," 1944, MPL; Milwaukee Housing Council, "Facing the Housing Problem," 1938, MPL; Milwaukee Board of Public Land Commissioners, "Control of Population Density through Zoning," 1936, LRB.

24. "Population Changes by Census Tracts, 1920–1940," Milwaukee Board of Public Land Commissioners, MPL.

25. Milwaukee County Regional Planning Department, "Residential Development in the Unincorporated Areas of Milwaukee County–Wisconsin," 1946, pp. 41–43, MPL.

26. Ibid., 51.

27. Clarence Stein, "Greendale and the Future," *The American City* (June 1948): 109.

28. Milwaukee County Regional Planning Department, "Residential Development in the Unincorporated Areas," 1946, chap. 4.

29. Letter, E. A. Howard to Milwaukee County Park Commission, undated, in Milwaukee County Regional Planning Department, "Residential Development in the Unincorporated Areas of Milwaukee County–Wisconsin," 1946, MPL.

30. Eugene A. Howard, "Twenty Three Years of Planning for Milwaukee County," Park Commission Folder, Box 1, Milwaukee County Regional Planning Department Files, MCHS.

31. Ibid.

32. "It's Elbow Room, Not Lower Taxes, that Lures City Folk to Rural Lots," *Milwaukee Journal,* September 22, 1946, City Planning Clipping File, MPL.

33. "Milwaukee Plans to Make Postwar Dreams Come True," *Providence Sunday Journal,* July 20, 1947, Folder 4, Box 5, William George Bruce Papers, Milwaukee Manuscript Collection CU and Milwaukee Micro Collection 60, MARC, GML.

34. Minutes of the First Meeting of the Board of Directors of the 1948 Corporation, November 30, 1945, Folder 3, Box 5, William George Bruce Papers, Milwaukee Manuscript Collection CU and Milwaukee Micro Collection 60, MARC, GML.

35. "Bohn, Wendt Irked by Anderson's Idea," *Milwaukee Journal,* March 13, 1946, City Planning Clipping File, MPL.

36. "Mayor's Postwar Message to Common Council," April 16, 1946, Folder 3, Box 5, William George Bruce Papers, Milwaukee Manuscript Collection CU and Milwaukee Micro Collection 60, MARC, GML.

37. "The 1948 Corporation: What It Is, What It Is Doing, What It Proposes to Do," Folder 4, Box 5, William George Bruce Papers, Milwaukee Manuscript Collection CU and Milwaukee Micro Collection 60, MARC, GML.

38. "Whitnall Quits City Land Post" *Milwaukee Journal,* September 24, 1943, and "Planning Director Issues a Reply," *Milwaukee Journal,* February 29, 1944, City Planning Clipping File, MPL.

39. "Realtors Seek Idea on Plan," *Milwaukee Journal,* March 26, 1944, City Planning Clipping File, MPL.

40. As quoted in Elmer Krieger, "A Master Plan for the City of Milwaukee," submitted to the Board of Public Land Commissioners, January 11, 1947, p. 16, MPL.

41. Ibid., 30.

42. "Suggestions Acclaimed by Most Leaders of City, County; a Few Are Critical," *Milwaukee Journal,* January 13, 1947, City Planning Clipping File, MPL.

43. Krieger, "A Master Plan for the City of Milwaukee," 46.

44. An excellent and penetrating overview of the debt referendum campaign is Eric Fure-Slocum, "Cities with Class?: Growth Politics, the Working-Class City, and Debt in Milwaukee during the 1940s," *Social Science History* 24, no. 1 (Spring 2000): 257–305.

45. Frank Zeidler, interview with author, September 13, 2002; "Biographical Sketch of Honorable Frank P. Zeidler, Mayor of Milwaukee," Folder 7, Box 118, Zeidler Papers, MPL.

46. As quoted in "Development in Need of Cities," *Milwaukee Journal*, October 10, 1951. A transcript of Zeidler's speech to NAHO can also be found in Zeidler, "Redevelopment in Milwaukee—What We Did," Folder 2, Box 107, Zeidler Papers, MPL.

47. Letter, Frank Zeidler, March 26, 1958, Folder 5, Box 191, Zeidler Papers, MPL.

48. "Making Urban Renewal More Effective," Ninth Report, by Frank Zeidler, Folder 6, Box 344, Zeidler Papers, MPL.

49. "Making Urban Renewal More Effective," p. 13, Third Report, Folder 9, Box 343, Zeidler Papers, MPL.

50. "Making Urban Renewal More Effective," p. 46, Second Report, Folder 8, Box 343, Zeidler Papers, MPL.

51. Fure-Slocum, "Challenge of the Working Class City," 333.

52. "Platforms and Planks of the Public Enterprise Committee," Folder 3, Box 99, Zeidler Papers, MPL.

53. Memo, Milwaukee Housing Authority to Milwaukee Common Council, May 22, 1947, in "Low-Rent Housing Units—Alleviation of Housing Shortage in Milwaukee," pp. 2–3, MPL; "A Review of Building Activities in Milwaukee during 1940," Milwaukee Building Inspector, Folder 8, Box 5, Zeidler Papers, MPL. An excellent analysis of the role developers played in fostering annexation can be found in Arnold Fleischmann, "The Territorial Expansion of Milwaukee: Historical Lessons for Contemporary Urban Policy and Research," *Journal of Urban History* 14, no. 2 (February 1988): 147–76. See also "Protest Bans on Annexing," *Milwaukee Journal*, April 2, 1951, Annexation Clipping File, MPL.

54. George Saffran, Milwaukee Budget Supervisor, "Annexation Practices in Milwaukee: An Administrative Analysis," prepared for the Administrative Survey Committee, June 1952, MPL.

55. Memo to Walter Swietlik, Commissioner of Public Works, August 22, 1947, Folder 2, Box 124, Zeidler Papers, MPL; "Asks Annexation for Home Building," *Milwaukee Journal*, January 20, 1948, Annexation Clipping File, MPL; Letter, Elton A. Schultz to Frank Zeidler, July 14, 1948, Folder 1, Box 77, Zeidler Papers, MPL.

56. For examples of letters to Zeidler regarding the postwar housing shortage, see Folders 5–8, Box 78, Zeidler Papers, MPL. On the lack of vacant lots, see letter from Arthur Werba to Frank Zeidler, May 5, 1948, Folder 1, Box 175, Zeidler Papers, MPL.

57. Handwritten Notes, Milwaukee Folder, Carton 33, Catherine Bauer Wurster Papers, Bancroft Library, University of California-Berkeley (BL-UCB).

58. "Renews Policy on Annexation," *Milwaukee Journal*, May 12, 1946, Annexation Clipping File, MPL.

59. Werba, "Making Milwaukee Mightier," 50–51, MPL.

60. As quoted from John Gurda, *The Making of Milwaukee* (Milwaukee County Historical Society Press, 1999), 338.

61. "Report of the Commission on the Economic Study of Milwaukee, 1948," p. 107, MPL; D. W. Knight, "Subsidization of Industry in Forty Selected Cities in Wisconsin: 1930–1946," *Wisconsin Commerce Studies* 1, no. 2 (1947): 185.

62. "Factory Land Choking Industry Here," *Milwaukee Journal*, April 24, 1949, Annexation Clipping File, MPL.

63. "Report of the Commission on the Economic Study of Milwaukee, 1948," pp. 1–6, MPL.

64. Goff, "The Politics of Governmental Integration in Metropolitan Milwaukee," 96.

65. "Building Plan Stymies Eyed," *Milwaukee Journal*, August 27, 1947.

66. "Continue Plan of Annexation," *Milwaukee Journal*, November 23, 1949, Annexation Clipping File, MPL.

67. For a national overview of urban politics and the role of growth coalitions, see John Mollenkopf, *The Contested City* (Princeton, N.J.: Princeton University Press, 1983). For an overview of urban renewal in northern cities, see Jon C. Teaford, *Rough Road to Renaissance: Urban Revitalization in America, 1940–1985* (Baltimore: Johns Hopkins University Press, 1990).

68. For Pittsburgh's postwar redevelopment, see Roy S. Lubove, *Twentieth Century Pittsburgh: Government, Business and Environmental Change* (New York: Wiley Publishing, 1969); and Michael Weber, *Don't Call Me Boss: David L. Lawrence, Pittsburgh's Renaissance Mayor* (Pittsburgh: University of Pittsburgh Press, 1988). For Chicago, see Carl W. Condit, *Chicago, 1930–1970: Building, Planning, and Urban Technology* (Chicago: University of Chicago Press, 1974); and Arnold R. Hirsch, *Making the Second Ghetto: Race and Housing in Chicago, 1940–1960* (Cambridge and New York: Cambridge University Press, 1983).

69. Thomas Sugrue, *Origins of the Urban Crisis: Race and Inequality in Postwar Detroit* (Princeton, N.J.: Princeton University Press, 1995); June Manning Thomas, *Redevelopment and Race: Planning a Finer City in Postwar Detroit* (Baltimore: Johns Hopkins University Press, 1997); Kevin Fox-Gotham, *Race, Real Estate, and Uneven Development: The Kansas City Experience, 1900–2000* (Albany: State University of New York Press, 2002).

70. For example, see Jon C. Teaford, *Cities of the Heartland: The Rise and Fall of the Industrial Midwest* (Bloomington: Indiana University Press, 1993); *The Rough Road to Renaissance: Urban Revitalization in America, 1940–1985* (Baltimore: Johns Hopkins University Press, 1985); Anthony Orum, *City Building in America* (Boulder, Colo.: Westview Press, 1995); Roy Lubove, *Twentieth Century Pittsburgh: Government, Politics, and Environmental Change* (New York: Wiley Publishing, 1969); Eric Sandweiss, *St. Louis: The Evolution of an American Urban Landscape* (Philadelphia: Temple University Press, 2001); and Sugrue, *Origins of the Urban Crisis.*

71. Fogelson, *Downtown: Its Rise and Fall, 1880–1950,* chap. 5.

72. The best study that refutes the "growth coalition" model as applicable to Milwaukee is Fure-Slocum, "Challenge of the Working Class City."

73. As quoted in *The American City,* May 1950, pp. 5–6. This urban renewal mindset is also discussed in Joel Rast, "Annexation Policy in Milwaukee: An Historical Institutionalist Approach," *Polity* 39: 56–57. Rast argues that annexation was most effective when city government acted independently of special interests, which the city could not free itself of in the 1920s (under Hoan), but was able to in the 1950s (under Zeidler). In contrast, I argue in chapters 2, 5, and 6 that Milwaukee's leaders were never completely free of special interests (especially in the real estate community) in their pursuit of growth, that there was more continuity than major differences between Hoan's and Zeidler's annexation programs (as exemplified by Werba), and that annexation deserves more attention as a planning tool.

74. Zeidler, "A Liberal in City Government," 61–62, MPL.

5—The Rise and Fall of the Satellite City

1. For example, see Michael Dudley, "Sprawl as Strategy: City Planners Face the Bomb," *Journal of Planning Education and Research* 21, no. 1: 52–63; Jennifer Light, *From Warfare to Welfare: Defense Intellectuals and Urban Problems in Cold War America* (Baltimore: Johns Hopkins University Press, 2003), 10–31; Tom Vanderbilt, *Survival City: Adventures among the Ruins of Atomic America* (Princeton, N.J.: Princeton Architectural Press, 2002), 75–79; and Matthew Farish, "Disaster and Decentralization: American Cities and the Cold War," *Cultural Geographies* 10, no. 2 (2003): 125–48. For a thoroughgoing analysis of civil defense in one American city, see David F. Krugler, *This Is only a Test: How Washington, D.C. Prepared for Nuclear War* (New York: Palgrave, 2006). For a critique on civil defense,

see Laura McEnaney, *Civil Defense Begins at Home: Militarization Meets Everyday Life in the Fifties* (Princeton, N.J.: Princeton University Press, 2000).

2. Dudley, "Sprawl as Strategy," 53.

3. "United States Strategic Bombing Survey: Summary Report," July 1946, 36, accessed in 1941–1943, 1945–1947 Correspondence Folder, Whitnall Papers, MCHS.

4. Tracy Augur, "Decentralization Can't Wait," *Appraisal Journal* (January 1949), 108. See also Krugler, "This Is only a Test," 28–35.

5. National Security Resources Board, "National Security Factors in Industrial Location," *Bulletin of the Atomic Scientist*, October 1948, 317.

6. Augur, "Decentralization Can't Wait," 110.

7. Tracy Augur, "The Dispersal of Cities as a Defense Measure," *Bulletin of the Atomic Scientist*, May 1948, 132.

8. "Ralph E. Lapp, Nuclear Scientist," Obituary, *Washington Post*, September 13, 2004. The full text of the Szilard Petition can be accessed. Folder #76, Harrison-Bundy File, Manhattan Engineer District, Records of the Chief of Engineers, Record Group #77, U.S. National Archives.

9. Ralph E. Lapp, *Must We Hide?* (Cambridge, Mass.: Addison-Wesley Press, 1949), 162–68.

10. J. Marchak, E. Teller, and L. R. Klein, "Dispersal of Cities and Industries," *Bulletin of the Atomic Scientist*, April 1948, 13–16.

11. As quoted in a letter from Harry Bogner and Fritz Grossman to Frank Zeidler, January 24, 1949, Folder 3, Box 142, Zeidler Papers, MPL.

12. Letter, Ralph Olson to Freedoms Foundation, Inc., November 21, 1950, Folder 9, Box 87, Zeidler Papers, MPL.

13. "1960 Directory and Report of the Common Council," p. 1, Marquette University Library (MUL).

14. "1955 Directory and Report of the Common Council," p. 44, Marquette Memorial Library, MUL.

15. "1961 Directory and Report of the Common Council," p. 44, MUL.

16. "1953 Directory and Report of the Common Council," p. 41, Marquette Memorial Library.

17. "Civil Defense Program of Development, 1955–1956," MUL.

18. Frank Zeidler, "Observer's Report of Atomic Test at Nevada Proving Ground," 1952, MPL.

19. Letter, Zeidler to Ralph E. Lapp, April 4, 1951, Folder 7, Box 142, Zeidler Papers, MPL.

20. Letter, Krieger to Zeidler, July 18, 1949, Folder 2, Box 191, Zeidler Papers, MPL.

21. Letter, John Kugler to Zeidler, August 2, 1949, Folder 3, Box 142, Zeidler Papers, MPL.

22. Alanen and Eden, *Main Street Ready Made*, 76.

23. Ibid., 78.

24. Letter, Zeidler to Richard Perrin, July 7, 1948, Folder 6, Box 176, Zeidler Papers, MPL.

25. Letter, Zeidler to Walter Mattison, September 14, 1948, Folder 4, Box 176, Zeidler Papers, MPL.

26. Statement by Frank Zeidler, October 15, 1948, Folder 4, Box 176, Zeidler Papers, MPL.

27. "Vote $300,000 for Greendale," *Milwaukee Journal,* December 7, 1948; Alanen and Eden, *Main Street Ready Made,* 79.

28. Joe Arnold, *The New Deal in the Suburbs,* 234–35; Greendale Village Board Minutes, April 19, 1949, Book 2, Greendale Village Hall, Greendale, Wisconsin.

29. Letter, Zeidler to Walter Kroening, February 9, 1949, Folder 2, Box 190, Zeidler Papers, MPL.

30. Letter, Krieger to Zeidler, February 14, 1949, Folder 2, Box 191, Zeidler Papers, MPL.

31. Letter, Krieger to Zeidler, May 20, 1949, Folder 2, Box 191, Zeidler Papers, MPL.

32. For example, see letter from Zeidler to Senator Joseph McCarthy, November 30, 1948, Folder 7, Box 177, Zeidler Papers, MPL.

33. "An Open Letter to Mayor Frank Zeidler," *Greendale Review,* July 22, 1949. This same passage is also quoted in Alanen and Eden, *Main Street Ready Made,* 83.

34. "Editorial," *Greendale Review,* July 22, 1949.

35. "Greendale Waves a Flag," *Milwaukee Journal,* August 24, 1949.

36. "G.V.C.H.A. Slate Sweeps Greendale Election April 4th," *Greendale Review,* April 14, 1950.

37. Memo, Greendale Village Board to Frank Zeidler, December 8, 1948, Folder 7, Box 177, Zeidler Papers, MPL; "Wire Protest on Greendale," *Milwaukee Journal,* December 9, 1948.

38. Greendale Village Board Minutes, April 19, 1949, Book 2, Greendale Village Hall, Greendale, Wisconsin; *Greendale Review,* April 29, 1949.

39. See "Where Does He Stand?" *Greendale Review,* September 3, 1948; "Home Purchase Plans," *Greendale Review,* September 17, 1948; and "We Still Want to Know!" *Greendale Review,* March 4, 1949.

40. "Mass Meeting of Greendale Tenants," *Greendale Review,* July 22, 1949.

41. Letter, Zeidler to Robert Eppley, Greendale Village Manager, December 10, 1948, Folder 7, Box 177, Zeidler Papers, MPL.

42. Memo, Arthur Werba to the Milwaukee Common Council, July 15, 1949, Folder 7, Box 177, Zeidler Papers, MPL.

43. Arnold, *The New Deal in the Suburbs,* 235; Alanen and Eden, *Main Street Ready Made,* 83–88.

44. "New Communities Projected by City," *Milwaukee Journal,* December 11, 1948, City Planning Clipping File, MPL.

45. Untitled Memo, February 1, 1949, Folder 2, Box 190, Zeidler Papers, MPL; "Vote $25,000 for Land Deals," *Milwaukee Journal,* April 13, 1949.

46. Memo, Mayor's Office to Krieger, February 9, 1949, Folder 2, Box 190, Zeidler Papers, MPL; Letter, Zeidler to Andrew Biemiller, March 8, 1949, Folder 7, Box 115, Zeidler Papers, MPL; Letter, Catherine Bauer to Zeidler, January 6, 1950, Folder 2, Box 191, Zeidler Papers, MPL. See also Letter, William Wheaton to Zeidler, February 8, 1954, Folder 3, Box 177, Zeidler Papers, MPL.

47. Krieger, "A Northwest Community Development Plan," December 1949, Wisconsin—Milwaukee Folder, Carton 33, Catherine Bauer Wurster Papers, BL, UCB.

48. Letter, Zeidler to Paul Betters, U.S. Conference of Mayors, and Lee Johnson, National Housing Conference, February 11, 1949, Folder 1, Box 177, Zeidler Papers, MPL.

49. "City Clearance 'Best in Nation,'" *Milwaukee Journal,* December 13, 1949.

50. Letter, Catherine Bauer to Frank Zeidler, January 6, 1950, Folder 2, Box 191, Zeidler Papers, MPL.

51. Catherine Bauer, "Redevelopment and Public Housing," transcript of speech to the American Society of Planning Officials Conference, August 15, 1950, Carton 3, Catherine Bauer Wurster Papers, BL, UCB. The speech is also mentioned in an undated memo from Elmer Krieger to the Board of Public Land Commissioners, Folder 5, Box 19, Zeidler Papers, MPL.

52. Letter, Krieger to Zeidler, March 27, 1950, Folder 2, Box 191, Zeidler Papers, MPL.

53. George Parkinson, "Dispersion Planning in Milwaukee," Folder 5, Box 190, Zeidler Papers, MPL.

54. "Village Makes Bid to Become Part of City," *Milwaukee Sentinel,* February 22, 1930, Annexation Clipping File, LRB.

55. "Points Butler Way to Water," *Milwaukee Journal,* December 4, 1946; "Werba Sees Annexation of Hampton Rd Area," *Milwaukee Sentinel,* December 15, 1946; "Milwaukee's Welcome Mat Laid Out for Butler Village," *Milwaukee Sentinel,* December 16, 1946, Annexation Clipping File, MPL.

56. "New Milwaukee Plans Include Five Counties," *Milwaukee Journal,* February 1, 1951.

57. "Expansion Plan Due for Serious Study," *Milwaukee Sentinel,* July 16, 1950, Annexation Clipping File, MPL.

58. Elmer Krieger, "Coordination of Plans for the City's Expansion and the Civil Defense Program," March 10, 1951, Folder 5, Box 190, Zeidler Papers, MPL.

59. Ibid., 9.

60. "Plan Protects City by Scattering It," *Milwaukee Sentinel,* March 11, 1951.

61. Krieger, "Coordination of Plans for the City's Expansion and the Civil Defense Program," Folder 5, Box 190, Zeidler Papers, MPL, p. 5.

62. Ibid., 4.

63. "Plan Hearings on Proposal of City Extension," *Milwaukee Journal,* March 12, 1951.

64. The most comprehensive history of Butler can be found in "A History of Butler," compiled by Hugh Swaford III, Butler Public Library, Butler, Wisc.

65. "Village of Butler Seeks Annexation Hearing Dec. 14," *Milwaukee Sentinel,* December 4, 1946, Annexation Clipping File, MPL.

66. "Judge Upholds City's Addition of Butler Area," *Milwaukee Sentinel,* March 7, 1950, Annexation Clipping File, MPL.

67. "Appeal Slated on Annexation," *Milwaukee Journal,* June 27, 1950; "Block to Annexation Backfires," *Milwaukee Sentinel,* July 7, 1950; "9 'Befriend' High Court in Annexation Battle," *Milwaukee Journal,* March 8, 1951, all in Annexation Clipping File, MPL.

68. "Protest Annexation to City of Milwaukee," *Menomonee Falls News,* March 22, 1951, Menomonee Falls Library, Menomonee Falls, Wisc. (MFL).

69. Minutes of Butler Village Board, October 17, 1950, Village Hall, Butler, Wisconsin; Minutes of Town of Menomonee Annual Meeting, April 8, 1952, Menomonee Falls Village Hall, Menomonee Falls, Wisc.

70. "Ask Fairness in Annexation Trial," *Milwaukee Journal,* March 1, 1951.

71. "High Court Ruling Blocks City's Plan," *Milwaukee Journal,* April 4, 1951; "High Court Rulings Jolt 2 Annex Plans," *Milwaukee Sentinel,* April 4, 1951.

72. Statement by Frank Zeidler, given to *Milwaukee Sentinel,* April 5, 1951, Folder 9, Box 89, Zeidler Papers, MPL.

73. Zeidler, "A Liberal in City Government," 21; Elmer Krieger, "Milwaukee Coordinates Expansion and Civil-Defense Plans," *American City,* June 1951, 118–19.

74. "Waukesha County Group Calls City 'Dictatorship,'" *Milwaukee Journal,* March 29, 1951, Annexation Clipping File, MPL.

75. Richard E. Perrin, "Public Housing in Milwaukee," 2nd edition, 1966, MPL; "Truman Approves $7,046,000 to Build Westlawn Project," *Milwaukee Journal,* July 5, 1950.

76. Board Meeting Minutes, February 27, 1946, Folder 11, Box 2, Milwaukee Metropolitan Association of Commerce, Minutes 1915–1964, Milwaukee Manuscript Collection 14, State Historical Society of Wisconsin, MARC, GML.

77. Letter, Affiliated Taxpayers' Committee to Milwaukee Common Council, January 24, 1945, in "Milwaukee Speaks on Housing and Blight Elimination," p. 8, MPL.

78. For an excellent account of the anti–public housing campaign, including the strategies used by the ATC and other groups, see Fure-Slocum, "The Challenge of the Working Class City," 484–562. For other coverage of the referenda, see "Voters Facing Housing Issue," *Milwaukee Journal,* March 28, 1951; "Is There a Real Housing Shortage in Milwaukee?" *Milwaukee Journal,* March 29, 1951; "Housing Story Told to Voters," *Milwaukee Journal,* March 30, 1951; "How Does Referendum Affect Slum Clearance?" *Mil-*

waukee Journal, April 2, 1951; "Public Housing, Slum Removal both Favored at Polls," *Milwaukee Journal,* April 4, 1951.

79. "Protest Annexation to City of Milwaukee," *Menomonee Falls News,* March 22, 1951, MFL.

80. Stein, "Greendale and the Future," 109. The article is also reprinted in Clarence S. Stein, *Toward New Towns for America* (Cambridge, Mass.: MIT Press, 1957), 187. To further understand Stein's sense of urbanism after WWII, see Kristin Larsen, "Cities to Come: Clarence Stein's Postwar Regionalism," *Journal of Planning History* 4, no. 1 (2005): 33–51.

6—Municipal Mercantilism

1. George Saffran, Milwaukee Budget Supervisor, "Annexation Practices in Milwaukee: An Administrative Survey," prepared for the Administrative Survey Committee, June 1952, MPL.

2. "Progress Report on the City's Administrative Survey," speech by Norman Gill, Citizens' Governmental Research Bureau, to the Milwaukee Board of Realtors, May 29, 1951, Folder 8, Box 48, Zeidler Papers, MPL.

3. Ibid.

4. Griffenhagen and Associates, "City of Milwaukee Report #16—Board of Public Land Commissioners," November 16, 1949, MPL.

5. George Saffran, Milwaukee Budget Supervisor, "Annexation Practices in Milwaukee: An Administrative Survey," prepared for the Administrative Survey Committee, June 1952, MPL.

6. For example, see Letter, Krieger to Zeidler, February 14, 1949, Folder 2, Box 191, Zeidler Papers, MPL; Letter, Krieger to Zeidler, May 20, 1949, Folder 2, Box 191, Zeidler Papers, MPL; Letter, Krieger to Zeidler, July 18, 1949, Folder 2, Box 191, Zeidler Papers, MPL; Letter, Krieger to Zeidler, September 30, 1953, Folder 5, Box 190, Zeidler Papers, MPL.

7. Letter, Werba to Zeidler, December 1, 1948, Folder 2, Box 124, Zeidler Papers, MPL.

8. "Annexation Means Good Planning," *Milwaukee Sentinel,* June 13, 1951, Annexation Clipping File, MPL.

9. Some penetrating studies of "uneven development" include Kevin Fox-Gotham, *Race, Real Estate, and Uneven Development: The Kansas City Experience, 1900–2000* (Albany: SUNY Press, 2002); Joe R. Feagin and Robert Parker, *Building American Cities: The Urban Real Estate Game* (Englewood Cliffs, N.J.: Prentice Hall, 1990); Joe T. Darden, *Detroit: Race and Uneven Development* (Philadelphia: Temple University Press, 1987).

10. Donald Curran, *Metropolitan Financing: The Milwaukee Experience, 1920–1970* (Madison: University of Wisconsin Press, 1973), 44.

11. Ibid., 146.

12. Robert C. Wood, *1400 Governments: The Political Economy of the New York Metropolitan Region* (Cambridge, Mass.: Harvard University Press, 1961).

13. An excellent overview of redevelopment in St. Louis is Joe Heathcott and Maire Murphy, "Corridors of Flight, Zones of Renewal: Industry, Planning, and Policy in the Making of Metropolitan St. Louis, 1940–1980," *Journal of Urban History* 31, no. 2, 151–89. For Pittsburgh, see Roy S. Lubove, *Twentieth Century Pittsburgh: Government, Business, and Environmental Change* (New York: Wiley Books, 1969). For Detroit and its annexation problems, see June Manning-Thomas, *Redevelopment and Race: Planning a Finer City in Postwar Detroit* (Baltimore: Johns Hopkins University Press, 1997), 31–32.

14. Curran, *Metropolitan Financing,* 37–38.

15. Ibid., 82.

16. "To the Farmers Living in the Town of Lake" by the Taxpayers and Voters League of the Town of Lake, Folder 1, Box 9, City Club of Milwaukee, Records 1909–

1975, Milwaukee Manuscript Collection AS and Milwaukee Micro Collection 69, WHS, MARC; *Milwaukee Sentinel*, May 13, 1931.

17. "High Court Ruling Blocks City's Plans," *Milwaukee Journal*, April 3, 1951, Annexation Clipping File, MPL.

18. Milwaukee Community Development Corporation, "Report on City-Suburban Relations," 1957, MPL.

19. Curran, *Metropolitan Financing,* 144.

20. For example, see "Firms' Annexation Plan Perils Town's Revenues," *Milwaukee Journal,* April 9, 1950, Annexation Clipping File, MPL.

21. "Metropolitan Area Fact Book, 1940, 1950, 1960," p. 43, MPL.

22. "Glendale: Rich Past, Bright Future, Fifty Years, 1950–2000," MPL.

23. "High Court Ruling Blocks City's Plan," *Milwaukee Journal*, April 3, 1951, Annexation Clipping File, MPL.

24. Curran, *Metropolitan Financing,* 146.

25. Introduction to the Collection, Milwaukee Metropolitan Association of Commerce Minutes, 1915–1964, Milwaukee Manuscript Collection 14, MARC, GML.

26. By 1949, the MAC counted 3,077 business and professional firms as official dues-paying members. Folder 14, Box 2, Milwaukee Metropolitan Association of Commerce, Minutes 1915–1964, Milwaukee Manuscript Collection 14, MARC, GML.

27. Executive Committee Meeting, July 16, 1949, Folder 15, Box 3, Milwaukee Metropolitan Association of Commerce Minutes 1915–1964, Milwaukee Manuscript Collection 14, MARC, GML.

28. Letter, Clifford Randall to MMAC Board of Directors, March 17, 1950, Folder 1, Box 3, Milwaukee Metropolitan Association of Commerce; Minutes 1915–1964, Milwaukee Manuscript Collection 14, MARC, GML.

29. Elizabeth Fones-Wolf, *Selling Free Enterprise: The Business Assault on Labor and Liberalism, 1945–1960* (Urbana: University of Illinois Press, 1994).

30. *Milwaukee Journal,* October 17, 1952; October 9, 1953; October 14, 1954.

31. "Report to the Board of Directors, February 23, 1956," Milwaukee Metropolitan Association of Commerce, Minutes 1915–1964, Milwaukee Manuscript Collection 14, State Historical Society of Wisconsin.

32. Milwaukee Association of Commerce, "Milwaukee Has Everything—for Profitable Industry, for Enjoyable Living," MPL.

33. For an excellent overview of labor's problems at Allis Chalmers and the 1946 strike, see Stephen Meyer, *Stalin over Wisconsin: The Making and Unmaking of Militant Unionism, 1900–1950* (New Brunswick, N.J.: Rutgers University Press, 1992). See also Anthony Orum, *City Building in America* (Boulder, Colo.: Westview Press, 1995), 105.

34. "Industries Division Report," January 24, 1950, Folder 1, Box 3, Milwaukee Metropolitan Association of Commerce Minutes 1915–1964, Milwaukee Manuscript Collection 14, MARC, GML.

35. Memo and Letter, Arthur Werba to Frank Zeidler, November 24, 1950, Folder 4, Box 124, Zeidler Papers, MPL.

36. "Village Adds to Industries," *Milwaukee Journal,* June 20, 1950, Annexation Clipping File, MPL.

37. For the squabbling over General Electric's site, see "Firms' Annexation Plan Perils Town's Revenues," *Milwaukee Journal,* April 9, 1950; "Towns Ask Firms to Stay," *Milwaukee Journal,* April 11, 1950. For the conflict over American Can, see Letter, Zeidler to Swietlik, December 1, 1948, Folder 2, Box 124, Zeidler Papers, MPL; Letter, Walter Swietlik to E. M. Boerke, December 8, 1948, Folder 2, Box 124, Zeidler Papers, MPL; "Town Maps Annex Fight," *Milwaukee Journal,* September 28, 1951.

38. Zeidler, "A Liberal in City Government," 61–62; Bertil Hanson, "A Report on the Politics of Milwaukee," 1960, V-4, MPL.

39. Mollenkopf, *The Contested City*; Teaford, *The Rough Road to Renaissance.*

40. Letter, Werba to Zeidler, April 14, 1950, Folder 4, Box 124, Zeidler Papers, MPL; Zeidler, "A Liberal in City Government," 35.

41. "Kohler Signs Bills Easing Annexation," *Milwaukee Sentinel,* July 9, 1951, Annexation Clipping File, MPL.

42. "Plan Annexing to Aid Transit," *Milwaukee Journal,* September 15, 1951.

43. Bill Vandervoort, "Milwaukee Interurban Railways," accessed online at http://hometown.aol.com/chirailfan/histmke3.html.

44. "Milwaukee County Highway Commission, Milwaukee County Expressway System: General Plan," 1, MPL.

45. Quoted in Zeidler's 1953 speech to the Common Council, Folder 10, Box 55, Zeidler Collection, MPL. Zeidler came to lament the demise of the interurban lines. He later recalled that his "biggest regret" as mayor was choosing not to more deeply explore rapid transit's salvation in the early 1950s; interview with author, September 13, 2002.

46. "Milwaukee Accused of 'Grabbing Land,'" *Menomonee Falls News,* September 20, 1951, MFL; "Transit Annex Called a Bluff," *Milwaukee Journal,* September 19, 1951, Annexation Clipping File, MPL.

47. "Suburbs Lash Plan to Annex Large Tracts," *Milwaukee Journal,* September 28, 1951, Annexation Clipping File, MPL.

48. Ibid.

49. On West Allis's annexations, see "Posting Clash in Greenfield Opens Battle," *Milwaukee Journal,* October 2, 1951, Annexation Clipping File, MPL. For Hales Corners, see "H.C. Votes for Incorporation," *The Tri-Town News,* January 31, 1952. For Wauwatosa and Butler, see "Two More Links in the Iron Ring," *Milwaukee Journal,* March 14, 1952, Annexation Clipping File, MPL. For Bayside, see "Hearing on Bayside Set," *Milwaukee Journal,* April 6, 1952, Annexation Clipping File, MPL.

50. Frank Zeidler, "Annual Speech to Milwaukee Common Council, 1952," Folder 9, Box 55, Zeidler Papers, MPL.

51. "Public Hearing, Regular Meeting of the Legislative Council," June 16, 1952, Council Minutes, Citizens Governmental Research Bureau, Metropolitan Problems Committee, Summary of Meetings, 1953–1954, C-1.14, Series 2-NNG, Gill Collection, Marquette University Archives, Marquette University (MUA).

52. "Public Hearing, Regular Meeting of the Legislative Council," June 16, 1952, p. 5, Council Minutes, Citizens Governmental Research Bureau, Metropolitan Problems Committee, Summary of Meetings, 1953–1954, C-1.14, Series 2-NNG, Gill Collection, MUA.

53. Ibid.

54. "Public Hearing, Regular Meeting of the Legislative Council," June 16, 1952, p. 11, Council Minutes, Citizens Governmental Research Bureau, Metropolitan Problems Committee, Summary of Meetings, 1953–1954, C-1.14, Series 2-NNG, Gill Collection, MUA.

55. "Public Hearing, Regular Meeting of the Legislative Council," June 16, 1952, p. 13, Council Minutes, Citizens Governmental Research Bureau, Metropolitan Problems Committee, Summary of Meetings, 1953–1954, C-1.14, Series 2-NNG, Gill Collection, MUA.

56. *Milwaukee Journal,* March 27, 1949, in Saffran, "Annexation Practices in Milwaukee: An Administrative Analysis," June 1952, MPL.

57. "Won a Backer by $435 Fee," *Milwaukee Journal,* June 12, 1952, Annexation Clipping File, MPL. A broader analysis of the role that developers played in fostering annexation can also be found in Fleischmann, "The Territorial Expansion of Milwaukee," *Journal of Urban History* 14, no. 2 (February 1988): 147–76.

58. "Hits Payment in Annexation," *Milwaukee Journal,* June 14, 1952, Annexation Clipping File, MPL.

59. "Annexing Plan of City Is Hit," *Milwaukee Journal,* October 11, 1952, Annexation Clipping File, MPL.

60. "We're Committing Suicide with Our Annexation Policy," *Milwaukee Sentinel,* September 5, 1952, Annexation Clipping File, MPL.

61. "List Benefits of Annexation," *Milwaukee Journal,* November 28, 1953, Annexation Clipping File, MPL, Citizens' Governmental Research Bureau, vol. 42, no. 9, May 26, 1954, Folder 9, Box 48, Zeidler Papers, MPL.

62. "Cities Are Obsolete," *Tri-Town News,* July 22, 1954.

63. Robert O. Self, *American Babylon: Race and the Struggle for Postwar Oakland* (Princeton, N.J.: Princeton University Press, 2003), 129.

64. Ibid., 96.

65. Ibid., 119.

66. "We Are Not 'SUB-urban,'" *West Allis Star,* August 8, 1957, Suburbs Clipping File, LRB.

67. Orum, *City Building in America,* 79–80.

68. "Two More Links in the Iron Ring," *Milwaukee Sentinel,* March 14, 1952, Annexation Clipping File, MPL.

69. "City an 'Octupus' and 'Hitler,' State Group Is Told," *Milwaukee Sentinel,* May 21, 1952, Annexation Clipping File, MPL.

70. William H. Bowman, "The Incorporation of Greenfield," in Esther L. Fisher, "A Brief History of the City of Greenfield," MPL, 135.

71. Hanson, "A Report on the Politics of Milwaukee," 1960, part IV, MPL.

72. For the background to the Lakeside power plant, see Letter, Werba to Zeidler, October 3, 1950, Folder 4, Box 124, Zeidler Papers, MPL. For Hibicke's annexation run-ins with Milwaukee, see "Pressure Told in Annexation," *Milwaukee Journal,* April 6, 1947; and "Hibicke Rips Annexation Move," *Milwaukee Sentinel,* February 27, 1951, in Annexation Clipping File, MPL.

73. As quoted in Milwaukee Community Development Corporation, "Report on City-Suburban Relations," 1957, MPL.

74. "Town of Lake Considers Consolidation with City of Milwaukee on its 116th Birthday," *Citizens Governmental Research Bureau Bulletin,* vol. 42, no. 7, April 1, 1954, Folder 9, Box 48, Zeidler Papers, MPL.

75. "Would Block Any Expansion by St. Francis," *Milwaukee Sentinel,* August 2, 1951, Annexation Clipping File, MPL.

76. Milwaukee Office of Budget Supervisor, "Consolidation? Cooperation? Advantages and Disadvantages of the Consolidation of the Town of Lake with the City of Milwaukee," 1953, MPL. See also "Mayor, Officials Predict Benefits to Both Communities if Plan Goes Through," *Milwaukee Journal,* June 12, 1953, Annexation Clipping File, MPL.

77. "Town of Lake Folks Call for Action," *Milwaukee Sentinel,* June 12, 1953, Annexation Clipping File, MPL.

78. *Citizens Governmental Research Bureau Bulletin,* vol. 42, no. 7, April 1, 1954, Folder 9, Box 48, Zeidler Papers, MPL.

79. Minutes of Milwaukee Association of Commerce Board of Directors Meeting, September 28, 1951, Folder 2, Box 3, Milwaukee Metropolitan Association of Commerce, Minutes 1915–1964, Milwaukee Manuscript Collection 14, MARC, GML.

80. Norbert Stefaniak, "Industrial Location within the Urban Area: A Case Study of the Locational Characteristics of 950 Manufacturing Plants in the Milwaukee Area," *Wisconsin Commerce Reports* VI, no. 5, August 1962.

81. *Citizens Governmental Research Bureau Bulletin,* vol. 43, no. 15, September 25, 1954, Folder 3, Box 187, Zeidler Papers, MPL; Curran, *Metropolitan Financing,* 44.

82. "Town of Oak Creek's 114th Anniversary—Milwaukee County's Future Low Tax Community," *Citizens Governmental Research Bureau Bulletin,* vol. 43, no. 15, September 25, 1954, Folder 3, Box 187, Zeidler Papers, MPL.

83. "Favor a City for Oak Creek," *Milwaukee Journal,* June 16, 1955; "Reaffirm

Vote on Oak Creek," *Milwaukee Journal*, June 23, 1955. See also Fleischmann, "The Politics of Annexation and Urban Development," 100–50.

84. Letter, Gerald Caffrey to Zeidler, December 14, 1955, Folder 3, Box 79, Zeidler Papers, MPL.

85. "Blame Oak Creek Law for Milwaukee Trouble," *Milwaukee Journal*, January 18, 1957; Fleischmann, "The Politics of Annexation and Urban Development," 130–45.

86. Letter, Frank Zeidler to Joe Lamping, July 12, 1957, Folder 9, Box 56, Zeidler Papers, MPL.

87. *Milwaukee Journal*, November 1, 1955; *Milwaukee Journal*, January 18, 1957.

88. *Milwaukee Journal*, July 26, 1955.

89. John Gurda, *The Making of Milwaukee* (Milwaukee: Milwaukee County Historical Society, 1999), 341–42.

90. "Mayor Seeks County Unity," *Milwaukee Journal*, August 26, 1956.

91. Memo, Gerald Caffrey to Zeidler, January 25, 1956, Folder 2, Box 181, Zeidler Papers, MPL.

92. The term "fragmented metropolis" was first used by Robert Fogelson in *The Fragmented Metropolis: Los Angeles, 1850–1930* (Cambridge, Mass.: Harvard University Press, 1967). See also Jon C. Teaford, *City and Suburb: The Political Fragmentation of Metropolitan America, 1850–1970* (Baltimore: Johns Hopkins University Press, 1979).

7—Selective Metropolitanism

1. The term "Late Great Migration" comes from Paul Edward Geib, "The Late, Great Migration: A Case Study of Southern Black Migration to Milwaukee, 1940–1970," M.A. Thesis, University of Wisconsin-Milwaukee, 1993.

2. Joe William Trotter, Jr., *Black Milwaukee: The Making of an Industrial Proletariat, 1915–1945* (Urbana: University of Illinois Press, 1985).

3. For the Sixth Ward and the zoning ordinance, see Trotter, *Black Milwaukee*, 181–82. For realtors and intentional segregation, see "Proposes City Negro District," *Milwaukee Journal*, September 16, 1924. For African American neighborhoods and 1930s slum clearance, see Keith Robert Schmitz, "Milwaukee and Its Black Community, 1930–1942," M.A. Thesis, University of Wisconsin-Milwaukee, 1979.

4. William Slayton, "Population Changes by Census Tract, City of Milwaukee, 1920–1940," MPL.

5. For an example of how city officials conflated race and blight during the 1940s, see Milwaukee Health Commissioner, "Observations on Housing Conditions in Milwaukee's Sixth Ward: A Report to Mayor John Bohn and the Common Council," 1944, MPL.

6. "Waukesha County Group Calls City 'Dictatorship,'" *Milwaukee Journal*, March 29, 1951, Annexation Clipping File, MPL.

7. National Affairs Committee Meeting, July 7, 1955, Folder 6, Box 3, Milwaukee Metropolitan Association of Commerce, Minutes 1915–1964, Milwaukee Manuscript Collection 14, MARC, GML.

8. "Designed for Export?" *New York Post*, March 15, 1956, in Folder 11, Box 47, Zeidler Papers, MPL.

9. Jack Dougherty, *More than One Struggle: The Evolution of Black School Reform in Milwaukee* (Chapel Hill: University of North Carolina Press, 2004), 51–52.

10. Memo, Zeidler to Common Council, December 23, 1952, Folder 11, Box 47, Zeidler Papers, MPL; Zeidler, "A Liberal in City Government."

11. Anonymous letter to Frank Zeidler, Folder 11, Box 47, Zeidler Papers, MPL.

12. *The Wauwatosa News-Times*, August 6, 1953, in Folder 5, Box 159, Zeidler Papers, MPL.

13. Very sound interpretations of the 1956 election in terms of race can be found in Dougherty, *More than One Struggle,* 57–58; and Patrick D. Jones, "'The Selma of the North': Race Relations and Civil Rights Insurgency in Milwaukee, 1958–1970," Ph.D. Diss., University of Wisconsin (2002), 33–34.

14. "The Shame of Milwaukee," *Newsweek,* April 2, 1953, 23. "Designed for Export?" *New York Post,* March 15, 1956, in Folder 11, Box 47, Zeidler Papers, MPL; "Here Are the Facts about Milton J. McGuire, Candidate for Mayor of Milwaukee," McGuire for Mayor Club, Folder 2, Box 48, Zeidler Papers, MPL, Anonymous letter to Frank Zeidler, Folder 11, Box 47, Zeidler Papers, MPL.

15. "To the Voters of Milwaukee," Folder 11, Box 47, Zeidler Papers, MPL; "Here Are the Facts about Milton J. McGuire," Folder 2, Box 48, Zeidler Papers, MPL.

16. As of February 27, 1956, fifty-eight of Milton McGuire's individual campaign contributions came from people who resided outside of Milwaukee, compared to only thirty contributors who lived in the city; Folder 14, Box 47, Zeidler Papers, MPL.

17. "Think, Milwaukee Voters!" Folder 2, Box 48, Zeidler Papers, MPL.

18. "Which do You Want? Americanism or Socialism?" *Milwaukee Sentinel,* March 23, 1956.

19. "Council-Mayor Discord Evident," *Milwaukee Sentinel,* March 16, 1956.

20. Board of Directors Meeting, November 22, 1955, Folder 6, Box 3, Milwaukee Metropolitan Association of Commerce, Minutes 1915–1964, Milwaukee Manuscript Collection 14, MARC, GML.

21. Board of Directors Meeting Minutes, March 8, 1956, Folder 7, Box 3, Milwaukee Metropolitan Association of Commerce, Minutes 1915–1964, Milwaukee Manuscript Collection 14, MARC, GML.

22. Memo, E. E. Woerfel to Woerfel Corporation Employees, March 20, 1956, Folder 2, Box 48, Zeidler Papers, MPL.

23. Bill Lueders, "Last of a Breed," *Milwaukee Magazine,* November 1985; *Milwaukee Labor Press,* March 15, 1956, Folder 1, Box 48, Zeidler Papers, MPL; *New York Post,* March 15, 1956, Folder 11, Box 47, Zeidler Papers, MPL; "1956 Mayoral Campaign Analysis," Board of Election Commissioners, City of Milwaukee, Folder 3, Box 48, Zeidler Papers, MPL.

24. "People You Should Know," *Pittsburgh Courier—Midwest Edition,* April 7, 1956, Folder 12, Box 47, Zeidler Papers, MPL; Speech by Joseph Clark, November 14, 1955, Folder 12, Box 48, Zeidler Papers, MPL; Speech by David Lawrence, undated, Folder 1, Box 48, Zeidler Paper, MPL.

25. Dougherty, *More Than One Struggle,* 57–60; Jones, "'The Selma of the North,'" 35.

26. Statement of Frank Zeidler, February 27, 1956, Folder 12, Box 47, Zeidler Papers, MPL.

27. For a specific example of how city officials viewed "metropolitan cooperation" as a suburban water grab, see Letter, William Kneuse and George Schmus to Robert Dineen, December 6, 1956, Folder 1, Box 160, Zeidler Papers, MPL.

28. For a comprehensive, start-to-finish account of the MSC, see Henry Schmandt and William Standing, *The Milwaukee Metropolitan Study Commission* (Bloomington: Indiana University Press, 1965), 73–78.

29. Ibid., 82–87; Letter, Zeidler to Phil Drotning, Secretary to Governor Walter Kohler, October 1, 1956, Folder 1, Box 160, Zeidler Papers, MPL.

30. Letter, Zeidler to Horace Wilkie, January 31, 1957, Folder 7, Box 159, Zeidler Papers, MPL.

31. Schmandt and Standing, *The Milwaukee Metropolitan Study Commission,* 301–8.

32. George A. Parkinson, "Proposal Regarding Metropolitan Government," Folder 8, Box 159, Zeidler Papers, MPL; "Resolution Setting Forth the City's Position Concerning Questions Proposed in the December 31, 1958 Communication from the Metropolitan Study Commission Concerning Metropolitan Governmental Organization," Folder 3, Box 160, Zeidler Papers, MPL.

33. Letter, John Lobb to Board of Directors, June 13, 1958, Folder 9, Box 3, Milwaukee Metropolitan Association of Commerce, Minutes 1915–1964, Milwaukee Manuscript Collection 14, MARC, GML.

34. Transcript of Presentation, Leo Tiefenthaler to the Milwaukee Metropolitan Survey Committee, October 19, 1956, Folder 6, Box 159, Zeidler Papers, MPL.

35. This and many other official statements from other area suburbs can be found in Land Use and Zoning Committee Folder, Box 2, Metropolitan Study Commission Collection, Wisconsin Series 1720, MARC, GML.

36. "More Metro Double Talk," *West Allis Star,* April 23, 1958, in Folder 8, Box 159, Zeidler Papers, MPL.

37. Letter, Zeidler to Lamping, July 12, 1957, Folder 9, Box 56, Zeidler Papers, MPL.

38. Land Use and Zoning Committee, MSC, "Proposed Findings and Conclusions Concerning Zoning in Milwaukee County," Folder 5, Box 6, Zeidler Papers, MPL.

39. Charles Beveridge, "History of the Water Supply in the Milwaukee Area: Submitted to the Committee on Metropolitan Functions, Metropolitan Study Commission," 1958, Marquette Memorial Library.

40. "Report of the Metropolitan Functions Committee Relating to Statement of the Wisconsin Board of Health Relating to Problems of Water Pollution in Private Wells in the Milwaukee Metropolitan Area," Folder 7, Box 160, Zeidler Papers, MPL.

41. Statement of Frank Zeidler, March 27, 1958, Folder 8, Box 159, Zeidler Papers, MPL.

42. Memo, Municipal League of Milwaukee County to Robert Dineen, December 6, 1956, Folder 1, Box 160, Zeidler Papers, MPL.

43. See "Response to Petition of City of Wauwatosa: Submitted to the Public Service Commission of Wisconsin," Folder 5, Box 161, Zeidler Papers, MPL. For Zeidler's political remarks, see Zeidler, "A Liberal in City Government," 158–64, MPL.

44. "City of Franklin Resolution," Folder 4, Box 2, Metropolitan Study Commission Collection, Wisconsin Series 1720, Metropolitan Study Commission Collection, Wisconsin Series 1720, MARC, GML.

45. "City of Hales Corners Resolution," City of St. Francis Resolution, Folder 4, Box 2, Metropolitan Study Commission Collection, Wisconsin Series 1720, Metropolitan Study Commission Collection, Wisconsin Series 1720, MARC, GML.

46. "Existing Planning Agencies for Zoning and Platting," Folder 1, Box 161, Zeidler Papers, MPL.

47. For a first-person overview of both Milwaukee's annexation problems and the creation of SEWRPC, see Richard Cutler, *Greater Milwaukee's Growing Pains, 1950–2000: An Insider's View* (Milwaukee: Milwaukee County Historical Society, 2001). Cutler, an attorney, served on the MSC and while he often represented suburbs in annexation litigation, he chaired the MSC's Land Use and Zoning Committee and acted as somewhat of a mediator between the city and its suburbs in the creation of SEWRPC. For the failure of both city and suburb to find common ground on "metropolitan impact" see "Summary of Public Hearing of Land Use and Zoning Board," October 20, 1959, Folder 6, Box 2, Metropolitan Study Commission Collection, Wisconsin Series 1720, MARC, GML. For land absorption, see David Rusk, "Creating Livable Communities: Are We Going to Live Together?" Web site, accessed at http://www.gamaliel.org/Strategic/StrategicpartnersRuskMadisonArticle.htm.

48. Land Use and Zoning Committee, MSC, "Proposed Findings and Conclusions Concerning Zoning in Milwaukee County," Folder 5, Box 6, Zeidler Papers, MPL.

49. Ibid.

50. For example, see "State Tax Climate under Fire at Annual Meeting," *Milwaukee Commerce,* vol. 37, no. 20, November 25, 1958, Folder 1, Box 37, Zeidler Papers, MPL.

51. Land Use and Zoning Committee, MSC, "Proposed Findings and Conclusions Concerning Zoning in Milwaukee County," Folder 5, Box 6, Zeidler Papers, MPL.

52. "Distinct: That's Wauwatosa," *Milwaukee Journal*, August 1, 1920, Suburbs Clipping File, Legislative Reference Bureau, Milwaukee, Wisconsin.

53. *Citizens Governmental Reference Bureau Bulletin*, vol. 43, no. 9, October 8, 1955, p. 3, Folder 9, Box 48, Zeidler Papers, MPL. "A History of the Briggs and Stratton Corporation," 1985, MPL.

54. *1957 Official Bulletin of the City of Wauwatosa*, Folder 1, Box 2, Wauwatosa Collection, MCHS.

55. *Citizens Governmental Research Bureau Bulletin*, vol. 43, no. 9, October 8, 1955, Folder 9, Box 48, Zeidler Papers, MPL; *1957 Official Bulletin of the City of Wauwatosa*, Folder 1, Box 2, Wauwatosa Collection, MCHS.

56. *Milwaukee Journal*, January 14, 1957.

57. Ibid.

58. *Milwaukee Journal*, January 20, 1957.

59. Gurda, *The Making of Milwaukee*, 352; Orum, *City Building in America*, 117.

60. Michael Johns, *Moment of Grace: The American City in the 1950's* (Berkeley: University of California Press, 2003); T. Sugrue, *Origins of the Urban Crisis*, 143.

61. Lois M. Quinn and John Pawasarat, *A Block Level Analysis of Racial Integration in Urban America: A Block Level Analysis of African American and White Housing Patterns*, Employment and Training Institute, School of Continuing Education, University of Wisconsin-Milwaukee, December 2002, revised January 2003.

62. "Hypersegregation Label Distorts Social Reality," *Milwaukee Journal-Sentinel*, January 13, 2003.

63. "Complaints Not Really about Our Methodology," *Milwaukee Journal-Sentinel*, January 18, 2003.

64. Zeidler, "A Liberal in City Government," 107, MPL.

65. Gurda, *The Making of Milwaukee*, 366–67.

66. Ibid., 374.

67. For Maier's personal insights into race and metropolitics, see Henry Maier, *The Mayor Who Made Milwaukee Famous* (Lanham, Md.: Madison Books, 1993).

68. Orum, *City Building in America*, 140.

69. David M. P. Freund, *Colored Property: State Policy and White Racial Politics in Suburban America* (Chicago: University of Chicago Press, 2007).

70. "Economic Fact Book on Metropolitan Milwaukee," Urban Research and Development Division, Metropolitan Milwaukee Association of Commerce, 1972, MUL; Nordberg Manufacturing Company, Folder 9, Box 30, Founding Industries of Wisconsin (Survey project), Records 1880–1993, UWM Manuscript Collection 41, MARC, GML.

71. For Allen Bradley, see "Changing with the Times: A History of the Allen-Bradley Company," 1987, MPL, and Allen-Bradley Folder 7, Box 1, Founding Industries of Wisconsin (Survey Project), Records 1880–1993, UWM Manuscript Collection 41; University Manuscript Collections. Golda Meir Library. University of Wisconsin--Milwaukee Founding Industries of Wisconsin (Survey project), Records 1880–1993. UWM Manuscript Collection 41. University Manuscript Collections, MARC, GML; *Milwaukee Journal-Sentinel*, December 5, 2004.

72. Sammis White, Jr., et al., "City and Suburban Impacts of the Industrial Changes in Milwaukee, 1979–1987," The Urban Research Center, University of Wisconsin-Milwaukee, 1989, pp. 3–4.

73. Sam Bass Warner, *The Private City: Philadelphia in Its Three Periods of Growth* (Philadelphia: University of Pennsylvania Press, 1968).

Works Cited

Periodicals

The American City
American Review of Reviews
Charities and Commons
Greendale Review
Journal of the American Institute of Architects
Menomonee Falls News
Milwaukee Daily News
Milwaukee Journal
Milwaukee Journal-Sentinel (The *Milwaukee Journal* and the *Milwaukee Sentinel* merged in
    1995)
Milwaukee Labor Press
Milwaukee Leader
Milwaukee Magazine
Milwaukee News
Milwaukee Sentinel
Newsweek
The New York Post
The New York Times
The North Milwaukee Annexationist
Once a Year (Milwaukee Press Club)
Pittsburgh Courier
Providence Sunday Journal
Racine Journal-Times
The Survey
The Survey Graphic
Tri-Town News
Wauwatosa News
Wauwatosa News-Times
West Allis Star
Wisconsin News

Manuscript Sources

Archives and Abbreviations

Bancroft Library, University of California-Berkeley (BL, UCB)
City of Menomonee Falls (CMF)
Division of Rare and Manuscript Records, Cornell University Library (CUL)
Legislative Reference Bureau, City of Milwaukee (LRB)
Marquette University Archives, Marquette Library (MUA)
Milwaukee Area Research Center, Golda Meir Library, University of Wisconsin-Milwau-
    kee (MARC, GML)
Milwaukee County Historical Society (MCHS)
Milwaukee Public Library (MPL)
Village of Butler (VB)
Village of Greendale (VG)

Collections and Abbreviations

American Society of Planning Officials Records, CUL
Board of Public Land Commissioners, Annual Reports, MPL
Catherine Bauer Wurster Papers, BL, UCB
Charles Whitnall Papers, MCHS
City Club of Milwaukee Records, MARC, GML
City of Milwaukee, Department of Building Inspector Records, MPL
Clarence Stein Papers, CUL
Clifford Randall Papers, MARC, GML
Daniel W. Hoan Papers, MCHS
Elbert Peets Papers, CUL
Emil Seidel Papers, MCHS
Founding Industries of Wisconsin, MARC, GML
Frank and Carl Zeidler Papers, MPL
Frank Zeidler Papers, MARC, GML
Gordon and Brysis Whitnall Papers, CUL
Greendale Development File, MARC, GML
Henry Wright Papers, CUL
Jerome Dretzka Papers, MCHS
Metropolitan Milwaukee Association of Commerce Collection, MARC, GML
Metropolitan Study Commission Collection, MARC, GML
Milwaukee County Park Commission Records, MCHS
Milwaukee County Real Estate Board, MCHS
Milwaukee County Regional Planning Department Records, MCHS
Milwaukee County Suburbs Collection, MCHS
Norman Gill Papers, MUA
Parklawn Collection, MCHS
Real Estate Collection, MCHS
Richard Perrin Papers, MCHS
Town of Menomonee Records, CMF
Village of Butler Records, VB
Village of Greendale Records, VG
Wauwatosa Collection, MCHS
William George Bruce Papers, MARC, GML

Unpublished Materials

Beveridge, Charles. "History of the Water Supply in the Milwaukee Area: Submitted to the Committee on Metropolitan Functions, Metropolitan Study Commission" 1958, Marquette Memorial Library.

Bradley, Allen. "Changing with the Times: A History of the Allen-Bradley Company," 1987, Milwaukee Public Library.

Clas, Alfred. "Civic Improvement in Milwaukee," 1916, Legislative Reference Bureau.

Crane, Jacob. "Greendale: The General Plan," Transcript of Paper for American City Planning Institute Meeting, Milwaukee, Wisconsin, October 24, 1936, Suburbs Clipping File, Legislative Reference Bureau.

Fisher, Esther L. "A Brief History of the City of Greenfield," 1975, Milwaukee Public Library.

"Glendale: Rich Past, Bright Future, Fifty Years, 1950–2000," Milwaukee Public Library.

Griffenhagen and Associates. "City of Milwaukee Report #16—Board of Public Land Commissioners," 1949, Milwaukee Public Library.

Gurda, John. "The West End: Merrill Park, Pigsville, Concordia: Milwaukee," 1980, Marquette Memorial Library.

Hanson, Bertil. "A Report on the Politics of Milwaukee," 1960, Milwaukee Public Library.

Hegemann, Werner. "City Planning for Milwaukee: What It Means and Why It Must Be Secured," 1916, Milwaukee Public Library.

"A History of the Briggs and Stratton Corporation," 1985, Milwaukee Public Library.

Joint Committee on City-County Consolidation in Milwaukee County. "Metropolitan Milwaukee: One Trade Area Burdened with 93 Local Governments," 1934, Milwaukee Public Library.

Krieger, Elmer. "A Master Plan for the City of Milwaukee," 1947, Milwaukee Public Library.

McClellan and Junkersfeld, Inc. "Milwaukee Transportation Survey," 1926, Milwaukee Public Library.

"Metropolitan Area Fact Book, 1940, 1950, 1960," Milwaukee Public Library.

Metropolitan Milwaukee Association of Commerce. Urban Research and Development Division. "Economic Fact Book on Metropolitan Milwaukee," 1972, Marquette Memorial Library.

Metropolitan Park Commission. "First Tentative Report," 1909, Legislative Reference Bureau.

———. "Third Tentative Report," 1910, Legislative Reference Bureau.

Milwaukee Association of Commerce. "Milwaukee Has Everything—for Profitable Industry, for Enjoyable Living," 1945, Milwaukee Public Library.

Milwaukee Board of Public Land Commissioners. "Annual Report," 1926, Milwaukee Public Library.

———. "Annual Report," 1929, Milwaukee Public Library.

———. "Control of Population Density through Zoning," 1936, Legislative Reference Bureau.

———. "Control of Population Density through Zoning," 1944, Legislative Reference Bureau.

———. "Platting Guide, City of Milwaukee," 1924, Milwaukee Public Library.

———. "Population Changes by Census Tracts, 1920–1940," Milwaukee Public Library.

———. "Restricted Heights of Buildings," 1920, Milwaukee Public Library.

———. "Zoning for Milwaukee: Tentative Report of the Board of Public Land Commissioners," 1920, Legislative Reference Bureau.

Milwaukee Budget Supervisor. "Annexation Practices in Milwaukee: An Administrative Analysis Prepared for the Administrative Survey Committee," 1952, Milwaukee Public Library.

Milwaukee Building Inspector. "Annual Report, Inspector of Buildings," 1926, Legislative Reference Bureau.

———. "Annual Report, Inspector of Buildings," 1928, Legislative Reference Bureau.

———. "Buildings Operations, Year 1920," Legislative Reference Bureau.

Milwaukee Citizens Governmental Research Bureau. "Report Made to the Research Clearinghouse of Milwaukee," 1947, Milwaukee Public Library.

Milwaukee Common Council. "1953 Directory and Report of the Common Council," Marquette Memorial Library.

———. "1955 Directory and Report of the Common Council," Marquette Memorial Library.

———. "1960 Directory and Report of the Common Council," Marquette Memorial Library.

———. "1961 Directory and Report of the Common Council," Marquette Memorial Library.

Milwaukee Community Development Corporation. "Report on City-Suburban Relations," 1957, Milwaukee Public Library.

Milwaukee County Highway Commission. "Milwaukee County Expressway System: General Plan," 1946, Milwaukee Public Library.

Milwaukee County Regional Planning Department. "Residential Development in the Unincorporated Areas of Milwaukee County—Wisconsin," 1946, Milwaukee Public Library.

Milwaukee Health Commissioner. "Observations on Housing Conditions in Milwaukee's Sixth Ward: A Report to Mayor John Bohn and the Common Council," 1944, Milwaukee Public Library.

Milwaukee Housing Council. "Facing the Housing Problem," 1938, Milwaukee Public Library.

"Milwaukee Speaks on Housing and Blight Elimination," 1945, Milwaukee Public Library.

Milwaukee Urban Observatory. "Metropolitan Milwaukee Fact Book: 1970," Marquette University Library.

National Conference on City Planning. "Proceedings, 1909–1924," Hillman Library, University of Pittsburgh.

Olmsted, Frederick Law, Jr., and John Nolen. "Report on Civic Center as proposed by the Metropolitan Park Commission," 1909, Legislative Reference Bureau.

"Report of the Commission on the Economic Study of Milwaukee," 1948, Milwaukee Public Library.

Roll, Richard. "Report of Richard O. Roll, Director of Real Property Survey on Substandard Housing in Milwaukee," 1944, Milwaukee Public Library.

Saffran, George. "Annexation Practices in Milwaukee: An Administrative Analysis," prepared for the Administrative Survey Committee, June 1952, Milwaukee Public Library.

Schulson, Florence. "A History of Planning Activity in Milwaukee, 1892–1952," 1952, Milwaukee Public Library.

Slayton, William. "Population Changes by Census Tract, City of Milwaukee, 1920–1940," 1946, Milwaukee Public Library.

Swaford, Hugh III. "A History of Butler," Butler Public Library, Butler, Wisconsin.

Tobin, Howard, et al. "Proposals for Downtown Milwaukee," The Urban Land Institute, 1941, Milwaukee Public Library.

Werba, Arthur. "Making Milwaukee Mightier," 1929, Milwaukee Public Library.

White, Sammis, Jr., et al. "City and Suburban Impacts of the Industrial Changes in Milwaukee, 1979–1987," Urban Research Center, University of Wisconsin-Milwaukee, 1989.

Whitnall, Charles. "The First Plans for a Parkway System for Milwaukee County," 1924, Milwaukee Public Library.

————. "Milwaukee City Planning," 1911, Legislative Reference Bureau.
————. "Milwaukee's Automobile Problems," 1938, Milwaukee Public Library.
Zeidler, Frank. "A Liberal in City Government: My Experience as Mayor of Milwaukee," 1962, Milwaukee Public Library.
————. "Observer's Report of Atomic Test at Nevada Proving Ground," 1952, Milwaukee Public Library.

Interviews

Cutler, Richard. Interview with author, March 8, 2003, Milwaukee.
Saltzstein, Arthur. Interview with author, June 22, 2007, Milwaukee.
Zeidler, Frank. Interview with author, September 13, 2002, Milwaukee.

Web-based Sources

Milwaukee Neighborhoods: Photos and Maps, 1885–1992. Digital Collection, Golda Meir Library, University of Wisconsin-Milwaukee, accessed online at http://www.uwm.edu/Library/digilib/Milwaukee/index.html.
Rusk, David. "Creating Livable Communities: Are We Going to Live Together?" accessed online at http://www.gamaliel.org/Strategic/StrategicpartnersRusk MadisonArticle.htm.
U.S. Bureau of the Census. "Population of the 100 Largest Urban Populations: 1920," accessed online at http://www.census.gov/population/documentation/twps0027/tab15.txt Internet. Release date June 15, 1998.
Vandervoort, Bill. "Milwaukee Interurban Railways," accessed online at http://hometown.aol.com/chirailfan/histmke3.html.

Published Sources

Aderman, Ralph M., ed. *Trading Post to Metropolis: Milwaukee County's First 150 Years.* Milwaukee: Milwaukee County Historical Society, 1987.
Alanen, Arnold, and Joseph Eden. *Main Street Ready Made: The New Deal Community of Greendale.* Madison: The State Historical Society of Wisconsin, 1987.
Arnold, Joe. *The New Deal in the Suburbs: A History of the Greenbelt Town Program.* Columbus: Ohio State University Press, 1971.
Attoe, Wayne, and Mark Latus. "The First Public Housing: Sewer Socialism's Garden City for Milwaukee." *The Journal of Popular Culture* X, no. 1 (Summer 1976).
Augur, Tracy. "Decentralization Can't Wait," *Appraisal Journal* (January 1949).
————. "The Dispersal of Cities as a Defense Measure." *Bulletin of the Atomic Scientist,* May 1948.
Axelrod, Jeremiah B. C. "'Keep the "L" Out of Los Angeles': Race, Discourse, and Urban Modernity in 1920s Southern California." *Journal of Urban History* 34 (2007): 3–37.
Barnett, Jonathan. *The Fractured Metropolis: Improving the New City, Restoring the Old City, Reshaping the Region.* New York: Harper-Collins, 1995.
Bassett, Edward. *Zoning: The Laws, Administration, and Court Decisions during the First Twenty Years.* New York: Russell Sage Foundation, 1936.
Bauman, John F. *Public Housing, Race, and Renewal: Urban Planning in Philadelphia, 1920–1974.* Philadelphia: Temple University Press, 1988.
Bauman, John F., and Edward K. Muller. *Before Renaissance: Planning in Pittsburgh, 1890–1940.* Pittsburgh: University of Pittsburgh Press, 2006.

————. "The Planning Technician as Urban Visionary: Frederick Bigger and American Planning, 1881–1963." *Journal of Planning History* 1, no. 2 (2002): 124–53.

Bauman, John J., Kristin M. Szylvian, and Roger Biles. *From Tenements to the Taylor Homes: In Search of an Urban Housing Policy in Twentieth-Century America.* University Park: Pennsylvania State University Press, 2000.

Bloom, Nicholas Dagen. "Architects, Architecture, and Urbanism." *Journal of Planning History* 7, no. 1 (Februry 2008): 76.

Booth, Douglas E. "Municipal Socialism and Government Reform: The Milwaukee Experience, 1910–1940." *Journal of Urban History* 12, no. 1 (November 1985): 51–74.

Boyer, M. Christine. *Dreaming the Rational City: The Myth of American City Planning.* Cambridge, Mass.: MIT Press, 1990.

Buder, Stanley. *Visionaries and Planners: The Garden City Movement and the Modern Community.* New York and Oxford: Oxford University Press, 1990.

Burgess, Patricia. *Planning for the Private Interest: Land Use Controls and Residential Patterns in Columbus, Ohio, 1900–1970.* Columbus: Ohio State University Press, 1994.

Caro, Robert. *The Power Broker: Robert Moses and the Fall of New York.* New York: Knopf, 1974.

Collins, Christine Craeseman. *Werner Hegemann and the Search for Universal Urbanism.* New York: W.W. Norton and Co., 2005.

Condit, Carl W. *Chicago, 1930–1970: Building, Planning, and Urban Technology.* Chicago: University of Chicago Press, 1974.

Contosta, David R. *Suburb in the City: Chestnut Hill, Philadelphia, 1850–1990.* Columbus: Ohio State University Press, 1992.

Curran, Donald. *Metropolitan Financing: The Milwaukee Experience, 1920–1970.* Madison: University of Wisconsin Press, 1973.

Cutler, Richard. *Greater Milwaukee's Growing Pains, 1950–2000: An Insider's View.* Milwaukee: Milwaukee County Historical Society, 2001.

Darden, Joe T., et al. *Detroit: Race and Uneven Development.* Philadelphia: Temple University Press, 1987.

Dougherty, Jack. *More than One Struggle: The Evolution of Black School Reform in Milwaukee.* Chapel Hill: University of North Carolina Press, 2004.

Duany, Andres, Elizabeth Plater-Zyberk, and Jeff Speck. *Suburban Nation: The Rise of Sprawl and the Decline of the American Dream.* New York: North Point Press, 2000.

Dudley, Michael. "Sprawl as Strategy: City Planners Face the Bomb." *Journal of Planning Education and Research* 21, no. 1 (Fall 2001).

England, George A. "Milwaukee's Socialist Government." *American Review of Reviews* (October 1910): 451.

Fairbanks, Robert. *Making Better Citizens: Housing Reform and the Community Development Strategy in Cincinnati, 1890–1960.* Urbana and Chicago: University of Illinois Press, 1988.

Farish, Matthew. "Disaster and Decentralization: American Cities and the Cold War." *Cultural Geographies* 10, no. 2 (2003): 125–48.

Feagin, Joe, and Robert Parker. *Building American Cities: The Urban Real Estate Game.* Englewood Cliffs, N.J.: Prentice Hall, 1990.

Fishman, Robert. *Bourgeois Utopias: The Rise and Fall of Suburbia.* New York: Basic Books, 1987.

————, ed. *The American Planning Tradition: Culture and Policy.* Baltimore: Johns Hopkins University Press, 2000.

Fleischmann, Arnold. "The Territorial Expansion of Milwaukee: Historical Lessons for Contemporary Urban Policy and Research." *Journal of Urban History* 14, no. 2 (February 1988): 147–76.

Fogelson, Robert. *Downtown: Its Rise and Fall, 1880–1950*. New Haven, Conn.: Yale University Press, 2001.

———. *The Fragmented Metropolis: Los Angeles, 1850–1930*. Cambridge, Mass.: Harvard University Press, 1967.

Fogelsong, Richard E. *Planning the Capitalist City: The Colonial Era to the 1920s*. Princeton, NJ: Princeton University Press, 1986.

Fones-Wolf, Elizabeth. *Selling Free Enterprise: The Business Assault on Labor and Liberalism, 1945–1960*. Urbana: University of Illinois Press, 1994.

Foss-Mollan, Kate. *Hard Water: Politics and Water Supply in Milwaukee, 1870–1995*. West Lafayette, Ind.: Purdue University Press, 2001.

Foster, Mark S. *From Streetcar to Superhighway: American City Planners and Urban Transportation, 1900–1940*. Philadelphia: Temple University Press, 1981.

Fox-Gotham, Kevin. *Race, Real Estate, and Uneven Development: The Kansas City Experience, 1900–2000*. Albany: State University of New York Press, 2002.

Freund, David M. P. *Colored Property: State Policy and White Racial Politics in Suburban America*. Chicago: University of Chicago Press, 2007.

Fure-Slocum, Eric. "Cities with Class?: Growth Politics, the Working-Class City, and Debt in Milwaukee during the 1940s." *Social Science History* 24, no. 1 (Spring 2000): 257–305.

George, Henry. *Progress and Poverty: An Inquiry into the Cause of Industrial Depressions and of Increase of Want with Increase of Wealth: The Remedy*. Garden City, N.Y.: Doubleday, Page & Co., 1912.

Gurda, John. *The Making of Milwaukee*. Milwaukee: Milwaukee County Historical Society, 1999.

Gutfreund, Owen. *Twentieth Century Sprawl: Highways and the Reshaping of the American Landscape*. New York: Oxford University Press, 2004.

Hall, Peter. *Cities of Tomorrow: An Intellectual History of Urban Planning and Design in the Twentieth Century*. 2nd edition. New York: Blackwell Publishing, 2002.

Harman, Ruth, and Charlotte Lekachman. "The 'Jacobs House.'" *The Wisconsin Magazine of History* 16, no. 3, March 1933.

Heathcott, Joe. "The City Quietly Remade: National Priorities and Local Agendas in the Movement to Clear the Slums." *Journal of Urban History* 34, no. 2, 221–242.

Heathcott, Joe, and Maire Murphy. "Corridors of Flight, Zones of Renewal: Industry, Planning, and Policy in the Making of Metropolitan St. Louis, 1940–1980." *Journal of Urban History* 31, no. 2, 151–89.

Hegemann, Werner, and Elbert Peets. *The American Vitruvius: An Architects' Handbook of Civic Art*. New York: Architectural Book Publishing Co., 1922.

Hirsch, Arnold R. *Making the Second Ghetto: Race and Housing in Chicago, 1940–1960*. New York: Cambridge University Press, 1983.

Hise, Greg. *Magnetic Los Angeles: Planning the Twentieth Century Metropolis*. Baltimore: Johns Hopkins University Press, 1997.

Holli, Melvin G. *The American Mayor: The Best and Worst Big-City Leaders*. University Park: Pennsylvania State University Press, 1999.

Howard, Ebenezer. *Garden Cities of Tomorrow*. Cambridge, Mass.: MIT Press, 1965.

Hunt, D. Bradford. "Was the 1937 Housing Act a Pyrrhic Victory?" *Journal of Planning History* 4, no. 3 (August 2005): 195–221.

Isenberg, Alison. *Downtown America: A History of the Place and the People Who Made It*. Chicago: University of Chicago Press, 2004.

Jablonsky, Thomas, ed. *Milwaukee Stories*. Milwaukee: Marquette University Press, 2005.

Jackson, Kenneth. *Crabgrass Frontier: The Suburbanization of the United States*. New York: Oxford University Press, 1985.

Jacobs, Jane. *The Death and Life of Great American Cities.* New York: Random House, 1961.

Johns, Michael. *Moment of Grace: The American City in the 1950's.* Berkeley: University of California Press, 2003.

Jozwiak, Elizabeth. "Politics in Play: Socialism, Free Speech, and Social Centers in Milwaukee." *Wisconsin Magazine of History,* Spring 2003.

Judd, Richard W. *Socialist Cities: Municipal Politics and the Grass Roots of American Socialism.* Albany: State University of New York Press, 1989.

Katz, Bruce, and Jennifer Bradley. "Divided We Sprawl," Part 2. *Atlantic Monthly,* 26–42.

Keating, Ann Durkin. *Building Chicago: Suburban Developers and the Creation of a Divided Metropolis.* Columbus: Ohio State University Press, 1988.

Kennedy, David. *Freedom from Fear: The American People in Depression and War, 1929–1945.* New York: Oxford University Press, 1999.

Kenny, Judith T. "Polish Routes to Americanization: House Form and Landscape on Milwaukee's South Side." In T. Vale and R. Ostergren, eds. *Wisconsin Land and Life.* Madison: University of Wisconsn Press, 1996.

Kerstein, Edward. *Milwaukee's All-American Mayor: A Portrait of Daniel Webster Hoan.* Englewood Cliffs, N.J.: Prentice-Hall, 1966.

Knight, D. W. "Subsidization of Industry in Forty Selected Cities in Wisconsin: 1930–1946." *Wisconsin Commerce Studies* 1, no. 2 (1947).

Krueckeberg, Donald, ed. *The American Planner: Biographies and Recollections.* New York: Routledge Press, 1983.

Krugler, David F. *This Is Only a Test: How Washington, D.C., Prepared for Nuclear War.* New York: Palgrave, 2006.

Kunstler, James Howard. *The Geography of Nowhere: The Rise and Decline of America's Man-Made Landscape.* New York; Touchstone Press, 1993.

Lapp, Ralph E. *Must We Hide?* Cambridge, Mass.: Addison-Wesley Press, 1949.

Larsen, Kristin. "Cities to Come: Clarence Stein's Postwar Regionalism." *Journal of Planning History* 4, no. 1 (2005): 33–51.

Leavitt, Judith Walzer. *The Healthiest City: Milwaukee and the Politics of Health Reform.* Princeton, N.J.: Princeton University Press, 1982.

Lewis, Nelson. *The Planning of the Modern City.* New York: Wiley and Sons, 1923.

Light, Jennifer. *From Warfare to Welfare: Defense Intellectuals and Urban Problems in Cold War America.* Baltimore: Johns Hopkins University Press, 2003.

Lubove, Roy S. *Community Planning in the 1920s: The Contributions of the Regional Planning Association of America.* Pittsburgh: University of Pittsburgh Press, 1963.

———. *The Progressives and the Slums: Tenement House Reform in New York City, 1890–1917.* Pittsburgh: University of Pittsburgh Press, 1962.

———. *Twentieth Century Pittsburgh: Government, Business, and Environmental Change.* New York: Wiley Books, 1969.

Lueders, Bill. "Last of a Breed." *Milwaukee Magazine,* November 1985.

Maier, Henry. *The Mayor Who Made Milwaukee Famous.* Lanham, Md.: Madison Books, 1993.

Manning-Thomas, June. *Redevelopment and Race: Planning a Finer City in Postwar Detroit.* Baltimore: Johns Hopkins University Press, 1997.

Marchak, J., E. Teller, and L. R. Klein. "Dispersal of Cities and Industries." *Bulletin of the Atomic Scientist,* April 1948.

Marcuse, Peter. "Housing in Early City Planning." *Journal of Urban History* 6, no. 2 (February 1980): 153–76.

McEnaney, Laura. *Civil Defense Begins at Home: Militarization Meets Everyday Life in the Fifties.* Princeton, N.J.: Princeton University Press, 2000.

McShane, Clay. *Technology and Reform: Street Railways and the Growth of Milwaukee,*

1887–1900. Madison: State Historical Society of Wisconsin, 1975.

Meyer, Stephen. *Stalin over Wisconsin: The Making and Unmaking of Militant Unionism, 1900–1950.* New Brunswick, N.J.: Rutgers University Press, 1992.

Miller, Sally M. *Race, Ethnicity, and Gender in Early Twentieth-Century American Socialism.* New York and London: Garland Publishing, 1996.

———. *Victor Berger and the Promise of Constructive Socialism, 1910–1920.* Westport, Ct.: Greenwood Press, 1973.

Miller, Zane, and Bruce Tucker. *Changing Plans for America's Inner Cities: Cincinnati's Over-the-Rhine and Twentieth-Century Urbanism.* Columbus: Ohio State University Press, 1998.

Mollenkopf, John. *The Contested City.* Princeton, N.J.: Princeton University Press, 1983.

Mumford, Lewis. *The City in History: Its Origins, Its Transformations, and Its Prospects.* New York: Harcourt, Brace, and World, 1961.

———. *The Culture of Cities.* New York: Harcourt, Brace, & Co., 1938.

National Security Resources Board. "National Security Factors in Industrial Location." *Bulletin of the Atomic Scientist,* October 1948.

Norquist, John. *The Wealth of Cities: Revitalizing the Centers of American Life.* Reading, Mass.: Addison & Wesley, 1998.

Orum, Anthony. *City Building in America.* Boulder, Colo.: Westview Press, 1995.

Ososfsky, Gilbert. *Harlem: The Making of a Ghetto; Negro New York, 1890–1930.* New York: Harper & Row, 1971.

Ostergren, Robert C., and Thomas Vale, eds. *Wisconsin Land and Life.* Madison: University of Wisconsin Press, 1997.

Page, Max. *The Creative Destruction of Manhattan, 1900–1940.* Chicago: University of Chicago Press, 1999.

Parsons, Kermit C., and David Schuyler, eds. *From Garden City to Green City: The Legacy of Ebenezer Howard.* Baltimore: Johns Hopkins University Press, 2002.

Perrin, Richard W. E., "Resurgent Classicism: Wisconsin Architecture in the Wake of the Columbian Exposition." *Wisconsin Magazine of History,* Winter 1962–1963, 119–23.

Peterson, Jon A. *The Birth of City Planning in the United States, 1840–1917.* Baltimore: Johns Hopkins University Press, 2003.

Pifer, Richard. *A City at War: Milwaukee Labor during World War II.* Madison: Wisconsin Historical Society Press, 2003.

Radford, Gail. *Modern Housing for America: Policy Struggles in the New Deal Era.* Chicago: University of Chicago Press, 1996.

Rast, Joel. "Annexation Policy in Milwaukee: An Historical Institutionalist Approach." *Polity* 39 (2007): 55–78.

———. "Governing the Regimeless City: The Frank Zeidler Administration in Milwaukee, 1948–1960." *Urban Affairs Review* 42: 81–112.

Revell, Keith. *Building Gotham: Civic Culture and Public Policy in New York City, 1898–1938.* Baltimore: Johns Hopkins University Press, 2003.

Rodgers, Daniel T. *Atlantic Crossings: Social Politics in a Progressive Age.* Cambridge, Mass.: Harvard University Press, 1998.

Rusk, David. *Cities without Suburbs.* Washington, D.C.: Woodrow Wilson Center Press, 1993.

Salvatore, Nick. *Eugene Debs: Citizen and Socialist.* 2nd edition. Urbana: University of Illinois Press, 2007.

Sandweiss, Eric. *St. Louis: The Evolution of an American Urban Landscape.* Philadelphia: Temple University Press, 2001.

Schaeffer, Daniel. *Garden Cities for America: The Radburn Experience.* Philadelphia: Temple University Press, 1982.

Schmandt, Henry J., and William H. Standing. *The Milwaukee Metropolitan Study Commission.* Bloomington: Indiana University Press, 1965.

Schultz, Stanley. *Constructing Urban Culture: American Cities and City Planning, 1800–1920.* Philadelphia: Temple University Press, 1989.

Schuyler, David. *A City Transformed: Redevelopment, Race, and Suburbanization in Lancaster, Pennsylvania, 1940–1980.* University Park: Pennsylvania State University Press, 2002.

Scott, Mel. *American City Planning since 1890.* Berkeley: University of California Press, 1969.

Self, Robert O. *American Babylon: Race and the Struggle for Postwar Oakland.* Princeton, N.J.: Princeton University Press, 2003.

Sies, Mary Corbin, and Christopher Silver, eds. *Planning the Twentieth Century American City.* Baltimore: Johns Hopkins University Press, 1996.

Simon, Roger. *The City-Building Process: Housing and Services in New Milwaukee Neighborhoods, 1880–1910.* Philadelphia: American Philosophical Society, 1996.

Smith, Carl. *The Plan of Chicago: Daniel Burnham and the Remaking of the American City.* Chicago: University of Chicago Press, 2006.

Spain, Daphne. *How Women Saved the City.* Minneapolis: University of Minnesota Press, 2000.

Spann, Edward K. *Designing Modern America: The Regional Planning Association of America and Its Members.* Columbus: Ohio State University Press, 1996.

Stave, Bruce, ed. *Socialism and the Cities.* Port Washington, N.Y.: Kennikat Press, 1975.

Stefaniak, Norbert. "Industrial Location within the Urban Area: A Case Study of the Locational Characteristics of 950 Manufacturing Plants in the Milwaukee Area." *Wisconsin Commerce Reports* VI, no. 5 (August 1962).

Steffens, Lincoln. *The Shame of the Cities.* New York: Hill and Wang, 1904.

Stein, Clarence S. *Toward New Towns for America.* Cambridge, Mass.: MIT Press, 1957.

Still, Bayard. *Milwaukee: The History of a City.* Madison: State Historical Society of Wisconsin, 1948.

Sugrue, Thomas. *Origins of the Urban Crisis: Race and Inequality in Postwar Detroit.* Princeton, N.J.: Princeton University Press, 1996.

Talen, Emily. "Beyond the Front Porch: Regionalist Ideals in the New Urbanist Movement." *Journal of Planning History* 7, no. 1 (2008), 20–47.

———. *New Urbanism and American Planning: The Conflict of Cultures.* New York and London: Routledge Press, 2005.

Teaford, Jon C. *Cities of the Heartland: The Rise and Fall of the Industrial Midwest.* Bloomington: Indiana University Press, 1993.

———. *City and Suburb: The Political Fragmentation of Metropolitan America, 1850–1970.* Baltimore: Johns Hopkins University Press, 1979.

———. *The Metropolitan Revolution: The Rise of Post-Urban America.* New York: Columbia University Press, 2006.

———. *The Rough Road to Renaissance: Urban Revitalization in America, 1940–1985.* Baltimore: Johns Hopkins University Press, 1985.

Trotter, Joe William, Jr. *Black Milwaukee: The Making of an Industrial Proletariat, 1915–1945.* Urbana: University of Illinois Press, 1985.

Vale, Thomas R., and Robert C. Ostergren, eds. *Wisconsin Land and Life.* Madison: University of Wisconsin Press, 1996.

Vanderbilt, Tom. *Survival City: Adventures among the Ruins of Atomic America.* Princeton, N.J.: Princeton Architectural Press, 2002.

Von Hoffman, Alexander. "The End of the Dream: The Political Struggle of America's Public Housers." *Journal of Planning History* 4 (August 2005).

Wachman, Marvin. *History of the Social-Democratic Party in Milwaukee, 1897–1910.* Urbana: University of Illinois Press, 1945.

Warner, Sam Bass. *The Private City: Philadelphia in Its Three Periods of Growth*. Philadelphia: University of Pennsylvania Press, 1968.

Weber, Michael. *Don't Call Me Boss: David L. Lawrence, Pittsburgh's Renaissance Mayor*. Pittsburgh: University of Pittsburgh Press, 1988.

Weiner, Ronald R. *Lake Effects: A History of Urban Policy Making in Cleveland, 1825–1929*. Columbus: Ohio State University Press, 2005.

Weiss, Marc A. *The Rise of the Community Builders: The American Real Estate Industry and Urban Land Planning*. New York: Columbia University Press, 1987.

Wells, Robert. *This Is Kilbourntown*. Milwaukee: Times Holding Co., Inc., 1971.

Wilson, William H. *The City Beautiful Movement*. Baltimore: Johns Hopkins University Press, 1994.

Wood, Edith Elmer. "Slums and Blighted Areas of the United States." *Housing Division Bulletin*, no. 1, Federal Emergency Administration of Public Works.

Wood, Robert C. *1400 Governments: The Political Economy of the New York Metropolitan Region*. Cambridge, Mass.: Harvard University Press, 1961.

Dissertations and Theses

Cady, David Barry. "The Influence of the Garden City Ideal on American Housing and Planning Reform, 1900–1940." Ph.D. Diss., University of Wisconsin-Madison, 1970.

Casey, Tim. "The 1912 Non-Partisan Election Law: Reform, Social Democrats, and Reaction." M.A. Thesis, Marquette University, 2000.

Christian, Marvin, "The Milwaukee Park Movement: A History of Its Origins and Development." M.A. Thesis, University of Wisconsin-Milwaukee, 1967.

Cole, Mary Susan. "Catherine Bauer and the Public Housing Movement, 1926–1937." Ph.D. Diss., George Washington University, 1975.

Fleischmann, Arnold. "The Politics of Annexation and Urban Development: A Clash of Two Paradigms." Ph.D. Diss., University of Texas at Austin, 1984.

Fure-Slocum, Eric. "The Challenge of the Working Class City: Recasting Growth Politics and Liberalism in Milwaukee, 1937–1952." Ph.D. Diss., University of Iowa, 2001.

Geib, Paul Edward. "The Late, Great Migration: A Case Study of Southern Black Migration to Milwaukee, 1940–1970." M.A. Thesis, University of Wisconsin-Milwaukee, 1993.

Goff, Charles. "The Politics of Governmental Integration in Metropolitan Milwaukee." Ph.D. Diss., Northwestern University, 1952.

Jones, Patrick D. "'The Selma of the North': Race Relations and Civil Rights Insurgency in Milwaukee, 1958–1970." Ph.D. Diss., University of Wisconsin, 2002.

Miller, Christopher Mark. "Milwaukee's First Suburbs: A Re-Interpretation of Suburban Incorporation in Nineteenth-Century Milwaukee County." Ph.D. Diss., Marquette University, 2007.

Olson, Frederick. "The Milwaukee Socialists, 1897–1941." Ph.D. Diss., Harvard University, 1952.

Reisser, Steven. "Immigrants and House Form in Northeast Milwaukee, 1885–1916." M.A. Thesis, University of Wisconsin-Milwaukee, 1977.

Schmitz, Keith Robert. "Milwaukee and Its Black Community: 1930–1942." M.A. Thesis, University of Wisconsin-Milwaukee, 1979.

Stachowski, Floyd John. "The Political Career of Daniel Webster Hoan." Ph.D. Diss., Northwestern University, 1966.

Wassmansdorf, Gregg. "Public-Private Dialectics in the Planning and Development of Los Angeles, 1781–1993." M.A. Thesis, University of Southern California, 1994.

Acknowledgments

Although probably neither man would admit it, two remarkable historians are largely responsible for my academic career. When I was an undergraduate at Bethany College in West Virginia, I switched majors, choosing History almost entirely due to the brilliant teaching of Gary Kappel. When I was a young graduate student at Marquette University, Thomas Jablonsky believed in me when he did not have to, illuminated the historical puzzles of American cities, and served as my dissertation advisor, pushing me to intellectual places I never believed I was capable of reaching. This book is an outgrowth of my doctoral dissertation, and my greatest intellectual and professional debt is to "Dr. J," whose advice and friendship I continue to cherish.

Marquette, where I received my graduate degrees, is blessed with a remarkable History Department. James Marten is simultaneously kind and challenging, and his outside shot remains, by all accounts, still dangerous. I also owe considerable intellectual debts to Steven Avella, Alan Ball, Robert Hay, John Krugler, and Athan Theoharis. Fellow graduate students Tim Casey, Brigitte Charaus, Robert Donnelly, Jodi Eastberg, John Eastberg, Ann Ostendorf, Wayne Riggs, Steven Servais, Edward Schmitt, and Daryl Webb provided friendship that far outlasts any academic calendar. Christopher Miller and I tried to turn the city of Milwaukee inside-out, discussed every aspect of urban history we could think of, and visited as many cities and baseball parks (not necessarily in that order) as our meager budgets allowed. Christopher's insights and friendship have been and remain particularly invaluable.

Many colleagues have provided helpful observations and comments on the research that underpins this book. They include Heather Barrow, John Bauman, Allen Dietrich-Ward, Owen Gutfreund, Judith Kenny, Tim Lacy, Clay McShane, Zane Miller, Edward Muller, Maire Murphy, Tim Neary,

Anthony Orum, Amanda Seligman, and Andrew Wiese. When I moved back to Pittsburgh, Edward Muller and Joel Tarr generously welcomed me into that city's rich community of urban historians. My current colleagues in the Robert Morris University Department of Social Sciences have made my professional life enjoyable and rewarding over the past several years.

I have presented sections of this project in a variety of terrific historical forums. They include the Urban History Association's Biennial Meeting, the Society of American City and Regional Planning Historians' (SACRPH) National Conference on Planning History, The Northern Great Plains History Conference, The Organization of American Historians Annual Meeting, The Pittsburgh Urban and Regional Renewal Summit, and the Newberry Library's Urban History Dissertation Group. Material from chapters 1 and 2 appeared previously in the *Michigan Historical Review*.

Historians rely heavily on the abilities of librarians and archivists, and I have been fortunate to work with many terrific people in these fields. They include the staffs at the Milwaukee Public Library's Special Collections Department (especially Virginia Schwartz and Judy Turner), the City of Milwaukee's Legislative Reference Bureau, the State Historical Society of Wisconsin's Area Research Center at the University of Wisconsin-Milwaukee's Golda Meir Library, The Milwaukee County Historical Society (especially Steven Dailey and Kevin Abing), the Carl A. Kroch Library at Cornell University, and the Bancroft Library at the University of California-Berkeley. The reference librarians at Marquette University, the University of Wisconsin-Milwaukee, Robert Morris University, and Carnegie Mellon University were also extremely patient and helpful.

The process of turning a manuscript into a book has been made far easier by a variety of people. At Northern Illinois University Press, Mary Lincoln first shepherded this project, and I am indebted to her. The two anonymous readers at NIU Press both provided invaluable feedback and suggestions that are, hopefully, reflected in the forthcoming pages. Alex Schwartz, Sara Hoerdeman, Susan Bean, Linda Manning, and Julia Fauci at NIU Press also have been remarkably patient and supportive. Tom Willcockson created the four annexation maps that appear in this book. Thanks also go to the Milwaukee County Historical Society, Cornell University's Kroch Library's Department of Special Collections, the Milwaukee Public Library, the City of Milwaukee's Legislative Reference Bureau, and the Wisconsin Historical Society for allowing permission to publish the images that appear in this book.

Financial support also proved crucial in the research and writing of this book. I am especially indebted to Marquette University, which supported my research through its John Raynor Fellowship, and Robert Morris University, which supported my research and writing through two Summer Research Fellowships and several course reductions. The Robert Morris University School of Education and Social Sciences Dean's Fund generously defrayed costs for the creation of this book's maps. For this I am especially indebted to Kathy Dennick-Brecht and John Graham.

Finally, I would like to thank the members of my family. My parents, Tom and Barb McCarthy, are too wonderful for words to describe. My brother, Joe, my sister-in-law, Dottie, my sister, Sarah, my mother-in-law, Lynne, my father-in-law, Bob, and my large extended family are a sustaining source of strength. This book is dedicated to my wife and best friend, Ann McCarthy. Countless times, she has provided encouragement, support, humor, and advice. Her patience, kindness, and strength are inspirational and a continuous blessing. Dedicating this book to her is the merest thanks I can give.

Index